MW00466026

LIBRARY   main
with music

1458

782.27   84105
B349B
            The BBC hymn book

84105

SILVER LAKE COLLEGE LIBRARY
2406 SOUTH ALVERNO ROAD
MANITOWOC, WI 54220

THE
BBC HYMN BOOK

With Music

Published for the
BRITISH BROADCASTING CORPORATION
LONDON
OXFORD UNIVERSITY PRESS
NEW YORK   TORONTO

SILVER LAKE COLLEGE LIBRARY
2406 SOUTH ALVERNO ROAD
MANITOWOC, WI 54220

Oxford University Press, Ely House, London W. 1

GLASGOW NEW YORK TORONTO MELBOURNE WELLINGTON
CAPE TOWN IBADAN NAIROBI DAR ES SALAAM LUSAKA ADDIS ABABA
DELHI BOMBAY CALCUTTA MADRAS KARACHI LAHORE DACCA
KUALA LUMPUR SINGAPORE HONG KONG TOKYO

ISBN 0 19 231301 0

First published 1951
Eighth impression 1973

*All rights reserved. No part of this publication may be repro-
duced, stored in a retrieval system, or transmitted, in any form
or by any means, electronic, mechanical, photocopying, recording,
or otherwise, without the prior permission of Oxford University
Press*

*Printed in Great Britain
at the University Press, Oxford
by Vivian Ridler
Printer to the University*

SILVER LAKE COLLEGE LIBRARY
2406 SOUTH ALVERNO ROAD
MANITOWOC, WI 54220

782.27
B349B

5-15-96 Gift - Ed. Hugdahl

84105

PREFACE

HYMNS are the most popular element in Christian worship to-day, and broadcast services rightly include many of them. Attentive listeners like to follow the words, but often this is difficult unless what is heard can be supplemented by what is seen in print. Many different hymn books, however, are in use in the various Christian churches; the number of hymns common to all the main books is small and their selection ill-balanced, and there are many variations in the printed texts. It is not surprising, therefore, that the BBC should have received a steady stream of letters suggesting the compilation of a hymn book for use in studio services, and particularly at the Daily Service.

The first step towards meeting this demand was taken in May 1937 when Dr. F. A. Iremonger, as 'Director of Religion', wrote a memorandum to Sir John Reith (as he then was), the Director-General. Dr. Iremonger suggested that an effort should be made to compile a book in which the 'good popular' might be preserved and the 'bad popular' omitted. (This distinction was one on which Sir Walford Davies never tired of insisting.) Secondly, he suggested that the corpus of hymns known to a wide public might be enriched by the inclusion of a number of new hymns not to be found in most of the standard books. Thirdly, he pointed out that the BBC was in a position to compile a hymn book which would make a wide and inclusive appeal.

The Director-General approved the proposal, and Dr. Iremonger then called together a small interdenominational committee consisting of the Venerable Leslie Hunter (now Bishop of Sheffield), and Mr. R. Ellis Roberts, Anglicans; the late Dr. W. T. Cairns, Church of Scotland; the late Dr. A. W. Harrison, Methodist; Dr. Hugh Martin, Baptist; the late Dr. Albert Peel, Congregationalist; the late Reverend W. T. Elmslie,

PREFACE

Presbyterian Church of England. The members of this committee were asked to make a critical survey of the hymns most frequently used in the worship of their respective denominations, and to recommend a selection for inclusion in a new book. In this way a first list of about five hundred hymns was compiled.

This list was then sent for comment to several hymnologists and musicians. These were Canon G. W. Briggs, the late Dr. W. T. Cairns, the late Sir Walford Davies, Dr. J. Dykes Bower, the Reverend A. D. Kelly, S.S.M., Dr. H. G. Ley, the late Mr. A. S. Owen, Dr. Millar Patrick, and (within the BBC) Mr. Trevor Harvey, Dr. W. K. Stanton, and Dr. R. S. Thatcher. On the outbreak of war in 1939 work on the book was suspended until 1941, when a new committee was appointed to complete it. Its members were Dr. F. A. Iremonger, Dr. W. K. Stanton (Editor-in-Chief), Dr. G. Thalben-Ball, Dr. R. S. Thatcher, Dr. J. W. Welch, and the Reverend Cyril Taylor, and they are referred to in this Preface as 'the Compilers'. Sir Hugh Allen was appointed Chairman, and held the post until his death in 1946. The service he rendered was invaluable. His long experience and technical knowledge, his pungent criticism and discriminating taste made him an ideal Chairman, and he was not too much encumbered by traditional estimates or intimate associations to pass an independent judgment on the merits alike of words and tunes.

A draft of the words was sent for comment to the Very Reverend E. Milner-White and to Dr. Millar Patrick. The Compilers adopted many of their suggestions, but are, of course, solely responsible for the final form of the book.

THE WORDS

Many hymns in the standard books are not printed exactly as the authors wrote them. Of some it is not easy to trace the original, or to know how far changes were made with the authors' consent. Editors have often made alterations, either for theological reasons, or to secure, as they supposed, a higher standard of versification. But the changes of British taste in hymnody, which can be traced through several centuries, have occasionally brought the wheel full circle to prove the author a better poet than his editors. The Compilers have not, therefore, adhered to any hard and fast rule in this matter. Of some hymns they have preferred to print emended versions which have become familiar through long usage; of others, to restore the original, or to produce their own version. When the last of these courses has been adopted the intention has been to make the meaning of the words more intelligible without changing their theology.

There is no section of 'General Hymns'. All the hymns are classified under definite headings, to help those who order public worship. Metrical Psalms and Paraphrases of other parts of the Bible are arranged in separate sections. Biblical references are attached also to those hymns which, though not close paraphrases, are based on specific passages of Scripture. It will be noticed that, in addition to hymns for use in services broadcast from a BBC studio, others—e.g. some of the Communion hymns and those for Baptism, Confirmation, and Marriage—have been included in order to complete the book, and to make it suitable for use in churches.

In long hymns the sign * is prefixed to those verses which may be most conveniently omitted.

In a book intended for general use there is no room to make adequate provision for young children, i.e. those under nine or ten. The few hymns in this book which are suitable only for them are included in their appropriate sections and are headed 'For Young Children'. For children over ten the Compilers advocate full, though discriminating, use of the hymns sung by adults. This treats the older children as they would wish to be treated, and it makes them familiar with the hymns which they will find in use when they become regular members of the adult congregation.

PREFACE

The book contains several new hymns, and some which are not at present widely known. The Compilers hope that they have succeeded in their effort to add something to the common stock of good hymns.

THE MUSIC

No indications of speed are given. The appropriate speed for any hymn is determined by three things:

(*a*) the mood of the words;

(*b*) the size of the congregation;

(*c*) the acoustics of the building in which it is sung.

The last section of the book (Nos. 499-542) contains settings which are intended for use primarily by the BBC Singers at the Daily Service. Many of these will be found suitable for use by experienced church choirs as anthems, and it will be noticed that there is considerable variation of difficulty within the section.

The accompaniments to the plainsong melodies are the work of Dr. E. T. Cook, C.B.E. (Organist of Southwark Cathedral).

The BBC is most grateful to the Compilers—in particular to Dr. Iremonger, who fostered the development of the book from its earliest stages, to Dr. Stanton, who prepared the draft for the press, and to all those who gave their advice during the many years in which the book was in preparation. Special thanks are also due to the staff of the Oxford University Press for their patience and ready co-operation.

BROADCASTING HOUSE
1950

ACKNOWLEDGEMENTS

PERMISSION to insert material has kindly been granted by authors, composers, publishers, or present owners of copyright according to the following list. In a few instances exact ownership is obscure. If for this reason, or through inadvertence, any rights still surviving have not been acknowledged, it is hoped that the owners will overlook the omission. Special acknowledgements are due to the Editors of *Songs of Praise* and to the Oxford University Press for allowing their material to be used, and to the O.U.P. Hymn Copyright Department for negotiating all the copyright permissions in the book.

In this list, a blank in the second column indicates that the author or composer is also the owner of the copyright, or that permission was granted in the lifetime of authors now dead.

WORDS

AUTHOR	PERMISSION GRANTED BY	NO. OF HYMN
AINGER, A. C.	S.P.C.K.	177
Alington, C. A.		270, 294
"	The Proprietors of *Hymns A. & M.*	103, 222, 327
Alston, A. E.	Bishop Alston	167
Andrew, Father, S. D. C.	Messrs. Mowbray & Co., Ltd.	358
Anon.		515
Arlott, J.		431, 435, 440
BARING-GOULD, S.	Messrs. J. Curwen & Sons, Ltd.	186, 419, 420
Bayly, A. F.		181
Bell, Miss M. A.	Oxford University Press	385
Bell, M. F.	English Hymnal Company, Ltd.	266
Birkbeck, W. J.	English Hymnal Company, Ltd.	511
Bourne, G. H.	Mr. A. Cyprian Bourne-Webb	206
Bridges, R.	Mrs. Bridges and the Clarendon Press, Oxford (from *The Yattendon Hymnal*) . . . 86, 113, 274, 285, 299, 314, 330, 395, 427, 433, 463, 590, 509, 521, 522, 523, 525, 527, 533	
Bright, W.	The Warden of Keble College, Oxford	198, 214, 402
Brooke, S. A.	Mrs. Leslie Brooke	71
Brownlie, J.	Messrs. Marshall, Morgan & Scott, Ltd.	158
Burkitt, F. C.	S.P.C.K.	161
Butler, H. M.	The Exors. of the late Mr. E. M. Butler	326
CHESTERTON, G. K.	Lady Sykes	394
Clare, J.	Mr. S. Sefton.	70
Coles, V. S. S.	The Proprietors of *Hymns A. & M.*	219
Cooke, G.	Messrs. Joseph Williams, Ltd.	261
Crum, J. M. C.	Oxford University Press	109
DAISLEY, G. W.	Messrs. Breitkopf & Härtel	505, 513, 516, 519, 529
Dearmer, G.		542
Dearmer, P.	English Hymnal Company, Ltd.	72, 215, 389, 405, 536
"	Lady Sykes	315
Draper, W. H.	Messrs. J. Curwen & Sons, Ltd. (Curwen Edition No. 80649)	2
FOSDICK, H. E.	The Fleming H. Revell Company	391
GEDGE, P.		343
Gill, T. H.	Mr. E. W. B. Gill	255
HENSLEY, L.	Oxford University Press	27
Holland, H. S.	English Hymnal Company, Ltd.	393
Horne, C. S.	The Hon. Mrs. K. M. Horne	242
Housman, L.	English Hymnal Company, Ltd.	60
Hull, Miss E.	Dr. Hull and Messrs. Chatto & Windus	316
Hunter, J.	Bishop Hunter	319
Hymns A. & M., Compilers of	The Proprietors of *Hymns A. & M.*	409

ACKNOWLEDGEMENTS

AUTHOR	PERMISSION GRANTED BY	NO. OF HYMN
Jervois, W. H. H.	Mr. Peter Martineau.	220, 535
Lacey, T. A.	English Hymnal Company, Ltd.	104, 174, 342, 346
Leachman, E. W.	Mrs. F. M. Tapp	350
Lowry, S. C.	Mr. H. V. Lowry	377
Macbean, L.	The Fifeshire Advertiser, Ltd.	45
Maclagan, W. D.	Sir Eric Maclagan	82
Mann, F.	Messrs. A. W. Ridley & Co.	357
Mason, A. J.	The Proprietors of Hymns A. & M.	205
Matheson, G.	Oxford University Press	175
Merrill, W. P.		364
Merrington, E. N.		390
Muirhead, L.	Oxford University Press	183
Nevill, Miss M.	The de Rusette Centre.	265
Page, T. E.	Miss B. D. Page	195
Palmer, E. S.	English Hymnal Company, Ltd.	449, 539
Parsons, R. G.		218, 540
Penn, W. J.		320
Pierpoint, F. S.	Oxford University Press	272
Piggott, W. C.	Oxford University Press	243
Pott, F.	The Proprietors of Hymns A. & M.	114, 256
Rawnsley, H. D.	Mrs. Rawnsley	381
Rees, T. R.	Messrs. A. R. Mowbray & Co., Ltd.	7, 231
"	Community of the Resurrection, Mirfield, Yorks.	85, 273
Riley, A.	English Hymnal Company, Ltd.	209, 288
Roberts, R. E.	English Hymnal Company, Ltd.	162
Romanis, W.	Mr. W. H. C. Romanis	422
Scott, Lesbia		353
Scott, R. B. Y.	Association Press, New York	24
Shillito, E.		99
Smith, H.	Mr. Nowell Smith	430
Smith, W. C.	Oxford University Press	10
Stevenson, Miss L.		138, 139
Struther, Jan.	Oxford University Press	309
Tearle, Mrs. M.		192
Thomas, H. A.	The relatives of the late Dr. H. A. Thomas	380
Thring, G.	Mr. L. G. P. Thring	65, 124 (part), 383
Tucker, F. Bland		79, 119, 201
Turton, W. H.	The Proprietors of Hymns A. & M.	213
Tweedy, H. H.	Hymn Society of America	23
Waddell, Miss H.	Messrs. Constable & Co., Ltd. (from *Medieval Latin Lyrics*).	246, 502
Wallis, S. J., S.S.J.E.		154
Walmsley, D.	Mrs. M. D. Farrar	260
Welch, E. A.	Lady Salmon	223
Woodward, G. R.	Messrs. Schott & Co., Ltd. (from *Songs of Syon*)	280, 418, 447
"	Messrs. A. R. Mowbray & Co., Ltd.	115
Young, A.		437

TUNES

COMPOSER	PERMISSION GRANTED BY	NO. OF HYMN
Allen, H. P.	Lady Allen	206, 339
Armes, P.	The Proprietors of Hymns A. & M.	460
Baring-Gould, S.	Messrs. J. Curwen & Sons, Ltd.	203(i), 419, 420
Blanchet, A.	Miss C. Morley Horder	20
Brown, A. H.	Oxford University Press	292(i)

ACKNOWLEDGEMENTS

COMPOSER	PERMISSION GRANTED BY	NO. OF HYMN
Buck, P. C.	Mr. A. F. Buck	91(ii), 515
,,	Messrs. Stainer & Bell, Ltd.	282
Chadwyck-Healey, H. P.	The Royal School of Church Music	273(ii)
Cocker, N.		211, 243
Cooke, G.	Messrs. Joseph Williams, Ltd.	261
Creed, J. E. H.		462
Davies, H. Walford	Miss C. Morley Horder	532
,,	Lady Davies and Mr. John Wilson	158, 410
Dyer, H. A.	Lady Popham	235, 275
Elliott, J. W.	Messrs. Novello & Co., Ltd.	26
Ett, C.	The Abbot of Downside	284, 445(ii)
Evans, D.		272
Ferguson, W. H.		65, 120, 230, 345, 360, 425, 448
,,	Royal School of Church Music	117
Foster, M. B.	The Proprietors of *Hymns A. & M.*	178, 381
Gatty, N.	Mrs. M. H. Gatty	5(ii), 113(ii), 130
George, G.	The H. W. Gray Company, Inc.	89(i)
Greatorex, W.		326
Harris, W. H.	Oxford University Press	306(i)
Harwood, B.		34, 187
Heath-Gracie, G. H.		531
Holst, G.	The Exors. of the late Gustav Holst	51, 244
Hopkins, J. H.	The Church Pension Fund. Church Hymnal Corporation, New York	353
Hopkirk, J.		24
Hunt, J. E.		539(ii)
Kirkpatrick, W. J.	The Hope Publishing Co. Chicago, Illinois, U.S.A. (Copyright 1923 Renewal)	43(ii)
Lahee, H.	Miss C. Morley Horder	122
Law, J.	Oxford University Press	107(ii)
Ley, H. G.	A. & C. Black, Ltd.	302(ii)
Mendelssohn-Bartholdy, F.	Messrs. Novello & Co., Ltd.	50
Murrill, H.		273(i), 351(ii)
Naylor, E. W.	Mr. Bernard Naylor	365
Parry, C. H. H.	The Exors. of the late Sir Hubert Parry and Messrs. J. Curwen & Sons, Ltd. (Curwen Edition, No. 40062)	387
,,	The Proprietors of *Hymns A. & M.*	376
,,	Messrs. Novello & Co., Ltd.	279, 351(i), 537
Parry, J.	Hymn Committee of the Union of Welsh Independents (Incorporated)	264(i)
,,	Messrs. Hughes A'I Fab	145(i)
Pettman, E.	Messrs. A. W. Ridley & Co.	53, 350
Russell, S. L.		389
Scholefield, C. C.	English Hymnal Company, Ltd.	426(ii)
Scott, J. S.		388
Selby, B. L.	The Proprietors of *Hymns A. & M.*	164
Shaw, M.	Messrs. J. Curwen & Sons, Ltd. (Curwen Edition Nos. 80634 and 80631)	33, 186
Slater, G.	Oxford University Press	320
Smith, A. M.		202
Somervell, A.	The Exors. of the late Sir Arthur Somervell.	39, 438
Stanford, C. V.	Messrs. Stainer & Bell, Ltd.	119
Stanton, W. K.		29, 59(ii), 63(ii), 76, 93(ii), 99, 109, 139, 161, 177, 181, 253, 262, 270, 287(i), 302(i), 309(ii), 314(i), 340, 390, 397, 443, 502, 512, 523, 539(i)
Stewart, C. Hylton	Messrs. J. Curwen & Sons, Ltd. (Curwen Edition, No. 80632)	492

ACKNOWLEDGEMENTS

COMPOSER	PERMISSION GRANTED BY	NO. OF HYMN
Stewart, C. Hylton.	Oxford University Press	124
Taylor, C. V.	4, 14, 98, 106(ii), 154, 175, 179, 180, 192, 242, 291, 309(i), 368(i), 386, 423, 437, 491	
„	Novello & Co. Ltd.	308
Terry, R. R.	Oxford University Press	7, 176
Thalben-Ball, G.	The Exors. of the late Sir Richard Terry	32
		9, 21, 59(i), 63(i), 195, 256, 265, 271, 278, 292(ii), 295, 409(ii), 417
Thatcher, R. S.		25, 172
Thiman, E. H.		416
Vaughan Williams, R.	English Hymnal Company, Ltd.	149, 227
Warrack, G.		23
Williams, T. J.	Messrs. W. Gwenlyn Evans & Son	197
Wood, C.	Oxford University Press	507
Yin-Lan, S.	Christian Literature Society for China	538

Thanks are also due to the following, who have kindly allowed the inclusion of versions and harmonizations of traditional and other melodies, which are their copyright:

Mrs. Bridges and the Clarendon Press, Oxford (from the *Yattendon Hymnal*): 509.
Educational Company of Ireland, Ltd.: 316.
English Hymnal Co., Ltd.: 2, 108, 260, 288, 328, 357, 385.
Enlarged Songs of Praise, Musical Editors of: 56, 60, 75, 81, 301, 315, 316, 319, 352, 371, 394, 431.
Evans, D.: 148, 191, 300.
     „   Exors. of: 540.
Karpeles, Miss M.: 254, 322.
Lengnick, A. & Co., Ltd.: 266
Mowbray, A. R. & Co., Ltd.: 115.
Novello & Co., Ltd., 511.
Oxford University Press: 143, 168, 183, 440.
Pritchard, T. C. L.: 469, 480.
Schott & Co., Ltd., London (from *Songs of Syon*): 530.
Shaw, Mrs. Geoffrey: 1, 182, 424.
Stainer & Bell, Ltd.: 136, 170, 475(ii).
Tatton, J. Meredith (from *Songs of Syon*): 404.

The following tunes have been harmonized or adapted by the musical editors: 13, 18, 19, 20, 23, 31(i), 31(ii), 32, 35, 36, 37(i), 40, 41, 42, 43(i), 43(ii), 44, 45, 47(i), 47(ii), 48, 53, 54(i), 54(ii), 56, 57, 60, 67(i), 69(i), 69(ii), 73, 75, 79, 80(ii), 87, 89(i), 90(i), 90(ii), 91(i), 96, 100, 102, 103, 104(i), 104(ii), 107(i), 107(ii), 110, 111(i), 111(ii), 113(i), 119, 125, 132, 133, 134, 135, 136, 138, 143, 147, 151(i), 151(ii), 155, 159, 162(i), 162(ii), 165(i), 165(ii), 167(i), 167(ii), 168, 170, 174, 185, 186, 188, 191, 196, 199, 200, 201, 204, 205, 206, 208(i), 208(ii), 209, 212(i), 215, 216, 217, 219, 220(i), 220(ii), 221, 222, 225, 227, 228, 232(i), 232(ii), 234, 235, 237, 239(i), 239(ii), 250(i), 252, 257, 258, 259, 260, 263, 264(i), 266, 267, 272, 280, 281(i), 285, 292(i), 293, 297(i), 299, 300, 301, 303, 304, 305, 306(ii), 311, 312, 315, 316, 323(i), 331, 332, 336, 342(i), 343(i), 343(ii), 346(i), 346(ii), 347, 351(i), 352, 354, 355, 358, 359(i), 359(ii), 361, 370, 371, 373, 374, 378, 380, 382, 383, 385, 389, 391, 395, 396, 400, 405, 409(i), 413(i), 413(ii), 418, 421(i), 421(ii), 426(i), 427(a), 430, 431, 432, 434, 435, 440, 445(i), 446, 447, 453, 454, 458, 463, 464, 466, 468, 469, 476, 487, 492, 498, 501(b), 503, 504, 517, 522, 528.

CONTENTS

I. GOD

HYMNS

1. THE ETERNAL FATHER

(a) His nature, providence, and works .   1–22

(b) His kingdom   23–28

2. THE LORD JESUS CHRIST

(a) His advent   29–40

(b) His birth   41–61

(c) His manifestation   62–69

(d) His life and ministry .   .   .   70–75

(e) His suffering and death .   .   .   76–97

(f) His resurrection   98–116

(g) His reign and priesthood .   .   117–134

(h) His presence and power .   .   135–146

3. THE HOLY SPIRIT .   .   .   147–164

4. THE HOLY TRINITY .   .   .   165–170

II. THE CHURCH OF GOD

1. Its commission and work .   .   171–187

2. The Holy Scriptures .   .   .   188–191

3. Holy Baptism   192–194

4. Confirmation   195

5. Holy Communion. .   .   .   196–220

6. Marriage   221–223

7. The Ministry   224–225

8. Saints' Days and other Holy Days .   .   226–240

9. The Communion of Saints .   .   241–255

III. CHRISTIAN LIFE AND DUTY

1. TOWARDS GOD

(a) Preparation for worship .   .   256–268

CONTENTS

HYMNS

(b) Worship, thanksgiving, love . . 269–288

(c) Repentance and forgiveness . . 289–296

(d) Faith and trust . . . 297–315

(e) Aspiration 316–338

(f) Prayer and self-discipline . . 339–348

(g) Dedication and discipleship . . 349–372

2. TOWARDS MAN

(a) Love, unity, peace . . . 373–377

(b) Those in need 378–383

(c) The absent, and travellers . . 384–386

(d) Service and citizenship . . 387–395

IV. TIMES, SEASONS, OCCASIONS

1. Sunday 396–400

2. Morning 401–410

3. Evening 411–428

4. New Year 429–430

5. Plough Sunday 431

6. Rogationtide 432–435

7. Lammas 436–438

8. Harvest 439–444

9. Dedication Festival . . . 445–446

10. Burial 447–449

V. METRICAL PSALMS . . . 450–483

VI. BIBLE PARAPHRASES . . . 484–498

VII. CHOIR SETTINGS . . . 499–542

CONTENTS

INDEXES

Hymns for use in procession
Scripture passages
Original first lines of translated hymns
Tunes (alphabetical)
Tunes (metrical)
Composers, arrangers, and sources of tunes
Authors, translators, and sources of words
First lines

GOD: THE ETERNAL FATHER

2 LASST UNS ERFREUEN   88.44.88. and Alleluias.

Melody from *Geistliche Kirchengesang*
(Cologne, 1623)

O praise him, O praise him, Al-le-lu-ia, Al-le-lu-ia, Al-le-lu-ia!

GOD: THE ETERNAL FATHER

Melody by Charles Hutcheson
(1792–1860)

1 STRACATHRO C.M.

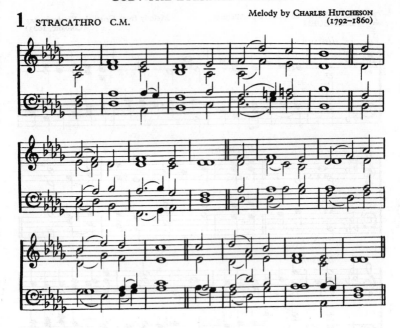

ALL as God wills, who wisely heeds
 To give or to withhold,
And knoweth more of all my needs
 Than all my prayers have told.

2 Enough that blessings undeserved
 Have marked my erring track;
That, wheresoe'er my feet have swerved,
 His chastening turned me back;

3 That more and more a providence
 Of love is understood,
Making the springs of time and sense
 Sweet with eternal good;

4 That death seems but a covered way
 Which opens into light,
Wherein no blinded child can stray
 Beyond the Father's sight.

5. And so the shadows fall apart,
 And so the west winds play;
And all the windows of my heart
 I open to the day.

John Greenleaf Whittier (1807–92)

B

HIS NATURE, PROVIDENCE, AND WORKS

Laudato sia Dio mio Signore

ALL creatures of our God and King,
Lift up your voice and with us sing
    Alleluia, Alleluia!
Thou burning sun with golden beam,
Thou silver moon with softer gleam,

*   O praise him, O praise him,*
*   Alleluia, Alleluia, Alleluia!*

2*Thou rushing wind that art so strong,
Ye clouds that sail in heaven along,
    O praise him, Alleluia!
Thou rising morn, in praise rejoice,
Ye lights of evening, find a voice:

3*Thou flowing water, pure and clear,
Make music for thy Lord to hear,
    Alleluia, Alleluia!
Thou fire so masterful and bright,
That givest man both warmth and light:

4 Dear mother earth, who day by day
Unfoldest blessings on our way,
    O praise him, Alleluia!
The flowers and fruits that in thee grow,
Let them his glory also show:

5 And all ye men of tender heart,
Forgiving others, take your part,
    O sing ye, Alleluia!
Ye who long pain and sorrow bear,
Praise God and on him cast your care:

6 And thou most kind and gentle death,
Waiting to hush our latest breath,
    O praise him, Alleluia!
Thou leadest home the child of God,
And Christ our Lord the way hath trod:

7. Let all things their Creator bless,
And worship him in humbleness;
    O praise him, Alleluia!
Praise, praise the Father, praise the Son,
And praise the Spirit, Three in One:

'Cantico di fratre sole', *S. Francis of Assisi* (1182–1226)
Par. William Henry Draper (1855–1933)

3 ALL THINGS BRIGHT AND BEAUTIFUL

76.76. D.

WILLIAM HENRY MONK
(1823–89)

ALL things bright and beautiful,
All creatures great and small,
All things wise and wonderful,
The Lord God made them all.

2 Each little flower that opens,
Each little bird that sings,
He made their glowing colours,
He made their tiny wings:

3 The purple-headed mountain,
The river running by,
The sunset, and the morning
That brightens up the sky:

4 The cold wind in the winter,
The pleasant summer sun,
The ripe fruits in the garden,
He made them every one:

5. He gave us eyes to see them,
And lips that we might tell
How great is God Almighty
Who has made all things well:

Cecil Frances Alexander (1818–95)

4 JABBOK 88.88.88.

CYRIL V. TAYLOR (1907–)

COME, O thou Traveller un-
      known,
  Whom still I hold but cannot see;
My company before is gone,
  And I am left alone with thee;
With thee all night I mean to stay,
And wrestle till the break of day.

2 In vain thou strugglest to get free,
    I never will unloose my hold;
  Art thou the man that died for me?
    The secret of thy love unfold;
  Wrestling, I will not let thee go,
  Till I thy name, thy nature know.

3 Yield to me now, for I am weak,
    But confident in self-despair;
  Speak to my heart, in blessings
      speak;
    Be conquered by my instant
        prayer!
  Speak, or thou never hence shalt
      move,
  And tell me if thy name is love?

4. 'Tis love, 'tis love, thou diedst for
      me!
    I hear thy whisper in my heart!
  The morning breaks, the shadows
      flee;
    Pure universal love thou art;
  To me, to all, thy mercies move;
  Thy nature and thy name is love.

Charles Wesley (1707–88)
Based on Genesis 32, 22–30

See also No. 348

5 LLANGOLLEN L.M.
(LLEDROD)

Welsh Hymn Melody

TUGWOOD L.M.

NICHOLAS GATTY (1874–1946)

FROM all that dwell below the skies
Let the Creator's praise arise:
Let the Redeemer's name be sung
Through every land, by every tongue.

2. Eternal are thy mercies, Lord;
Eternal truth attends thy word:
Thy praise shall sound from shore to shore,
Till suns shall rise and set no more.

Isaac Watts (1674–1748)
Based on Psalm 117

6 WARRINGTON L.M.

RALPH HARRISON (1748-1810)

GIVE to our God immortal praise,
Mercy and truth are all his ways;
Wonders of grace to God belong,
Repeat his mercies in your song.

2 Give to the Lord of lords renown;
The King of kings with glory crown:
His mercies ever shall endure,
When lords and kings are known no more.

3 He fills the sun with morning light,
He bids the moon direct the night:
His mercies ever shall endure,
When suns and moons shall shine no more.

4 He sent his Son with power to save
From guilt and darkness and the grave:
Wonders of grace to God belong,
Repeat his mercies in your song.

5. Through this vain world he guides our feet,
And leads us to his heavenly seat:
His mercies ever shall endure,
When this vain world shall be no more.

Isaac Watts (1674-1748)
Based on Psalm 136

SILVER LAKE COLLEGE-LIBRARY
2406 SOUTH ALVERNO ROAD
MANITOWOC, WI. 54220

See also No. 461

GOD: THE ETERNAL FATHER

7 ABBOT'S LEIGH 87.87. D.

CYRIL V. TAYLOR (1907–)

SILVER LAKE COLLEGE LIBRARY
2406 SOUTH ALVERNO ROAD
MANITOWOC, WI. 54220

GOD is love: let heaven adore him;
   God is love: let earth rejoice;
Let creation sing before him,
   And exalt him with one voice.
He who laid the earth's foundation,
   He who spread the heavens above,
He who breathes through all creation,
   He is love, eternal love.

2 God is love: and he enfoldeth
   All the world in one embrace;
With unfailing grasp he holdeth
   Every child of every race.
And when human hearts are breaking
   Under sorrow's iron rod,
All the sorrow, all the aching,
   Wrings with pain the heart of God.

3. God is love: and though with blindness
   Sin afflicts the souls of men,
God's eternal loving-kindness
   Holds and guides them even then.
Sin and death and hell shall never
   O'er us final triumph gain;
God is love, so love for ever
   O'er the universe must reign.

Timothy Rees, C.R. (1874–1939) and Compilers

8 LONDON NEW C.M.

Scottish Psalter (1635)
as given in PLAYFORD'S *Psalms* (1671)

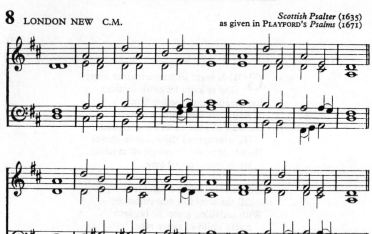

GOD moves in a mysterious way
    His wonders to perform;
He plants his footsteps in the sea,
    And rides upon the storm.

2 Deep in unfathomable mines
    Of never-failing skill
He treasures up his bright designs,
    And works his sovereign will.

3 Ye fearful saints, fresh courage take;
    The clouds ye so much dread
Are big with mercy, and shall break
    In blessings on your head.

4 Judge not the Lord by feeble sense
    But trust him for his grace;
Behind a frowning providence
    He hides a smiling face.

5. Blind unbelief is sure to err,
    And scan his work in vain;
God is his own interpreter,
    And he will make it plain.

William Cowper (1731–1800)

9 ORLANDO L.M.

GEORGE THALBEN-BALL

HIGH in the heavens, eternal God,
  Thy goodness in full glory shines;
Thy truth shall break through every cloud
  That veils and darkens thy designs.

2 For ever firm thy justice stands,
    As mountains their foundations keep;
  Wise are the wonders of thy hands;
    Thy judgments are a mighty deep.

3 My God, how excellent thy grace,
    Whence all our hope and comfort springs!
  The sons of Adam in distress
    Fly to the shadow of thy wings.

4. Life, like a fountain, rich and free,
    Springs from the presence of the Lord;
  And in thy light our souls shall see
    The glories promised in thy word.

Isaac Watts (1674–1748)
Based on Psalm 36, 5–9

See also No. 482

10 S. DENIO II.II.II.II.

Welsh Melody

IMMORTAL, invisible, God only wise,
In light inaccessible hid from our eyes,
Most blessèd, most glorious, the Ancient of Days,
Almighty, victorious, thy great name we praise.

2 Unresting, unhasting, and silent as light,
Nor wanting, nor wasting, thou rulest in might;
Thy justice like mountains high soaring above
Thy clouds which are fountains of goodness and love.

3 To all life thou givest, to both great and small;
In all life thou livest, the true life of all;
We blossom and flourish as leaves on the tree,
And wither and perish; but naught changeth thee.

4. Great Father of glory, pure Father of light,
Thine angels adore thee, all veiling their sight;
All laud we would render: O help us to see
'Tis only the splendour of light hideth thee.

Walter Chalmers Smith (1824–1908)
Based on 1 Timothy 1, 17

11 UFFINGHAM L.M.

JEREMIAH CLARKE (1670–1707)

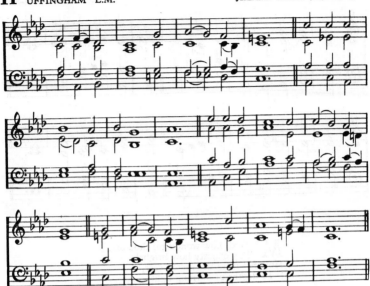

LORD of all being, throned afar,
Thy glory flames from sun and star;
Centre and soul of every sphere,
Yet to each loving heart how near!

2 Sun of our life, thy quickening ray
Sheds on our path the glow of day;
Star of our hope, thy softened light
Cheers the long watches of the night.

3 Our midnight is thy smile withdrawn,
Our noontide is thy gracious dawn,
Our rainbow arch thy mercy's sign;
All, save the clouds of sin, are thine.

4 Lord of all life, below, above,
Whose light is truth, whose warmth is love,
Before thy ever-blazing throne
We ask no lustre of our own.

5. Grant us thy truth to make us free,
And kindling hearts that burn for thee,
Till all thy living altars claim
One holy light, one heavenly flame.

Oliver Wendell Holmes (1809–94)

12 WESTMINSTER C.M.

JAMES TURLE (1802–82)

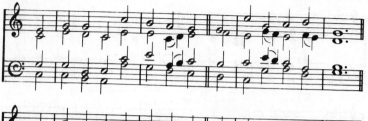

MY God, how wonderful thou art,
    Thy majesty how bright!
How beautiful thy mercy-seat,
    In depths of burning light!

2 How dread are thine eternal years,
    O everlasting Lord,
By prostrate spirits day and night
    Incessantly adored!

3 How wonderful, how beautiful,
    The sight of thee must be,
Thine endless wisdom, boundless power,
    And aweful purity!

4 O, how I fear thee, living God,
    With deepest, tenderest fears,
And worship thee with trembling hope,
    And penitential tears!

5 Yet I may love thee too, O Lord,
    Almighty as thou art,
For thou hast stooped to ask of me
    The love of my poor heart.

6 No earthly father loves like thee,
    No mother, e'er so mild,
Bears and forbears as thou hast done
    With me, thy sinful child.

7. My God, how wonderful thou art,
    Thy majesty how bright!
How beautiful thy mercy-seat,
    In depths of burning light!

Frederick William Faber (1814–63)

13 S. BARTHOLOMEW L.M.

Melody by HENRY DUNCALF (18th cent.)

MY God, my King, thy various praise
Shall fill the remnant of my days;
Thy grace employ my humble tongue,
Till death and glory raise the song.

2 The wings of every hour shall bear
Some thankful tribute to thine ear,
And every setting sun shall see
New works of duty done for thee.

3 Thy truth and justice I'll proclaim;
Thy bounty flows, an endless stream:
Thy mercy swift, thine anger slow,
But dreadful to the stubborn foe.

4. But who can speak thy wondrous deeds?
Thy greatness all our thoughts exceeds;
Vast and unsearchable thy ways,
Vast and immortal be thy praise.

Isaac Watts (1674–1748)
Based on Psalm 145

See also Nos. 19, 470

14 PORTLAND 888.4.

Cyril V. Taylor (1907–)

O LORD of heaven and earth and sea,
To thee all praise and glory be;
How shall we show our love to thee,
Who givest all?

2 The golden sunshine, vernal air,
Sweet flowers and fruit thy love declare;
When harvests ripen, thou art there,
Who givest all.

3 For peaceful homes and healthful days,
For all the blessings earth displays,
We owe thee thankfulness and praise,
Who givest all.

4 Thou didst not spare thine only Son,
But gav'st him for a world undone,
And freely with that blessèd one
Thou givest all.

5 Thou giv'st the Spirit's blessèd dower,
Spirit of life and love and power,
And dost his sevenfold graces shower
Upon us all.

6. For souls redeemed, for sins forgiven,
For means of grace and hopes of heaven,
Father, all praise to thee be given,
Who givest all.

Christopher Wordsworth (1807–85)

15 PRAISE MY SOUL 87.87.87. JOHN GOSS (1800–80)

1 Praise, my soul, the King of hea - ven; To his
feet thy tri-bute bring. Ransomed, healed, re - stored, for-
-giv - en, Who like me his praise should sing? Praise him!
Praise him! Praise him! Praise him! Praise the ev-er-last-ing King.

GOD: THE ETERNAL FATHER

Harmony

2 Praise him for his grace and fa - vour
  To our fa - thers in dis - tress;
  Praise him still the same for ev - er,
  Slow to chide and swift to bless.
  Praise him! Praise him! Praise him! Praise him!
  Glo - rious in his faith-ful - ness.

3 Fa - ther - like, he tends and spares us;
  Well our fee - ble frame he knows;
  In his hands he gen - tly bears us,
  Res - cues us from all our foes.
  Praise him! Praise him! Praise him! Praise him!
  Wide - ly as his mer - cy flows.

4. Angels, help us to adore him; Ye behold him face to face; Sun and moon, bow down before him, Dwellers all in time and space. Praise him! Praise him! Praise him! Praise him! Praise with us the God of grace.

Henry Francis Lyte (1793-1847)
Based on Psalm 103

16 AUSTRIAN HYMN 87.87. D. Franz Joseph Haydn (1732–1809)

PRAISE the Lord! ye heavens, adore him;
    Praise him, angels, in the height;
Sun and moon, rejoice before him,
    Praise him, all ye stars and light.
Praise the Lord! for he hath spoken:
    Worlds his mighty voice obeyed;
Laws, which never shall be broken,
    For their guidance he hath made.

2. Praise the Lord! for he is glorious;
    Never shall his promise fail;
God hath made his saints victorious,
    Sin and death shall not prevail.
Praise the God of our salvation;
    Hosts on high, his power proclaim;
Heaven and earth and all creation,
    Laud and magnify his name!

Foundling Hospital Collection (1796)
Based on Psalm 148

See also Nos. 478, 483

17 LOBE DEN HERREN 14.14.4.7.8.

Melody from *Stralsund Gesangbuch* (1665)
as given in the
Chorale Book for England (1863)

Lobe den Herren

PRAISE to the Lord, the Almighty, the King of creation;
O my soul, praise him, for he is thy health and salvation:
All ye who hear,
Brothers and sisters, draw near,
Praise him in glad adoration.

2 Praise to the Lord, who o'er all things so wondrously reigneth,
Shelters thee under his wings, yea, so gently sustaineth:
Hast thou not seen?
All that is needful hath been
Granted in what he ordaineth.

3 Praise to the Lord, who doth prosper thy work and defend thee;
Surely his goodness and mercy here daily attend thee:
Ponder anew
What the Almighty can do,
Who with his love doth befriend thee.

4. Praise to the Lord, O let all that is in me adore him!
All that hath life and breath come now with praises before him!
Let the amen
Sound from his people again:
Gladly for aye we adore him!

Joachim Neander (1650–80). *Tr. Catherine Winkworth* (1827–78) *and Compilers*
Based on Psalms 103 & 150

See also No. 534 (CS)

18 NUN FREUT EUCH 87.87.887.

Christliche Lieder (Wittenberg, 1524)

Sei Lob und Ehr' dem höchsten Gut

SING praise to God who reigns above,
　The God of all creation,
The God of power, the God of love,
　The God of our salvation;
With healing balm my soul he fills,
And every faithless murmur stills:
　To God all praise and glory!

2*The angel host, O King of kings,
　Thy praise for ever telling,
In earth and sky all living things
　Beneath thy shadow dwelling,
Adore the wisdom which could span,
And power which formed creation's plan:
　To God all praise and glory!

3 What God's almighty power hath made
　His gracious mercy keepeth;
By morning glow or evening shade
　His watchful eye ne'er sleepeth:
Within the kingdom of his might
Lo, all is just, and all is right:
　To God all praise and glory!

4 Then all my gladsome way along
　I sing aloud thy praises,
That men may hear the grateful song
　My voice unwearied raises:
Be joyful in the Lord, my heart;
Both soul and body bear your part:
　To God all praise and glory!

5. O ye who name Christ's holy name,
　Give God all praise and glory:
All ye who own his power, proclaim
　Aloud the wondrous story.
Cast each false idol from his throne,
The Lord is God, and he alone:
　To God all praise and glory!

Johann Jakob Schutz (1640–90). Tr. Frances Elizabeth Cox (1812–97)

19 SOLEMNIS HAEC FESTIVITAS L.M.

Angers Melody

SING to the Lord a joyful song;
  Lift up your hearts, your voices raise;
To us his gracious gifts belong,
  To him our songs of love and praise.

2 For life and love, for rest and food,
  For daily help and nightly care,
Sing to the Lord, for he is good,
  And praise his name, for it is fair.

3 For strength to those who on him wait,
  His truth to prove, his will to do,
Praise ye our God, for he is great;
  Trust in his name, for it is true.

4 For joys untold, which from above
  Cheer those who love his high employ,
Sing to our God, for he is love,
  Exalt his name, for it is joy.

5. Sing to the Lord of heaven and earth,
  Whom angels serve and saints adore,
The Father, Son, and Holy Ghost,
  To whom be praise for evermore. Amen.

John Samuel Bewley Monsell (1811–75)
Based on Psalm 145, 1–2

See also Nos. 13, 470

20 ANIMAE HOMINUM 87.87.   ALFRED BLANCHET (1868–1926)

Unison

SOULS of men, why will ye scatter
   Like a crowd of frightened sheep?
Foolish hearts, why will ye wander
   From a love so true and deep?

2 There's a wideness in God's mercy,
   Like the wideness of the sea;
There's a kindness in his justice,
   Which is more than liberty.

3 For the love of God is broader
   Than the measures of man's mind;
And the heart of the Eternal
   Is most wonderfully kind.

4. If our love were but more simple,
   We should take him at his word;
And our lives be filled with glory
   From the glory of the Lord.

Frederick William Faber (1814–63) *and Compilers*

20 ANIMAE HOMINUM 87.87.   ALFRED BLANCHET (1868–1926)

SOULS of men, why will ye scatter
 Like a crowd of frightened sheep?
Foolish hearts, why will ye wander
 From a love so true and deep?

2 There's a wideness in God's mercy,
 Like the wideness of the sea;
There's a kindness in his justice,
 Which is more than liberty.

3 For the love of God is broader
 Than the measures of man's mind;
And the heart of the Eternal
 Is most wonderfully kind.

4. If our love were but more simple,
 We should take him at his word;
And our lives be filled with glory
 From the glory of the Lord.

Frederick William Faber (1814–63) *and Compilers*

21 SIRIUS D.L.M.

GEORGE THALBEN-BALL

THE spacious firmament on high,
With all the blue ethereal sky,
And spangled heavens, a shining frame,
Their great Original proclaim.
The unwearied sun from day to day
Does his Creator's power display,
And publishes to every land
The works of an almighty hand.

2 Soon as the evening shades prevail,
The moon takes up the wondrous tale,
And nightly to the listening earth
Repeats the story of her birth;
Whilst all the stars that round her burn,
And all the planets in their turn,
Confirm the tidings, as they roll,
And spread the truth from pole to pole.

3. What though in solemn silence all
Move round the dark terrestrial ball;
What though nor real voice nor sound
Amid their radiant orbs be found;
In reason's ear they all rejoice,
And utter forth a glorious voice,
For ever singing as they shine,
'The hand that made us is divine.'

Joseph Addison (1672–1719)
Based on Psalm 19, 1–6

22 BELGRAVE C.M.   WILLIAM HORSLEY (1774-1858)

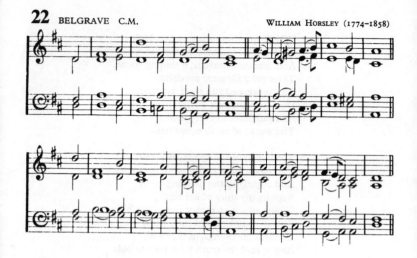

WHEN all thy mercies, O my God,
  My rising soul surveys,
Transported with the view, I'm lost
  In wonder, love, and praise.

2 Unnumbered comforts to my soul
    Thy tender care bestowed,
  Before my infant heart conceived
    From whom those comforts flowed.

3 When in the slippery paths of youth
    With heedless steps I ran,
  Thine arm unseen conveyed me safe,
    And led me up to man.

4 Ten thousand thousand precious gifts
   My daily thanks employ;
Nor is the least a cheerful heart,
   That tastes those gifts with joy.

5 Through every period of my life
   Thy goodness I'll pursue,
And after death in distant worlds
   The glorious theme renew.

6. Through all eternity to thee
   A joyful song I'll raise;
But O! eternity's too short
   To utter all thy praise.

Joseph Addison (1672–1719)

See also

299	All my hope		467	O God, our help
450	All people that on earth		470	O Lord, thou art my God
300	Awake, our souls		312	O thou in all thy might
452	Before the almighty Father's throne		471	O worship the King
272	For the beauty of the earth		474	The God of love
513	God liveth still	(CS)	475	The King of love
456	God's law is perfect		476	The Lord doth reign
491	Hast thou not known		26	The Lord is King!
461	Let us, with a gladsome mind		477	The Lord my pasture
265	Might and glory		478	The Lord of heaven confess
463	My soul, praise the Lord!		480	The Lord's my Shepherd
464	Now Israel may say		481	Through all the changing scenes
277	Now thank we all our God		482	Thy mercy, Lord
495	O God of Bethel		483	Ye boundless realms of joy

23 WELLINGTON SQUARE D.C.M.

GUY WARRACK (1900–)

ETERNAL God, whose power upholds
  Both flower and flaming star,
To whom there is no here nor there,
  No time, no near nor far,
No alien race, no foreign shore,
  No child unsought, unknown,
O send us forth, thy prophets true,
  To make all lands thine own!

HIS KINGDOM

2 O God of love, whose spirit wakes
    In every human breast,
Whom love, and love alone, can know,
    In whom all hearts find rest,
Help us to spread thy gracious reign,
    Till greed and hate shall cease,
And kindness dwell in human hearts,
    And all the earth find peace!

3 O God of truth, whom science seeks
    And reverent souls adore,
Who lightest every earnest mind
    Of every clime and shore,
Dispel the gloom of error's night,
    Of ignorance and fear,
Until true wisdom from above
    Shall make life's pathway clear!

4 O God of beauty, oft revealed
    In dreams of human art,
In speech that flows to melody,
    In holiness of heart;
Teach us to ban all ugliness
    That blinds our eyes to thee,
Till all shall know the loveliness
    Of lives made fair and free.

5. O God of righteousness and grace,
    Seen in the Christ, thy Son,
Whose life and death reveal thy face,
    By whom thy will was done,
Inspire thy heralds of good news
    To live thy life divine,
Till Christ is formed in all mankind,
    And every land is thine!

Henry Hallam Tweedy (1868–1953)

24 BELLWOODS S.M.

JAMES HOPKIRK (1908–)

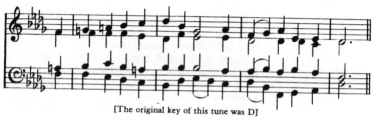

[The original key of this tune was D]

O DAY of God, draw nigh
In beauty and in power,
Come with thy timeless judgment now
To match our present hour.

2 Bring to our troubled minds,
Uncertain and afraid,
The quiet of a steadfast faith,
Peace of a call obeyed.

3 Bring justice to our land,
That all may dwell secure,
And build for all the days to come
Foundations that endure.

4 Bring to our world of strife
Thy sovereign word of peace,
That war may haunt the earth no more
And desolation cease.

5. O day of God, draw nigh,
As at creation's birth,
Let there be light again, and set
Thy judgments in the earth.

Robert Balgarnie Young Scott (1899–) *and Compilers*

25 SHERE S.M.   ERIC HARDING THIMAN (1900–   )

O LORD our God, arise!
  The cause of truth maintain,
And wide o'er all the peopled world
  Extend her blessèd reign.

2   Thou Prince of life, arise!
      Nor let thy glory cease;
  Far spread the conquests of thy grace,
      And bless the earth with peace.

3   O Holy Ghost, arise!
      Spread forth thy quickening wing,
  And o'er a dark and ruined world
      Let light and order spring.

4.   All on the earth, arise!
      To God the Saviour sing;
  From shore to shore, from earth to heaven,
      Let echoing anthems ring.

Ralph Wardlaw (1779–1853) *and Compilers*

26 CHURCH TRIUMPHANT L.M.   JAMES WILLIAM ELLIOTT (1833–1915)

T HE Lord is King! lift up thy voice,
   O earth, and all ye heavens, rejoice;
From world to world the joy shall ring,
'The Lord omnipotent is King!'

2 The Lord is King! who then shall dare
Resist his will, distrust his care,
Or murmur at his wise decrees,
Or doubt his royal promises?

3 The Lord is King! child of the dust,
The Judge of all the earth is just;
Holy and true are all his ways:
Let every creature speak his praise.

4. He reigns! ye saints, exalt your strains;
Your God is King, your Father reigns;
Through earth and heaven one song shall ring,
'The Lord omnipotent is King!'

Josiah Conder (1789–1855)

27 S. CECILIA 66.66.　　　　　　　　LEIGHTON GEORGE HAYNE (1836–83)

THY kingdom come, O God;
　Thy rule, O Christ, begin;
Break with thine iron rod
　The tyrannies of sin.

2 Where is thy reign of peace,
　And purity and love?
When shall all hatred cease,
　As in the realms above?

3 When comes the promised time
　That war shall be no more,
And lust, oppression, crime,
　Shall flee thy face before?

4 We pray thee, Lord, arise,
　And come in thy great might;
Revive our longing eyes,
　Which languish for thy sight.

5 Men scorn thy sacred name,
　And wolves devour thy fold;
By many deeds of shame
　We learn that love grows cold.

6. O'er lands both near and far
　Thick darkness broodeth yet:
Arise, O morning star,
　Arise, and never set.

Lewis Hensley (1824–1905) and Compilers

GOD: THE ETERNAL FATHER

Melody from *A Collection of Hymns and Sacred Poems* (Dublin, 1749)

28 IRISH C.M.

'THY kingdom come!' On bended knee
    The passing ages pray;
And faithful souls have yearned to see
    On earth that kingdom's day.

2 But the slow watches of the night
    Not less to God belong;
And for the everlasting right
    The silent stars are strong.

3 And lo, already on the hills
    The flags of dawn appear;
Gird up your loins, ye prophet souls,
    Proclaim the day is near;

4 The day in whose clear-shining light
    All wrong shall stand revealed;
When justice shall be throned in might,
    And every hurt be healed;

5. When knowledge, hand in hand with peace,
    Shall walk the earth abroad;
The day of perfect righteousness,
    The promised day of God.

Frederick Lucian Hosmer (1840–1929)

See also

452 Before the almighty Father's throne
485 Behold, the mountain
30 Come, thou long-expected Jesus
7 God is love

34 Lift up your heads, ye mighty gates
35 Lo! he comes
476 The Lord doth reign
479 The Lord will come

Many hymns under *The Lord Jesus Christ, His reign and priesthood* (Nos. 117–134) are also suitable.

THE LORD JESUS CHRIST

29 LICHFIELD 88.88. D.

WALTER K. STANTON (1891–)

ALL glory to God in the sky,
　And peace upon earth be restored;
O Jesus, exalted on high,
　Appear our omnipotent Lord;
Who, meanly in Bethlehem born,
　Didst stoop to redeem a lost race,
Once more to thy creatures return,
　And reign in thy kingdom of grace.

2 O wouldst thou again be made known,
　Again in thy Spirit descend,
And set up in each of thine own
　A kingdom that never shall end.
Thou only art able to bless,
　And make all the nations obey,
And bid the dire enmity cease,
　And bow the whole world to thy sway.

3. Come then to thy servants again,
    Who long thy appearing to know;
Thy quiet and peaceable reign
    In mercy establish below;
All sorrow before thee shall fly,
    And anger and hatred be o'er,
And envy and malice shall die,
    And discord afflict us no more.

Charles Wesley (1707–88) and Compilers

30 STUTTGART 87.87.

Adapted from a melody in
Psalmodia Sacra (Gotha, 1715)

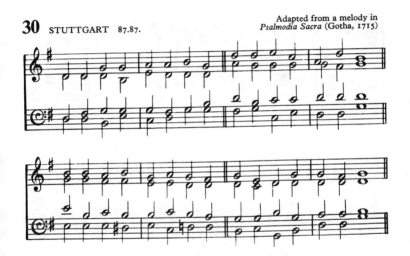

COME, thou long-expected Jesus,
    Born to set thy people free;
From our fears and sins release us,
    Let us find our rest in thee.

2 Israel's strength and consolation,
    Hope of all the earth thou art;
Dear desire of every nation,
    Joy of every longing heart.

3 Born thy people to deliver,
    Born a child, and yet a king;
Born to reign in us for ever,
    Now thy gracious kingdom bring.

4. By thine own eternal Spirit
    Rule in all our hearts alone;
By thine all-sufficient merit
    Raise us to thy glorious throne.

Charles Wesley (1707–88)

31

Mode iv

PSALM 125   L.M.

Allison's *Psalter* (1599)

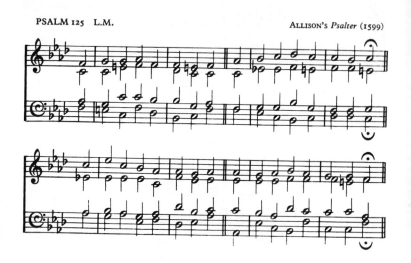

Conditor alme siderum

CREATOR of the starry height,
  Thy people's everlasting light,
Jesu, Redeemer of us all,
Hear thou thy servants when they call.

2 To thee the travail deep was known
  That made the whole creation groan,
  Till thou, Redeemer, shouldest free
  Thine own in glorious liberty.

3 When earth was near its evening hour,
  Thou didst, in love's redeeming power,
  Like bridegroom from his chamber, come
  From out a Virgin Mother's womb.

4 At thy great name, exalted now,
  All knees in lowly homage bow;
  All things in heaven and earth adore,
  And own thee King for evermore.

5 To thee, O Holy One, we pray,
  Our judge in that tremendous day,
  Ward off, while yet we dwell below,
  The weapons of our crafty foe.

6. To God the Father, God the Son,
  And God the Spirit, Three in One,
  Praise, honour, might, and glory be
  From age to age eternally. Amen.

7th cent. Tr. John Mason Neale (1818–66)

A - men.

32 HIGHWOOD 11.10.11.10.   RICHARD RUNCIMAN TERRY (1865–1938)

Unison

HARK what a sound, and too divine for hearing,
 Stirs on the earth and trembles in the air!
Is it the thunder of the Lord's appearing?
 Is it the music of his people's prayer?

2 Surely he cometh, and a thousand voices
 Shout to the saints, and to the deaf are dumb;
Surely he cometh, and the earth rejoices,
 Glad in his coming who hath sworn, 'I come.'

3 This hath he done, and shall we not adore him?
 This shall he do, and can we still despair?
Come, let us quickly fling ourselves before him,
 Cast at his feet the burden of our care.

4. Yea, through life, death, through sorrow and through sinning
 He shall suffice me, for he hath sufficed:
Christ is the end, for Christ was the beginning,
 Christ the beginning, for the end is Christ.

Frederic William Henry Myers (1843–1901)

33 LITTLE CORNARD 66.66.88.

Martin Shaw (1875–1958)

ORGAN

HIS ADVENT

HILLS of the north, rejoice;
   River and mountain-spring,
Hark to the advent voice;
   Valley and lowland, sing!
Though absent long, your Lord is nigh;
He judgment brings and victory.

2   Isles of the southern seas,
   Deep in your coral caves
Pent be each warring breeze,
   Lulled be your restless waves:
He comes to reign with boundless sway,
And makes your wastes his great highway.

3   Lands of the east, awake,
   Soon shall your sons be free;
The sleep of ages break,
   And rise to liberty.
On your far hills, long cold and grey,
Has dawned the everlasting day.

4   Shores of the utmost west,
   Ye that have waited long,
Unvisited, unblest,
   Break forth to swelling song;
High raise the note, that Jesus died,
Yet lives and reigns, the Crucified.

5.   Shout, while ye journey home!
   Songs be in every mouth!
Lo, from the north we come,
   From east and west and south.
City of God, the bond are free,
We come to live and reign in thee!

Charles Edward Oakley (1832–65)

34 LOWER MARLWOOD 84.84.884.

BASIL HARWOOD (1859-1949)

Macht hoch die Thür, das Thor macht weit

LIFT up your heads, ye mighty gates,
      Alleluia!
Behold, the King of glory waits;
      Alleluia!
The King of kings is drawing near,
The Saviour of the world is here.
      Alleluia!

2 O blest the land, the city blest,
      Alleluia!
Where Christ the ruler is confessed.
      Alleluia!
O happy hearts and happy homes
To whom this King in triumph comes.
      Alleluia!

3 Fling wide the portals of your heart,
      Alleluia!
Make it a temple set apart
      Alleluia!
From earthly use for heaven's employ,
Adorned with prayer and love and joy.
      Alleluia!

4. Redeemer, come! with us abide,
      Alleluia!
Our hearts to thee we open wide,
      Alleluia!
Let us thy inner presence feel,
Thy grace and love in us reveal.
      Alleluia!

Georg Weissel (1590–1635)
Tr. Catherine Winkworth (1827–78)

35 HELMSLEY 87.87.47.

English Melody (18th cent.)

LO! he comes with clouds descending,
Once for favoured sinners slain;
Thousand thousand saints attending
Swell the triumph of his train:
Alleluia!
Christ appears, in power to reign.

2 Every eye shall now behold him
Robed in dreadful majesty;
Those who set at naught and sold him,
Pierced and nailed him to the tree,
Deeply wailing,
Shall the true Messiah see.

3 Those dear tokens of his Passion
Still his dazzling body bears;
Cause of endless exultation
To his ransomed worshippers;
With what rapture
Gaze we on those glorious scars!

4. Yea, amen, let all adore thee,
High on thine eternal throne;
Saviour, take the power and glory:
Claim the kingdom for thine own:
Alleluia!
Thou shalt reign, and thou alone.

John Cennick (1718–55)
Charles Wesley (1707–88)
Martin Madan (1726–90)

36 VENI, IMMANUEL 88.88.88.

Melody adapted by THOMAS HELMORE (1811–90)
from a French Missal

Veni, veni, Immanuel

O COME, O come, Immanuel,
And ransom captive Israel,
That mourns in lonely exile here,
Until the Son of God appear.
Rejoice, rejoice! Immanuel
Shall come to thee, O Israel.

2 O come, O come, thou Lord of might,
Who to thy tribes, on Sinai's height,
In ancient times didst give the law
In cloud and majesty and awe:

3 O come, thou Rod of Jesse, free
Thine own from Satan's tyranny;
From depths of hell thy people save,
And give them victory o'er the grave:

4 O come, thou Dayspring, come and cheer
Our spirits by thine advent here;
Disperse the gloomy clouds of night,
And death's dark shadows put to flight:

5. O come, thou Key of David, come
And open wide our heavenly home;
Make safe the way that leads on high,
And close the path to misery:

From the Great O Antiphons (12th–13th cent.)
Tr. John Mason Neale (1818–66)

37 VERBUM SUPERNUM
(O SALUTARIS)

Mode viii (Mechlin Version)

UFFINGHAM L.M.

JEREMIAH CLARKE (1670–1707)

Verbum supernum prodiens

O HEAVENLY Word, eternal Light,
 Begotten of the Father's might,
Who in these latter days art born
For succour to a world forlorn;

2 Our hearts enlighten from above,
  And kindle with thine own true love;
  That we who hear thy call to-day
  May cast earth's vanities away.

3 And when as Judge thou drawest nigh,
  The secrets of all hearts to try;
  When sinners meet their aweful doom,
  And saints attain their heavenly home;

4 O let us not, for evil past,
  Be driven from thy face at last;
  But with thy saints for evermore
  Behold thee, love thee, and adore.

5. To God the Father, God the Son,
   And God the Spirit, Three in One,
   Praise, honour, might, and glory be
   From age to age eternally. Amen.

c. 10th cent.
Tr. Compilers of Hymns A. & M. and others

THE LORD JESUS CHRIST

38 WINCHESTER NEW L.M.
(CRASSELIUS)

Adapted from a Chorale in
Musikalisches Handbuch (Hamburg, 1690)

Jordanis oras praevia

ON Jordan's bank the Baptist's cry
Announces that the Lord is nigh;
Awake and hearken, for he brings
Glad tidings of the King of kings.

2 Then cleansed be every breast from sin,
Make straight the way for God within;
Prepare we in our hearts a home,
Where such a mighty guest may come.

3 For thou art our salvation, Lord,
Our refuge and our great reward;
Without thy grace we waste away
Like flowers that wither and decay.

4 To heal the sick stretch out thine hand,
And bid the fallen sinner stand;
Shine forth, and let thy light restore
Earth's own true loveliness once more.

5. All praise, eternal Son, to thee
Whose advent sets thy people free,
Whom with the Father we adore,
And Holy Ghost, for evermore. Amen.

Charles Coffin (1676–1749)
Tr. John Chandler (1806–76)
and Compilers of Hymns A. & M.

39 WINDERMERE S.M. ARTHUR SOMERVELL (1863–1937)

Instantis adventum Dei

THE advent of our King
Our prayers must now employ,
And we must hymns of welcome sing
In strains of holy joy.

2 The everlasting Son
Incarnate deigns to be;
Himself a servant's form puts on,
To set his servants free.

3 Daughter of Sion, rise
To meet thy lowly King;
Nor let thy faithless heart despise
The peace he comes to bring.

4. As Judge, on clouds of light,
Our King will come again,
And his true members all unite
With him in heaven to reign.

Charles Coffin (1676–1749)
Tr. John Chandler (1806–76) and others

THE LORD JESUS CHRIST

40 WACHET AUF Irregular. Melody adapted from PHILIPP NICOLAI (1556–1608)

WACHET AUF Irregular. Harmonized by JOHANN SEBASTIAN BACH (1685–1750)

Wachet auf! ruft uns die Stimme

'WAKE, O wake! for night is flying,'
 The watchmen on the heights are crying,
 'Awake, Jerusalem, at last!'
Midnight hears the welcome voices,
And at the thrilling cry rejoices:
 'Come forth, ye virgins, night is past!
 The Bridegroom comes; awake!
 Your lamps with gladness take;
 Alleluia!
 And for his marriage feast prepare,
 For ye must go to meet him there.'

2. Sion hears the watchmen singing,
 And all her heart with joy is springing;
 She wakes, she rises from her gloom;
For her Lord comes down all-glorious,
The strong in grace, in truth victorious;
 Her star is risen, her light is come.
 O come, thou blessèd one,
 God's own belovèd Son;
 Alleluia!
 We follow till the halls we see
 Where thou hast bid us sup with thee.

Philipp Nicolai (1556–1608)   *Tr. Catherine Winkworth* (1827–78)
Based on S. Matthew 25, 1–13

See also

484 Behold the amazing gift
340 Christian, seek not yet repose
457 Hail to the Lord's Anointed
490 Hark, the glad sound
460 Jesus shall reign
 24 O day of God
 25 O Lord our God, arise!

253 Ten thousand times ten thousand
479 The Lord will come
185 Thou whose almighty word
 27 Thy kingdom come, O God
 28 'Thy kingdom come!' On bended knee
372 Ye servants of the Lord

THE LORD JESUS CHRIST

41 ES IST EIN' ROS' 76.76.676.   German Melody. Harmonized by MICHAEL
ENTSPRUNGEN   PRAETORIUS (1571–1621)

And peace on⸺ earth to men.

And peace on earth to men.

Μέγα καὶ παράδοξον θαῦμα.

A GREAT and mighty wonder,
  A full and holy cure:
The Virgin bears the Infant
  With virgin-honour pure.
    Repeat the hymn again!
    'To God on high be glory,
    And peace on earth to men.'

2 The Word becomes incarnate
  And yet remains on high.
The angel host sings anthems
  To shepherds, from the sky:

3 While thus they sing your Monarch,
  Those bright angelic bands,
Rejoice, ye vales and mountains,
  Ye oceans, clap your hands!

4 Since all he comes to ransom,
  By all he be adored,
The Infant born in Bethlem,
  The Saviour and the Lord:

5. All idol forms shall perish,
  All error shall decay,
And Christ shall wield his sceptre,
  Our Lord and God for aye:

S. Germanus (634–732)
Tr. John Mason Neale (1818–66) *and Compilers*

42 IRIS 87.87.47. French or Flemish Melody

Come and wor - ship, wor-ship Christ, the new - born King.

ANGELS, from the realms of
   glory,
  Wing your flight o'er all the earth;
Ye who sang creation's story,
  Now proclaim Messiah's birth:
    Come and worship,
Worship Christ, the new-born King.

2 Shepherds, in the field abiding,
   Watching o'er your flocks by
    night,
God with man is now residing,
  Yonder shines the infant Light:

3 Sages, leave your contemplations,
  Brighter visions beam afar;
Seek the great Desire of nations,
  Ye have seen his natal star:

4. All creation, join in praising
  God the Father, Spirit, Son,
Evermore your voices raising
  To the eternal Three in One:

James Montgomery (1771–1854)

43 NORMANDY 11.11.11.11.

Normandy Carol

First Tune

[vv 1-2] [v. 3]

For Young Children

AWAY in a manger, no crib for a bed,
The little Lord Jesus laid down his sweet head.
The stars in the bright sky looked down where he lay,
The little Lord Jesus asleep on the hay.

2 The cattle are lowing, the baby awakes,
But little Lord Jesus no crying he makes.
I love thee, Lord Jesus; look down from the sky,
And stay by my bedside till morning is nigh.

3. Be near me, Lord Jesus; I ask thee to stay
Close by me for ever, and love me, I pray.
Bless all the dear children in thy tender care,
And fit us for heaven, to live with thee there.

Anon.

43 CRADLE SONG 11.11.11.11.

Melody by WILLIAM JAMES KIRKPATRICK
(1838–1921)

Second Tune

For Young Children

AWAY in a manger, no crib for a bed,
The little Lord Jesus laid down his sweet head.
The stars in the bright sky looked down where he lay,
The little Lord Jesus asleep on the hay.

2 The cattle are lowing, the baby awakes,
But little Lord Jesus no crying he makes.
I love thee, Lord Jesus; look down from the sky,
And stay by my bedside till morning is nigh.

3. Be near me, Lord Jesus; I ask thee to stay
Close by me for ever, and love me, I pray.
Bless all the dear children in thy tender care,
And fit us for heaven, to live with thee there.

Anon.

THE LORD JESUS CHRIST

44 THIS ENDRIS NYGHT C.M.

English Carol (15th century)

BEHOLD, the great Creator makes
　　Himself a house of clay;
A robe of human flesh he takes
　　Which he will wear for aye.

2 Hark, hark, the wise eternal Word
　　Like a weak infant cries!
In form of servant is the Lord,
　　And God in cradle lies.

3 This wonder struck the world amazed,
　　It shook the starry frame;
Squadrons of spirits stood and gazed,
　　Then down in troops they came.

4 Glad shepherds ran to view this sight;
　　A choir of angels sings,
And eastern sages with delight
　　Adore this King of kings.

5. Join then, all hearts that are not stone,
　　And all our voices prove,
To celebrate this holy one,
　　The God of peace and love.

Thomas Pestel (c. 1584–c. 1659)

45 BUNESSAN 55.53.D.

Gaelic Melody

Leanabh an aigh

CHILD in the manger,
  Infant of Mary;
Outcast and stranger
  Lord of all;
Child who inherits
  All our transgressions,
All our demerits
  On him fall.

2 Once the most holy
  Child of salvation
Gently and lowly
  Lived below;
Now as our glorious
  Mighty Redeemer,
See him victorious
  O'er each foe.

3. Prophets foretold him,
  Infant of wonder;
Angels behold him
  On his throne;
Worthy our Saviour
  Of all their praises;
Happy for ever
  Are his own.

Mary Macdonald (1817–c. 1890)
Tr. Lachlan Macbean (1853–1931)

46 YORKSHIRE 10.10.10.10.10.10. JOHN WAINWRIGHT (1723–68)

CHRISTIANS, awake, salute the happy morn,
Whereon the Saviour of the world was born;
Rise to adore the mystery of love,
Which hosts of angels chanted from above;
With them the joyful tidings first begun
Of God incarnate and the Virgin's Son.

2 Then to the watchful shepherds it was told,
Who heard the⌢angelic herald's voice, 'Behold,
'I bring good tidings of a Saviour's birth
'To you and all the nations on the earth;
'This day hath God fulfilled his promised word,
'This day is born a Saviour, Christ the Lord.'

3 To Bethlem straight the⌢enlightened shepherds ran,
To see the wonder God had wrought for man,
And found, with Joseph and the blessèd Maid,
Her Son, the Saviour, in a manger laid;
Joyful, the wondrous story they proclaim,
The first apostles of his infant fame.

4. O may we keep and ponder in our mind
God's wondrous love in saving lost mankind;
Trace we the Babe, who hath retrieved our loss,
From his poor manger to his bitter cross;
Saved by his love, incessant we shall sing
Eternal praise to heaven's almighty King.

John Byrom (1692–1763) and Compilers
Based on S. Luke 2, 8–17

THE LORD JESUS CHRIST

Mode iii

HERR JESU CHRIST L.M.

Nürnberg Gesangbuch (1676)

A solis ortus cardine

FROM east to west, from shore to shore,
Let every heart awake and sing
The holy Child whom Mary bore,
The Christ, the everlasting King.

2 Behold, the world's Creator wears
The form and fashion of a slave;
Our very flesh our Maker shares,
His fallen creature, man, to save.

3 For this how wondrously he wrought!
A maiden, in her lowly place,
Became, in ways beyond all thought,
The chosen vessel of his grace.

4 He shrank not from the oxen's stall,
He lay within the manger bed,
And he, whose bounty feedeth all,
At Mary's breast himself was fed.

5 And while the angels in the sky
Sang praise above the silent field,
To shepherds poor the Lord most high,
The one great Shepherd, was revealed.

6. All glory for this blessèd morn
To God the Father ever be;
All praise to thee, O Virgin-born,
All praise, O Holy Ghost, to thee. Amen.

Caelius Sedulius (died c. 450)
Tr. John Ellerton (1826–93) and Compilers of Hymns A. & M.

48 VOM HIMMEL HOCH L.M.

Melody attributed to
MARTIN LUTHER (1483–1546)

Vom Himmel hoch da komm ich her

GIVE heed, my heart, lift up thine eyes:
  Who is it in yon manger lies?
Who is this child so young and fair?
The blessèd Christ-child lieth there.

2 Dear Lord, who hast created all,
  How hast thou made thee weak and small,
  That thou must choose thy infant bed
  Where ass and ox but lately fed.

3 Were earth a thousand times as fair,
  Beset with gold and jewels rare,
  She yet were far too poor to be
  A narrow cradle, Lord, for thee.

4. O dearest Jesus, holy Child,
  Make thee a bed, soft, undefiled,
  Within my heart, that it may be
  A quiet chamber kept for thee.

Martin Luther (1483–1546)
Tr. Catherine Winkworth (1827–78) and Compilers

49 S. GEORGE S.M.
(GAUNTLETT)

HENRY JOHN GAUNTLETT (1805–76)

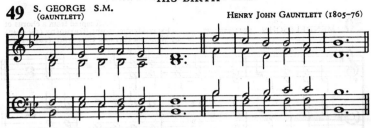

Jam desinant suspiria

GOD from on high hath heard;
  Let sighs and sorrows cease;
Lo, from the opening heaven descends
  To man the promised peace.

2 Hark, through the silent night
     Angelic voices swell;
   Their joyful songs proclaim that God
     Is born on earth to dwell.

3 See how the shepherd-band
     Speed on with eager feet;
   Come to the hallowed cave with them
     The holy Babe to greet.

4 But O, what sight appears
     Within that lowly door!
   A manger, stall, and swaddling clothes,
     A Child, and Mother poor!

5 Art thou the Christ? the Son?
     The Father's image bright?
   And see we him whose arm upholds
     Earth and the starry height?

6 Yea, faith can pierce the cloud
     Which veils thy glory now;
   We hail thee God, before whose throne
     The angels prostrate bow.

7. Our sinful pride to cure
     With that pure love of thine,
   O be thou born within our hearts,
     Most holy Child divine.

Charles Coffin (1676–1749)
Tr. James Russell Woodford (1820–85)

THE LORD JESUS CHRIST

50 MENDELSSOHN 7777.7777.77.

Adapted from a chorus of
FELIX MENDELSSOHN-BARTHOLDY (1809–47)
by WILLIAM HAYMAN CUMMINGS (1831–1915)

ORGAN

HARK, the herald-angels sing
'Glory to the new-born King;
Peace on earth, and mercy mild,
God and sinners reconciled!'
Joyful, all ye nations, rise,
Join the triumph of the skies,
With the angelic host proclaim,
'Christ is born in Bethlehem.'
Hark, the herald-angels sing,
'Glory to the new-born King'.

2 Christ, by highest heaven adored,
Christ, the everlasting Lord,
Late in time behold him come,
Offspring of a Virgin's womb.
Veiled in flesh the Godhead see;
Hail, the incarnate Deity,
Pleased as Man with man to dwell,
Jesus, our Immanuel!

3. Hail, the heaven-born Prince of peace!
Hail, the Sun of righteousness!
Light and life to all he brings,
Risen with healing in his wings.
Mild he lays his glory by,
Born that man no more may die,
Born to raise the sons of earth,
Born to give them second birth:

Charles Wesley (1707–88)
George Whitefield (1714–70)
Martin Madan (1726–90) *and others*

51 CRANHAM Irregular.

GUSTAV HOLST (1874–1934)

HIS BIRTH

IN the bleak mid-winter
   Frosty wind made moan;
Earth stood hard as iron,
   Water like a stone;
Snow had fallen, snow on snow,
   Snow on snow,
In the bleak mid-winter,
   Long ago.

2 Our God, heaven cannot hold him,
   Nor earth sustain;
Heaven and earth shall flee away
   When he comes to reign:
In the bleak mid-winter
   A stable-place sufficed
The Lord God Almighty,
   Jesus Christ.

3 Angels and archangels
   May have gathered there,
Cherubim and Seraphim
   Thronged the air:
But only his Mother,
   In her maiden bliss,
Worshipped the Belovèd
   With a kiss.

4. What can I give him,
   Poor as I am?
If I were a shepherd
   I would bring a lamb;
If I were a wise man
   I would do my part;
Yet what I can I give him—
   Give my heart.

Christina Rossetti (1830–94)

52 NOEL D.C.M.

English Traditional Melody arranged by
ARTHUR SEYMOUR SULLIVAN (1842–1900)

I ᵀ came upon the midnight clear,
   That glorious song of old,
From angels bending near the earth
   To touch their harps of gold:
'Peace on the earth, good will to men,
   From heaven's all-gracious King!'
The world in solemn stillness lay
   To hear the angels sing.

2 Still through the cloven skies they come,
   With peaceful wings unfurled;
And still their heavenly music floats
   O'er all the weary world;
Above its sad and lowly plains
   They bend on hovering wing;
And ever o'er its Babel sounds
   The blessèd angels sing.

3 Yet with the woes of sin and strife
    The world has suffered long;
Beneath the angel-strain have rolled
    Two thousand years of wrong;
And man, at war with man, hears
      not
    The love-song which they bring:
O hush the noise, ye men of strife,
    And hear the angels sing.

4. For lo, the days are hastening on,
    By prophet-bards foretold,
When, with the ever-circling years,
    Comes round the age of gold;
When peace shall over all the earth
    Its ancient splendours fling,
And all the world give back the song
    Which now the angels sing.

Edmund Hamilton Sears (1810–76) and Compilers
Based on S. Luke 2, 13–14

53 LOVE INCARNATE 67.67.

EDGAR PETTMAN (1865–1943)

L OVE came down at Christmas,
    Love all lovely, Love divine;
Love was born at Christmas,
    Star and angels gave the sign.

2 Worship we the Godhead,
    Love incarnate, Love divine;
Worship we our Jesus:
    But wherewith for sacred sign?

3. Love shall be our token,
    Love be yours and love be mine,
Love to God and all men,
    Love for plea and gift and sign.

Christina Rossetti (1830–94)

54

Mode i

Christe, Redemptor omnium

O CHRIST, Redeemer of our race,
   Thou brightness of the Father's face,
Of him, and with him ever One,
Ere times and seasons had begun;

2 Thou that art very Light of light,
   Unfailing hope in sin's dark night,
   Hear thou the prayers thy people pray
   The wide world o'er, this blessèd day.

3 Remember, Lord of life and grace,
   How once, to save a ruined race,
   Thou didst our very flesh assume
   In Mary's undefilèd womb.

4 This day, as year by year its light
   Sheds o'er the world a radiance bright,
   Tells how, descending from the throne,
   Thou savedst man, and thou alone.

5 Thou by the Father's will didst come
   To call his banished children home.
   Redeemed the new-made song we sing;
   It is the birthday of our King.

6. O Lord, the Virgin-born, to thee
   Eternal praise and glory be,
   Whom with the Father we adore,
   And Holy Ghost, for evermore. Amen.

6th cent. Tr. Henry Williams Baker (1821–77) and Compilers of Hymns A. & M.

A - men.

Another setting of this hymn will be found overleaf

54 S. BARTHOLOMEW L.M.

Melody by HENRY DUNCALF (18th cent.)

Christe, Redemptor omnium

O CHRIST, Redeemer of our race,
    Thou brightness of the Father's face,
Of him, and with him ever One,
Ere times and seasons had begun.;

2 Thou that art very Light of light,
    Unfailing hope in sin's dark night,
    Hear thou the prayers thy people pray
    The wide world o'er, this blessèd day.

3 Remember, Lord of life and grace,
    How once, to save a ruined race,
    Thou didst our very flesh assume
    In Mary's undefilèd womb.

4 This day, as year by year its light
    Sheds o'er the world a radiance bright,
    Tells how, descending from the throne,
    Thou savedst man, and thou alone.

5 Thou by the Father's will didst come
    To call his banished children home.
    Redeemed the new-made song we sing;
    It is the birthday of our King

6. O Lord, the Virgin-born, to thee
    Eternal praise and glory be,
    Whom with the Father we adore,
    And Holy Ghost, for evermore. Amen.

6th cent. Tr. Henry Williams Baker (1821–77) and Compilers of Hymns A. & M.

A - men.

THE LORD JESUS CHRIST

55 ADESTE FIDELES Irregular.

18th-century Melody

HIS BIRTH

Adeste, fideles

O COME, all ye faithful,
Joyful and triumphant,
O come ye, O come ye to Bethlehem:
Come and behold him,
Born the King of angels:
O come, let us adore him,
O come, let us adore him,
O come, let us adore him, Christ the Lord!

2 God of God,
Light of light,
Lo, he abhors not the Virgin's womb;
Very God,
Begotten, not created:

3* See how the shepherds,
Summoned to his cradle,
Leaving their flocks, draw nigh with lowly fear;
We too will thither
Bend our joyful footsteps:

4* Lo, star-led chieftains,
Wise men, Christ adoring,
Offer him incense, gold, and myrrh;
We to the Christ-child
Bring our hearts' oblations:

5* Child, for us sinners
Poor and in the manger,
Fain we embrace thee, with awe and love;
Who would not love thee,
Loving us so dearly?

6 Sing, choirs of angels,
Sing in exultation,
Sing, all ye citizens of heaven above;
Glory to God
In the highest:

7 Yea, Lord, we greet thee,
Born this happy morning,
Jesu, to thee be glory given;
Word of the Father,
Now in flesh appearing:

Before 18th cent. Tr. Frederick Oakeley (1802–80), W. T. Brooke and others

56 FOREST GREEN D.C.M. Irregular.

English Traditional Melody

HIS BIRTH

O LITTLE town of Bethlehem,
How still we see thee lie!
Above thy deep and dreamless sleep
The silent stars go by.
Yet in thy dark streets shineth
The everlasting light;
The hopes and fears of all the years
Are met in thee to-night.

2 O morning stars, together
Proclaim the holy birth,
And praises sing to God the King,
And peace to men on earth.
For Christ is born of Mary;
And, gathered all above,
While mortals sleep, the angels keep
Their watch of wondering love.

3 How silently, how silently,
The wondrous gift is given!
So God imparts to human hearts
The blessings of his heaven.
No ear may hear his coming;
But in this world of sin,
Where meek souls will receive him, still
The dear Christ enters in.

4 Where children pure and happy
Pray to the blessèd Child,
Where misery cries out to thee,
Son of the Mother mild;
Where charity stands watching,
And faith holds wide the door,
The dark night wakes, the glory breaks,
And Christmas comes once more.

5. O holy Child of Bethlehem,
Descend to us, we pray;
Cast out our sin, and enter in,
Be born in us to-day.
We hear the Christmas angels
The great glad tidings tell:
O come to us, abide with us,
Our Lord Immanuel.

Phillips Brooks (1835–93)

See also No. 532 (CS)

57 DIVINUM MYSTERIUM 87.87.877. Melody from *Piae Cantiones* (1582)

HIS BIRTH

Corde natus ex Parentis

OF the Father's love begotten
 Ere the worlds began to be,
He is Alpha and Omega,
 He the source, the ending he,
Of the things that are, that have been,
 And that future years shall see,
  Evermore and evermore.

2 O that birth for ever blessèd,
 When the Virgin, full of grace,
By the Holy Ghost conceiving,
 Bare the Saviour of our race,
And the Babe, the world's Redeemer,
 First revealed his sacred face,
  Evermore and evermore.

3 This is he whom seers of old time
 Chanted of with one accord;
Whom the voices of the prophets
 Promised in their faithful word;
Now he shines, the long-expected;
 Let creation praise its Lord,
  Evermore and evermore.

4 O ye heights of heaven, adore him;
 Angel hosts, his praises sing;
All dominions, bow before him,
 And extol our God and King;
Let no tongue on earth be silent,
 Every voice in concert ring,
  Evermore and evermore.

5. Christ, to thee, with God the Father,
 And, O Holy Ghost, to thee,
Hymn and chant and high thanksgiving,
 And unwearied praises be,
Honour, glory, and dominion,
 And eternal victory,
  Evermore and evermore. Amen.

Aurelius Clemens Prudentius (348–c. 410)
Tr. John Mason Neale (1818–66) and Henry Williams Baker (1821–77)

58 IRBY 87.87.77.

HENRY JOHN GAUNTLETT (1805–76)

HIS BIRTH

ONCE in royal David's city
    Stood a lowly cattle shed,
Where a Mother laid her baby
    In a manger for his bed;
Mary was that Mother mild,
Jesus Christ her little Child.

2 He came down to earth from heaven
    Who is God and Lord of all,
And his shelter was a stable,
    And his cradle was a stall;
With the poor and mean and lowly,
Lived on earth our Saviour holy.

3 And he is our childhood's pattern:
    Day by day like us he grew;
He was little, weak, and helpless;
    Tears and smiles like us he knew;
And he feeleth for our sadness,
And he shareth in our gladness.

4 And our eyes at last shall see him
    Through his own redeeming love,
For that Child so dear and gentle
    Is our Lord in heaven above;
And he leads his children on
To the place where he is gone.

5. Not in that poor lowly stable,
    With the oxen standing by,
We shall see him; but in heaven,
    Set at God's right hand on high;
When like stars his children crowned
All in white shall wait around.

Cecil Frances Alexander (1818–95)

59 JUBILATE DEO 77.77.77.

GEORGE THALBEN-BALL

LOXTON 77.77.77.

WALTER K. STANTON (1891–   )

S<small>ING</small>, O sing, this blessèd morn!
Unto us a Child is born,
Unto us a Son is given,
God himself comes down from heaven;
Sing, O sing, this blessèd morn,
Jesus Christ to-day is born.

2 God of God, and Light of light,
Comes with mercies infinite,
Joining in a wondrous plan
Heaven to earth and God to man:

3 God with us, Immanuel,
Deigns for ever now to dwell;
He on Adam's fallen race
Sheds the fullness of his grace:

4 God comes down that man may rise,
Lifted by him to the skies,
Christ is Son of Man that we
Sons of God in him may be:

5. O renew us, Lord, we pray,
With thy Spirit day by day,
That we ever one may be,
With the Father and with thee:

Christopher Wordsworth (1807–85)

THE LORD JESUS CHRIST

English Traditional Melody

THE maker of the sun and moon,
   The maker of our earth,
Lo, late in time, a fairer boon,
   Himself is brought to birth.

2 How blest was all creation then,
   When God so gave increase;
And Christ, to heal the hearts of men,
   Brought righteousness and peace.

3 His human form, by man denied,
   Took death for human sin;
His endless love, through faith descried,
   Still lives the world to win.

4. O perfect love, outpassing sight,
   O light beyond our ken,
Come down through all the world to-night,
   And heal the hearts of men!

Laurence Housman (1865–1959)

Verses 1–3 may be used at any season of the Church's year.

61 WINCHESTER OLD C.M.　　　　　　　　　　ESTE's *Psalter* (1592)

WHILE shepherds watched their
　　flocks by night,
All seated on the ground,
The angel of the Lord came down
And glory shone around.

2 'Fear not,' said he (for mighty dread
　　Had seized their troubled mind);
'Glad tidings of great joy I bring
　To you and all mankind.

3 'To you in David's town this day
　　Is born of David's line
A Saviour, who is Christ the Lord;
　And this shall be the sign:

4 'The heavenly Babe you there shall
　　find
　To human view displayed,
All meanly wrapped in swathing
　　bands,
　　And in a manger laid.'

5 Thus spake the seraph; and forthwith
　　Appeared a shining throng
Of angels praising God, who thus
　Addressed their joyful song:

6. 'All glory be to God on high,
　　And to the earth be peace;
Good-will henceforth from heaven to men
　Begin and never cease.'

Nahum Tate (1652–1715)
Based on S. Luke 2, 8–14

See also

501　All my heart　　　　　　(CS)
515　Into this world　　　　　(CS)
72　Jesus, good above all other

529　O Jesu, so meek　　　　(CS)
532　O little town　　　　　　(CS)
315　To us in Bethlem city

THE LORD JESUS CHRIST

62 DIX 77.77.77.

Abridged from a Chorale by
CONRAD KOCHER (1786–1872)

HIS MANIFESTATION

AS with gladness men of old
  Did the guiding star behold,
As with joy they hailed its light,
Leading onward, beaming bright;
So, most gracious Lord, may we
Evermore be led to thee.

2 As with joyful steps they sped,
  Saviour, to thy lowly bed,
  There to bend the knee before
  Thee whom heaven and earth adore;
  So may we with willing feet
  Ever seek thy mercy-seat.

3 As they offered gifts most rare,
  At thy cradle rude and bare;
  So may we with holy joy,
  Pure and free from sin's alloy,
  All our costliest treasures bring,
  Christ, to thee, our heavenly King.

4 Holy Jesus, every day
  Keep us in the narrow way;
  And, when earthly things are past,
  Bring our ransomed souls at last
  Where they need no star to guide,
  Where no clouds thy glory hide.

5. In the heavenly country bright
  Need they no created light;
  Thou its light, its joy, its crown,
  Thou its sun which goes not down:
  There for ever may we sing
  Alleluias to our King.

William Chatterton Dix (1837-58)
Based on S. Matthew 2, 1-11

63 JESMIAN 11.10.11.10.

GEORGE THALBEN-BALL

First Tune

BRIGHTEST and best of the sons of the morning,
　　Dawn on our darkness, and lend us thine aid;
Star of the east, the horizon adorning,
　　Guide where our infant Redeemer is laid.

2 Cold on his cradle the dew-drops are shining;
　　Low lies his head with the beasts of the stall;
Angels adore him in slumber reclining,
　　Maker and Monarch and Saviour of all.

3 Say, shall we yield him, in costly devotion,
　　Odours of Edom, and offerings divine,
Gems of the mountain, and pearls of the ocean,
　　Myrrh from the forest, or gold from the mine?

4. Vainly we offer each ample oblation,
　　Vainly with gifts would his favour secure:
Richer by far is the heart's adoration,
　　Dearer to God are the prayers of the poor.

Reginald Heber (1783–1826)

63 READY TOKEN 11.10.11.10. WALTER K. STANTON (1891–)

Second Tune

BRIGHTEST and best of the sons of the morning,
  Dawn on our darkness, and lend us thine aid;
Star of the east, the horizon adorning,
  Guide where our infant Redeemer is laid.

2 Cold on his cradle the dew-drops are shining;
  Low lies his head with the beasts of the stall;
Angels adore him in slumber reclining,
  Maker and Monarch and Saviour of all.

3 Say, shall we yield him, in costly devotion,
  Odours of Edom, and offerings divine,
Gems of the mountain, and pearls of the ocean,
  Myrrh from the forest, or gold from the mine?

4. Vainly we offer each ample oblation,
  Vainly with gifts would his favour secure:
Richer by far is the heart's adoration,
  Dearer to God are the prayers of the poor.

Reginald Heber (1783–1826)

64 STUTTGART 87.87.

Adapted from a melody in
Psalmodia Sacra (Gotha, 1715)

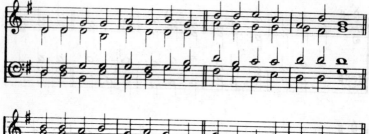

O sola magnarum urbium

EARTH has many a noble city;
  Bethlem, thou dost all excel:
Out of thee the Lord from heaven
  Came to rule his Israel.

2 Fairer than the sun at morning
  Was the star that told his birth,
To the world its God announcing,
  Seen in fleshly form on earth.

3 Eastern sages at his cradle
  Make oblations rich and rare;
See them give, in deep devotion,
  Gold and frankincense and myrrh.

4 Sacred gifts of mystic meaning:
  Incense doth their God disclose,
Gold the King of kings proclaimeth,
  Myrrh his sepulchre foreshows.

5. Holy Jesus, in thy brightness
    To the Gentile world displayed,
  With the Father and the Spirit
    Endless praise to thee be paid. Amen.

Aurelius Clemens Prudentius (348–c. 410)
Tr. Edward Caswall (1814–78)
Based on S. Matthew 2, 1–11

A - men.

65 CUDDESDON 65.65. D.   WILLIAM HAROLD FERGUSON (1874-1950)

FROM the eastern mountains
   Pressing on they come,
Wise men in their wisdom,
   To his humble home;
Stirred by deep devotion,
   Hasting from afar,
Ever journeying onward,
   Guided by a star.

2 There their Lord and Saviour
   Meek and lowly lay,
Wondrous light that led them
   Onward on their way,
Ever now to lighten
   Nations from afar,
As they journey homeward
   By that guiding star.

3 Thou who in a manger
   Once hast lowly lain,
Who dost now in glory
   O'er all kingdoms reign,

Gather in the peoples,
   Who in lands afar
Have not seen the brightness
   Of thy guiding star.

4 Gather in the outcasts,
   All who've gone astray;
Throw thy radiance o'er them,
   Guide them on their way;
Those who never knew thee,
   Those who've wandered far,
Guide them by the brightness
   Of thy guiding star.

5. Onward through the darkness
   Of the lonely night,
Shining still before them
   With thy kindly light,
Guide them, Jew and Gentile,
   Homeward from afar,
Young and old together,
   By thy guiding star.

Godfrey Thring (1823-1903) and Compilers
Based on S. Matthew 2, 1-10

E

66 MERTON 87.87.   WILLIAM HENRY MONK (1823–89)

HAIL, thou source of every blessing,
  Sovereign Father of mankind!
Gentiles now, thy grace possessing,
  In thy courts admission find.

2 Once far off, but now invited,
    We approach thy sacred throne;
  In thy covenant united,
    Reconciled, redeemed, made one.

3 Now revealed to eastern sages,
    See the star of mercy shine,
  Mystery hid in former ages,
    Mystery great of love divine.

4. Hail, thou universal Saviour!
    Gentiles now their offerings bring,
  In thy temple seek thy favour,
    Jesus Christ, our Lord and King.

Basil Woodd (1760–1831)

67

A Patre unigenitus

T̲HE Father's sole-begotten Son
　　Was born, the Virgin's child, on earth;
His Cross for us adoption won,
　　The life and grace of second birth.

2 Forth from the height of heaven he came,
　　In form of man with man abode;
Redeemed his world from death and shame,
　　The joys of endless life bestowed.

3 Redeemer, come with power benign,
　　Dwell in the souls that look for thee;
O let thy light within us shine,
　　That we may thy salvation see.

4. Eternal glory, Lord, to thee,
　　Whom, now revealed, our hearts adore;
To God the Father glory be,
　　And Holy Spirit, evermore. Amen.

Latin Acrostic Poem
Tr. Thomas Benson Pollock (1836–1896) and Compilers of Hymns A. & M.

Metrical tune and words overleaf.

THE LORD JESUS CHRIST

Later version of melody by
WILLIAM KNAPP (1698–1768)

A Patre unigenitus

THE Father's sole-begotten Son
    Was born, the Virgin's child, on earth;
His Cross for us adoption won,
    The life and grace of second birth.

2 Forth from the height of heaven he came,
    In form of man with man abode;
Redeemed his world from death and shame,
    The joys of endless life bestowed.

3 Redeemer, come with power benign,
    Dwell in the souls that look for thee;
O let thy light within us shine,
    That we may thy salvation see.

4. Eternal glory, Lord, to thee,
    Whom, now revealed, our hearts adore;
To God the Father glory be,
    And Holy Spirit, evermore. Amen.

Latin Acrostic Poem
Tr. Thomas Benson Pollock (1836–1896) and Compilers of Hymns A. & M.

A - men.

68 TALLIS' ORDINAL C.M.   THOMAS TALLIS (*c.* 1510–*c.* 1585)

Satus Dei, volens tegi

THE Son of God his glory hides
   With parents mean and poor;
And he, who made the heavens, abides
   In village home obscure.

2 Those mighty hands that bear the sky
   No earthly toil refuse;
And he who set the stars on high
   A humble trade pursues.

3 He in whose sight the angels stand,
   At whose behest they fly,
Now yields himself to man's command
   And lays his glory by.

4. For this thy lowliness revealed,
   Jesu, we thee adore,
And praise to God the Father yield,
   And Spirit evermore. Amen.

Jean-Baptiste de Santeuil (1630–97) *Tr. John Chandler* (1806–76) *and others*
Based on S. Luke 2, 51

A - men.

69

Mode ii

AFFECTION L.M.

GREENWOOD'S *Psalmody*

HIS MANIFESTATION

Quae stella sole pulchrior

WHAT star is this with beams so bright,
More beauteous than the noon-day light?
It heralds forth the King of kings,
And Gentiles to his cradle brings.

2 See now fulfilled what God decreed,
'From Jacob shall a star proceed';
And eastern sages with amaze
Upon the wondrous vision gaze.

3 The guiding star above is bright,
Within them shines a clearer light,
Which leads them on with power benign
To seek the giver of the sign.

4 True love can brook no dull delay,
Nor toil nor dangers stop their way;
Home, kindred, fatherland, and all
They leave at their Creator's call.

5 While now the shining star of grace
Draws us, O Christ, to seek thy face,
Let not our slothful hearts refuse
The guidance of that light to use.

6. To God the Father, heavenly Light,
To Christ, revealed in earthly night,
To God the Holy Ghost, we raise
Our equal and unceasing praise. Amen.

Charles Coffin (1676–1749)
Tr. John Chandler (1806–76) and others
Based on Numbers 24, 17, and S. Matthew 2, 1–10

See also

117, 118	All hail the power	460	Jesus shall reign
120	At the name of Jesus	178	Lift up your heads, ye gates of brass
172	Christ for the world	523	Love, unto thine own (CS)
177	God is working his purpose out	267	O worship the Lord
455	God of mercy	496	The race that long in darkness pined
457	Hail to the Lord's Anointed	185	Thou whose almighty word
141	How brightly beams		

THE LORD JESUS CHRIST

70 SURREY 88.88.88.

HENRY CAREY (1690-1743)

A STRANGER once did bless the earth
    Who never caused a heart to mourn,
Whose very voice gave sorrow mirth—
    And how did earth his worth return?
It spurned him from its lowliest lot,
The meanest station owned him not.

2 An outcast thrown in sorrow's way,
    A fugitive that knew no sin,
Yet in lone places forced to stray—
    Men would not take the stranger in.
Yet peace, though much himself he mourned,
Was all to others he returned.

3 His presence was a peace to all,
    He bade the sorrowful rejoice.
Pain turned to pleasure at his call,
    Health lived and issued from his voice;
He healed the sick, and sent abroad
The dumb rejoicing in the Lord.

4 The blind met daylight in his eye,
    The joys of everlasting day;
The sick found health in his reply;
    The cripple threw his crutch away.
Yet he with troubles did remain,
And suffered poverty and pain.

5. It was for sin he suffered all
    To set the world-imprisoned free,
To cheer the weary when they call—
    And who could such a stranger be?
The God, who hears each human cry,
And came, a Saviour, from on high.

John Clare (1793–1864) *and Compilers*

THE LORD JESUS CHRIST

71 FITZWILLIAM 888.6.

English Traditional Melody

I T fell upon a summer day,
   When Jesus walked in Galilee,
The mothers from a village brought
   Their children to his knee.

2 He took them in his arms, and laid
   His hands on each remembered head;
'Suffer these little ones to come
   To me,' he gently said.

3 'Forbid them not; unless ye bear
   The childlike heart your hearts within,
Unto my kingdom ye may come,
   But may not enter in.'

4 Master, I fain would enter there;
   O let me follow thee, and share
Thy meek and lowly heart, and be
   Freed from all worldly care.

5 Of innocence and love and trust,
   Of quiet work and simple word,
Of joy, and thoughtlessness of self,
   Build up my life, good Lord.

6. O happy thus to live and move!
   And sweet this world, where I shall find
God's beauty everywhere, his love,
   His good in all mankind.

Stopford Augustus Brooke (1832–1916)
Based on S. Mark 10, 13–16

72 QUEM PASTORES
LAUDAVERE 888.7.

Melody from a 14th-century German MS.

JESUS, good above all other,
　Gentle child of gentle mother,
In a stable born our brother,
　Give us grace to persevere.

2 Jesus, cradled in a manger,
　For us facing every danger,
　Living as a homeless stranger,
　　Make we thee our King most dear.

3 Jesus, for thy people dying,
　Risen Master, death defying,
　Lord in heaven, thy grace supplying,
　　Keep us to thy presence near.

4 Jesus, who our sorrows bearest,
　All our thoughts and hopes thou sharest;
　Thou to man the truth declarest;
　　Help us all thy truth to hear.

5. Lord, in all our doings guide us;
　Pride and hate shall ne'er divide us;
　We'll go on with thee beside us,
　　And with joy we'll persevere!

Percy Dearmer (1867-1936)

73 EISENACH L.M.

Later form of melody by
JOHANN HERMANN SCHEIN (1586–1630)

O amor quam ecstaticus

O LOVE, how deep, how broad, how high!
It fills the heart with ecstasy,
That God, the Son of God, should take
Our mortal form for mortals' sake.

2 For us he was baptized, and bore
His holy fast, and hungered sore;
For us temptations sharp he knew;
For us the tempter overthrew.

3 For us he prayed, for us he taught,
For us his daily works he wrought,
By words and signs and actions, thus
Still seeking not himself but us.

4 For us to wicked men betrayed,
Scourged, mocked, in purple robe arrayed,
He bore the shameful cross and death;
For us at length gave up his breath.

5. For us he rose from death again,
For us he went on high to reign,
For us he sent his Spirit here,
To guide, to strengthen, and to cheer.

? Thomas à Kempis (1379–1471) Tr. Benjamin Webb (1820–85)

74 DAS NEUGEBORNE
KINDELEIN 88.88.88.

Melody by MELCHIOR VULPIUS (1609)
Harmony chiefly by JOHANN SEBASTIAN BACH
(1685–1750)

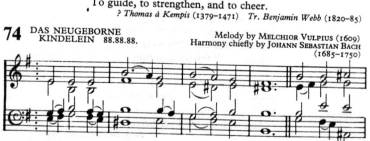

WE saw thee not when thou didst come
    To this poor world of sin and death,
Nor e'er beheld thy cottage home
    In that despisèd Nazareth;
But we believe thy footsteps trod
Its streets and plains, thou Son of God.

2 We did not see thee lifted high
    Amid that wild and savage crew,
Nor heard thy meek imploring cry:
    'Forgive, they know not what they do';
Yet we believe the deed was done,
Which shook the earth and veiled the sun.

3 We stood not by the empty tomb
    Where late thy sacred body lay,
Nor sat within that upper room,
    Nor met thee in the open way:
But we believe that angels said
'Why seek the living with the dead?'

4 We did not mark the chosen few,
    When thou didst through the clouds ascend,
First lift to heaven their wondering view,
    Then to the earth all prostrate bend;
Yet we believe that mortal eyes
Beheld that journey to the skies.

5 And now that thou art throned above,
    And dost from heaven thy people bless,
Thy promised Spirit's light and love
    Still shine upon our wilderness.
For we believe thy faithful word,
And trust in our redeeming Lord.

John Hampden Gurney (1802–62) *and Compilers*

THE LORD JESUS CHRIST

75 RESONET IN LAUDIBUS 77.88. and Refrain.

German Carol Melody (14th century)

Unison

(vv 2-4-6 end here)

At his feet we hum-bly fall; Crown him, crown him Lord of all.

At his feet we hum-bly fall—the Lord of all. Crown him,

crown him, crown him, crown him, crown him Lord of all.

WHO is he in yonder stall,
    At whose feet the shepherds fall?
'Tis the Lord, O wondrous story!
'Tis the Lord, the King of glory!
At his feet we humbly fall;
Crown him, crown him Lord of all.

2 Who is he in deep distress,
   Fasting in the wilderness?
'Tis the Lord, O wondrous story!
'Tis the Lord, the King of glory!

3 Who is he the gathering throng
   Greet with loud triumphant song?
'Tis the Lord, O wondrous story!
'Tis the Lord, the King of glory!
At his feet we humbly fall;
Crown him, crown him Lord of all.

4 Lo, at midnight, who is he
   Prays in dark Gethsemane?
'Tis the Lord, O wondrous story!
'Tis the Lord, the King of glory!

5 Who is he on yonder tree
   Dies in shame and agony?
'Tis the Lord, O wondrous story!
'Tis the Lord, the King of glory!
At his feet we humbly fall;
Crown him, crown him Lord of all.

6 Who is he that from the grave
   Comes to heal and help and save?
'Tis the Lord, O wondrous story!
'Tis the Lord, the King of glory!

7. Who is he that from his throne
   Rules through all the world alone?
'Tis the Lord, O wondrous story!
'Tis the Lord, the King of glory!
At his feet we humbly fall;
Crown him, crown him Lord of all.

Benjamin Russell Hanby (1833–67) and Compilers

See also

341 Forty days and forty nights
 81 It is a thing most wonderful
343 Lone in the desert

 83 Lord, who throughout
 84 My song is love unknown

76 MYLOR L.M.

WALTER K. STANTON (1891–)

Good Friday

A TIME to watch, a time to pray,
A day of wonders is to-day:
The saddest, yet the gladdest too,
That ever man or angel knew.

2 The saddest—for our Saviour bore
His death, that man might die no more:
The agony, the scourge, the fear,
The crown of thorns, the cross, the spear;

3 And yet the gladdest—for to-day
Our load of sin was borne away:
And hopes of joy that never dies
Hang on our Saviour's sacrifice.

4. O Saviour, blessèd be thy name!
Thine is the glory, ours the shame;
By all the pain thy love endured
Let all our many sins be cured.

John Mason Neale (1818–66) and Compilers

77 S. THEODULPH 76.76.D.

MELCHIOR TESCHNER (c. 1613)

Fine

Palm Sunday

Gloria, laus, et honor

ALL glory, laud, and honour
  To thee, Redeemer, King,
To whom the lips of children
  Made sweet hosannas ring.
Thou art the King of Israel,
  Thou David's royal Son,
Who in the Lord's name comest,
  The King and blessèd one.

2 The company of angels
   Are praising thee on high,
And mortal men and all things
   Created make reply.
The people of the Hebrews
   With palms before thee went;
Our praise and prayer and anthems
   Before thee we present.

3 To thee before thy Passion
   They sang their hymns of praise;
To thee now high exalted
   Our melody we raise.
Thou didst accept their praises;
   Accept the prayers we bring,
Who in all good delightest,
   Thou good and gracious King.

4. All glory, laud, and honour
   To thee, Redeemer, King,
To whom the lips of children
   Made sweet hosannas ring.

S. Theodulph of Orléans (died 821)
Tr. John Mason Neale (1818–66)

See also No. 78

78 S. THEODULPH 76.76.

MELCHIOR TESCHNER (*c.* 1613)

Palm Sunday

Gloria, laus, et honor

*A*LL glory, laud, and honour
  To thee, Redeemer, King,
To whom the lips of children
Made sweet hosannas ring.

2 Thou art the King of Israel,
    Thou David's royal Son,
  Who in the Lord's name comest,
    The King and blessèd one:

3 The company of angels
    Are praising thee on high,
  And mortal men and all things
    Created make reply:

4 The people of the Hebrews
    With palms before thee went;
  Our praise and prayer and anthems
    Before thee we present:

5 To thee before thy Passion
    They sang their hymns of praise;
  To thee now high exalted
    Our melody we raise:

6. Thou didst accept their praises;
    Accept the prayers we bring,
  Who in all good delightest,
    Thou good and gracious King:

S. Theodulph of Orléans (died 821)
Tr. John Mason Neale (1818–66)

See also No. 77

79 BANGOR C.M. WILLIAM TANZER, *Harmony of Sion* (1734)

Solus ad victimam procedis, Domine

Alone thou goest forth, O Lord,
  In sacrifice to die;
Is thy dread sorrow naught to us
  Who pass unheeding by?

2 Our sins, not thine, thou bearest, Lord;
    Make us thy sorrow feel,
  Till through our pity and our shame
    Love answers love's appeal.

3 Thou, in each darkest hour of earth,
    Canst light and life restore;
  Then let all praise be given to thee
    Who livest evermore.

4. Grant us to suffer with thee, Lord,
    That, as we share this hour,
  Thy Cross may bring us to thy joy
    And resurrection power.

Peter Abelard (1079–1142)
Tr. F. Bland Tucker (1895–) *and Compilers*

Another translation of these words will be found at No. 502 (CS)

80 STABAT MATER 887. D.

French Melody

Verses 1, 3, 5

CHRISTI MUTTER STUND VOR SCHMERZEN 887. D.

Melody from CORNER's *Gesangbuch* (1625)

Verses 2, 4

Either tune may be used for the whole hymn.

Stabat Mater dolorosa

AT the Cross, her station keeping,
   Stood the mournful Mother weeping,
     Where he hung, the dying Lord;
For her soul, of joy bereavèd,
Bowed with anguish, deeply grievèd,
     Felt the sharp and piercing sword.

2 O how sad and sore distressèd
   Now was she, that Mother blessèd
     Of the sole-begotten one;
Deep the woe of her affliction
When she saw the crucifixion
     Of her ever-glorious Son.

3 Who, on Christ's dear Mother gazing,
   Pierced by anguish so amazing,
     Born of woman, would not weep?
Who, on Christ's dear Mother thinking,
Such a cup of sorrow drinking,
     Would not share her sorrows deep?

4 She beheld his tribulation
   For the sins of every nation,
     Saw him scourged and led to death,
Saw her Child, in death forsaken,
All his comfort from him taken,
     Till he yielded up his breath.

5. Jesu, may her deep devotion
   Stir in me the same emotion,
     Fount of love, Redeemer kind;
That my heart, fresh ardour gaining,
And a purer love attaining,
     May with thee acceptance find.

13th cent. Tr. Edward Caswall (1814–78) and others

81 HERONGATE L.M.   English Traditional Melody

I T is a thing most wonderful,
  Almost too wonderful to be,
That God's own Son should come from heaven,
  And die to save a child like me.

2 And yet I know that it is true:
  He chose a poor and humble lot,
And wept and toiled and mourned and died,
  For love of those who loved him not.

3 But even could I see him die,
  I could but see a little part
Of that great love, which, like a fire,
  Is always burning in his heart.

4 It is most wonderful to know
  His love for me so free and sure;
But 'tis more wonderful to see
  My love for him so faint and poor.

5. And yet I want to love theé, Lord;
  O light the flame within my heart,
And I will love thee more and more,
  Until I see thee as thou art.

William Walsham How (1823–97)

82 AD INFEROS 87.87.   WALTER HAY SANGSTER (1835–99)

I T is finished! blessèd Jesus,
   Thou hast breathed thy latest sigh,
Teaching us, the sons of Adam,
How the Son of God can die.

2 Lifeless lies the piercèd body,
   Resting in its rocky bed;
Thou hast left the cross of anguish
For the mansions of the dead.

3 In the hidden realms of darkness
   Shines a light unseen before,
When the Lord of dead and living
Enters at the lowly door.

4 Now in spirit, rich in mercy
   Comes he from the world above,
Preaching to the souls in prison
Tidings of his dying love.

5 Lo, the heavenly light around him,
   As he draws his people near;
All amazed they come rejoicing
At the gracious words they hear.

6 Patriarch and Priest and Prophet
   Gather round him as he stands,
In adoring faith and gladness
Hearing of the piercèd hands.

7 There in lowliest joy and wonder
   Stands the robber by his side,
Reaping now the blessèd promise
Spoken by the Crucified.

8. Jesus, Lord of our salvation,
   Let thy mercy rest on me;
Grant me too, when life is finished,
Rest in Paradise with thee.

William Dalrymple Maclagan (1826–1910) and Compilers
Based on 1 Peter 3, 18–19

83 S. MARY C.M.

PRYS' *Psalter* (1621)

LORD, who throughout these forty days
    For us didst fast and pray,
Teach us with thee to mourn our sins,
    And at thy side to stay.

2 As thou with Satan didst contend,
    And didst the victory win,
O give us strength in thee to fight,
    In thee to conquer sin.

3 As thirst and hunger thou didst bear,
    So teach us, gracious Lord,
To die to self, and daily live
    By thy most holy word.

4. And through these days of penitence,
    And through thy Passiontide,
Yea, evermore, in life and death,
    Lord Christ, with us abide.

Claudia Frances Hernaman (1838–98) and Compilers

84 PSALM 47 66.66.44.44.

Melody by HENRY LAWES (1595–1662)

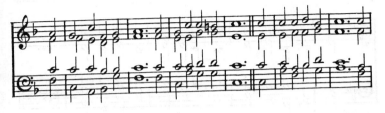

M Y song is love unknown,
  My Saviour's love to me,
Love to the loveless shown,
  That they might lovely be.
    O who am I,
      That for my sake
      My Lord should take
    Frail flesh and die?

2 He came from his blest throne,
    Salvation to bestow:
  But men made strange, and none
    The longed-for Christ would
        know.
    But O, my friend,
      My friend indeed,
      Who at my need
    His life did spend!

3 Sometimes they strew his way,
    And his sweet praises sing;
  Resounding all the day
    Hosannas to their King.
    Then 'Crucify!'
      Is all their breath,
      And for his death
    They thirst and cry.

4 In life, no house, no home
    My Lord on earth might have;
  In death, no friendly tomb
    But what a stranger gave.
    What may I say?
      Heaven was his home:
      But mine the tomb
    Wherein he lay.

5. Here might I stay and sing,
    No story so divine;
  Never was love, dear King,
    Never was grief like thine!
    This is my friend,
      In whose sweet praise
      I all my days
    Could gladly spend.

Samuel Crossman (1624–83)

THE LORD JESUS CHRIST

85 LLANGLOFFAN 76.86.D.

Welsh Melody

O CRUCIFIED Redeemer,
   Whose life-blood we have spilt,
To thee we raise our guilty hands,
   And humbly own our guilt.
To-day we see thy Passion
   Spread open to our gaze;
The crowded street, the country cot,
   Its Calvary displays.

2 Wherever love is outraged,
   Wherever hope is killed,
Where man still wrongs his brother man,
   Thy Passion is fulfilled.
We see thy tortured body,
   We see the wounds that bleed,
Where brotherhood hangs crucified,
   Nailed to the cross of greed.

3 We hear thy cry of anguish,
   We see thy life outpoured,
Where battlefield runs red with blood,
   Our brothers' blood, O Lord.
And in that bloodless battle,
   The fight for daily bread,
Where might is right and self is king,
   We see thy thorn-crowned head.

4. The groaning of creation,
   Wrung out by pain and care;
The anguish of a million hearts
   That break in dumb despair:
O crucified Redeemer,
   These are thy cries of pain;
O may they break our selfish hearts,
   And love come in to reign.

Timothy Rees, C.R. (1874–1939), and Compilers

THE LORD JESUS CHRIST

Melody by HANS LEO HASSLER (1564–1612)
adapted and harmonized by
JOHANN SEBASTIAN BACH (1685–1750)

O Haupt voll Blut und Wunden

O SACRED head, sore wounded,
  Defiled and put to scorn;
O kingly head, surrounded
  With mocking crown of thorn:
What sorrow mars thy grandeur?
  Can death thy bloom deflower?
O countenance whose splendour
  The hosts of heaven adore!

2 In thy most bitter Passion
  My heart to share doth cry,
With thee for my salvation
  Upon the cross to die.
Ah, keep my heart thus movèd
  To stand thy cross beneath,
To mourn thee, well-belovèd,
  Yet thank thee for thy death.

3. My days are few, O fail not,
  With thine immortal power,
To hold me that I quail not
  In death's most fearful hour:
That I may fight befriended,
  And see in my last strife
To me thine arms extended
  Upon the cross of life.

From Salve caput cruentatum (? Arnulf von Loewen, 1200–50)
Tr. Paulus Gerhardt (1607–76). Par. Robert Bridges (1844–1930)

See also No. 533 (CS)

87 ENGEDI 86.886.   SAMUEL SEBASTIAN WESLEY (1810-76)

O SAVIOUR, where shall guilty man
  Find rest, except in thee?
Thine was the warfare with his foe,
The cross of pain, the cup of woe,
  And thine the victory.

2 How came the everlasting Son,
  The Lord of life, to die?
Why didst thou meet the tempter's power?
Why didst thou, in thy dying hour,
  Endure such agony?

3 To save us by thy precious blood,
  To make us one in thee,
That ours might be thy perfect life,
Thy thorny crown, thy cross, thy strife,
  And ours the victory.

4. O make us worthy, gracious Lord,
  Of all thy love to be;
To thy blest will our wills incline,
That unto death we may be thine,
  And ever live in thee.

                    Caroline Elizabeth May (1808-73) *and Compilers*

THE LORD JESUS CHRIST

88 RICHMOND C.M.

Adapted from THOMAS HAWEIS (1734–1820)
by SAMUEL WEBBE the younger (1770–1843)

PRAISE to the Holiest in the height,
    And in the depth be praise;
In all his words most wonderful,
    Most sure in all his ways.

2 O loving wisdom of our God!
    When all was sin and shame,
A second Adam to the fight
    And to the rescue came.

3 O wisest love! that flesh and blood,
    Which did in Adam fail,
Should strive afresh against the foe,
    Should strive and should prevail;

4 And that a higher gift than grace
    Should flesh and blood refine,
God's presence and his very self,
    And essence ali-divine.

5 O generous love! that he who smote
    In Man, for man, the foe,
The double agony in Man,
    For man, should undergo;

6 And in the garden secretly,
    And on the cross on high,
Should teach his brethren, and inspire
    To suffer and to die.

7. Praise to the Holiest in the height,
    And in the depth be praise;
In all his words most wonderful,
    Most sure in all his ways.

John Henry Newman (1801–90)

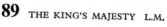

89 THE KING'S MAJESTY L.M.

GRAHAM GEORGE (1912–   )

WINCHESTER NEW L.M.
(CRASSELIUS)

Adapted from a Chorale in
Musikalisches Handbuch (Hamburg, 1690)

HIS SUFFERING AND DEATH

Palm Sunday

RIDE on! ride on in majesty!
  Hark, all the tribes 'Hosanna' cry;
O Saviour meek, pursue thy road
With palms and scattered garments strowed.

2 Ride on! ride on in majesty!
  In lowly pomp ride on to die;
  O Christ, thy triumphs now begin,
  O'er captive death and conquered sin.

3 Ride on! ride on in majesty!
  The angel armies of the sky
  Look down with sad and wondering eyes
  To see the^approaching sacrifice.

4 Ride on! ride on in majesty!
  Thy last and fiercest strife is nigh;
  The Father on his sapphire throne
  Awaits his own anointed Son.

5. Ride on! ride on in majesty!
  In lowly pomp ride on to die;
  Bow thy meek head to mortal pain,
  Then take, O God, thy power, and reign.

Henry Hart Milman (1791–1868)

F

90 PANGE, LINGUA   Mode iii

PANGE, LINGUA   Mode iii (Mechlin Version)

HIS SUFFERING AND DEATH

Passion Sunday

Pange, lingua, gloriosi proelium certaminis

SING, my tongue, the glorious battle,
　Sing the last, the dread affray;
O'er the Cross, the Victor's trophy,
　Sound the high triumphal lay:
How, the pains of death enduring,
　Earth's Redeemer won the day.

2 Faithful Cross! above all other,
　One and only noble tree!
None in foliage, none in blossom,
　None in fruit thy peer may be;
Sweetest wood and sweetest iron!
　Sweetest weight is hung on thee.

3 Bend, O lofty tree, thy branches,
　Thy too rigid sinews bend;
And awhile the stubborn hardness
　Which thy birth bestowed, suspend;
And the limbs of heaven's high Monarch
　Gently on thine arms extend.

4 Thou alone wast counted worthy
　This world's ransom to sustain,
That by thee a wrecked creation
　Might its ark and haven gain,
With the sacred blood anointed
　Of the Lamb that hath been slain.

5. Praise and honour to the Father,
　Praise and honour to the Son,
Praise and honour to the Spirit,
　Ever Three and ever One,
One in might and One in glory,
　While eternal ages run. Amen.

Venantius Fortunatus (c. 530–609)
Tr. John Mason Neale (1818–66) and others

Another setting of this hymn will be found overleaf

90 S. THOMAS 87.87.87.

Melody from SAMUEL WEBBE'S
Motetts or Antiphons (1792) and
An Essay on the Church Plain Chant (1782)

HIS SUFFERING AND DEATH

Passion Sunday

Pange, lingua, gloriosi proelium certaminis

SING, my tongue, the glorious battle,
   Sing the last, the dread affray;
O'er the Cross, the Victor's trophy,
   Sound the high triumphal lay:
How, the pains of death enduring,
   Earth's Redeemer won the day.

2 Faithful Cross! above all other,
   One and only noble tree!
None in foliage, none in blossom,
   None in fruit thy peer may be;
Sweetest wood and sweetest iron!
   Sweetest weight is hung on thee.

3 Bend, O lofty tree, thy branches,
   Thy too rigid sinews bend;
And awhile the stubborn hardness
   Which thy birth bestowed, suspend;
And the limbs of heaven's high Monarch
   Gently on thine arms extend.

4 Thou alone wast counted worthy
   This world's ransom to sustain,
That by thee a wrecked creation
   Might its ark and haven gain,
With the sacred blood anointed
   Of the Lamb that hath been slain.

5. Praise and honour to the Father,
   Praise and honour to the Son,
Praise and honour to the Spirit,
   Ever Three and ever One,
One in might and One in glory,
   While eternal ages run. Amen.

Venantius Fortunatus (c. 530–609)
Tr. John Mason Neale (1818–66) and others

A - men.

91 VEXILLA REGIS

Mode i

GONFALON ROYAL L.M.

Percy Carter Buck (1871–1947)

Unison

HIS SUFFERING AND DEATH

Vexilla Regis prodeunt

THE royal banners forward go;
The Cross shines forth in mystic glow,
Where he in flesh, our flesh who made,
Our sentence bore, our ransom paid.

2 There, whilst he hung, his sacred side
By soldier's spear was opened wide,
To cleanse us in the precious flood
Of water mingled with his blood.

3 Fulfilled is now what David told
In true prophetic song of old,
How God the nations' King should be;
For God is reigning from the Tree.

4 O Tree of glory, Tree most fair,
Ordained those holy limbs to bear,
How bright in purple robe it stood,
The purple of a Saviour's blood!

5 Upon its arms, like balance true,
He weighed the price for sinners due,
The price which none but he could pay,
And spoiled the spoiler of his prey.

6. To thee, eternal Three in One,
Let homage meet by all be done;
As by the Cross thou dost restore,
So rule and guide us evermore. Amen.

Venantius Fortunatus (c. 530–609)
Tr. John Mason Neale (1818–66) and Compilers of Hymns A. & M.

92 HORSLEY C.M.

WILLIAM HORSLEY (1774–1858)

THERE is a green hill far away,
  Without a city wall,
Where the dear Lord was crucified,
  Who died to save us all.

2 We may not know, we cannot tell
  What pains he had to bear;
But we believe it was for us
  He hung and suffered there.

3 He died that we might be forgiven,
  He died to make us good;
That we might go at last to heaven,
  Saved by his precious blood.

4 There was no other good enough
  To pay the price of sin,
He only could unlock the gate
  Of heaven, and let us in.

5. O dearly, dearly has he loved,
  And we must love him too,
And trust in his redeeming blood,
  And try his works to do.

Cecil Frances Alexander (1818–95)

93 ARFON 77.77.77.

Welsh Hymn Melody

WINSCOMBE 77.77.77.   WALTER K. STANTON (1891–   )

1 THRONED upon the aweful tree,
King of grief, I watch with thee.
Darkness veils thine anguished face:
None its lines of woe can trace,
None can tell what pangs unknown
Hold thee silent and alone;

2 Silent through those three dread
hours,
Wrestling with the evil powers,
Left alone with human sin,
Gloom around thee and within,
Till the appointed time is nigh,
Till the Lamb of God may die.

3 Hark the cry that peals aloud
Upward through the whelming
cloud!
Thou, the Father's only Son,
Thou, his own Anointed One,
Thou dost ask him—can it be?—
'Why hast thou forsaken me?'

4 Lord, should fear and anguish roll
Darkly o'er my sinful soul,
Thou, who once wast thus bereft
That thine own might ne'er be left,
Teach me by that bitter cry
In the gloom to know thee nigh.

John Ellerton (1826–93)
Based on Psalm 22, 1, and S. Matthew 27, 45–46

THE LORD JESUS CHRIST

94 S. GEORGE S.M.
(GAUNTLETT)

HENRY JOHN GAUNTLETT (1805–76)

Summi Parentis Filio

TO Christ, the Prince of peace,
And Son of God most high,
The fountain-source of heavenly life,
We lift our joyful cry.

2   Deep in his heart for us
The wound of love he bore,
That love which he enkindles still
In hearts that him adore.

3   O Jesu, victim blest,
What else but love divine
Could thee constrain to open thus
That sacred heart of thine?

4   O wondrous fount of love,
O well of waters free,
O heavenly flame, refining fire,
O burning charity!

5. Hide us in thy dear heart,
Jesu, our Saviour blest,
So shall we find thy plenteous grace,
And heaven's eternal rest.

? 18th cent. Tr. Edward Caswall (1814–78) and others

95 FULDA L.M.

GARDINER'S *Sacred Melodies* (1812)

WE sing the praise of him who died,
   Of him who died upon the cross;
The sinner's hope let men deride,
   For this we count the world but loss.

2 Inscribed upon the cross we see,
   In shining letters, 'God is love';
He bears our sins upon the tree;
   He brings us mercy from above.

3 The Cross! it takes our guilt away;
   It holds the fainting spirit up;
It cheers with hope the gloomy day,
   And sweetens every bitter cup.

4 It makes the coward spirit brave,
   And nerves the feeble arm for fight;
It takes its terror from the grave,
   And gilds the bed of death with light;

5. The balm of life, the cure of woe,
   The measure and the pledge of love,
The sinner's refuge here below,
   The angels' theme in heaven above.

Thomas Kelly (1769–1855)

96 O TRAURIGKEIT 447.76.

JOHANN SCHOP (c. 1664)

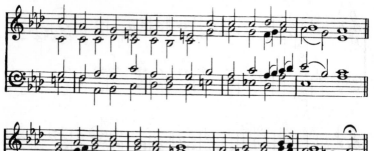

O Traurigkeit, O Herzeleid

WHAT sorrow sore
At my heart's core!
The Son of God now dieth.
He, the King whom I adore,
In the darkness lieth.

2 I cannot dare
His Cross to share,
Alone he doth endure it.
Mine the sin he beareth there,
Dying he doth cure it.

3 O ground of faith,
Laid low in death,
Blest lips now silent sleeping!
Surely all that live must mourn
Here with bitter weeping.

4 O happy he
Whose heart doth see
And rightly comprehendeth
Why the Lord of glory thus
To the grave descendeth.

5. O Jesu blest,
My help and rest,
I humbly pray, Lord, hear me;
Make me love thee to the last,
And in death be near me.

Johann Rist (1607–67)
Tr. Catherine Winkworth (1827–78) and Compilers

97 ROCKINGHAM L.M.   Adapted by EDWARD MILLER (1731-1807)

WHEN I survey the wondrous Cross
    On which the Prince of glory died,
My richest gain I count but loss,
    And pour contempt on all my pride.

2 Forbid it, Lord, that I should boast
    Save in the death of Christ, my God;
All the vain things that charm me most,
    I sacrifice them to his blood.

3 See, from his head, his hands, his feet,
    Sorrow and love flow mingled down;
Did e'er such love and sorrow meet,
    Or thorns compose so rich a crown?

4. Were the whole realm of nature mine,
    That were an offering far too small;
Love so amazing, so divine,
    Demands my soul, my life, my all.

Isaac Watts (1674-1748)
Based on Galatians 6, 14

See also

196	According to thy gracious word		517	Jesu, grant me this	(CS)
500	Ah, holy Jesus	(CS)	276	My God, I love thee	
502	Alone to sacrifice	(CS)	358	O dearest Lord, thy sacred head	
301	Beneath the cross of Jesus		530	O Lamb of God	(CS)
200	Bread of heaven		533	O sacred head	(CS)
503	Bread of the world	(CS)	296	Rock of ages	
303	God the Father's only Son	(CS)	369	Take up thy cross	
516	It is finishèd!		542	When Jesus Christ was yet a child	(CS)

98 MEAD HOUSE 87.87.D.

CYRIL V. TAYLOR (1907–)

HIS RESURRECTION

ALLELUIA, Alleluia!
    Hearts to heaven and voices raise;
Sing to God a hymn of gladness,
    Sing to God a hymn of praise;
He who on the cross a victim
    For the world's salvation bled,
Jesus Christ, the King of glory,
    Now is risen from the dead.

2 Now the iron bars are broken,
    Christ from death to life is born,
Glorious life, and life immortal,
    On this holy Easter morn.
Christ has triumphed, and we conquer
    By his mighty enterprise,
We with him to life eternal
    By his resurrection rise.

3 Christ is risen, Christ the first-fruits
    Of the holy harvest field,
Which will all its full abundance
    At his second coming yield;
Then the golden ears of harvest
    Will their heads before him wave,
Ripened by his glorious sunshine,
    From the furrows of the grave.

4. Christ is risen, we are risen;
    Shed upon us heavenly grace,
Rain and dew and gleams of glory
    From the brightness of thy face;
That, with hearts in heaven dwelling,
    We on earth may fruitful be,
And by angel hands be gathered,
    And be ever, Lord, with thee.

Christopher Wordsworth (1807–85) *and others*

99 EXULTATE DEO 88.86.46.   WALTER K. STANTON (1891–   )

Al - le - lu - ia!

AWAY with gloom, away with doubt!
　　With all the morning stars we sing;
With all the sons of God we shout
　　　The praises of a King,
　　　　Alleluia!
　　Of our returning King.

2 Away with death, and welcome life;
　　In him we died and live again;
And welcome peace, away with strife!
　　　For he returns to reign.
　　　　Alleluia!
　　The Crucified shall reign.

3. Then welcome beauty, he is fair;
　　And welcome youth, for he is young;
And welcome spring; and everywhere
　　　Let merry songs be sung!
　　　　Alleluia!
　　For such a King be sung!

Edward Shillito (1872–1948)

100 CHRISTUS IST ERSTANDEN 68.88.88.　　Melody from *Trier Gesangbuch* (1871)

CHRIST the Lord is risen!
　　Now is the hour of darkness past;
　Christ hath assumed his reigning power.
　　Behold the great accuser cast
　Down from the skies, to rise no more:
　　　Alleluia, Alleluia!

2. Christ the Lord is risen!
　　Rejoice, ye heavens! let every star
　Shine with new glories round the sky!
　　Saints, while ye sing the heavenly war,
　Raise your Redeemer's name on high!
　　　Alleluia, Alleluia!

Isaac Watts (1674-1748)

THE LORD JESUS CHRIST

101 WÜRTEMBURG 77.77.4.   JOHANN ROSENMÜLLER (1619–84)

Christus ist erstanden

CHRIST the Lord is risen again;
Christ hath broken every chain;
Hark! angelic voices cry,
Singing evermore on high,
Alleluia!

2 He who gave for us his life,
Who for us endured the strife,
Is our paschal Lamb to-day;
We too sing for joy, and say
Alleluia!

3 He who bore all pain and loss
Comfortless upon the cross,
Lives in glory now on high,
Pleads for us, and hears our cry.
Alleluia!

4. Now he bids us tell abroad
How the lost may be restored,
How the penitent forgiven,
How we too may enter heaven.
Alleluia!

Michael Weisse (c. 1480–1534)
Tr. Catherine Winkworth (1827–78)

102 AVE VIRGO VIRGINUM 76.76.D.   LEISENTRITT's *Gesangbuch* (1584)

Ἄίσωμεν πάντες λαοί

COME, ye faithful, raise the strain
   Of triumphant gladness;
God hath brought his Israel
   Into joy from sadness;
Loosed from Pharaoh's bitter yoke
   Jacob's sons and daughters;
Led them with unmoistened foot
   Through the Red Sea waters.

2 'Tis the spring of souls to-day;
   Christ hath burst his prison,
And from three days' sleep in death
   As a sun hath risen;

All the winter of our sins,
   Long and dark, is flying
From his light, to whom we give
   Laud and praise undying.

3. Neither might the gates of death,
   Nor the tomb's dark portal,
Nor the watchers, nor the seal,
   Hold thee as a mortal;
But arising, thou didst stand
   'Midst the twelve, bestowing
Thine own peace, which evermore
   Passeth human knowing.

S. John of Damascus (died c. 750)
Tr. John Mason Neale (1818–66) and Compilers

103 VULPIUS
(GELOBT SEI GOTT) 888.4.

Melody by MELCHIOR VULPIUS (1609)

Al - le - lu - ia,

Al - le - lu - ia, Al - le - lu - ia!

GOOD Christian men, rejoice and sing!
Now is the triumph of our King!
To all the world glad news we bring:
   Alleluia!

2 The Lord of life is risen for aye;
 Bring flowers of song to strew his way;
 Let all mankind rejoice and say
   Alleluia!

3 Praise we in songs of victory
 That love, that life which cannot die,
 And sing with hearts uplifted high
   Alleluia!

4. Thy name we bless, O risen Lord,
 And sing to-day with one accord
 The life laid down, the life restored:
   Alleluia!

Cyril Argentine Alington (1872–1955)

104

Metrical tune and words overleaf.

HIS RESURRECTION

Sermone blando Angelus

HIS cheering message from the grave
   An angel to the women gave:
'Full soon your Master ye shall see;
He goes before to Galilee.'

2 But while with flying steps they press
   To bear the news, all eagerness,
Their Lord, the living Lord, they meet,
And prostrate fall to kiss his feet.

3 So when his mourning followers heard
   The tidings of that faithful word,
Quick went they forth to Galilee,
Their loved and lost once more to see.

4 Maker of all, to thee we pray,
   Fulfil in us thy joy to-day;
When death assails, grant, Lord, that we
May share thy Paschal victory.

5. To thee who, dead, again dost live,
   All glory, Lord, thy people give;
All glory, as is ever meet,
To Father and to Paraclete. Amen.

4th or 5th cent.
Tr. Thomas Alexander Lacey (1853–1931)

104 SOLEMNIS HAEC FESTIVITAS L.M.

Angers Melody

HIS RESURRECTION

Sermone blando Angelus

HIS cheering message from the grave
An angel to the women gave:
'Full soon your Master ye shall see;
He goes before to Galilee.'

2 But while with flying steps they press
To bear the news, all eagerness,
Their Lord, the living Lord, they meet,
And prostrate fall to kiss his feet.

3 So when his mourning followers heard
The tidings of that faithful word,
Quick went they forth to Galilee,
Their loved and lost once more to see.

4 Maker of all, to thee we pray,
Fulfil in us thy joy to-day;
When death assails, grant, Lord, that we
May share thy Paschal victory.

5. To thee who, dead, again dost live,
All glory, Lord, thy people give;
All glory, as is ever meet,
To Father and to Paraclete. Amen.

4th or 5th cent.
Tr. Thomas Alexander Lacey (1853–1931)

A - men.

105 EASTER HYMN 74.74.D. Adapted from a melody in *Lyra Davidica* (1708)

HIS RESURRECTION

JESUS Christ is risen to-day,
   Our triumphant holy day,
Who did once, upon the cross,
Suffer to redeem our loss:
          Alleluia!

2 Hymns of praise then let us sing
   Unto Christ, our heavenly King,
Who endured the cross and grave,
Sinners to redeem and save:
          Alleluia!

3. But the anguish he endured
   Our salvation hath procured;
Now above the sky he's King,
Where the angels ever sing:
          Alleluia!

Lyra Davidica (1708)

106 S. ALBINUS 78.78.4. HENRY JOHN GAUNTLETT (1805–76)

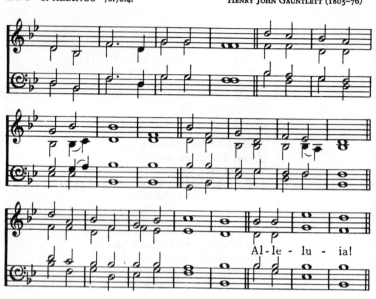

Al - le - lu - ia!

MOWSLEY 78.78.4. CYRIL V. TAYLOR (1907–)

Jesus lebt

JESUS lives! thy terrors now
    Can, O death, no more appal us;
Jesus lives! by this we know
    Thou, O grave, canst not enthral us:
        Alleluia!

2 Jesus lives! henceforth is death
    But the gate of life immortal;
This shall calm our trembling breath,
    When we pass its gloomy portal:
        Alleluia!

3 Jesus lives! for us he died;
    Then, alone to Jesus living,
Pure in heart may we abide,
    Praise to him and glory giving:
        Alleluia!

4 Jesus lives! our hearts know well
    Naught from us his love shall sever;
Life nor death nor powers of hell
    Tear us from his keeping ever:
        Alleluia!

5. Jesus lives! to him the throne
    High o'er heaven and earth is given;
May we go where he is gone,
    Live and reign with him in heaven:
        Alleluia!

Christian Fürchtegott Gellert (1715–69)
Tr. Frances Elizabeth Cox (1812–97) and others
Based on Romans 8, 11

107

Mode viii

MONTESANO L.M.

A. LEECH-WILKINSON (1899–   )

HIS RESURRECTION

Aurora lucis rutilat

LIGHT's glittering morn bedecks the sky;
Heaven thunders forth its victor-cry;
The glad earth shouts her triumph high,
And groaning hell makes wild reply.

2 While he, the King, the mighty King,
Despoiling death of all its sting,
And trampling down the powers of night,
Brings forth his ransomed saints to light.

3 His tomb of late the threefold guard
Of watch and stone and seal had barred;
But now, in pomp and triumph high,
He comes from death to victory.

4 The pains of hell are loosed at last;
The days of mourning now are past;
An angel robed in light hath said,
'The Lord is risen from the dead.'

5. All praise be thine, O risen Lord,
From death to endless life restored:
All praise to God the Father be,
And Holy Ghost eternally. Amen.

4th or 5th cent. Tr. John Mason Neale (1818–66)
and Compilers of Hymns A. & M

THE LORD JESUS CHRIST

108 LASST UNS
ERFREUEN 88.44.88. and Alleluias.

Melody from *Geistliche Kirchengesang*
(Cologne, 1623)

Unison

Harmony

Al-le - lu - ia, Al-le-lu - ia!

Unison

Harmony

Al-le - lu - ia, Al-le - lu - ia, Al-le -

Unison

-lu - ia, Al-le - lu - ia, Al-le-lu - ia!

HIS RESURRECTION

Easter Procession

Aurora lucis rutilat

LIGHT's glittering morn bedecks the sky;
Heaven thunders forth its victor-cry;
Alleluia!
The glad earth shouts her triumph high,
And groaning hell makes wild reply:
Alleluia!

2 While he, the King, the mighty King,
Despoiling death of all its sting,
Alleluia!
And trampling down the powers of night,
Brings forth his ransomed saints to light:
Alleluia!

3 His tomb of late the threefold guard
Of watch and stone and seal had barred;
Alleluia!
But now, in pomp and triumph high,
He comes from death to victory:
Alleluia!

4 The pains of hell are loosed at last;
The days of mourning now are past;
Alleluia!
An angel robed in light hath said,
'The Lord is risen from the dead':
Alleluia!

5 That Easter-tide with joy was bright,
The sun shone out with fairer light,
Alleluia!
When, to their longing eyes restored,
The Apostles saw their risen Lord:
Alleluia!

6 He bade them see his hands, his side,
Where yet the glorious wounds abide:
Alleluia!
The tokens true which made it plain
Their Lord indeed was risen again:
Alleluia!

7 Jesus, the King of gentleness,
Do thou thyself our hearts possess,
Alleluia!
That we may give thee all our days
The tribute of our grateful praise:
Alleluia!

8. All praise be thine, O risen Lord,
From death to endless life restored:
Alleluia!
All praise to God the Father be,
And Holy Ghost eternally:
Alleluia!

*4th or 5th cent. Tr. John Mason Neale (1818–66)
and Compilers of Hymns A. & M.*

For shorter versions of this hymn see Nos. 107 *and* 111

G

THE LORD JESUS CHRIST

WALTER K. STANTON (1891-)

HIS RESURRECTION

NOW the green blade riseth from the buried grain,
    Wheat that in dark earth many days has lain;
  Love lives again, that with the dead has been:
      Love is come again,
      Like wheat that springeth green.

2 In the grave they laid him, Love whom men had slain,
    Thinking that never he would wake again,
      Laid in the earth like grain that sleeps unseen:

3 Forth he came at Easter, like the risen grain,
    He that for three days in the grave had lain,
      Quick from the dead my risen Lord is seen:

4. When our hearts are wintry, grieving, or in pain,
    Thy touch can call us back to life again,
      Fields of our hearts that dead and bare have been:

John Macleod Campbell Crum (1872–1958)

110 O FILII ET FILIAE 888. and Alleluias.

Proper melody (modern version)
as given in WEBBE'S *Motetts* (1792)

Al - - le - lu - ia!

HIS RESURRECTION

O filii et filiae

O SONS and daughters, let us sing,
  The King of heaven, the glorious King,
O'er death has risen triumphing:
    Alleluia!

2 On Easter morn, at break of day,
  The faithful women went their way,
Their spices in the tomb to lay:
    Alleluia!

3 An angel clad in white they see,
  Who sat, and spake unto the three,
'Your Lord doth go to Galilee':
    Alleluia!

4 That night the Apostles met in fear,
  Amongst them came their Lord most dear,
And said 'My peace be on all here':
    Alleluia!

5 When Thomas first the tidings heard
  That they had seen the risen Lord,
He doubted the disciples' word:
    Alleluia!

6 'My piercèd side, O Thomas, see;
  My hands, my feet, I show to thee;
Not faithless, but believing be':
    Alleluia!

7 No longer Thomas then denied;
  He saw the feet, the hands, the side;
'Thou art my Lord and God', he cried:
    Alleluia!

8 How blest are they who have not seen,
  And yet whose faith has constant been,
For they eternal life shall win:
    Alleluia!

9. On this most holy day of days
  To God your hearts and voices raise
In laud and jubilee and praise:
    Alleluia!

Jean Tisserand (died 1494). Tr. John Mason Neale (1818–66) and others

111

Mode viii

DEUS TUORUM MILITUM L.M.

Grenoble Melody

HIS RESURRECTION

Claro paschali gaudio

THAT Easter-tide with joy was bright.
The sun shone out with fairer light,
When, to their longing eyes restored,
The Apostles saw their risen Lord.

2 He bade them see his hands, his side,
Where yet the glorious wounds abide:
The tokens true which made it plain
Their Lord indeed was risen again.

3 Jesus, the King of gentleness,
Do thou thyself our hearts possess,
That we may give thee all our days
The tribute of our grateful praise.

4. All praise be thine, O risen Lord,
From death to endless life restored:
All praise to God the Father be,
And Holy Ghost eternally. Amen.

4th or 5th cent. Tr. John Mason Neale (1818–66)
and Compilers of Hymns A. & M.

112 ELLACOMBE 76.76.D.

Mainz Gesangbuch (1833)

HIS RESURRECTION

Ἀναστάσεως ἡμέρα

THE day of Resurrection,
　Earth, tell it out abroad;
The passover of gladness,
　The passover of God.
From death to life eternal,
　From earth unto the sky,
Our Christ hath brought us over
　With hymns of victory.

2 Our hearts be pure from evil,
　That we may see aright
The Lord in rays eternal
　Of resurrection-light;
And, listening to his accents,
　May hear, so calm and plain,
His own 'All hail', and, hearing,
　May raise the victor strain.

3. Now let the heavens be joyful,
　And earth her song begin,
The round world keep high triumph,
　And all that is therein;
Let all things seen and unseen
　Their notes of gladness blend,
For Christ the Lord is risen,
　Our joy that hath no end.

S. John of Damascus (died c. 750)
Tr. John Mason Neale (1818–66)

113

Mode viii

TUGWOOD L.M.

NICHOLAS GATTY (1874-1946)

HIS RESURRECTION

Ad cenam Agni providi

THE Lamb's high banquet doth invite
Our souls arrayed in garments white;
Let us, whom through the sea he led,
Rejoice in song to Christ our Head;

2 Whose holiest body on the rood
Parchèd in death to be our food,
And for our wine his life-red blood
Tasting again we live in God.

3 'Twas he that on our Easter night
Turned the destroying angel's might;
From Pharaoh's bondage tyrannous
For evermore delivered us.

4 Now Christ our sacrifice shall be,
Our spotless paschal Lamb is he:
And he our pure unleavened bread
Himself for us is offerèd.

5 O true and worthy victim thou,
By whom hell's power is broken now,
By whom thy captive folk set free
Return to life and liberty.

6 See, Christ arising from the tomb
Comes crowned with glory out of gloom.
Our tyrant foe he hath enchained,
And Paradise for man regained.

7. To thee, O Christ, be glory paid,
Who hast arisen from the dead:
Thee with the Father we adore,
And Holy Spirit, evermore. Amen.

7th cent. Tr. Robert Bridges (1844-1930)

THE LORD JESUS CHRIST

First three lines adapted from
GIOVANNI PIERLUIGI DA PALESTRINA (1525–94)
'Alleluia' by WILLIAM HENRY MONK (1823–99)

114 VICTORY 888.4.

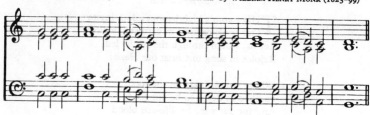

Finita jam sunt proelia

THE strife is o'er, the battle done;
Now is the Victor's triumph won;
Now let the song of joy be sung:
 Alleluia!

2 Death's mightiest powers have done their worst,
But Jesus hath his foes dispersed;
Let shouts of praise and joy outburst:
 Alleluia!

3 On the third morn he rose again
Glorious in majesty to reign;
O let us swell the joyful strain:
 Alleluia!

4 He closed the yawning gates of hell;
The bars from heaven's high portals fell;
Let hymns of joy his triumph tell:
 Alleluia!

5. Lord, by the stripes which wounded thee,
From death's dread sting thy servants free,
That we may live, and sing to thee:
 Alleluia!

From Symphonia Sirenum (Cologne, 1695)
Tr. Francis Pott (1832–1909) and Compilers

115 VRUECHTEN 67.67. D.

Dutch Melody (17th cent.)

Had Christ, that once was slain, Ne'er burst his three-day pri - son,

Our faith had been in vain: But now hath Christ a - ris - en, a -

-ris - en, a - ris - en, a - ris - - - - en.

THIS joyful Eastertide,
  Away with sin and sorrow.
My Love, the Crucified,
  Hath sprung to life this morrow:
  Had Christ, that once was slain,
  Ne'er burst his three-day
    prison,
  Our faith had been in vain:
  But now hath Christ arisen.

2 My flesh in hope shall rest,
    And for a season slumber:
  Till trump from east to west
    Shall wake the dead in number:

3. Death's flood hath lost his chill,
    Since Jesus crossed the river:
  Lover of souls, from ill
    My passing soul deliver:

George Ratcliffe Woodward (1848–1934)

THE LORD JESUS CHRIST

116 S. FULBERT C.M.

HENRY JOHN GAUNTLETT (1805–76)

Chorus novae Jerusalem

YE choirs of new Jerusalem,
　Your sweetest notes employ,
The paschal victory to hymn
　In strains of holy joy.

2 For Judah's Lion bursts his chains,
　Crushing the serpent's head;
And cries aloud through death's
　　domains,
　To wake the imprisoned dead.

3 Devouring depths of hell their prey
　At his command restore;
His ransomed hosts pursue their way
　Where Jesus goes before.

4 Triumphant in his glory now
　To him all power is given;
To him in one communion bow
　All saints in earth and heaven.

5 While we, his soldiers, praise our
　　King,
　His mercy we implore,
Within his palace bright to bring
　And keep us evermore.

6. All glory to the Father be,
　All glory to the Son,
All glory, Holy Ghost, to thee,
　While endless ages run.　Amen.

S. Fulbert of Chartres (died 1028)
Tr. Robert Campbell (1814–68)

A - men.

486	Blest be the everlasting God		141	How brightly beams (verse 2)
45	Child in the manger		72	Jesus, good above all other
505	Christ, our helper	(CS)	206	Lord, enthroned in heavenly splendour
397	Come, let us with our Lord arise		398	Most glorious Lord of life
123	Come, ye faithful, raise the anthem		497	The Saviour died
488	Father of peace		400	This is the day the Lord hath made

117 LADYWELL D.C.M. WILLIAM HAROLD FERGUSON (1874-1950)

1 All hail the power of Je-sus' name, Let an-gels prostrate fall;

Bring forth the roy-al di-a-dem, And crown him Lord of all.

Crown him, ye morning stars of light, Who formed this floating ball,

Now hail the great Cre-a-tor's might, And crown him Lord of all.

117 (*continued*)

2 Hail him, ye heirs of God's de-sign, Ye ransomed of the Fall; Hail God in-car-nate, Man di-vine, And crown him Lord of all. Sin-ners, whose love can ne'er for-get The worm-wood and the gall, Go

HIS REIGN AND PRIESTHOOD

spread your tro-phies at his feet, And crown him Lord of all.

Unison

3. Crown him, ye ser-vants of your God, Who answered at his call; Ex - tol him in whose path ye trod, And crown him Lord of all. Let ev - 'ry tribe and

117 (*continued*)

ev - 'ry tongue Be - fore him prostrate fall; And

shout in un - i - ver-sal song The crownèd Lord of all.

Edward Perronet(1726–92)
John Rippon (1751–1836) *and Compilers*

118 MILES LANE C.M.

WILLIAM SHRUBSOLE (1760–1806)
(Modern form of second line)

ALL hail the power of Jesus' name,
  Let angels prostrate fall;
Bring forth the royal diadem,
  And crown him Lord of all.

2 Crown him, ye morning stars of light,
    Who fixed this floating ball,
  Now hail the strength of Israel's might,
    And crown him Lord of all.

3 Ye seed of Israel's chosen race,
    Ye ransomed of the Fall;
  Hail him who saves you by his grace,
    And crown him Lord of all.

4 Hail him, ye heirs of David's line,
    Whom David Lord did call;
  The God incarnate, Man divine,
    And crown him Lord of all.

5 Sinners, whose love can ne'er forget
    The wormwood and the gall;
  Go spread your trophies at his feet,
    And crown him Lord of all.

6. Let every tribe and every tongue
    Before him prostrate fall;
  And shout in universal song
    The crownèd Lord of all.

Edward Perronet (1726–92)
John Rippon (1751–1836)

THE LORD JESUS CHRIST

119 ENGELBERG 10.10.10. with Alleluias.

CHARLES VILLIERS STANFORD
(1852–1924)

ALL praise to thee, for thou, O King divine,
Didst yield the glory that of right was thine,
That in our darkened hearts thy grace might shine:
    Alleluia!

2 Thou cam'st to us in lowliness of thought;
By thee the outcast and the poor were sought,
And by thy death was God's salvation wrought:
    Alleluia!

3 Let this mind be in us which was in thee,
Who wast a servant that we might be free,
Humbling thyself to death on Calvary:
    Alleluia!

4 Wherefore, by God's eternal purpose, thou
Art high exalted o'er all creatures now,
And given the name to which all knees shall bow:
    Alleluia!

5. Let every tongue confess with one accord
In heaven and earth that Jesus Christ is Lord;
And God the Father be by all adored:
    Alleluia!

F. Bland Tucker (1895–   )
Based on Philippians 2, 5–11

120 CUDDESDON 65.65. D. WILLIAM HAROLD FERGUSON (1874–1950)

AT the name of Jesus
  Every knee shall bow,
Every tongue confess him
  King of glory now;
'Tis the Father's pleasure
  We should call him Lord,
Who from the beginning
  Was the mighty Word.

2 Humbled for a season,
    To receive a name
  From the lips of sinners
    Unto whom he came,
  Faithfully he bore it
    Spotless to the last;
  Brought it back victorious,
    When from death he passed.

3 In your hearts enthrone him;
    There let him subdue
  All that is not holy,
    All that is not true:
  Crown him as your captain
    In temptation's hour;
  Let his will enfold you
    In its light and power.

4. Brothers, this Lord Jesus
    Shall return again,
  With his Father's glory,
    With his angel train;
  For all wreaths of empire
    Meet upon his brow,
  And our hearts confess him
    King of glory now.

Caroline Maria Noel (1817–77)
Based on Philippians 2, 9–11

121 NORMAN 87.87. Melody from DOLES' *Choralbuch* (Leipzig, 1785)

Aeterne Rex altissime

CHRIST, above all glory seated,
　King triumphant, strong to save!
Dying, thou hast death defeated;
　Buried, thou hast spoiled the grave.

2 Thou art gone where now is given
　　What no mortal might could gain,
On the eternal throne of heaven,
　　In thy Father's power to reign.

3 There thy kingdoms all adore thee,
　　Heaven above and earth below;
While the depths of hell before thee,
　　Trembling and defeated, bow.

4 We, O Lord, with hearts adoring,
　　Follow thee above the sky;
Hear our prayers, thy grace imploring;
　　Lift our souls to thee on high.

5 So when thou again in glory
　　On the clouds of heaven shalt shine,
We thy flock may stand before thee,
　　Owned for evermore as thine.

6. Hail, all hail! in thee confiding,
　　Jesus, thee shall all adore,
In thy Father's might abiding
　　With one Spirit evermore. Amen.

c. 5th cent. Tr. James Russell Woodford (1820–85)

A - men.

122 NATIVITY C.M.   HENRY LAHEE (1826–1912)

COME, let us join our cheerful songs
    With angels round the throne;
Ten thousand thousand are their tongues,
    But all their joys are one.

2 'Worthy the Lamb that died', they cry,
    'To be exalted thus';
'Worthy the Lamb', our lips reply,
    'For he was slain for us'.

3 Jesus is worthy to receive
    Honour and power divine;
And blessings, more than we can give,
    Be, Lord, for ever thine.

4. Let all creation join in one
    To bless the sacred name
Of him that sits upon the throne,
    And to adore the Lamb.

Isaac Watts (1674–1748)
Based on Revelation 5, 11–13

123 NEANDER 87.87.87.   From a Chorale by JOACHIM NEANDER (1640–80)

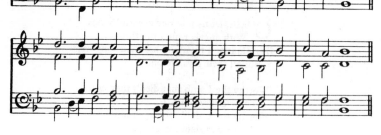

COME, ye faithful, raise the anthem,
  Cleave the skies with shouts of praise;
Sing to him who found the ransom,
  Ancient of eternal days,
God of God, the Word incarnate,
  Whom the heaven of heaven obeys.

2 Ere he raised the lofty mountains,
  Formed the seas, or built the sky,
Love eternal, free, and boundless,
  Moved the Lord of life to die,
Fore-ordained the Prince of princes
  For the throne of Calvary.

3 There, for us and our redemption,
  See him all his life-blood pour!
There he wins our full salvation,
  Dies that we may die no more;
Then, arising, lives for ever,
  Reigning where he was before.

4. Laud and honour to the Father,
  Laud and honour to the Son,
Laud and honour to the Spirit,
  Ever Three and ever One,
One in might and One in glory,
  While unending ages run. Amen.

Job Hupton (1762–1849)
John Mason Neale (1818–66)

A - men.

THE LORD JESUS CHRIST

124 CORONA D.S.M.   CHARLES HYLTON STEWART (1884–1932)

HIS REIGN AND PRIESTHOOD

CROWN him with many crowns,
The Lamb upon his throne;
Hark how the heavenly anthem drowns
All music but its own.
Awake, my soul, and sing
Of him who died for thee;
And hail him as thy matchless King
Through all eternity.

2   Crown him the Virgin's Son,
The God incarnate born,
Whose conquering arm those trophies won
Which now his brow adorn;
The Saviour long foretold,
The Branch of Jesse's stem,
The eternal Shepherd of his fold,
The Babe of Bethlehem.

3   Crown him the Lord of life,
Who triumphed o'er the grave,
And rose victorious in the strife
For those he came to save.
His glories now we sing
Who died and rose on high,
Who died eternal life to bring,
And lives that death may die.

4   Crown him the Lord of heaven,
Enthroned in worlds above,
The King of kings to whom is given
The wondrous name of Love.
Hail him the Prince of peace,
Whose power a sceptre sways
From pole to pole, that wars may cease,
And all be love and praise.

5.   Crown him the Lord of years,
The Potentate of time,
Creator of the rolling spheres,
Ineffably sublime:
All hail, Redeemer, hail!
For thou hast died for me:
Thy praise shall never, never fail
Throughout eternity.

Matthew Bridges (1800–94)
Godfrey Thring (1823–1903) and others

125 LLANFAIR 74.74. D.

Melody by ROBERT WILLIAMS (1781–1821)

1. HAIL the day that sees him rise,
To his throne above the skies;
Christ, awhile to mortals given,
Enters now the highest heaven:
    Alleluia!

2. There for him high triumph waits:
Lift your heads, eternal gates;
Christ hath conquered death and sin;
Take the King of glory in:
    Alleluia!

3. Lo, the heaven its Lord receives,
Yet he loves the earth he leaves;
Though returning to his throne,
Still he calls mankind his own:
    Alleluia!

4. See, he lifts his hands above;
See, he shows the prints of love;
Hark, his gracious lips bestow
Blessings on his Church below:
    Alleluia!

5. Still for us he intercedes,
His prevailing death he pleads,
Near himself prepares our place,
He the first-fruits of our race:
    Alleluia!

6. Lord, though parted from our sight,
Far above the starry height,
Grant our hearts may thither rise,
Seeking thee above the skies:
    Alleluia!

Charles Wesley (1707–88)
Thomas Cotterill (1779–1823) and others

126 METZLER'S REDHEAD C.M.   RICHARD REDHEAD (1820–1901)

Jesu, nostra redemptio

JESU, our hope, our heart's desire,
  Thy work of grace we sing;
Redeemer of the world art thou,
  Its Maker and its King.

2 How vast the mercy and the love
   Which laid our sins on thee,
 And led thee to a cruel death,
   To set thy people free!

3 But now the bonds of death are burst:
   The ransom has been paid;
 And thou art on thy Father's throne,
   In majesty arrayed.

4 O may thy mighty love prevail
   Our sinful souls to spare!
 O may we stand around thy throne,
   And see thy glory there!

5. Jesu, our only joy be thou,
   As thou our prize wilt be;
 In thee be all our glory now,
   And through eternity.

7th–8th cent. Tr. John Chandler (1806–76)
and Compilers of Hymns A. & M.

127 REGENT SQUARE 87.87.87.   HENRY SMART (1813–79)

LOOK, ye saints, and see how glorious
   Reigns the Man of Sorrows now;
From the fight returned victorious,
   Every knee to him shall bow:
Crown him, crown him! crown him, crown him!
   Crowns become the victor's brow.

2 Crown the Saviour, angels, crown him;
   Rich the trophies Jesus brings;
In the seat of power enthrone him,
   While the vault of heaven rings:
Crown him, crown him! crown him, crown him!
   Crown the Saviour King of kings.

3 Sinners in derision crowned him,
   Mocking their Messiah's claim;
Saints and angels throng around him,
   Own his title, praise his name.
Crown him, crown him! crown him, crown him!
   Spread abroad the victor's fame!

4. Hark, those bursts of acclamation!
   Hark, those loud triumphal chords!
Jesus takes the highest station,
   O what joy the sight affords!
Crown him, crown him! crown him, crown him!
   King of kings, and Lord of lords.

Thomas Kelly (1769–1855) and Compilers

128 GOPSAL 66.66.88.

GEORGE FREDERICK HANDEL (1685–1759)

REJOICE! the Lord is King;
   Your Lord and King adore;
Mortals, give thanks and sing,
   And triumph evermore:
     Lift up your heart, lift up your voice;
     Rejoice, again I say, rejoice.

2 Jesus, the Saviour, reigns,
   The God of truth and love;
When he had purged our stains,
   He took his seat above:

3 His kingdom cannot fail;
   He rules o'er earth and heaven;
The keys of death and hell
   Are to our Jesus given:

4. He sits at God's right hand
   Till all his foes submit,
And bow to his command,
   And fall beneath his feet:

                    Charles Wesley (1707–88)

H

129 REX GLORIAE 87.87.D.

HENRY SMART (1813–79)

SEE the Conqueror mounts in triumph,
　　See the King in royal state
Riding on the clouds his chariot
　　To his heavenly palace gate;
Hark, the choirs of angel voices
　　Joyful alleluias sing,
And the portals high are lifted
　　To receive their heavenly King.

2 Who is this that comes in glory,
　　With the trump of jubilee?
Lord of battles, God of armies,
　　He has gained the victory;
He who on the cross did suffer,
　　He who from the grave arose,
He has vanquished sin and Satan,
　　He by death has spoiled his foes.

3 He has raised our human nature
　　In the clouds to God's right hand;
There we sit in heavenly places,
　　There with him in glory stand;
Jesus reigns, adored by angels;
　　Man with God is on the throne;
Mighty Lord, in thine ascension
　　We by faith behold our own.

4. Glory be to God the Father;
　　Glory be to God the Son,
Dying, risen, ascending for us,
　　Who the heavenly realm has won;
Glory to the Holy Spirit;
　　To One God in Persons Three;
Glory both in earth and heaven,
　　Glory, endless glory, be. Amen.

Christopher Wordsworth (1807–85) and Compilers

A - men.

130 TUGWOOD L.M.

NICHOLAS GATTY (1874-1946)

Hymnum canamus gloriae

SING we triumphant hymns of praise,
New hymns to heaven exulting raise:
Christ, by a road before untrod,
Ascendeth to the throne of God.

2 O grant that we may thither tend,
And with unwearied hearts ascend
Toward thy kingdom's throne, where thou,
As we believe, art seated now.

3 Be thou our joy and strong defence,
Who art our future recompense:
So shall the light that springs from thee
Be ours through all eternity.

4. O risen Christ, ascended Lord,
All praise to thee let earth accord,
Who art, while endless ages run,
With Father and with Spirit One. Amen.

The Venerable Bede (673-735)
Tr. Benjamin Webb (1820-85) and Compilers

A - men.

131 S. LEONARD C.M.   HENRY SMART (1813–79)

THE eternal gates lift up their heads,
    The doors are opened wide;
The King of glory is gone up
    Unto his Father's side.

2 And ever on our earthly path
    A gleam of glory lies;
A light still breaks behind the cloud
    That veils thee from our eyes.

3 Lift up our hearts, lift up our minds,
    And let thy grace be given,
That, while we live on earth below,
    Our treasure be in heaven;

4. That, where thou art at God's right hand,
    Our hope, our love may be:
Dwell in us now, that we may dwell
    For evermore in thee.

Cecil Frances Alexander (1818–95) and Compilers

132 S. MAGNUS C.M.
(NOTTINGHAM)

Probably by JEREMIAH CLARKE (1670–1707)

THE head that once was crowned with thorns
  Is crowned with glory now;
A royal diadem adorns
  The mighty victor's brow.

2 The highest place that heaven affords
  Is his, is his by right,
The King of kings and Lord of lords,
  And heaven's eternal Light;

3 The joy of all who dwell above,
  The joy of all below,
To whom he manifests his love,
  And grants his name to know.

4 To them the Cross with all its shame,
  With all its grace, is given;
Their name an everlasting name,
  Their joy the joy of heaven.

5 They suffer with their Lord below,
  They reign with him above,
Their profit and their joy to know
  The mystery of his love.

6. The Cross he bore is life and health,
  Though shame and death to him;
His people's hope, his people's wealth,
  Their everlasting theme.

Thomas Kelly (1769–1855)

133 ASCENDIT DEUS 887. D.   JOHANN GOTTFRIED SCHICHT (1753-1823)

THE Lord ascendeth up on high,
The Lord hath triumphed gloriously,
  In power and might excelling;
The grave and hell are captive led,
Lo, he returns, our glorious Head,
  To his eternal dwelling.

2 The heavens with joy receive their Lord,
By saints, by angel hosts adored;
  O day of exultation!
O earth, adore thy glorious King,
His rising, his ascension sing,
  With grateful adoration.

3. Our great High Priest now goes before,
Upon his Church his grace to pour,
  And still his love he giveth:
O may our hearts to him ascend;
May all within us upward tend
  To him who ever liveth.

Arthur Tozer Russell (1806-74) and Compilers

THE LORD JESUS CHRIST

134 CLIFTON C.M.

JOHN CHARLES CLIFTON (1781–1841)

W ITH joy we meditate the grace
   Of our High Priest above;
His heart is made of tenderness,
   And ever yearns with love.

2 Touched with a sympathy within,
   He knows our feeble frame;
He knows what sore temptations
      mean,
   For he hath felt the same.

3 He in the days of feeble flesh
   Poured out his cries and tears;
And, though exalted, feels afresh
   What every member bears.

4 He'll never quench the smoking
      flax,
   But raise it to a flame;
The bruisèd reed he never breaks,
   Nor scorns the meanest name.

5. Then let our humble faith address
      His mercy and his power:
   We shall obtain delivering grace
      In every needful hour.

Isaac Watts (1674–1748) and others
Based on Hebrews 4, 15–16

See also

29	All glory to God	35	Lo! he comes
197	Alleluia! sing to Jesus	206	Lord, enthroned in heavenly splendour
45	Child in the manger	214	Once, only once
30	Come, thou long-expected Jesus	15	Praise, my soul, the King of heaven
457	Hail to the Lord's Anointed	183	The Church of God a kingdom is
489	Hark how the adoring hosts,	496	The race that long
490	Hark, the glad sound	497	The Saviour died
33	Hills of the north, rejoice	218	We hail thy presence
460	Jesus shall reign	498	Where high the heavenly temple stands
325	King of glory	287	Ye servants of God
34	Lift up your heads, ye mighty gates		

135 ABRIDGE C.M.   ISAAC SMITH (c. 1725–c. 1800)

B E thou my guardian and my guide,
    And hear me when I call;
Let not my slippery footsteps slide,
    And hold me lest I fall.

2 The world, the flesh, and Satan dwell
    Around the path I tread;
O save me from the snares of hell,
    Thou quickener of the dead.

3 And if I tempted am to sin,
    And outward things are strong,
Do thou, O Lord, keep watch within,
    And save my soul from wrong.

4. Still let me ever watch and pray,
    And feel that I am frail;
That if the tempter cross my way,
    Yet he may not prevail.

                    Isaac Williams (1802–65)

THE LORD JESUS CHRIST

136 DEIRDRE 88.88. (Trochaic)

Irish Melody

Crist lim, Crist reum, Crist im degaid.

*'A corslet of faith for the protection of body
and soul against devils, and men, and vices.'*

CHRIST be with me, Christ within me,
  Christ behind me, Christ before me,
Christ beside me, Christ to win me,
  Christ to comfort and restore me.

2. Christ beneath me, Christ above me,
  Christ in quiet, Christ in danger,
Christ in hearts of all that love me,
  Christ in mouth of friend and stranger.

*8th cent. or later
Tr. Cecil Frances Alexander (1818–95)*

137 RATISBON 77.77.77.

WERNER, *Choralbuch* (1815)

CHRIST, whose glory fills the skies,
  Christ, the true, the only light,
Sun of righteousness, arise,
  Triumph o'er the shades of night;
Dayspring from on high, be near;
Daystar, in my heart appear.

2 Dark and cheerless is the morn
    Unaccompanied by thee;
  Joyless is the day's return,
    Till thy mercy's beams I see;
  Till they inward light impart,
  Glad my eyes, and warm my heart.

3. Visit then this soul of mine,
    Pierce the gloom of sin and grief;
  Fill me, radiancy divine,
    Scatter all my unbelief;
  More and more thyself display,
  Shining to the perfect day.

Charles Wesley (1707–88)

138 SCHÖNSTER HERR JESU 569.558.   Silesian Folk-song (1842)

For Young Children

Schönster Herr Jesu

FAIREST Lord Jesus,
Lord of all creation,
Jesus, of God and Mary the Son;
Thee will I cherish,
Thee will I honour,
O thou my soul's delight and crown.

2 Fair are the meadows,
Fairer still the woodlands,
Robed in the verdure and bloom of spring.
Jesus is fairer,
Jesus is purer,
He makes the saddest heart to sing.

3. Fair are the flowers,
Fairer still the sons of men,
In all the freshness of youth arrayed:
Yet is their beauty
Fading and fleeting;
My Jesus, thine will never fade.

Anon. (Münster, 1677)
Tr. Lilian Stevenson (1870–1960)

139 SILCHESTER 569.558.

WALTER K. STANTON (1891–   )

Schönster Herr Jesu

FAIREST Lord Jesus,
  Lord of all creation,
    Jesus, of God and Mary the Son;
Thee will I cherish,
Thee will I honour,
    O thou my soul's delight and crown.

2 Fair are the meadows,
  Fairer still the woodlands,
    Robed in the verdure and bloom of spring.
Jesus is fairer,
Jesus is purer,
    He makes the saddest heart to sing.

3 Fair are the flowers,
  Fairer still the sons of men,
    In all the freshness of youth arrayed:
Yet is their beauty
Fading and fleeting;
    My Jesus, thine will never fade.

4. When I lie dying,
  Still on thee relying,
    Suffer me not from thine arms to fall:
At my last hour
Be thou my power,
    For thou, Lord Jesus, art my all.

Anon. (Münster, 1677)
Tr. Lilian Stevenson (1870–1960)

THE LORD JESUS CHRIST

140 PILGRIMAGE 87.87.47.

GEORGE JOB ELVEY (1816–93)

BRYN CALFARIA 87.87.47.

Melody by WILLIAM OWEN (1814–93)

Arglwydd arwain 'trwy'r anialwch

GUIDE me, O thou great Redeemer,
    Pilgrim through this barren land;
I am weak, but thou art mighty,
    Hold me with thy powerful hand;
        Bread of heaven,
    Feed me till I want no more.

2 Open now the crystal fountain
    Whence the healing stream doth flow:
Let the fire and cloudy pillar
    Lead me all my journey through;
        Strong deliverer,
    Be thou still my strength and shield.

3. When I tread the verge of Jordan,
    Bid my anxious fears subside;
Death of death, and hell's destruction,
    Land me safe on Canaan's side;
        Songs and praises
    I will ever give to thee.

William Williams (1716–91)
Tr. Peter Williams (1723–96) *and others*

141 WIE SCHÖN LEUCHTET
887. D. 84.48.

Melody by PHILIPP NICOLAI (1556–1608)
Harmonized by FELIX MENDELSSOHN-BARTHOLDY
(1809–47)

Wie schön leuchtet der Morgenstern

HOW brightly beams the morning star!
What sudden radiance from afar
  Doth glad us with its shining?
Brightness of God, that breaks our night
And fills the darkened souls with light,
  Who long for truth were pining.
Newly, truly, God's word feeds us,
      Rightly leads us,
      Life bestowing,
Praise, O praise such love o'erflowing!

2. All praise to him who came to save,
Who conquered death and scorned the grave;
  Each day new praise resoundeth
To him the Life who once was slain,
The friend whom none shall trust in vain,
  Whose grace for aye aboundeth;
Sing then, ring then, tell the story
      Of his glory,
      Till his praises
Flood with light earth's darkest places!

Philipp Nicolai (1556–1608), Johann Adolf Schlegel (1721–93)
Tr. Catherine Winkworth (1827–78)

See also No. 541 (CS)

142 S. PETER C.M. ALEXANDER ROBERT REINAGLE (1799–1877)

HOW sweet the name of Jesus sounds
   In a believer's ear!
It soothes his sorrows, heals his wounds,
   And drives away his fear.

2 It makes the wounded spirit whole,
   And calms the troubled breast;
'Tis manna to the hungry soul,
   And, to the weary, rest.

3 Dear name! the rock on which I build,
   My shield and hiding-place,
My never-failing treasury filled
   With boundless stores of grace.

4 Jesus, my shepherd, brother, friend,
   My prophet, priest, and king,
My lord, my life, my way, my end,
   Accept the praise I bring.

5 Weak is the effort of my heart,
   And cold my warmest thought;
But when I see thee as thou art,
   I'll praise thee as I ought.

6. Till then I would thy love proclaim
   With every fleeting breath;
And may the music of thy name
   Refresh my soul in death.

John Newton (1725–1807) and Compilers

143 KINGSFOLD D.C.M.

From an English Traditional Melody, noted
by LUCY BROADWOOD

I HEARD the voice of Jesus say,
  'Come unto me and rest;
Lay down, thou weary one, lay
    down
  Thy head upon my breast.'
I came to Jesus as I was,
  Weary, and worn, and sad;
I found in him a resting-place,
  And he has made me glad.

2 I heard the voice of Jesus say,
  'Behold, I freely give
The living water, thirsty one:
  Stoop down, and drink, and live.'

I came to Jesus, and I drank
  Of that life-giving stream;
My thirst was quenched, my soul
    revived,
  And now I live in him.

3. I heard the voice of Jesus say,
  'I am this dark world's light:
Look unto me, thy morn shall rise,
  And all thy day be bright.'
I looked to Jesus, and I found
  In him my star, my sun;
And in that light of life I'll walk
  Till travelling days are done.

Horatius Bonar (1808–89)

144 SEELENBRÄUTIGAM 55.88.55.   ADAM DRESE (1620–1701)

Jesu, geh' voran

JESU, guide our way
   To eternal day:
So shall we, no more delaying,
Follow thee, thy voice obeying:
   Lead us by the hand
   To our Father's land.

2 When we danger meet,
   Steadfast make our feet;
Lord, preserve us uncomplaining
'Mid the darkness round us reigning:
   Through adversity
   Lies our way to thee.

3. Order all our way
   Through the mortal day:
In our toil, with aid be near us;
In our need, with succour cheer us:
   Till we safely stand
   In our Father's land.

Nicolaus Ludwig von Zinzendorf (1700–60)
Tr. Arthur Tozer Russell (1806–74) and Compilers

145 ABERYSTWYTH 77.77.D.

JOSEPH PARRY (1841–1903)

HOLLINGSIDE 77.77.D.

JOHN BACCHUS DYKES (1823–76)

HIS PRESENCE AND POWER

JESU, lover of my soul,
  Let me to thy bosom fly,
While the nearer waters roll,
  While the tempest still is high:
Hide me, O my Saviour, hide,
  Till the storm of life is past;
Safe into the haven guide,
  O receive my soul at last.

2 Other refuge have I none;
  Hangs my helpless soul on thee;
Leave, ah, leave me not alone,
  Still support and comfort me.
All my trust on thee is stayed,
  All my help from thee I bring;
Cover my defenceless head
  With the shadow of thy wing.

3. Plenteous grace with thee is found,
  Grace to cover all my sin;
Let the healing streams abound;
  Make and keep me pure within.
Thou of life the fountain art;
  Freely let me take of thee;
Spring thou up within my heart,
  Rise to all eternity.

Charles Wesley (1707–88)

146 BUCKLAND 77.77.   LEIGHTON GEORGE HAYNE (1836–83)

For Young Children

LOVING Shepherd of thy sheep,
    Keep thy lamb, in safety keep;
Nothing can thy power withstand,
None can pluck me from thy hand.

2 Loving Saviour, thou didst give
Thine own life that we might live,
And the hands outstretched to bless
Bear the cruel nails' impress.

3 I would praise thee every day,
Gladly all thy will obey,
Like thy blessèd ones above
Happy in thy precious love.

4 Loving Shepherd, ever near,
Teach thy lamb thy voice to hear,
Suffer not my steps to stray
From the straight and narrow way.

5. Where thou leadest I would go,
Walking in thy steps below,
Till before my Father's throne
I shall know as I am known.

Jane Eliza Leeson (1807–82)

See also

197	Alleluia! sing to Jesus	323	Jesu, thou joy
351	Dear Lord and Father	72	Jesus, good above all other
259	Dear Shepherd of thy people	519	Jesus is this dark world's light (CS)
517	Jesu, grant me this (CS)	262	Jesus, stand among us
518	Jesu, priceless treasure (CS)	263	Jesus, where'er thy people meet
322	Jesu, the very thought	74	We saw thee not

GOD: THE HOLY SPIRIT

147 NEW YEAR'S DAY 555.11.

Adapted from a melody in THOMAS BUTTS
Harmonia Sacra (c. 1753)

AWAY with our fears,
  Our troubles and tears,
  The Spirit is come,
The witness of Jesus returned to his home.

2   The pledge of our Lord
  To his heaven restored,
  Is sent from the sky,
And tells us our Head is exalted on high.

3   Our glorified Head
  His Spirit hath shed,
  With his people to stay,
And never again will he take him away.

4   Our heavenly Guide
  With us shall abide,
  His comforts impart,
And set up his kingdom of love in the heart.

5.   The heart that believes
  His kingdom receives,
  His power and his peace,
His life, and his joy's everlasting increase.

Charles Wesley (1707–88)

148 HAMPTON S.M.   WILLIAMS' *Psalmody* (c. 1770)

BREATHE on me, Breath of God,
Fill me with life anew,
That I may love what thou dost love,
And do what thou wouldst do.

2 Breathe on me, Breath of God,
Until my heart is pure,
Until with thee I will one will,
To do and to endure.

3 Breathe on me, Breath of God,
Blend all my soul with thine,
Until this earthly part of me
Glows with the fire divine.

4. Breathe on me, Breath of God,
So shall I never die,
But live with thee the perfect life
Of thine eternity.

Edwin Hatch (1835–89)

149 DOWN AMPNEY 66.11.D.   RALPH VAUGHAN WILLIAMS (1872–1958)

GOD: THE HOLY SPIRIT

Discendi, Amor santo

COME down, O Love divine,
  Seek thou this soul of mine,
And visit it with thine own ardour glowing;
  O Comforter, draw near,
  Within my heart appear,
And kindle it, thy holy flame bestowing.

2   O let it freely burn,
  Till earthly passions turn
To dust and ashes in its heat consuming;
  And let thy glorious light
  Shine ever on my sight,
And clothe me round, the while my path illuming.

3   Let holy charity
  Mine outward vesture be,
And lowliness become mine inner clothing;
  True lowliness of heart,
  Which takes the humbler part,
And o'er its own shortcomings weeps with loathing.

4.   And so the yearning strong,
  With which the soul will long,
Shall far outpass the power of human telling;
  For none can guess its grace,
  Till he become the place
Wherein the Holy Spirit makes his dwelling.

Bianco da Siena (died 1434)
Tr. Richard Frederick Littledale (1833–90)

150 HAWKHURST L.M.　　　　　　　HENRY JOHN GAUNTLETT (1805-76)

COME, gracious Spirit, heavenly Dove,
With light and comfort from above;
Be thou our guardian, thou our guide,
O'er every thought and step preside.

2 The light of truth to us display,
And make us know and choose thy way;
Plant holy fear in every heart,
That we from God may ne'er depart.

3 Lead us to Christ, the living Way;
Nor let us from his pastures stray:
Lead us to holiness, the road
That we must take to dwell with God.

4. Lead us to heaven, that we may share
Fullness of joy for ever there;
Lead us to God, our final rest,
To be with him for ever blest.

Simon Browne (1680-1732)

151 VENI CREATOR

Mode viii

Praise to thy e - ter-nal me-rit, Fa-ther, Son, and Ho - ly Spi-rit.

Veni, Creator Spiritus

COME, Holy Ghost, our souls
    inspire,
And lighten with celestial fire;
Thou the anointing Spirit art,
Who dost thy sevenfold gifts impart.

2 Thy blessèd unction from above
Is comfort, life, and fire of love;
Enable with perpetual light
The dullness of our blinded sight:

3 Anoint and cheer our soilèd face
With the abundance of thy grace:
Keep far our foes, give peace at
    home;
Where thou art guide no ill can
    come.

4. Teach us to know the Father, Son,
And thee, of both, to be but One;
That through the ages all along
This may be our endless song:

Praise to thy eternal merit,
Father, Son, and Holy Spirit. Amen.

? *9th cent. Par. John Cosin* (1594–1672)

A - men.

Another setting of this hymn will be found overleaf

151 VENI CREATOR

Mode viii (Mechlin Version)

After Verse 4

Veni, Creator Spiritus

COME, Holy Ghost, our souls inspire,
And lighten with celestial fire;
Thou the anointing Spirit art,
Who dost thy sevenfold gifts impart.

2 Thy blessèd unction from above
Is comfort, life, and fire of love;
Enable with perpetual light
The dullness of our blinded sight:

3 Anoint and cheer our soilèd face
With the abundance of thy grace:
Keep far our foes, give peace at home;
Where thou art guide no ill can come.

4. Teach us to know the Father, Son,
And thee, of both, to be but One;
That through the ages all along
This may be our endless song:

Praise to thy eternal merit,
Father, Son, and Holy Spirit. Amen.

? 9th cent. Par. John Cosin (1594–1672)

See also No. 508 (CS)

A - men.

152 VENI, SANCTE SPIRITUS 777.D.   SAMUEL WEBBE the elder (1740–1816)

Veni, sancte Spiritus

COME, thou Holy Spirit, come,
  And from thy celestial home
    Send thy light and brilliancy:
Father of the poor, draw near;
Giver of all gifts, be here;
    Come, the soul's true radiancy.

2 Thou of Comforters the best,
  Thou the soul's most welcome
        guest,
    Sweet refreshment here below;
In our labour rest most sweet,
Grateful coolness in the heat,
    Solace in the midst of woe.

3 O most blessèd Light divine,
  Shine within these hearts of thine,
    And our inmost being fill;
Where thou art not, man hath
        naught,
Nothing good in deed or thought,
    Nothing free from taint of ill.

4 Heal our wounds; our strength
        renew;
  On our dryness pour thy dew;
    Wash the stains of guilt away:
Bend the stubborn heart and will;
Melt the frozen, warm the chill;
    Guide the steps that go astray.

5. On the faithful, who adore
    And confess thee, evermore
      In thy sevenfold gifts descend:
    Give them virtue's sure reward,
    Give them thy salvation, Lord,
      Give them joys that never end.

13th cent. Tr. Edward Caswall (1814–78)
John Mason Neale (1818–66)
and Compilers of Hymns A. & M.

153 CAPETOWN 77.75.   Adapted from a Chorale by Friedrich Filitz (1804–76)

GRACIOUS Spirit, Holy Ghost,
  Taught by thee, we covet most
Of thy gifts at Pentecost,
    Holy, heavenly love.

2 Love is kind, and suffers long,
  Love is meek, and thinks no wrong,
Love than death itself more strong;
    Therefore give us love.

3 Prophecy will fade away,
  Melting in the light of day;
Love will ever with us stay;
    Therefore give us love.

4 Faith will vanish into sight;
  Hope be emptied in delight;
Love in heaven will shine more bright;
    Therefore give us love.

5. Faith and hope and love we see
  Joining hand in hand agree;
But the greatest of the three,
    And the best, is love.

Christopher Wordsworth (1807–85)
Based on 1 Corinthians 13

154 MARSTON STREET 88.88.7. CYRIL V. TAYLOR (1907–)

Whitsunday Procession

HAIL, blest Spirit, Lord eternal,
Love omnipotent, supernal,
Honour meet to thee we render,
Veneration deep and tender:
  Hail, Lord God the Holy Ghost!

2 Hail, free Spirit, all transcending,
Yet on mortal man descending;
At this festal tide we laud thee,
Praise and homage we accord thee:

3 Gracious Spirit, light diffusing,
Breath of life in man infusing;
Blessèd are the souls that know thee,
Joy and peace thy children owe thee:

4*Truth eternal, wise Creator,
   Fallen man's illuminator;
   Light of reason, hope, ambition,
   Fire of love and true contrition:

5*Spirit, sinful man reproving,
   Wayward hearts most gently moving;
   When by sin we sorely grieve thee,
   Naught but pleading love perceive we:

6 Purest Spirit, sanctifying
   Quickened souls, on grace relying;
   Cleanse, renew thy creatures lowly,
   Guide, inspire, and make us holy:

7 Spirit, Comforter indwelling,
   Mightiest earthly aid excelling;
   Lord, who in thy Church abidest,
   There to us thyself confidest:

8*Paraclete, anointing, sealing,
   Secret things of God revealing;
   Souls by inner light transforming,
   Heart and will to Christ conforming:

9. Lord, to thee who all sustainest,
   God, with Father, Son, who reignest,
   Glory be from all creation,
   Worship, love, and adoration:

Sydney James Wallis, S.S.J.E. (1870–1956)

155 GOTT SEI DANK 77.77. FREYLINGHAUSEN's *Geistreiches Gesangbuch* (1704)

HOLY Spirit, truth divine,
Dawn upon this soul of mine;
Word of God, and inward light,
Wake my spirit, clear my sight.

2 Holy Spirit, love divine,
Glow within this heart of mine:
Kindle every high desire;
Perish self in thy pure fire.

3 Holy Spirit, power divine,
Fill and nerve this will of mine;
By thee may I strongly live,
Bravely bear, and nobly strive.

4 Holy Spirit, peace divine,
Still this restless heart of mine;
Speak to calm this tossing sea,
Stayed in thy tranquillity.

5. Holy Spirit, right divine,
King within my conscience reign:
Be my law, and I shall be
Firmly bound, for ever free.

Samuel Longfellow (1819–92)

156 S. TIMOTHY C.M.

HENRY WILLIAMS BAKER (1821–77)
arranged by WILLIAM HENRY MONK (1823–89)

O HOLY Ghost, thy people bless
    Who long to feel thy might,
And fain would grow in holiness,
    As children of the light.

2 To thee we bring, who art the Lord,
    Our selves to be thy throne;
Let every thought and deed and word
    Thy pure dominion own.

3 Life-giving Spirit, o'er us move,
    As on the formless deep;
Give life and order, light and love,
    Where now is death or sleep.

4 Great gift of our ascended King,
    His saving truth reveal;
Our tongues inspire his praise to sing,
    Our hearts his love to feel.

5. O Holy Ghost, of sevenfold might,
    All graces come from thee;
Grant us to know and serve aright
    One God in Persons Three.

Henry Williams Baker (1821–77)

157 TALLIS' ORDINAL C.M.　　　　　THOMAS TALLIS (c. 1510–c. 1585)

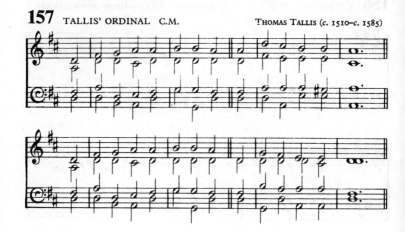

O fons amoris, Spiritus

O HOLY Spirit, Lord of grace,
　　Eternal fount of love,
Inflame, we pray, our inmost hearts
　　With fire from heaven above.

2. As thou in bond of love dost join
　　The Father and the Son,
So fill us all with mutual love,
　　And knit our hearts in one.

Charles Coffin (1676–1749)
Tr. John Chandler (1806–76)
and Compilers of Hymns A. & M.

158 TEMPLE 66.84.   HENRY WALFORD DAVIES (1869–1941)

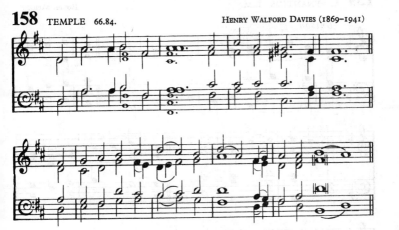

Βασιλεῦ οὐράνιε, Παράκλητε

O KING enthroned on high,
　Thou Comforter divine,
Blest Spirit of all truth, be nigh
　And make us thine.

2　Thou art the source of life,
　　Thou art our treasure-store;
Give us thy peace, and end our strife
　　For evermore.

3.　Descend, O heavenly Dove,
　　Abide with us alway;
And in the fullness of thy love
　　Cleanse us, we pray.

Pentecostarion (c. 8th cent.)
Tr. John Brownlie (1859–1925)

159 S. VENANTIUS L.M.

Rouen Melody

Unison

O SPIRIT of the living God,
    In all the fullness of thy grace,
Where'er the foot of man hath trod,
    Descend on our rebellious race.

2 Give tongues of fire and hearts of love
    To preach the reconciling word;
Give power and wisdom from above,
    Whene'er the joyful sound is heard.

3 Be darkness, at thy coming, light,
    Confusion order, in thy path;
Souls without strength inspire with might;
    Bid mercy triumph over wrath.

4 O Spirit of the Lord, prepare
    All the round earth her God to meet;
Breathe thou abroad like morning air,
    Till hearts of stone begin to beat.

5. Baptise the nations; far and nigh
    The triumphs of the Cross record;
The name of Jesus glorify
    Till every kindred call him Lord.

James Montgomery (1771–1854) and Compilers

160 S. CUTHBERT 86.84.   JOHN BACCHUS DYKES (1823–76)

OUR blest Redeemer, ere he breathed
　　His tender last farewell,
A guide, a comforter, bequeathed,
　　With us to dwell.

2 He came sweet influence to impart,
　　A gracious, willing guest,
While he can find one humble heart,
　　Wherein to rest.

3 And his that gentle voice we hear,
　　Soft as the breath of even,
That checks each fault, that calms each fear,
　　And speaks of heaven.

4 And every virtue we possess,
　　And every victory won,
And every thought of holiness,
　　Are his alone.

5. Spirit of purity and grace,
　　Our weakness, pitying, see;
O make our hearts thy dwelling-place,
　　And worthier thee.

Harriet Auber (1773–1862)
Based on S. John 14, 16

161 WOOD END 77.77. D.

WALTER K. STANTON (1891–)

*Last Verse ♯

GOD: THE HOLY SPIRIT

OUR Lord, his Passion ended,
  Hath gloriously ascended,
Yet though from him divided,
He leaves us not unguided;
    All his benefits to crown
    He hath sent his Spirit down,
    Burning like a flame of fire,
    His disciples to inspire.

2 God's Spirit is directing;
  No more they sit expecting,
But forth to all the nation
They go with exultation;
    That which God in them hath wrought
    Fills their life and soul and thought;
    So their witness now can do
    Work as great in others too.

3. The centuries go gliding,
  But still we have abiding
With us that Spirit holy,
To make us brave and lowly—
    Lowly, for we feel our need,
    God alone is strong indeed;
    Brave, for with the Spirit's aid
    We can venture unafraid.

Francis Crawford Burkitt (1864–1935)

162

Mode i

SAMSON L.M.   Adapted from GEORGE FREDERICK HANDEL (1685–1759)

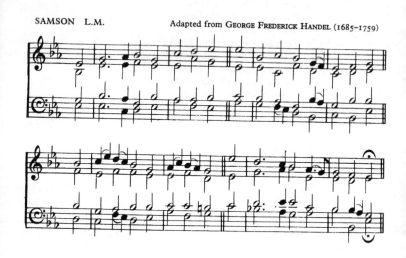

GOD: THE HOLY SPIRIT

Beata nobis gaudia

REJOICE! the year upon its way
  Has brought again that blessèd day,
When on the chosen of the Lord
The Holy Spirit was outpoured.

2 On each the fire, descending, stood
  In quivering tongues' similitude—
Tongues, that their words might ready prove,
And fire, to make them flame with love.

3 And now, O holy God, this day
  Regard us as we humbly pray,
And send us, from thy heavenly seat,
The blessings of the Paraclete.

4. To God the Father, God the Son,
  And God the Spirit, praise be done;
May Christ the Lord upon us pour
The Spirit's gift for evermore. Amen.

c. 4th cent. Tr. Richard Ellis Roberts (1879–1953)
Based on Acts 2, 1–4

163 MELCOMBE L.M.

SAMUEL WEBBE the elder (1740–1816)

SPIRIT of mercy, truth, and love,
O shed thine influence from above;
And still from age to age convey
The wonders of this sacred day.

2 In every clime, by every tongue,
Be God's surpassing glory sung;
Let all the listening earth be taught
The acts our great Redeemer wrought.

3. Unfailing Comfort, heavenly Guide,
Still o'er thy holy Church preside;
Still let mankind thy blessings prove,
Spirit of mercy, truth, and love.

Foundling Hospital Collection (1774)

GOD: THE HOLY SPIRIT

164 WHITSUN 886.   BERTRAM LUARD SELBY (1853–1918)

TO thee, O Comforter divine,
For all thy grace and power benign,
Sing we Alleluia!

2 To thee, whose faithful love had place
In God's great covenant of grace:

3 To thee, whose faithful voice doth win
The wandering from the ways of sin:

4 To thee, whose faithful power doth heal,
Enlighten, sanctify, and seal:

5 To thee, whose faithful truth is shown
By every promise made our own:

6 To thee, our teacher and our friend,
Our faithful leader to the end:

7 To thee, by Jesus Christ sent down,
Of all his gifts the sum and crown:

8. To thee, who art with God the Son
And God the Father ever One:

Frances Ridley Havergal (1836–79)

See also

508 Come, Holy Ghost   (CS)
321 Eternal Ruler
522 Love of the Father   (CS)

165

Mode iii

ILLSLEY L.M.

JOHN BISHOP (1665–1737)

GOD: THE HOLY TRINITY

Adesto, sancta Trinitas

BE near us, Holy Trinity,
  One God of equal majesty;
All things that are on thee depend,
Who art beginning without end.

2 The myriad armies of the sky
  Praise, worship, tell thy name most high:
  This triple frame—earth, air, and sea
  Doth bless thee everlastingly.

3 We also come, thy servants all,
  And at thy feet adoring fall:
  O join the vows and prayers we bring
  With those high hymns the angels sing.

4 Thee we confess one Light to be,
  Thee we adore, co-equal Three:
  Alpha and Omega we cry,
  And all things having breath reply.

5 Praise to the Father, made of none,
  Praise to his sole-begotten Son,
  Praise to the Holy Spirit be,
  Eternal Godhead, One in Three.   Amen.

c. 10th cent. Tr. Compilers of Hymns A. & M.

166 SANDYS S.M.

SANDYS' *Collection* (1833)

FATHER, in whom we live,
In whom we are, and move,
The glory, power, and praise receive
Of thy creating love.

2   Incarnate Deity,
Let all the ransomed race
Render in thanks their lives to thee,
For thy redeeming grace.

3   Spirit of holiness,
Let all thy saints adore
Thy sacred energy, and bless
Thine heart-renewing power.

4.   Eternal, Triune Lord,
Let all the hosts above,
Let all the sons of men, record
And dwell upon thy love.

Charles Wesley (1707–88)

167

O Pater sancte

FATHER most holy, merciful and loving,
　Jesus, Redeemer, ever to be worshipped,
Life-giving Spirit, Comforter most gracious,
　God everlasting;

2 Three in a wondrous unity unbroken,
　　One perfect Godhead, love that never faileth,
Light of the angels, succour of the needy,
　　Hope of all living;

3 All thy creation serveth its Creator;
　　Thee every creature praiseth without ceasing;
We too would sing thee psalms of true devotion;
　　Hear, we beseech thee.

4. Lord God Almighty, unto thee be glory,
　　One in Three Persons, over all exalted;
Thine, as is meet, be honour, praise, and blessing,
　　Now and for ever. Amen.

c. 10th cent. Tr. Alfred Edward Alston (1862–1927)

Metrical tune and words overleaf.

167 ISTE CONFESSOR 11.11.11.5.
(ANGERS)

Angers Melody

O Pater sancte

FATHER most holy, merciful and loving,
Jesus, Redeemer, ever to be worshipped,
Life-giving Spirit, Comforter most gracious,
God everlasting;

2 Three in a wondrous unity unbroken,
One perfect Godhead, love that never faileth,
Light of the angels, succour of the needy,
Hope of all living;

3 All thy creation serveth its Creator;
Thee every creature praiseth without ceasing;
We too would sing thee psalms of true devotion;
Hear, we beseech thee.

4. Lord God Almighty, unto thee be glory,
One in Three Persons, over all exalted;
Thine, as is meet, be honour, praise, and blessing,
Now and for ever. Amen.

c. 10th cent. Tr. Alfred Edward Alston (1862–1927)

168 SHIPSTON 87.87.

English Traditional Melody

FIRMLY I believe and truly
  God is Three, and God is One;
And I next acknowledge duly
  Manhood taken by the Son.

2 And I trust and hope most fully
  In that Manhood crucified;
And each thought and deed unruly
  Do to death, as he has died.

3 Simply to his grace and wholly
  Light and life and strength belong,
And I love supremely, solely,
  Him the holy, him the strong.

4 And I hold in veneration
  For the love of him alone,
Holy Church as his creation,
  And her teachings as his own.

5. Adoration aye be given,
  With and through the angelic host,
To the God of earth and heaven,
  Father, Son, and Holy Ghost. Amen.

John Henry Newman (1801–90)

A - men.

169 NICAEA 11.12.12.10.   JOHN BACCHUS DYKES (1823–76)

HOLY, holy, holy, Lord God Almighty!
    Early in the morning our song shall rise to thee:
Holy, holy, holy, merciful and mighty,
    God in Three Persons, blessèd Trinity!

2 Holy, holy, holy! all the saints adore thee,
    Casting down their golden crowns around the glassy sea,
Cherubim and Seraphim falling down before thee,
    Which wert, and art, and evermore shalt be.

3 Holy, holy, holy! though the darkness hide thee,
    Though the eye of sinful man thy glory may not see,
Only thou art holy; there is none beside thee,
    Perfect in power, in love, and purity.

4. Holy, holy, holy, Lord God Almighty!
    All thy works shall praise thy name in earth and sky and sea;
Holy, holy, holy, merciful and mighty,
    God in Three Persons, blessèd Trinity!

Reginald Heber (1783–1826)
Based on Revelation 4, 8–11

170 S. PATRICK D.L.M.

Irish Melody

Atomriug indiu niurt tren

I BIND unto myself to-day
   The strong name of the Trinity,
By invocation of the same,
   The Three in One, and One in Three.

2 I bind unto myself to-day
      The power of God to hold and lead,
   His eye to watch, his might to stay,
      His ear to hearken to my need.

vv. 3 and 4 overleaf

170 (*continued*)

3 The wisdom of my God to teach,
    His hand to guide, his shield to ward,
  The Word of God to give me speech,
    His heavenly host to be my guard.

GOD: THE HOLY TRINITY

Verse 4. Unison

4. I bind unto myself to-day
    The strong name of the Trinity,
   By invocation of the same,
    The Three in One, and One in Three.

8th cent. or later. Tr. Cecil Frances Alexander (1818–95)

See also

269 Bright the vision
270 Come, ye people, rise and sing
290 Father of heaven

THE CHURCH OF GOD

171 LUCERNE 887. D.

Würtemberg Gesangbuch (1710)

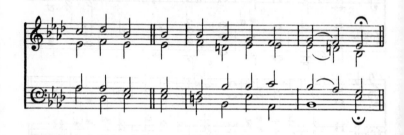

BEHOLD the temple of the Lord!
  The work of God, by man abhorred,
    Appearing fair and splendid:
It lifts its head in spite of foes,
And though a hostile world oppose,
    The work will yet be ended.

2 A building this, not made with hands;
  On firm foundations, lo, it stands,
    For God himself has laid them:
  The workmanship of God alone,
  The rich materials all his own:
    'Twas he himself that made them.

3 He builds it for his glory's sake,
  Its solid frame no force can shake,
    However men despise it:
  And time, that other work destroys,
  'Gainst this in vain its power employs;
    The work of God defies it.

4. From age to age his work goes on,
  The stones collected one by one;
    Ere long it will be finished:
  And when he works his grand design,
  The temple will for ever shine
    With lustre undiminished.

Thomas Kelly (1769–1855)

172 MILTON ABBAS 664.6664.

Eric Harding Thiman (1900–   )

CHRIST for the world we sing!
The world to Christ we bring
  With fervent prayer;
The wayward and the lost,
By restless passions tossed,
Redeemed at countless cost
  From dark despair.

2 Christ for the world we sing!
The world to Christ we bring
  With one accord;
With us the work to share,
With us reproach to dare,
With us the cross to bear,
  For Christ our Lord.

3. Christ for the world we sing!
  The world to Christ we bring
    With joyful song;
  The new-born souls, whose days,
  Reclaimed from error's ways,
  Inspired with hope and praise,
    To Christ belong.

Samuel Wolcott (1813–86)

173 RICHMOND C.M.

Adapted from THOMAS HAWEIS (1734–1820)
by SAMUEL WEBBE the younger (1770–1843)

CITY of God, how broad and far
  Outspread thy walls sublime!
The true thy chartered freemen are
  Of every age and clime.

2 One holy Church, one army strong,
    One steadfast, high intent;
  One working band, one harvest-song,
    One King omnipotent.

3 How purely hath thy speech come down
    From man's primeval youth!
  How grandly hath thine empire grown,
    Of freedom, love, and truth!

4 How gleam thy watch-fires through the night
    With never-fainting ray!
  How rise thy towers, serene and bright,
    To meet the dawning day!

5. In vain the surge's angry shock,
    In vain the drifting sands:
  Unharmed upon the^eternal Rock
    The^eternal City stands.

Samuel Johnson (1822–82)

174 PSALM 36 (68) 887.887.D.

Strasburg Psalter (1539)

Unison (vv. 1, 2, 4)

ITS COMMISSION AND WORK

FAITH of our fathers, taught of old
　By faithful shepherds of the fold,
　　The hallowing of our nation;
Thou wast through many⁀a wealthy year,
Through many⁀a darkened day of fear,
　　The rock of our salvation.
Arise, arise, good Christian men,
Your glorious standard raise again,
　　The cross of Christ who calls you;
Who bids you live and bids you die
For his great cause, and stands on high
　　To witness what befalls you.

2*Our fathers heard the trumpet call
　Through lowly cot and kingly hall
　　From oversea resounding;
They bowed with stubborn wills to learn
The truths that live, the thoughts that burn,
　　With new resolve abounding.
Arise, arise, good Christian men,
Your glorious standard raise again,
　　The cross of Christ who guides you;
Whose arm is bared to join the fray,
Who marshals you in stern array,
　　Fearless, whate'er betides you.

3*Our fathers held the faith received,
　By saints declared, by saints believed,
　　By saints in death defended;
Through pain of doubt and bitterness,
Through pain of treason and distress,
　　They for the right contended.
Arise, arise, good Christian men,
Your glorious standard raise again,
　　The cross of Christ who bought you;
Who leads you forth in this new age,
With long-enduring hearts to wage
　　The warfare he has taught you.

4. Though frequent be the loud alarms,
　Though still we march by ambushed arms
　　Of death and hell surrounded:
With Christ for chief we fear no foe;
Nor force nor craft can overthrow
　　The Church that he has founded.
Arise, arise, good Christian men,
Your glorious standard raise again,
　　The cross wherewith he signed you;
The King himself shall lead you on,
Shall watch you till the strife be done,
　　Then near his throne shall find you.

Thomas Alexander Lacey (1853-1931)

See overleaf for verse 3

THE CHURCH OF GOD

174 (*continued*) PSALM 36 (68) 887.887. D.   *Strasburg Psalter* (1539)

Harmony (*v. 3*)

F AITH of our fathers, taught of old
By faithful shepherds of the fold,
The hallowing of our nation;
Thou wast through many⁀a wealthy year,
Through many⁀a darkened day of fear,
The rock of our salvation.
Arise, arise, good Christian men,
Your glorious standard raise again,
The cross of Christ who calls you;
Who bids you live and bids you die
For his great cause, and stands on high
To witness what befalls you.

2*Our fathers heard the trumpet call
Through lowly cot and kingly hall
From oversea resounding;
They bowed with stubborn wills to learn
The truths that live, the thoughts that burn,
With new resolve abounding.
Arise, arise, good Christian men,
Your glorious standard raise again,
The cross of Christ who guides you;
Whose arm is bared to join the fray,
Who marshals you in stern array,
Fearless, whate'er betides you.

3*Our fathers held the faith received,
By saints declared, by saints believed,
By saints in death defended;
Through pain of doubt and bitterness,
Through pain of treason and distress,
They for the right contended.
Arise, arise, good Christian men,
Your glorious standard raise again,
The cross of Christ who bought you;
Who leads you forth in this new age,
With long-enduring hearts to wage
The warfare he has taught you.

4. Though frequent be the loud alarms,
Though still we march by ambushed arms
Of death and hell surrounded:
With Christ for chief we fear no foe;
Nor force nor craft can overthrow
The Church that he has founded.
Arise, arise, good Christian men,
Your glorious standard raise again,
The cross wherewith he signed you;
The King himself shall lead you on,
Shall watch you till the strife be done,
Then near his throne shall find you.

Thomas Alexander Lacey (1853–1931)

175 TAMBARAM 10.10.10.10.4. CYRIL V. TAYLOR (1907–)

Unison (vv. 1, 4)

Harmony (vv. 2, 3)

GATHER us in, thou love that fillest all:
    Gather our rival faiths within thy fold;
Rend each man's temple-veil and bid it fall,
    That we may know that thou hast been of old:
      Gather us in.

2 Gather us in: we worship only thee:
    In varied names we stretch a common hand;
In diverse forms a common soul we see;
    In many ships we seek one spirit-land;
      Gather us in.

3 Each sees one colour of thy rainbow-light,
    Each looks upon one tint and calls it heaven;
Thou art the fullness of our partial sight;
    We are not perfect till we find the seven;
      Gather us in.

4. Some seek a Father in the heavens above,
    Some ask a human image to adore,
Some crave a spirit vast as life and love;
    Within thy mansions we have all and more;
      Gather us in.

George Matheson (1842–1906)

K

THE CHURCH OF GOD

176 ABBOT'S LEIGH 87.87. D.

CYRIL V. TAYLOR (1907–   )

GLORIOUS things of thee are spoken,
   Sion, city of our God!
He whose word cannot be broken
   Formed thee for his own abode:
On the Rock of Ages founded,
   What can shake thy sure repose?
With salvation's walls surrounded,
   Thou mayst smile at all thy foes.

2 See, the streams of living waters,
   Springing from eternal love,
Well supply thy sons and daughters,
   And all fear of want remove.
Who can faint while such a river
   Ever flows their thirst to assuage—
Grace which, like the Lord the giver,
   Never fails from age to age.

3. Saviour, if of Sion's city
   I, through grace, a member am,
Let the world deride or pity,
   I will glory in thy name:
Fading is the worldling's pleasure,
   All his boasted pomp and show;
Solid joys and lasting treasure
   None but Sion's children know.

John Newton (1725–1807)
Based on Isaiah 33, 20–21 and Psalm 87

177 LIVINGSTONE Irregular.

WALTER K. STANTON (1891–)

GOD is working his purpose out, as year succeeds to year,
  God is working his purpose out, and the time is drawing near;
Nearer and nearer draws the time, the time that shall surely be,
When the earth shall be filled with the glory of God, as the waters cover
    the sea.

2 From utmost east to utmost west, where'er man's foot hath trod,
  By the mouth of many messengers goes forth the voice of God;
  'Give ear to me, ye continents; ye isles, give ear to me,
  That the earth may be filled with the glory of God, as the waters cover
      the sea.'

3 What can we do to work God's work, to prosper and increase
  The brotherhood of all mankind, the reign of the Prince of peace?
  What can we do to hasten the time, the time that shall surely be,
  When the earth shall be filled with the glory of God, as the waters cover
      the sea?

4 March we forth in the strength of God, with the banner of Christ unfurled,
  That the light of the glorious gospel of truth may shine throughout the
      world:
  Fight we the fight with sorrow and sin, to set their captives free,
  That the earth may be filled with the glory of God, as the waters cover
      the sea.

5. All we can do is nothing worth, unless God blesses the deed;
  Vainly we hope for the harvest-tide, till God gives life to the seed;
  Yet nearer and nearer draws the time, the time that shall surely be,
  When the earth shall be filled with the glory of God, as the waters cover
      the sea.

Arthur Campbell Ainger (1841–1919)
Based on Habakkuk 2, 14

178 CRUCIS VICTORIA C.M.

MYLES BIRKET FOSTER (1851–1922)

L IFT up your heads, ye gates of
     brass;
   Ye bars of iron, yield;
And let the King of glory pass;
   The Cross is in the field.

2 That banner, brighter than the star
   That leads the train of night,
Shines on the march, and guides
     from far
   His servants to the fight.

3 A holy war those servants wage;
   In that mysterious strife,
The powers of heaven and hell
     engage
   For more than death or life.

4 Ye armies of the living God,
   Sworn warriors of Christ's host,
Where hallowed footsteps never
     trod,
   Take your appointed post.

5 Though few and small and weak
     your bands,
   Strong in your Captain's strength,
Go to the conquest of all lands:
   All must be his at length.

6 O fear not, faint not, halt not now;
   Quit you like men, be strong;
To Christ shall every nation bow,
   And sing with you this song:

7. Uplifted are the gates of brass,
     The bars of iron yield;
   Behold the King of glory pass;
     The Cross hath won the field.

James Montgomery (1771–1854) *and others*

179 EIRENE 11.11.11.5.   CYRIL V. TAYLOR (1907–   )

Christe du Beistand

LORD of our life, and God of our salvation,
Star of our night, and hope of every nation,
Hear and receive thy Church's supplication,
    Lord God Almighty.

2 See round thine ark the hungry billows curling;
See how thy foes their banners are unfurling;
Lord, while their darts envenomed they are hurling,
    Thou canst preserve us.

3 Lord, thou canst help when earthly armour faileth,
Lord, thou canst save when deadly sin assaileth;
Christ, o'er thy Church nor death nor hell prevaileth;
    Grant us thy peace, Lord.

4. Grant us thy help till foes are backward driven;
Grant them thy truth, that they may be forgiven;
Grant peace on earth, and, after we have striven,
    Peace in thy heaven.

                    Matthäus Appelles von Löwenstern (1594–1648)
                         Par. Philip Pusey (1799–1855)

180 GOLDEN TREASURY 66.66.66.   CYRIL V. TAYLOR (1907–)

O THOU not made with hands,
   Not throned above the skies,
Nor walled with shining walls,
   Nor framed with stones of price,
More bright than gold or gem,
God's own Jerusalem!

2 Where'er the gentle heart
   Finds courage from above;
Where'er the heart forsook
   Warms with the breath of love;
Where faith bids fear depart,
City of God, thou art.

3 Thou art where'er the proud
   In humbleness melts down;
Where self itself yields up;
   Where martyrs win their crown;
Where faithful souls possess
Themselves in perfect peace.

4 Where in life's common ways
   With cheerful tread we go;
Where in his steps we tread,
   Who trod the way of woe;
Where he is in the heart,
City of God, thou art.

5. Not throned above the skies,
   Nor golden-walled afar,
But where Christ's two or three
   In his name gathered are,
Lo, in the midst of them,
God's own Jerusalem!

Francis Turner Palgrave (1824–97)

THE CHURCH OF GOD

181 NORTHUMBRIA 10.10.10.10.10.10. WALTER K. STANTON (1891-   )

REJOICE, O people, in the mounting years
    Wherein God's mighty purposes unfold:
From age to age his righteous reign appears,
    From land to land the love of Christ is told.
Rejoice, O people, in your glorious Lord,
    Lift up your hearts in jubilant accord.

2 Rejoice, O people, in the years of old,
    When prophets' glowing vision lit the way;
Till saint and martyr sped the venture bold,
    And eager hearts awoke to greet the day.
Rejoice in God's glad messengers of peace,
    Who bore the Saviour's gospel of release.

3*Rejoice, O people, in the deathless fame
    Won by the saints whose labours blessed our land;
And those who wrought for love of Jesus' name
    With art of builder's and of craftsman's hand.
Rejoice in him whose Spirit gave the skill
    To work in loveliness his perfect will.

4 Rejoice, O people, in this living hour:
    Low lies man's pride and human wisdom dies;
But on the cross God's love reveals his power;
    And from his waiting Church new hopes arise.
Rejoice that, while the sin of man divides,
    One Christian fellowship of love abides.

5 Rejoice, O people, in the days to be,
    When, o'er the strife of nations sounding clear,
Shall ring love's gracious song of victory,
    To east and west his kingdom bringing near.
Rejoice, rejoice, his Church on earth is one,
    And binds the ransomed nations 'neath the sun.

6. Rejoice, O people, in that final day
    When all the travail of creation ends;
Christ now attains his universal sway,
    O'er heaven and earth his royal word extends:
That word proclaimed where saints and martyrs trod:
    The glorious gospel of the blessèd God.

Albert F. Bayly (1901–   )

Harmony version overleaf

181 (*continued*) NORTHUMBRIA
10.10.10.10.10.10.

WALTER K. STANTON (1891–)

REJOICE, O people, in the mounting years
    Wherein God's mighty purposes unfold:
From age to age his righteous reign appears,
    From land to land the love of Christ is told.
Rejoice, O people, in your glorious Lord,
    Lift up your hearts in jubilant accord.

2 Rejoice, O people, in the years of old,
    When prophets' glowing vision lit the way;
Till saint and martyr sped the venture bold,
    And eager hearts awoke to greet the day.
Rejoice in God's glad messengers of peace,
    Who bore the Saviour's gospel of release.

3*Rejoice, O people, in the deathless fame
    Won by the saints whose labours blessed our land;
And those who wrought for love of Jesus' name
    With art of builder's and of craftsman's hand.
Rejoice in him whose Spirit gave the skill
    To work in loveliness his perfect will.

4 Rejoice, O people, in this living hour:
    Low lies man's pride and human wisdom dies;
But on the cross God's love reveals his power;
    And from his waiting Church new hopes arise.
Rejoice that, while the sin of man divides,
    One Christian fellowship of love abides.

5 Rejoice, O people, in the days to be,
    When, o'er the strife of nations sounding clear,
Shall ring love's gracious song of victory,
    To east and west his kingdom bringing near.
Rejoice, rejoice, his Church on earth is one,
    And binds the ransomed nations 'neath the sun.

6. Rejoice, O people, in that final day
    When all the travail of creation ends;
Christ now attains his universal sway,
    O'er heaven and earth his royal word extends:
That word proclaimed where saints and martyrs trod:
    The glorious gospel of the blessèd God.

Albert F. Bayly (1901–   )

182 MELLING 77.77.

JOHN FAWCETT (1789–1867)

Walte fürder, nah und fern

SPREAD, O spread, thou mighty word,
Spread the kingdom of the Lord,
Wheresoe'er his breath has given
Life to beings meant for heaven.

2 Tell them how the Father's will
Made the world, and keeps it still,
How he sent his Son to save
All who help and comfort crave.

3 Tell of our Redeemer's love,
Who for ever doth remove
By his holy sacrifice
All the guilt that on us lies.

4 Tell them of the Spirit given
Now to guide us up to heaven,
Strong and holy, just and true,
Working both to will and do.

5. Word of life, most pure and strong,
Lo, for thee the nations long;
Spread, till from its dreary night
All the world awakes to light.

Jonathan Friedrich Bahnmaier (1774–1841)
Tr. Catherine Winkworth (1827–78)

183 CAPEL C.M.

English Traditional Melody

THE Church of God a kingdom is,
   Where Christ in power doth reign,
Where spirits yearn till, seen in bliss,
   Their Lord shall come again.

2 Glad companies of saints possess
   This Church below, above;
And God's perpetual calm doth bless
   Their paradise of love.

3 An altar stands within the shrine
   Whereon, once sacrificed,
Is set, immaculate, divine,
   The Lamb of God, the Christ.

4 There rich and poor, from countless lands,
   Praise Christ on mystic rood;
There nations reach forth holy hands
   To take God's holy food.

5 There pure life-giving streams o'erflow
   The sower's garden-ground;
And faith and hope fair blossoms show,
   And fruits of love abound.

6. O King, O Christ, this endless grace
   To us and all men bring,
To see the vision of thy face
   In joy, O Christ, our King.

Lionel Muirhead (1845–1925)

THE CHURCH OF GOD

184 AURELIA 76.76. D.

SAMUEL SEBASTIAN WESLEY (1810–76)

THE Church's one foundation
  Is Jesus Christ, her Lord;
She is his new creation
  By water and the word:
From heaven he came and sought her
  To be his holy bride,
With his own blood he bought her
  And for her life he died.

2 Elect from every nation
  Yet one o'er all the earth,
Her charter of salvation
  One Lord, one faith, one birth;
One holy name she blesses,
  Partakes one holy food,
And to one hope she presses
  With every grace endued.

3 Though with a scornful wonder
  Men see her sore oppressed,
By schisms rent asunder,
  By heresies distressed,
Yet saints their watch are keeping,
  Their cry goes up, 'How long?'
And soon the night of weeping
  Shall be the morn of song.

4 'Mid toil and tribulation,
  And tumult of her war,
She waits the consummation
  Of peace for evermore;
Till with the vision glorious
  Her longing eyes are blest,
And the great Church victorious
  Shall be the Church at rest.

5. Yet she on earth hath union
  With God the Three in One,
And mystic sweet communion
  With those whose rest is won:
O happy ones and holy!
  Lord, give us grace that we,
Like them, the meek and lowly,
  On high may dwell with thee.

Samuel John Stone (1839–1900)

185 MOSCOW 664.6664.

Melody by FELICE DE GIARDINI (1716–96)

THOU, whose almighty word
Chaos and darkness heard,
  And took their flight;
Hear us, we humbly pray,
And where the gospel-day
Sheds not its glorious ray,
  Let there be light.

2 Thou, who didst come to bring,
On thy redeeming wing,
  Healing and sight,
Health to the sick in mind,
Sight to the inly blind,
O now to all mankind
  Let there be light.

3 Spirit of truth and love,
Life-giving, holy Dove,
  Speed forth thy flight;
Move on the waters' face,
Bearing the lamp of grace,
And in earth's darkest place
  Let there be light.

4. Blessed and holy Three,
Glorious Trinity,
  Wisdom, love, might;
Boundless as ocean's tide
Rolling in fullest pride,
Through the earth, far and wide,
  Let there be light.

John Marriott (1780–1825)
Based on Genesis 1, 3

186 MARCHING 87.87.   MARTIN SHAW (1875-1958)

Igjennem Nat og Trængsel

THROUGH the night of doubt and sorrow
Onward goes the pilgrim band,
Singing songs of expectation,
Marching to the promised land.

2 Clear before us through the darkness,
Gleams and burns the guiding light;
Brother clasps the hand of brother,
Stepping fearless through the night.

3 One the light of God's own presence
O'er his ransomed people shed,
Chasing far the gloom and terror,
Brightening all the path we tread.

4 One the object of our journey,
One the faith which never tires,
One the earnest looking forward,
One the hope our God inspires.

5 One the strain that lips of thousands
Lift as from the heart of one;
One the conflict, one the peril,
One the march in God begun.

6. One the gladness of rejoicing
On the far eternal shore,
Where the one almighty Father
Reigns in love for evermore.

Bernhardt Severin Ingemann (1789-1862)
Tr. Sabine Baring-Gould (1834-1924)

187 THORNBURY 76.76.D.   BASIL HARWOOD (1859-1949)

THY hand, O God, has guided
   Thy flock, from age to age;
The wondrous tale is written,
   Full clear, on every page;
Our fathers owned thy goodness,
   And we their deeds record;
And both of this bear witness,
   'One Church, one Faith, one Lord.'

2 Thy heralds brought glad tidings
   To greatest, as to least;
They bade men rise, and hasten
   To share the great King's feast;
And this was all their teaching,
   In every deed and word,
To all alike proclaiming
   'One Church, one Faith, one Lord.'

3 *See overleaf*

4 Through many a day of darkness,
   Through many a scene of strife,
The faithful few fought bravely,
   To guard the nation's life.
Their gospel of redemption,
   Sin pardoned, man restored,
Was all in this enfolded,
   'One Church, one Faith, one Lord.'

5 *See overleaf*

6. Thy mercy will not fail us,
   Nor leave thy work undone;
With thy right hand to help us,
   The victory shall be won;
And then by men and angels
   Thy name shall be adored,
And this shall be their anthem,
   'One Church, one Faith, one Lord.'

Edward Hayes Plumptre (1821–91)

Harmony version overleaf

187 (*continued*) THORNBURY 76.76. D. BASIL HARWOOD (1859–1949)

Harmony (*vv. 3, 5*)

one Faith, one Lord

3*When shadows thick were falling,
    And all seemed sunk in night,
Thou, Lord, didst send thy servants,
    Thy chosen sons of light.
On them and on thy people
    Thy plenteous grace was poured,
And this was still their message,
    'One Church, one Faith, one Lord.'

4 *See previous page*

5 And we, shall we be faithless?
    Shall hearts fail, hands hang down?
Shall we evade the conflict,
    And cast away our crown?
Not so; in God's deep counsels
    Some better thing is stored:
We will maintain, unflinching,
    'One Church, one Faith, one Lord.'

6. *See previous page*

See also

485	Behold, the mountain	469	O greatly blessed
23	Eternal God, whose power upholds	159	O spirit of the living God
201	Father, we thank thee	213	O thou, who at thy Eucharist
5	From all that dwell	161	Our Lord, his Passion ended
65	From the eastern mountains	472	Pray that Jerusalem
390	God of eternity	364	Rise up, O men of God!
273	God of love and truth	163	Spirit of mercy
455	God of mercy	426	The day thou gavest
33	Hills of the north, rejoice	255	We come unto our fathers' God
493	How glorious Sion's courts appear		

188 CLIFTON C.M.

JOHN CHARLES CLIFTON (1781–1841)

THE HOLY SCRIPTURES

ALMIGHTY God, thy word is
    cast
  Like seed into the ground;
Now let the dew of heaven descend
  And righteous fruits abound.

2 Let not the foe of Christ and man
    This holy seed remove,
  But give it root in every heart
    To bring forth fruits of love.

3 Let not the world's deceitful cares
    The rising plant destroy,
  But let it yield a hundredfold
    The fruits of peace and joy.

4. Great God, come down, and on thy
    word
    Thy mighty power bestow:
  That all whose souls the truth
    receive
    Its saving power may know.

John Cawood (1775–1852) and others
Based on S. Mark 4, 3–9

189 SOUTHWELL C.M.   HERBERT STEPHEN IRONS (1834-1905)

FATHER of mercies, in thy word
  What endless glory shines!
For ever be thy name adored
  For these celestial lines.

2 Here may the blind and hungry come,
  And light and food receive;
Here shall the lowliest guest have room,
  And taste and see and live.

3 Here springs of consolation rise
  To cheer the fainting mind,
And thirsting souls receive supplies,
  And sweet refreshment find.

4 Here the Redeemer's welcome voice
  Spreads heavenly peace around,
And life and everlasting joys
  Attend the blissful sound.

5 O may these heavenly pages be
  My ever dear delight;
And still new beauties may I see,
  And still increasing light.

.6. Divine Instructor, gracious Lord,
  Be thou for ever near;
Teach me to love thy sacred word,
  And view my Saviour here.

Anne Steele (1716-78)

190 RAVENSHAW 66.66.

Melody abridged by WILLIAM HENRY MONK (1823–89)
from *Ave Hierarchia* (MICHAEL WEISSE, 1480–1534)

LORD, thy word abideth,
And our footsteps guideth;
Who its truth believeth
Light and joy receiveth.

2 When our foes are near us,
Then thy word doth cheer us,
Word of consolation,
Message of salvation.

3 When the storms are o'er us
  And dark clouds before us,
  Then its light directeth
  And our way protecteth.

4 Who can tell the pleasure,
  Who recount the treasure,
  By thy word imparted
  To the simple-hearted?

5 Word of mercy, giving
  Succour to the living;
  Word of life, supplying
  Comfort to the dying.

6. O that we, discerning
   Its most holy learning,
   Lord, may love and fear thee,
   Evermore be near thee.

Henry Williams Baker (1821–77)

THE CHURCH OF GOD

191 NYLAND 76.76. D.

Finnish Melody

THE HOLY SCRIPTURES

O WORD of God incarnate,
   O wisdom from on high,
O truth unchanged, unchanging,
   O light of our dark sky,
We praise thee for the radiance
   That from the hallowed page,
A lantern to our footsteps,
   Shines on from age to age.

2 The Church from her dear Master
      Received the gift divine,
   And still that light she lifteth,
      O'er all the earth to shine;
   It is the golden casket
      Where gems of truth are stored;
   It is the heaven-drawn picture
      Of Christ, the living Word.

3. O make thy Church, dear Saviour,
      A lamp of purest gold,
   To bear before the nations
      Thy true light, as of old;
   O teach thy wandering pilgrims
      By this their path to trace,
   Till, clouds and darkness ended,
      They see thee face to face.

William Walsham How (1823–97)

See also

257 Blessèd Jesus, at thy word
456 God's law is perfect
182 Spread, O spread
473 Teach me, O Lord, the perfect way

THE CHURCH OF GOD

192 BEWELEY 66.66.

CYRIL V. TAYLOR (1907–)

HOLY BAPTISM

*'Defende and kepe the soul of thy litel seruaunt amonge so many perels of
this corruptible lyf and, thy grace goyng with, dresse hym by the way of pes
to the countrey of euer-lasting clernes.'*

DEFEND, O Lord, and keep
    Thy little servant's soul;
In *him* thy life plant deep,
    The life that makes *him* whole.

2 Throughout this mortal life,
    With perils all around,
Faithful in every strife,
    And strong may *he* be found.

3. Keep *him* in thy sure grace,
    And, when this life is past,
Lead *him* to that clear place,
    To peace with thee at last.

Versified by Mary Tearle (1911–)

193 S. STEPHEN C.M.
(NEWINGTON)

WILLIAM JONES (1726–1800)

IN token that thou shalt not fear
    Christ crucified to own,
We print the cross upon thee here,
    And stamp thee his alone.

2 In token that thou shalt not flinch
    Christ's combat to maintain,
But 'neath his banner manfully
    Firm at thy post remain;

3 In token that thou too shalt tread
    The path he travelled by,
Endure the cross, despise the shame,
    And sit thee down on high;

4. Thus outwardly and visibly
    We seal thee for his own;
And may the brow that wears his cross
    Hereafter share his crown.

Henry Alford (1810–71)

194 BUCKLAND 77.77.

LEIGHTON GEORGE HAYNE (1836–83)

LOVING Shepherd of thy sheep,
Keep thy lamb, in safety keep;
Nothing can thy power withstand,
None can pluck *him* from thy hand.

2 May *he* praise thee every day,
Gladly all thy will obey;
Like thy blessèd ones above,
Happy in thy precious love.

3 Loving Shepherd, ever near,
Teach thy lamb thy voice to hear;
Suffer not *his* steps to stray
From the straight and narrow way.

4. Where thou leadest may *he* go,
Walking in thy steps below,
Then, before thy Father's throne,
Saviour, claim *him* for thine own.

Jane Eliza Leeson (1807–82) *and Compilers*

See also

237 Around the throne of God
43 Away in a manger
484 Behold the^amazing gift
302 Fight the good fight

307 Lead us, heavenly Father
369 Take up thy cross
474 The God of love

195 VIGIL 87.83.

GEORGE THALBEN-BALL

SOLDIER, go! Thy vow is spoken:
   Counting earthly gain but loss,
Thou henceforth must bear the token
     Of the cross.

2 Strengthened with the sevenfold blessing
   Of the Spirit here outpoured,
Thou must dare to live confessing
     Christ thy Lord.

3 Trust in him: though sore temptation
   Oft thy fainting heart assail,
Yet the Prince of thy salvation
     Shall prevail.

4 Faithful in his service ever
   Fight, nor fear the battle's tide:
Hosts of hell can harm thee never
     At his side.

5 He, his mighty arm extending,
   Still hath power from sin to save,
Though thy warfare hath no ending
     But the grave.

6. Then, when over death victorious
   Thou shalt lay thine armour down,
With the saints in heaven glorious
     Take the crown.

Thomas Ethelbert Page (1850–1936)

See also

316	Be thou my Vision	406	Forth in thy name
484	Behold the amazing gift	244	From glory to glory
339	Christian, dost thou see them?	326	Lift up your hearts!
302	Fight the good fight	337	Soldiers, who are Christ's below
271	Fill thou my life		

Many hymns under *The Holy Spirit* (Nos. 147–164) and *Dedication and Discipleship*
(Nos. 349–372) are also suitable.

L

196 BANGOR C.M.   WILLIAM TANZER, *Harmony of Sion* (1734)

ACCORDING to thy gracious word,
   In meek humility
This will I do, my dying Lord,
   I will remember thee.

2 Thy body, broken for my sake,
      My bread from heaven shall be;
   Thy testamental cup I take,
      And thus remember thee.

3 Gethsemane can I forget,
      Or there thy conflict see,
   Thine agony and bloody sweat,
      And not remember thee?

4 When to the Cross I turn mine eyes
      And rest on Calvary,
   O Lamb of God, my sacrifice,
      I must remember thee:

5 Remember thee, and all thy pains,
      And all thy love to me;
   Yea, while a breath, a pulse remains,
      Will I remember thee.

6. And when these failing lips grow dumb,
      And mind and memory flee,
   When thou shalt in thy kingdom come,
      Jesu, remember me.

James Montgomery (1771–1854)

THE CHURCH OF GOD

197 EBENEZER 87.87.D.
(TON-Y-BOTEL)

THOMAS JOHN WILLIAMS (1869–1944)

[*By permission of W. Gwenlyn Evans & Son, Carnarvon.*]

ALLELUIA! sing to Jesus,
   His the sceptre, his the throne;
Alleluia! his the triumph,
   His the victory alone:
Hark! the songs of peaceful Sion
   Thunder like a mighty flood;
Jesus out of every nation
   Hath redeemed us by his blood.

2 Alleluia! not as orphans
   Are we left in sorrow now;
Alleluia! he is near us,
   Faith believes, nor questions how:
Though the cloud from sight received him
   When the forty days were o'er,
Shall our hearts forget his promise,
   'I am with you evermore'?

3 Alleluia! bread of angels,
   Thou on earth our food, our stay;
Alleluia! here the sinful
   Flee to thee from day to day;
Intercessor, friend of sinners,
   Earth's Redeemer, plead for me,
Where the songs of all the sinless
   Sweep across the crystal sea.

4. Alleluia! King eternal,
   Thee the Lord of lords we own;
Alleluia! born of Mary,
   Earth thy footstool, heaven thy throne:
Thou within the veil hast entered,
   Robed in flesh, our great High Priest;
Thou on earth both priest and victim
   In the Eucharistic feast.

William Chatterton Dix (1837–98)

198 UNDE ET MEMORES 10.10.10.10.10.10. WILLIAM HENRY MONK (1823–89)

HOLY COMMUNION

AND now, O Father, mindful of the love
That bought us, once for all, on Calvary's tree,
And having with us him that pleads above,
We here present, we here spread forth to thee
That only offering perfect in thine eyes,
The one true pure immortal sacrifice.

2 Look, Father, look on his anointed face,
And only look on us as found in him;
Look not on our misusings of thy grace,
Our prayer so languid, and our faith so dim;
For lo, between our sins and their reward
We set the Passion of thy Son our Lord.

3 And then for those, our dearest and our best,
By this prevailing presence we appeal;
O fold them closer to thy mercy's breast,
O do thine utmost for their souls' true weal;
From tainting mischief keep them white and clear,
And crown thy gifts with strength to persevere.

4. And so we come; O draw us to thy feet,
Most patient Saviour, who canst love us still;
And by this food, so aweful and so sweet,
Deliver us from every touch of ill:
In thine own service make us glad and free,
And grant us never more to part with thee.

William Bright (1824–1901)

199 GWEEDORE 66.66.88.   SAMUEL SEBASTIAN WESLEY (1810–76) (adapted)

AUTHOR of life divine,
   Who hast a table spread,
Furnished with mystic wine
And everlasting bread,
Preserve the life thyself hast given,
And feed and train us up for heaven.

2.   Our needy souls sustain
   With fresh supplies of love,
Till all thy life we gain,
   And all thy fullness prove,
And, strengthened by thy perfect grace,
Behold without a veil thy face.

Charles Wesley (1707–88)

200 CHARTERHOUSE 77.77.77.   Alexander Samuel Cooper (1835–1900)

BREAD of heaven, on thee we feed,
For thy flesh is meat indeed;
Ever may our souls be fed
With this true and living bread,
Day by day with strength supplied
Through the life of him who died.

2. Vine of heaven, thy blood supplies
This blest cup of sacrifice;
'Tis thy wounds our healing give,
To thy Cross we look and live:
Thou our life! O let us be
Rooted, grafted, built in thee.

Josiah Conder (1789–1855)

201 LES COMMANDEMENS
DE DIEU 98.98.

Composed or adapted by LOUIS BOURGEOIS in
Genevan Psalter (1547)

FATHER, we thank thee who hast planted
    Thy holy name within our hearts.
Knowledge and faith and life immortal
    Jesus thy Son to us imparts.

2 Thou, Lord, didst make all for thy pleasure,
    Didst give man food for all his days,
Giving in Christ the bread eternal;
    Thine is the power, be thine the praise.

3 Watch o'er thy Church, O Lord, in mercy,
    Save it from evil, guard it still,
Perfect it in thy love, unite it,
    Cleansed and conformed unto thy will.

4. As grain, once scattered on the hillsides,
    Was in the broken bread made one,
So may thy world-wide Church be gathered
    Into thy kingdom by thy Son.

From the Didache (2nd cent.)
Versified by F. Bland Tucker (1895–   ) and Compilers

202 SURSUM CORDA 10.10.10.10.   ALFRED M. SMITH

HERE, O my Lord, I see thee face to face;
  Here would I touch and handle things unseen,
Here grasp with firmer hand the eternal grace,
  And all my weariness upon thee lean.

2 Here would I feed upon the bread of God,
  Here drink with thee the royal wine of heaven;
Here would I lay aside each earthly load,
  Here taste afresh the calm of sin forgiven.

3. I have no help but thine; nor do I need
  Another arm save thine to lean upon;
It is enough, my Lord, enough indeed;
  My strength is in thy might, thy might alone.

Horatius Bonar (1808–89)

THE CHURCH OF GOD

203 EUDOXIA 65.65.

Sabine Baring-Gould (1834-1924)

Verses 1, 3, 5

CASWALL 65.65.

Friedrich Filitz (1804-76)

Verses 2, 4, 6

Choir only

JESUS, blessèd Saviour,
  God of love and power,
Thou thyself art dwelling
  In us at this hour.

Full Unison

2 Nature cannot hold thee,
    Heaven is all too strait
For thine endless glory
    And thy royal state.

Choir only

3 Out beyond the shining
    Of the furthest star
Thou art ever stretching
    Infinitely far.

Full Unison

4 Yet in us thy children
    Thou art dwelling now:
Fill us with thy goodness
    Till our hearts o'erflow.

Choir only

5 Multiply our graces,
    Chiefly love and fear,
And, dear Lord, the chiefest,
    Grace to persevere.

Full Unison

6. O how can we thank thee
    For a gift like this?
Gift that truly maketh
    Heaven's eternal bliss.

Frederick William Faber (1814–63)
and Compilers

THE CHURCH OF GOD

204 PICARDY   87.87.87.

French Traditional Carol

last verse

HOLY COMMUNION

Σιγησάτω πᾶσα σὰρξ βροτεία

LET all mortal flesh keep silence,
 And with fear and trembling stand;
Ponder nothing earthly-minded,
 For with blessing in his hand
Christ our God to earth descendeth,
 Our full homage to demand.

2 King of kings, yet born of Mary,
 As of old on earth he stood,
Lord of lords, in human vesture—
 In the body and the blood—
He will give to all the faithful
 His own self for heavenly food.

3 Rank on rank the host of heaven
 Spreads its vanguard on the way,
As the Light of light descendeth
 From the realms of endless day,
That the powers of hell may vanish
 As the darkness clears away.

4. At his feet the six-winged Seraph;
 Cherubim with sleepless eye,
Veil their faces to the Presence,
 As with ceaseless voice they cry,
'Alleluia, Alleluia,
 Alleluia, Lord most high'.

Liturgy of S. James
Tr. Gerard Moultrie (1829–85)

205 GLOUCESTER L.M.

EDWARD HODGES (1796–1867)

LOOK down upon us, God of grace,
And send from thy most holy place
The quickening Spirit all divine
On us and on this bread and wine.

2. O may his overshadowing
Make now for us this bread we bring
The body of thy Son our Lord,
This cup his blood for sinners poured.

Arthur James Mason (1851–1928)

206 KINGLEY VALE 87.87.47.

HUGH PERCY ALLEN (1869–1946)

LORD, enthroned in heavenly splendour,
 First-begotten from the dead,
Thou alone, our strong defender,
 Liftest up thy people's head.
  Alleluia!
 Jesu, true and living Bread.

2 Here our humblest homage pay we;
 Here in loving reverence bow;
Here for faith's discernment pray we,
 Lest we fail to know thee now.
  Alleluia!
 Thou art here, we ask not how.

3 Though the lowliest form doth veil thee,
 As of old in Bethlehem,
Here as there thine angels hail thee,
 Branch and Flower of Jesse's stem.
  Alleluia!
 We in worship join with them.

4 Paschal Lamb, thine offering, finished
 Once for all when thou wast slain,
In its fullness undiminished
 Shall for evermore remain,
  Alleluia!
 Cleansing souls from every stain.

5. Life-imparting, heavenly Manna,
 Stricken Rock with streaming side,
Heaven and earth with loud hosanna
 Worship thee, the Lamb who died,
  Alleluia!
 Risen, ascended, glorified.

George Hugh Bourne (1840–1925)

207 ROCKINGHAM L.M.   Adapted by EDWARD MILLER (1731–1807)

M^Y God, and is thy table spread,
 And doth thy cup with love o'erflow?
Thither be all thy children led,
 And let them all thy sweetness know.

2 Hail, sacred feast, which Jesus makes,
 Rich banquet of his flesh and blood!
Thrice happy he who here partakes
 That sacred stream, that heavenly food.

3. O let thy table honoured be,
 And furnished well with joyful guests;
And may each soul salvation see,
 That here its sacred pledges tastes.

Philip Doddridge (1702–51)

208 PANGE, LINGUA

Mode iii

PART I

Pange, lingua, gloriosi Corporis mysterium

NOW my tongue, the mystery telling,
  Of the glorious body sing,
And the blood, all price excelling,
  Which the Gentiles' Lord and King,
In a Virgin's womb once dwelling,
  Shed for this world's ransoming.

Given for us, and condescending
  To be born for us below,
He, with men in converse blending,
  Dwelt the seed of truth to sow,
Till he closed with wondrous ending
  His most patient life of woe.

3 That last night, at supper lying,
  'Mid the twelve, his chosen band,
Jesus, with the law complying,
  Keeps the feast its rites demand;
Then, more precious food supplying,
  Gives himself with his own hand.

4. Word-made-flesh true bread he maketh
  By his word his flesh to be;
Wine his blood; which whoso taketh
  Must from carnal thoughts be free;
Faith alone, though sight forsaketh,
  Shows true hearts the mystery.

S. Thomas Aquinas (1227–74)
Tr. Edward Caswall (1814–78)
and Compilers of Hymns A. & M.

Metrical tune and words overleaf.

208 (*continued*)

PANGE, LINGUA

Mode iii (Mechlin Version)

PART 1

Pange, lingua, gloriosi Corporis mysterium

NOW my tongue, the mystery telling,
    Of the glorious body sing,
And the blood, all price excelling,
    Which the Gentiles' Lord and King,
In a Virgin's womb once dwelling,
    Shed for this world's ransoming.

2 Given for us, and condescending
    To be born for us below,
He, with men in converse blending,
    Dwelt the seed of truth to sow,
Till he closed with wondrous ending
    His most patient life of woe.

3 That last night, at supper lying,
    'Mid the twelve, his chosen band,
Jesus, with the law complying,
    Keeps the feast its rites demand;
Then, more precious food supplying,
    Gives himself with his own hand.

4. Word-made-flesh true bread he maketh
    By his word his flesh to be;
Wine his blood; which whoso taketh
    Must from carnal thoughts be free;
Faith alone, though sight forsaketh,
    Shows true hearts the mystery.

208 *(continued)*

Melody from SAMUEL WEBBE'S
Motetts or Antiphons (1792) and
An Essay on the Church Plain Chant (1782)

S. THOMAS 87.87.87.

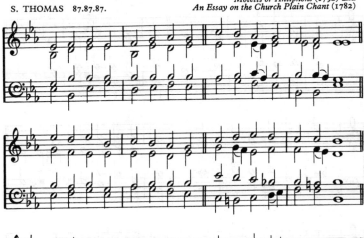

PART 2

Tantum ergo sacramentum

THEREFORE we, before him bending,
　　This great Sacrament revere;
Types and shadows have their ending,
　　For the newer rite is here;
Faith, our outward sense befriending,
　　Makes the inward vision clear.

2. Glory let us give, and blessing
　　To the Father, and the Son,
Honour, might, and praise addressing,
　　While eternal ages run;
Ever too his love confessing,
　　Who, from Both, with Both is One. Amen.

S. Thomas Aquinas (1227–74)
Tr. Edward Caswall (1814–78)
and Compilers of Hymns A. & M.

A - men.

209 IN ALLEN MEINEN
THATEN 776. D.

Sion's Harp, 1855 (from *Davidisches Harfen-und-Psalterspiel*, 1744)

O esca viatorum

O FOOD of men wayfaring,
The bread of angels sharing,
O manna from on high!
We hunger; Lord, supply us,
Nor thy delights deny us,
Whose hearts to thee draw nigh.

2 O stream of love past telling,
O purest fountain, welling
From out the Saviour's side!
We faint with thirst; revive us,
Of thine abundance give us,
And all we need provide.

3. O Jesu, by thee bidden,
We here adore thee, hidden
'Neath forms of bread and wine.
Grant, when the veil is riven,
We may behold in heaven
Thy countenance divine.

c. 1661. *Tr. John Athelstan Laurie Riley* (1858–1945)

210 S. FLAVIAN C.M.
(Psalm 132)

DAY's *Psalter* (1562)

O GOD unseen, yet ever near,
   Thy presence may we feel;
And thus inspired with holy fear,
   Before thine altar kneel.

2 Here may thy faithful people know
   The blessings of thy love,
The streams that through the desert flow,
   The manna from above.

3 We come, obedient to thy word,
   To feast on heavenly food;
Our meat the body of the Lord,
   Our drink his precious blood.

4. Thus may we all thy word obey,
   For we, O God, are thine;
And go rejoicing on our way,
   Renewed with strength divine.

Edward Osler (1798–1863)

See also No. 528 (CS)

211 RYBURN 88.88.88.

NORMAN COCKER (1889–1953)

HOLY COMMUNION

O LEAD my blindness by the hand,
   Lead me to thy familiar feast,
Not here or now to understand,
   Yet even here and now to taste
How the eternal Word of heaven
On earth in broken bread is given.

2 We, who this holy precinct round
   In one adoring circle kneel,
May we in one intent be bound,
   And one serene devotion feel;
And grow around thy sacred shrine
Like tendrils of the deathless vine.

3. We, who with one blest food are fed,
   Into one' body may we grow,
And one pure life from thee, the Head,
   Informing all the members flow;
One pulse be felt in every vein,
One law of pleasure and of pain.

William Ewart Gladstone (1809–98)

See also No. 531 (CS)

212 VERBUM SUPERNUM
(O SALUTARIS)

Mode viii (Mechlin Version)

First Tune

O salutaris hostia

O SAVING victim, opening wide
The gate of heaven to man below,
Our foes press hard on every side:
Thine aid supply, thy strength bestow.

2. All praise and thanks to thee ascend
For evermore, blest One in Three;
O grant us life that shall not end
In our true native land with thee. Amen.

212 O JESU CHRIST L.M.   *Melody from Haus Kirchen Cantorei (1587)*

O salutaris hostia

O SAVING victim, opening wide
    The gate of heaven to man below,
Our foes press hard on every side:
    Thine aid supply, thy strength bestow.

2. All praise and thanks to thee ascend
    For evermore, blest One in Three;
O grant us life that shall not end
    In our true native land with thee. Amen.

S. Thomas Aquinas (1227–74)
Tr. John Mason Neale (1818–66), Edward Caswall (1814–78)
and Compilers of Hymns A. & M.

A - men.

THE CHURCH OF GOD

213 SONG I 10.10.10.10.10.10.

Melody and Bass by
ORLANDO GIBBONS (1583–1625)

HOLY COMMUNION

O THOU, who at thy Eucharist didst pray
  That all thy Church might be for ever one,
Grant us at every Eucharist to say,
  With longing heart and soul, 'Thy will be done.'
O may we all one bread, one body be,
One through this sacrament of unity.

2 For all thy Church, O Lord, we intercede;
  Make thou our sad divisions soon to cease;
Draw us the nearer each to each, we plead,
  By drawing all to thee, O Prince of peace;
Thus may we all one bread, one body be,
One through this sacrament of unity.

3 We pray thee too for wanderers from thy fold;
  O bring them back, good Shepherd of the sheep,
Back to the faith which saints believed of old,
  Back to the Church which still that faith doth keep;
Soon may we all one bread, one body be,
One through this sacrament of unity.

4. So, Lord, at length when sacraments shall cease,
  May we be one with all thy Church above,
One with thy saints in one unbroken peace,
  One with thy saints in one unbounded love:
More blessèd still, in peace and love to be
One with the Trinity in Unity.

William Harry Turton (1856–1938)
Based on S. John 17, 11

214 ALBANO C.M.

VINCENT NOVELLO (1781–1861)

ONCE, only once, and once for all,
    His precious life he gave;
Before the Cross our spirits fall,
    And own it strong to save.

2 'One offering, single and complete',
    With lips and heart we say;
But what he never can repeat
    He shows forth day by day.

3 For as the priest of Aaron's line
    Within the holiest stood,
And sprinkled all the mercy-shrine
    With sacrificial blood;

4 So he who once atonement wrought,
    Our Priest of endless power,
Presents himself for those he bought
    In that dark noontide hour.

5 His manhood pleads where now it lives
    On heaven's eternal throne,
And where in mystic rite he gives
    Its presence to his own.

6. And so we show thy death, O Lord,
    Till thou again appear;
And feel, when we approach thy board,
    We have an altar here.

William Bright (1824–1901)
Based on Hebrews 10, 1–14

215 ACH GOTT UND HERR 87.87.

Melody Anon. (1625)

نْبِيلَا مَثْنُى اِتِبِا اِفِقِفِيت

STRENGTHEN for service, Lord, the hands
    That holy things have taken;
Let ears that now have heard thy songs
    To clamour never waken.

2 Lord, may the tongues which 'Holy' sang
    Keep free from all deceiving;
The eyes which saw thy love be bright,
    Thy blessèd hope perceiving.

3. The feet that tread thy holy courts
    From light do thou not banish;
The bodies by thy body fed
    With thy new life replenish.

Liturgy of Malabar
Tr. C. W. Humphreys, Percy Dearmer (1867–1936) and others

See also No. 536 (CS)

216 VERBUM SUPERNUM
(O SALUTARIS)

Mode viii (Mechlin Version)

Verbum supernum prodiens

THE heavenly Word, proceeding forth,
  Yet leaving not the Father's side,
Accomplishing his work on earth,
  Had reached at length life's eventide.

2 By false disciple to be given
    To foemen for his life athirst,
  Himself, the very bread of heaven,
    He gave to his disciples first.

3 He gave himself in either kind,
    His precious flesh, his precious blood;
  In love's own fullness thus designed
    Of the whole man to be the food.

4. By birth their fellow-man was he;
    Their meat, when sitting at the board;
  He died, their ransomer to be;
    He ever reigns, their great reward. Amen.

S. Thomas Aquinas (1227–74)
Tr. John Mason Neale (1818–66)
and Compilers of Hymns A. & M.

A - men.

217 ADORO TE DEVOTE 10.10.10.10.   Proper Melody (Solesmes Version)

Adoro te devote

THEE we adore, O hidden Saviour, thee,
Who in thy Sacrament art pleased to be;
Both flesh and spirit in thy presence fail,
Yet here thy presence we devoutly hail.

2 O blest memorial of our dying Lord,
Who living bread to men doth here afford!
O may our souls for ever feed on thee,
And thou, O Christ, for ever precious be.

3 Fountain of goodness, Jesus, Lord and God,
Cleanse us, unclean, with thy most cleansing blood;
Increase our faith and love, that we may know
The hope and peace which from thy presence flow.

4. O Christ, whom now beneath a veil we see,
May what we thirst for soon our portion be,
To gaze on thee unveiled, and see thy face,
The vision of thy glory and thy grace. Amen.

S. Thomas Aquinas (1227–74)
Tr. James Russell Woodford (1820–85)

A - men.

M

THE CHURCH OF GOD

218 WORDSWORTH 76.76.D.   WILLIAM HENRY MONK (1823–89)

WE hail thy presence glorious,
   O Christ, our great High Priest,
O'er sin and death victorious,
   At thy thanksgiving feast;
As thou art interceding
   For us in heaven above,
Thy Church on earth is pleading
   Thy perfect work of love.

2 Through thee in every nation
   Thine own their hearts upraise,
Offering one pure oblation,
   One sacrifice of praise:
With thee, in blest communion,
   The living and the dead
Are joined in closest union,
   One body with one Head.

3 O living bread from heaven,
   Jesu, our Saviour good,
Who thine own self hast given
   To be our souls' true food;

For us thy body broken
   Hung on the cross of shame;
This bread its hallowed token
   We break in thy dear name.

4 O stream of love unending,
   Poured from the one true vine,
With our weak nature blending
   The strength of life divine;
Our thankful faith confessing
   In thy life-blood outpoured,
We drink this cup of blessing,
   And praise thy name, O Lord.

5. May we, thy word believing,
   Thee through thy gifts receive,
That, thou within us living,
   We all to God may live;
Draw us from earth to heaven,
   Till sin and sorrow cease,
Forgiving and forgiven,
   In love and joy and peace.

Richard Godfrey Parsons (1882–1948)

See also No. 540 (CS)

219 MEIRIONYDD 76.76.D.   Melody by WILLIAM LLOYD (1785–1852)

WE pray thee, heavenly Father,
   To hear us in thy love,
And pour upon thy children
   Thy blessing from above;
That so in love abiding,
   From all defilement free,
We may in pureness offer
   Our Eucharist to thee.

2 Be thou our guide and helper,
   O Jesus Christ, we pray;
So may we well approach thee,
   If thou wilt be the way:
Thou, very truth, hast promised
   To help us in our strife,
Food of the weary pilgrim,
   Eternal source of life.

3 And thou, Creator Spirit,
   Look on us; we are thine;
Renew in us thy graces,
   Upon our darkness shine;
That, with thy benediction
   Upon our souls outpoured,
We may receive in gladness
   The body of the Lord.

4. O Trinity of Persons,
   O Unity most high,
On thee alone relying
   Thy servants would draw nigh:
Unworthy in our weakness,
   On thee our hope is stayed,
And, blessed by thy forgiveness,
   We will not be afraid.

Vincent Stuckey Stratton Coles (1845–1929)
and Compilers

220 CHRISTE FONS JUGIS 11.11.11.5.

Rouen Melody

Alternative Accompaniment

WHEREFORE, O Father, we thy humble servants
Here bring before thee Christ thy well-belovèd,
All-perfect offering, sacrifice immortal,
Spotless oblation.

2. See now thy children, making intercession
   Through him, our Saviour, Son of God incarnate,
   For all thy people, living and departed,
        Pleading before thee. *William Henry Hammond Jervois (1852–1905)*

See also

503	Bread of the world	(CS)	531	O lead my blindness	(CS)
506	Christ was the Word	(CS)	535	See, Father, thy belovèd Son	(CS)
510	Deck thyself	(CS)	536	Strengthen for service	(CS)
244	From glory to glory		538	The bread of life	(CS)
323	Jesu, thou joy		475	The King of love	
345	Not for our sins alone		540	We hail thy presence	(CS)
528	O God unseen	(CS)			

MARRIAGE

221 DANK SEI GOTT IN DER HÖHE 76.76. D.   Melody as in JOHANN SEBASTIAN BACH'S *Vierstimmige Choralgesänge* (1769)

O FATHER all creating,
    Whose wisdom, love, and power
First bound two lives together
    In Eden's primal hour,
The lives of these thy children
    With thy best gifts endue,
A home by thee made happy,
    A love by thee kept true.

2. Except thou build it, Father,
    The house is built in vain;
Except thou, Saviour, bless it,
    The joy will turn to pain;
But naught can break the marriage
    Of hearts in thee made one,
And love thy Spirit hallows
    Is endless love begun.

*John Ellerton (1826–93)
and Compilers*

222 ILLSLEY L.M.   JOHN BISHOP (1665–1737)

O FATHER, by whose sovereign sway
  The sun and stars in order move,
Yet who hast made us bold to say
  Thy nature and thy name is love:

2 O royal Son, whose every deed
  Showed love and love's divinity,
Yet didst not scorn the humblest need
  At Cana's feast in Galilee:

3 O Holy Spirit, who dost speak
  In saint and sage since time began,
Yet givest courage to the weak
  And teachest love to selfish man:

4. Be present in our hearts to-day,
  All powerful to bless, and give
To these thy children grace that they
  May love, and through their loving live.

Cyril Argentine Alington (1872–1955)

223 S. ALPHEGE 76.76.   HENRY JOHN GAUNTLETT (1805–76)

WE lift our hearts, O Father,
    To thee our voices raise,
For these thy suppliant servants,
    In mingled prayer and praise:

2 Praise for the joy of loving,
    All other joys above;
Praise for the priceless blessing
    Of love's response to love;

3 Prayer that the sweet surrender
    Of self may perfect be,
That each be one with other,
    And both be one in thee;

4 Prayer that thou wilt accomplish
    The promise of to-day,
And crown the years with blessing
    That shall not pass away;

5. Praise for the hope most glorious
    That looks beyond the veil,
Where faith and hope shall vanish,
    But love shall never fail.

Edward Ashurst Welch (1860–1932)

See also

149	Come down, O Love divine	307	Lead us, heavenly Father
352	Father, hear the prayer	328, 329	Love divine
271	Fill thou my life	157	O Holy Spirit, Lord of grace
272	For the beauty of the earth	158	O King enthroned on high
274	Happy are they	481	Through all the changing scenes

224 ANGELS' SONG L.M.
(SONG 34)

Melody and Bass by ORLANDO GIBBONS
(1583–1625)

THE MINISTRY

LORD, pour thy Spirit from on high,
 And thine ordainèd servants bless;
Graces and gifts to each supply,
 And clothe thy priests with righteousness.

2 Within thy temple when they stand,
 To teach the truth as taught by thee,
Saviour, like stars in thy right hand,
 Let all thy Church's pastors be.

3 Wisdom and zeal and faith impart,
 Firmness with meekness, from above,
To bear thy people in their heart,
 And love the souls whom thou dost love:

4 To watch and pray and never faint,
 By day and night their guard to keep,
To warn the sinner, cheer the saint,
 To feed thy lambs, and tend thy sheep.

5. Then, when their work is finished here,
 May they in hope their charge resign;
When the chief Shepherd shall appear,
 O God, may they and we be thine.

James Montgomery (1771–1854)

225 CROMER L.M.   JOHN AMBROSE LLOYD (1815–74)

O THOU who makest souls to shine
  With light from lighter worlds above,
And droppest glistening dew divine
  On all who seek a Saviour's love;

2 Do thou thy benediction give
  On all who teach, on all who learn,
That so thy Church may holier live,
  And every lamp more brightly burn.

3 Give those who teach pure hearts and wise,
  Faith, hope, and love, all warmed by prayer;
Themselves first training for the skies,
  They best will raise their people there.

4 Give those who learn the willing ear,
  The spirit meek, the guileless mind;
Such gifts will make the lowliest here
  Far better than a kingdom find.

5 O bless the shepherd; bless the sheep;
  That guide and guided both be one,
One in the faithful watch they keep,
  Until this hurrying life be done.

6. If thus, good Lord, thy grace be given,
  In thee to live, in thee to die,
Before we upward pass to heaven,
  We taste our immortality.

John Armstrong (1813–56)

THE CHURCH OF GOD

226 HANOVER 10.10.11.11.

Probably by WILLIAM CROFT (1678–1727)

Supreme quales arbiter

DISPOSER supreme, and Judge of the earth,
 Who choosest for thine the weak and the poor;
To frail earthen vessels and things of no worth
 Entrusting thy riches which aye shall endure.

2 Those vessels soon fail, though full of thy light,
 And at thy decree are broken and gone;
Then brightly appeareth the arm of thy might,
 As through the clouds breaking the lightnings have shone.

3 Like clouds are they borne to do thy great will,
 And swift as the winds about the world go;
The Word with his wisdom their spirits doth fill,
 They thunder, they lighten, like waters o'erflow.

4 Their sound goeth forth, 'Christ Jesus is Lord!'
 Then Satan doth fear, his citadels fall:
As when the dread trumpets went forth at thy word,
 And one long blast shattered the Canaanites' wall.

5 O loud be their trump, and stirring the sound,
 To rouse us, O Lord, from sin's deadly sleep;
May lights which thou kindlest in darkness around
 The dull soul awaken her vigils to keep.

6. All honour and praise, dominion and might,
 To thee, Three in One, eternally be,
Who, pouring around us thy glorious light,
 Dost call us from darkness thy glory to see. Amen.

Jean-Baptiste de Santeuil (1630–97)
Tr. Isaac Williams (1802–65) *and others*

227 SINE NOMINE 10.10.10.4.

RALPH VAUGHAN WILLIAMS (1872–1958)

FOR all the saints who from their labours rest,
Who thee by faith before the world confessed,
Thy name, O Jesu, be for ever blest:
    Alleluia!

2 Thou wast their rock, their fortress, and their might;
Thou, Lord, their captain in the well-fought fight;
Thou in the darkness drear their one true light:
    Alleluia!

3 O may thy soldiers, faithful, true, and bold,
Fight as the saints who nobly fought of old,
And win with them the victor's crown of gold:
    Alleluia!

Harmony
4 O blest communion, fellowship divine!
We feebly struggle, they in glory shine;
Yet all are one in thee, for all are thine:
    Alleluia!

Harmony
5 And when the strife is fierce, the warfare long,
Steals on the ear the distant triumph-song,
And hearts are brave again, and arms are strong:
    Alleluia!

Harmony
6 The golden evening brightens in the west;
Soon, soon to faithful warriors cometh rest;
Sweet is the calm of Paradise the blest:
    Alleluia!

7 But lo, there breaks a yet more glorious day;
The saints triumphant rise in bright array:
The King of glory passes on his way:
    Alleluia!

8. From earth's wide bounds, from ocean's farthest coast,
Through gates of pearl streams in the countless host,
Singing to Father, Son, and Holy Ghost:
    Alleluia!

William Walsham How (1823-97)

228 S. HELENA S.M. Melody adapted from BENJAMIN MILGROVE (1731–1810)

FOR all thy saints, O Lord,
Who strove in thee to live,
Who followed thee, obeyed, adored,
Our grateful hymn receive.

2 For all thy saints, O Lord,
Accept our thankful cry,
Who counted thee their great reward,
And strove in thee to die.

3 Jesu, thy name we bless,
And humbly pray that we
May follow them in holiness,
Who lived and died in thee.

4. Thine earthly members fit
To join thy saints above,
In one communion ever knit,
One fellowship of love.

Richard Mant (1776–1848) and others.

229 SONG 67 C.M. Melody and Bass by ORLANDO GIBBONS (1583–1625)

GIVE me the wings of faith to rise
　　Within the veil, and see
The saints above, how great their joys,
　　How bright their glories be.

2 Once they were mourning here below,
　　And wet their couch with tears;
They wrestled hard, as we do now,
　　With sins and doubts and fears.

3 I ask them whence their victory came;
　　They, with united breath,
Ascribe their conquest to the Lamb,
　　Their triumph to his death.

4 They marked the footsteps that he trod,
　　His zeal inspired their breast,
And, following their incarnate God,
　　Possess the promised rest.

5. Our glorious Leader claims our praise
　　For his own pattern given;
While the long cloud of witnesses
　　Show the same path to heaven.

Isaac Watts (1674–1748)

THE CHURCH OF GOD

230 LANCING L.M.

WILLIAM HAROLD FERGUSON (1874-1950)

Unison

Lo, round the throne, a glorious band,
The saints in countless myriads stand,
Of every tongue, redeemed to God,
Arrayed in garments washed in blood.

2 Through tribulation great they came;
They bore the cross, despised the shame;
From all their labours now they rest,
In God's eternal glory blest.

3 They see their Saviour face to face,
And sing the triumphs of his grace;
Him day and night they ceaseless praise,
To him the loud thanksgiving raise:

4 'Worthy the Lamb, for sinners slain,
Through endless years to live and reign;
Thou hast redeemed us by thy blood,
And made us kings and priests to God.'

5. O may we tread the sacred road
That saints and holy martyrs trod;
Wage to the end the glorious strife,
And win, like them, a crown of life.

Rowland Hill (1744-1833) and others
Based on Revelation 7, 13-17 and 5, 9-10

231 IN BABILONE 87.87.D.

Dutch Melody

LORD, who in thy perfect wisdom
    Times and seasons dost arrange,
Working out thy changeless purpose
    In a world of ceaseless change;
Thou didst form our ancient nation,
    Guiding it through all the days,
To unfold in it thy purpose
    To thy glory and thy praise.

2 To our shores remote, benighted,
    Barrier of the western waves,
Tidings in thy love thou sentest,
    Tidings of the Cross that saves.
Saints and heroes strove and suffered
    Here thy Gospel to proclaim;
We, the heirs of their endeavour,
    Tell the honour of their name.

3 Lord, we hold in veneration
    All the saints our land has known,
Bishops, Doctors, Priests, Confessors,
    Martyrs, standing round thy throne;
Alban, Anselm, Bede, Augustine—
    Sing the great heroic band!
Who of old by prayer and labour
    Hallowed this our fatherland.

4. Still thine ancient purpose standeth
    Every change and chance above;
Still thine ancient Church remaineth,
    Witness to thy changeless love.
Grant us vision, Lord, and courage
    To fulfil thy work begun;
In the Church and in the nation,
    King of kings, thy will be done.

Timothy Rees, C.R. (1874-1939) and Compilers

THE CHURCH OF GOD

232

Mode viii

First Tune

Deus tuorum militum

O GOD, thy soldiers' faithful Lord,
  Their portion, and their great reward,
From all transgressions set us free
Who sing thy Martyr's victory.

2 By wisdom taught he learned to know
  The vanity of all below,
  The fleeting joys of earth disdained,
  And everlasting glory gained.

3 Right manfully his cross he bore,
  And ran his race of torments sore;
  For thee he poured his life away,
  With thee he lives in endless day.

4. All praise to God the Father be,
  All praise, eternal Son, to thee,
  Whom with the Spirit we adore
  For ever and for evermore. Amen.

? S. Ambrose (c. 340–97)
Tr. John Mason Neale (1818–66)
and Compilers of Hymns A. & M.

232 DEUS TUORUM MILITUM L.M.

Second Tune

Grenoble Melody

Deus tuorum militum

O GOD, thy soldiers' faithful Lord,
　　Their portion, and their great reward,
From all transgressions set us free
Who sing thy Martyr's victory.

2 By wisdom taught he learned to know
　　The vanity of all below,
　　The fleeting joys of earth disdained,
　　And everlasting glory gained.

3 Right manfully his cross he bore,
　　And ran his race of torments sore;
　　For thee he poured his life away,
　　With thee he lives in endless day.

4. All praise to God the Father be,
　　All praise, eternal Son, to thee,
　　Whom with the Spirit we adore
　　For ever and for evermore. Amen.

? S. Ambrose (c. 340–97)
Tr. John Mason Neale (1818–66)
and Compilers of Hymns A. & M.

A - men.

233 DU FOND DE MA PENSÉE 76.76.D.
(PSALM 130)

Strasburg Psalter (1539)

In domo Patris

OUR Father's home eternal,
   O Christ, thou dost prepare
With many divers mansions,
   And each one passing fair;
They are the victors' guerdon,
   Who, through the hard-won fight,
Have followed in thy footsteps,
   And reign with thee in light.

2. The holy men and women,
   Their earthly struggle o'er,
With joy put off the armour
   That they shall need no more;
And every faithful servant,
   Made perfect in thy grace,
Hath each his fitting station
   'Mid those that see thy face.

? *Thomas à Kempis* (1379–1471)
Tr. John Mason Neale (1818–66) *and others*

234 AETERNA CHRISTI MUNERA L.M.

Melody from GUIDETTI,
Directorium Chori (1582)

Aeterna Christi munera

THE eternal gifts of Christ the King,
The apostles' glorious deeds, we sing;
And while due hymns of praise we pay,
Our thankful hearts cast grief away.

2 The Church in these her princes boasts,
These victor chiefs of warrior hosts;
The soldiers of the heavenly hall,
The lights that rose on earth for all.

3 'Twas thus the yearning faith of saints,
The unconquered hope that never faints,
The love of Christ that knows not shame,
The prince of this world overcame.

4 In these the Father's glory shone;
In these the will of God the Son;
In these exults the Holy Ghost;
Through these rejoice the heavenly host.

5. Redeemer, hear us of thy love,
That, with this glorious band above,
Hereafter, of thine endless grace,
Thy servants also may have place. Amen.

S. Ambrose (c. 340–97)
Tr. John Mason Neale (1818–66)

A - men.

235 BROMSGROVE C.M.

HERBERT ARTHUR DYER (1878–1918)

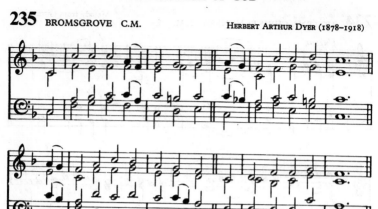

Alternative Accompaniment

Unison

THE Son of God goes forth to war,
  A kingly crown to gain;
His blood-red banner streams afar:
  Who follows in his train?

2 Who best can drink his cup of woe,
    Triumphant over pain,
  Who patient bears his cross below,
    He follows in his train.

3 The martyr first, whose eagle eye
    Could pierce beyond the grave;
  Who saw his Master in the sky,
    And called on him to save:

4 Like him, with pardon on his tongue
    In midst of mortal pain,
  He prayed for them that did the wrong:
    Who follows in his train?

5 A glorious band, the chosen few
    On whom the Spirit came,
  Twelve valiant saints, their hope they knew,
    And mocked the cross and flame.

6 They met the tyrant's brandished steel,
    The lion's gory mane,
  They bowed their necks the death to feel:
    Who follows in their train?

7. They climbed the steep ascent of heaven
    Through peril, toil, and pain;
  O God, to us may grace be given
    To follow in their train.

Reginald Heber (1783–1826)

THE CHURCH OF GOD

236 ALL SAINTS 87.87.77.

Darmstadt Gesangbuch (1698)

Wer sind die vor Gottes Throne

WHO are these, like stars appearing,
  These, before God's throne who stand?
Each a golden crown is wearing;
  Who are all this glorious band?
    Alleluia! hark, they sing,
    Praising loud their heavenly King.

2 Who are these, of dazzling brightness,
    These in God's own truth arrayed?
  Clad in robes of purest whiteness,
    Robes whose lustre ne'er shall fade,
      Ne'er be touched by time's rude hand—
      Whence comes all this glorious band?

3 These are they who have contended
    For their Saviour's honour long,
  Wrestling on till life was ended,
    Following not the sinful throng;
      These, who well the fight sustained,
      Triumph through the Lamb have gained.

4 These are they whose hearts were riven,
    Sore with woe and anguish tried,
  Who in prayer full oft have striven
    With the God they glorified;
      Now, their painful conflict o'er,
      God has bid them weep no more.

5. These like priests have watched and waited,
    Offering up to Christ their will,
  Soul and body consecrated
    Day and night to serve him still:
      Now, in God's most holy place
      Blest they stand before his face.

Heinrich Theobald Schenck (1656–1727)
Tr. Frances Elizabeth Cox (1812–97)
Based on Revelation 7, 13–17

See also

242	For the might of thine arm		251	O dear and heavenly city
244	From glory to glory		252	O what their joy
246	How mighty are the Sabbaths		253	Ten thousand times
353	I sing a song		254	There is a land
247	Jerusalem, my happy home		255	We come unto our fathers' God
248	Jerusalem the golden		286	Ye holy angels bright
249	Let saints on earth		288	Ye watchers
250	Light's abode			

Many hymns under *The Communion of Saints* (Nos. 241–255) are also suitable.

THE CHURCH OF GOD

237 SOLOTHURN L.M.

Swiss Traditional Melody

MICHAELMAS

AROUND the throne of God a band
Of glorious angels ever stand;
God's grace and glory they behold,
And on their heads are crowns of gold.

2 Some wait around him, ready still
To sing his praise and do his will;
And some, when he commands them, go
To guard his servants here below.

3 Lord, give thine angels every day
Command to guide us on our way,
And bid them every evening keep
Their watch around us while we sleep.

4. So shall no wicked thing draw near,
To do us harm or cause us fear;
And we shall dwell, when life is past,
With angels round thy throne at last.

John Mason Neale (1818–66) *and others*

MICHAELMAS

238 TRISAGION 10.10.10.10.   HENRY SMART (1813–79)

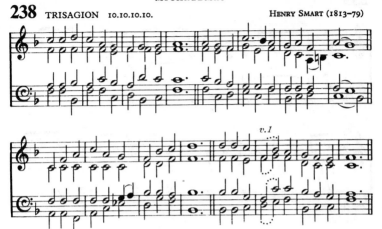

v.1

Φωστῆρες τῆς ἀΰλου

STARS of the morning, so gloriously bright,
   Filled with celestial virtue and light,
These that, where night never followeth day,
Raise the 'Thrice Holy' ever and aye:

2 These are thy ministers, these dost thou own,
  Lord God of Sabaoth, nearest thy throne;
  These are thy messengers, these dost thou send,
  Help of the helpless ones, man to defend.

3 These keep the guard amidst Salem's dear bowers,
  Thrones, principalities, virtues, and powers;
  Where, with the living ones, mystical four,
  Cherubim, Seraphim, bow and adore.

4 Then, when the earth was first poised in mid space,
  Then, when the planets first sped on their race,
  Then, when were ended the six days' employ,
  Then all the sons of God shouted for joy.

5. Still let them succour us; still let them fight,
  Lord of angelic hosts, battling for right;
  Till, where their anthems they ceaselessly pour,
  We with the angels may bow and adore.

S. Joseph the Hymnographer (died ? 883). Tr. John Mason Neale (1818–66)

See also

269	Bright the vision	282	Sing Alleluia forth
122	Come, let us join our cheerful	478	The Lord of heaven confess
	songs	541	What tongue can tell (CS)
489	Hark how the adoring hosts	483	Ye boundless realms
52	It came upon the midnight clear	286	Ye holy angels bright
279	O praise ye the Lord!	288	Ye watchers
16	Praise the Lord! ye heavens		

239

Mode ii

S. BARTHOLOMEW L.M.

Melody by HENRY DUNCALF (18th cent.)

THE BLESSED VIRGIN MARY

Quem terra, pontus, aethera

THE God whom earth and sea and sky
Adore and laud and magnify,
Whose might they own, whose praise they swell,
In Mary's womb vouchsafed to dwell.

2 The God whom sun and moon obey,
Whom all things serve from day to day,
Is borne upon a Maiden's breast,
By fullest heavenly grace possessed.

3 How blest that Mother, in whose shrine
The world's Creator, Lord divine,
Whose hand contains the earth and sky,
Once deigned, as in his ark, to lie!

4 Blest in the message Gabriel brought:
Blest by the work the Spirit wrought:
From whom the great Desire of earth
Took human flesh and human birth.

5. O Lord, the Virgin-born, to thee
Eternal praise and glory be,
Whom with the Father we adore,
And Holy Ghost, for evermore. Amen.

? Venantius Fortunatus (530–609)
Tr. John Mason Neale (1818–66) and Compilers

240 QUEM PASTORES
LAUDAVERE 88.77.

Melody from a 14th-century German MS.

v.2 eye That
v.3 blest, Who

VIRGIN-BORN, we bow before thee:
   Blessèd was the womb that bore thee;
      Mary, Mother meek and mild,
      Blessèd was she in her Child.

2 Blessèd was the breast that fed thee;
   Blessèd was the hand that led thee;
      Blessèd was the parent's eye
      That watched thy slumbering infancy.

3 Blessèd she by all creation,
   Who brought forth the world's salvation;
      Blessèd they, for ever blest,
      Who love thee most and serve thee best.

4. Virgin-born, we bow before thee:
   Blessèd was the womb that bore thee;
      Mary, Mother meek and mild,
      Blessèd was she in her Child.

Reginald Heber (1783–1826)

See also

41   A great and mighty wonder
318   Blest are the pure in heart
31   Creator of the starry height
47   From east to west
288   Ye watchers

241 S. ALPHEGE 76.76.   HENRY JOHN GAUNTLETT (1805–76)

Hic breve vivitur

BRIEF life is here our portion,
　Brief sorrow, short-lived care;
The life that knows no ending,
　The tearless life, is there.

2 There grief is turned to pleasure,
　Such pleasure as below
No human voice can utter,
　No human heart can know.

3 Thou hast no shore, fair ocean,
　Thou hast no time, bright day!
Dear fountain of refreshment
　To pilgrims far away!

4 The morning shall awaken,
　The shadows shall decay,
And each true-hearted servant
　Shall shine as doth the day.

5. Strive, man, to win that glory;
　Toil, man, to gain that light:
Send hope before to grasp it,
　Till hope be lost in sight.

From De Contemptu Mundi
Bernard of Cluny (12th cent.)
Tr. John Mason Neale (1818–66)

See also No. 248

242 TANWORTH Irregular.

CYRIL V. TAYLOR (1907–)

FOR the might of thine arm we bless thee, our God, our fathers' God;
Thou hast kept thy pilgrim people by the strength of thy staff and rod;
Thou hast called us to the journey which faithless feet ne'er trod;
For the might of thine arm we bless thee, our God, our fathers' God.

2 For the love of Christ constraining, that bound their hearts as one;
For the faith in truth and freedom in which their work was done;
For the peace of God's evangel wherewith their feet were shod;
For the might of thine arm we bless thee, our God, our fathers' God.

3 We are watchers of a beacon whose light must never die;
We are guardians of an altar that shows thee ever nigh;
We are children of thy freemen who sleep beneath the sod;
For the might of thine arm we bless thee, our God, our fathers' God.

THE COMMUNION OF SAINTS

4. May the shadow of thy presence around our camp be spread;
Baptize us with the courage thou gavest to our dead;
O keep us in the pathway their saintly feet have trod;
For the might of thine arm we bless thee, our God, our fathers' God.

Charles Silvester Horne (1865–1914)

243 RIPPONDEN 888.4. NORMAN COCKER (1889–1953)

FOR those we love within the veil,
  Who once were comrades of our way,
We thank thee, Lord; for they have won
    To cloudless day.

2 Free from the fret of mortal years,
  And knowing now thy perfect will,
With quickened sense and heightened joy
    They serve thee still.

3 O fuller, sweeter is that life,
  And larger, ampler is the air:
Eye cannot see nor heart conceive
    The glory there;

4 Nor know to what high purpose thou
  Dost yet employ their ripened powers,
Nor how at thy behest they touch
    This life of ours.

5. And life for them is life indeed,
  The splendid goal of earth's strait race;
And where no shadows intervene
    They see thy face.

William Charter Piggott (1872–1943)

244 SHEEN 14.14.14.15. GUSTAV HOLST (1874–1934)

ʼΑπὸ δόξης εἰς δόξαν πορευόμενοι

FROM glory to glory advancing, we praise thee, O Lord;
  Thy name, with the Father and Spirit, be ever adored.
From strength unto strength we go forward on Sion's highway,
To appear before God in the city of infinite day.

2. Thanksgiving and glory and worship and blessing and love,
One heart and one song have the saints upon earth and above.
Evermore, O Lord, to thy servants thy presence be nigh;
Ever fit us by service on earth for thy service on high.

Liturgy of S. James
Par. C. W. Humphreys

THE COMMUNION OF SAINTS

245 ANGELS' SONG L.M.
(SONG 34)

Melody and Bass by
ORLANDO GIBBONS (1583–1625)

HE wants not friends that hath thy love,
  And may converse and walk with thee,
And with thy saints here and above,
  With whom for ever I must be.

2 In the communion of the saints
  Is wisdom, safety, and delight;
And when my heart declines and faints,
  It's raisèd by their heat and light.

3 As for my friends, they are not lost;
  The several vessels of thy fleet,
Though parted now, by tempests tossed,
  Shall safely in the haven meet.

4 Still we are centred all in thee,
  Members, though distant, of one Head;
In the same family we be,
  By the same faith and spirit led.

5 Before thy throne we daily meet
  As joint-petitioners to thee;
In spirit we each other greet,
  And shall again each other see.

6. The heavenly hosts, world without end,
  Shall be my company above;
And thou, my best and surest Friend,
  Who shall divide me from thy love?

Richard Baxter (1615–91)

246 PEARSALL 76.76. D. ROBERT LUCAS PEARSALL (1795–1856)

O quanta qualia sunt illa Sabbata

HOW mighty are the Sabbaths,
  How mighty and how deep,
That the high courts of heaven
  To everlasting keep.
What peace unto the weary,
  What pride unto the strong,
When God in whom are all things
  Shall be all things to men.

2 Jerusalem is the city
  Of everlasting peace,
A peace that is surpassing
  And utter blessedness;
Where finds the dreamer waking
  Truth beyond dreaming far,
Nor there the heart's possessing
  Less than the heart's desire.

3*But of the courts of heaven
   And him who is the King,
The rest and the refreshing,
   The joy that is therein,
Let those that know it answer
   Who in that bliss have part,
If any word can utter
   The fullness of the heart.

4*But ours, with minds uplifted
   Unto the heights of God,
With our whole heart's desiring,
   To take the homeward road,
And the long exile over,
   Captive in Babylon,
Again unto Jerusalem,
   To win at last return.

5 There, all vexation ended,
   And from all grieving free,
We sing the song of Sion
   In deep security.
And everlasting praises
   For all thy gifts of grace
Rise from thy happy people,
   Lord of our blessedness.

6 There Sabbath unto Sabbath
   Succeeds eternally,
The joy that has no ending
   Of souls in holiday.
And never shall the rapture
   Beyond all mortal ken
Depart the eternal chorus
   That angels sing with men.

7. Now to the King eternal
   Be praise eternally,
From whom are all things, by whom
   And in whom all things be.
From whom, as from the Father,
   By whom, as by the Son,
In whom, as in the Spirit,
   The Lord God, Three in One. Amen.

Peter Abelard (1079–1142). *Tr. Helen Waddell* (1889–1965)

For another translation of these words see No. 252.

A - men.

247 S. AUSTIN C.M.

English Traditional Melody

JERUSALEM, my happy home,
   When shall I come to thee?
When shall my sorrows have an end?
   Thy joys when shall I see?

2 O happy harbour of the saints,
   O sweet and pleasant soil!
In thee no sorrow may be found,
   No grief, no care, no toil.

3 Thy gardens and thy gallant walks
   Continually are green;
There grow such sweet and pleasant flowers
   As nowhere else are seen.

4 Quite through the streets with silver sound
   The flood of life doth flow,
Upon whose banks on every side
   The wood of life doth grow.

5 There trees for evermore bear fruit,
   And evermore do spring;
There evermore the angels sit,
   And evermore do sing.

6 There David stands with harp in hand
   As master of the choir:
Ten thousand times that man were blest
   That might this music hear.

7. Jerusalem, Jerusalem,
   God grant I once may see
Thy endless joys, and of the same
   Partaker aye to be!

'F. B. P.' (*late 16th or early 17th cent.*)

248 EWING 76.76. D.

Melody by ALEXANDER EWING (1830–95)

Urbs Sion aurea

JERUSALEM the golden,
  With milk and honey blessed,
Beneath thy contemplation
  Sink heart and voice oppressed.
I know not, O I know not
  What joys await us there,
What radiancy of glory,
  What bliss beyond compare.

2 They stand, those halls of Sion,
  All jubilant with song,
And bright with many an angel,
  And all the martyr throng;
The Prince is ever in them,
  The daylight is serene:
The pastures of the blessèd
  Are decked in glorious sheen.

3. There is the throne of David
    And there, from care released,
  The shout of them that triumph,
    The song of them that feast;
  And they, who with their Leader
    Have conquered in the fight,
  For ever and for ever
    Are clad in robes of white.

From De Contemptu Mundi
Bernard of Cluny (12th cent.)
Tr. John Mason Neale (1818–66)

See also No. 241

249 FRENCH C.M.
(DUNDEE)

Scottish Psalter (1615)
as given in RAVENSCROFT'S *Psalter* (1621)

L ET saints on earth in concert sing
    With those whose work is done;
For all the servants of our King
    In heaven and earth are one.

2 One family, we dwell in him,
    One Church, above, beneath;
Though now divided by the stream,
    The narrow stream of death.

3 One army of the living God,
    To his command we bow;
Part of his host hath crossed the flood,
    And part is crossing now.

4 E'en now to their eternal home
    There pass some spirits blest;
While others to the margin come,
    Waiting their call to rest.

5. Jesu, be thou our constant guide;
    Then, when the word is given,
Bid Jordan's narrow stream divide,
    And bring us safe to heaven.

Charles Wesley (1707–88) *and others*

250

Mode ii

REGENT SQUARE 87.87.87.

HENRY SMART (1813–79)

Jerusalem luminosa

LIGHT's abode, celestial Salem,
　Vision whence true peace doth spring,
Brighter than the heart can fancy,
　Mansion of the highest King;
O how glorious are the praises
　Which of thee the prophets sing!

2 There for ever and for ever
    Alleluia is out-poured;
For unending, for unbroken
    Is the feast-day of the Lord;
All is pure and all is holy
    That within thy walls is stored.

3 There no cloud nor passing vapour
    Dims the brightness of the air;
Endless noon-day, glorious noon-day,
    From the Sun of suns is there;
There no night brings rest from labour,
    For unknown are toil and care.

4 O how glorious and resplendent,
    Fragile body, shalt thou be,
When endued with so much beauty,
    Full of health, and strong, and free,
Full of vigour, full of pleasure
    That shall last eternally!

5 Now with gladness, now with courage,
    Bear the burden on thee laid,
That hereafter these thy labours
    May with endless gifts be paid,
And in everlasting glory
    Thou with brightness be arrayed.

6. Laud and honour to the Father,
    Laud and honour to the Son,
Laud and honour to the Spirit,
    Ever Three and ever One,
One in might and One in glory,
    While unending ages run. Amen.

Thomas à Kempis (1379–1471)
Tr. John Mason Neale (1818–66)

251 CHRISTUS DER IST
MEIN LEBEN 76.76.

Melody by MELCHIOR VULPIUS
(c. 1560–1616)

Coelestis O Jerusalem

O DEAR and heavenly city
    Which ever shalt abide,
Thrice blessèd are the people
Who in thy courts reside.

2 In thee is peace for ever,
    There saints have perfect rest,
There dwells the King eternal,
    By men and angels blest.

3 There God for ever reigneth,
　　Himself of all the crown;
　The Lamb a sun that shineth
　　And never goeth down.

4 Naught to this seat approacheth
　　Their sweet peace to molest;
　They sing their God for ever,
　　Nor day nor night they rest.

5 Sure hope doth thither lead us,
　　Our longings thither tend;
　May short-lived toil ne'er daunt us
　　For joys that cannot end.

6. To Christ the sun that lightens
　　His Church above, below,
　To Father and to Spirit
　　All things created bow. Amen.

Paris Breviary (1822)
Tr. Isaac Williams (1802–65) *and Compilers*

See also No. 526 (CS)

A - men.

252 REGNATOR ORBIS 10.10.10.10.

Melody by
FRANÇOIS LA FEILLÉE (1808)

THE COMMUNION OF SAINTS

O quanta qualia sunt illa Sabbata

O WHAT their joy and their glory must be,
Those endless Sabbaths the blessèd ones see!
Crown for the valiant; to weary ones rest;
God shall be all, and in all ever blest.

2 What are the Monarch, his court, and his throne?
What are the peace and the joy that they own?
O that the blest ones, who in it have share,
All that they feel could as fully declare!

3*Truly Jerusalem name we that shore,
Vision of peace, that brings joy evermore;
Wish and fulfilment can severed be ne'er,
Nor the thing prayed for come short of the prayer.

4*There, where no troubles distraction can bring,
We the sweet anthems of Sion shall sing;
While for thy grace, Lord, their voices of praise
Thy blessèd people eternally raise.

5 There dawns no Sabbath, no Sabbath is o'er,
Those Sabbath-keepers have one evermore;
One and unending is that triumph-song
Which to the angels and us shall belong.

6 Now in the meanwhile, with hearts raised on high,
We for that country must yearn and must sigh;
Seeking Jerusalem, dear native land,
Through our long exile on Babylon's strand.

7. Low before him with our praises we fall,
Of whom, and in whom, and through whom are all;
Of whom, the Father; and in whom, the Son;
Through whom, the Spirit, with them ever One. Amen.

Peter Abelard (1079-1142)
Tr. John Mason Neale (1818-66)

For another translation of these words see No. 246.

A - men.

THE CHURCH OF GOD

253 EASTLEACH 76.86. D.   WALTER K. STANTON (1891–   )

TEN thousand times ten thousand,
In sparkling raiment bright,
The armies of the ransomed saints
Throng up the steeps of light:
'Tis finished! all is finished,
Their fight with death and sin;
Fling open wide the golden gates,
And let the victors in.

2 What rush of alleluias
 Fills all the earth and sky!
What ringing of a thousand harps
 Bespeaks the triumph nigh!
O day, for which creation
 And all its tribes were made!
O joy, for all its former woes
 A thousand-fold repaid!

3. Bring near thy great salvation,
 Thou Lamb for sinners slain,
Fill up the roll of thine elect,
 Then take thy power and reign:
Appear, Desire of nations,
 Thine exiles long for home;
Show in the heavens thy promised
 sign;
 Thou Prince and Saviour, come.

Henry Alford (1810–71)

254 MENDIP C.M.   **English Traditional Melody**

THERE is a land of pure delight
 Where saints immortal reign;
Infinite day excludes the night,
 And pleasures banish pain.

2 There everlasting spring abides,
 And never-withering flowers;
Death, like a narrow sea, divides
 This heavenly land from ours.

3 Sweet fields beyond the swelling flood
 Stand dressed in living green;
So to the Jews old Canaan stood
 While Jordan rolled between.

4. Could we but climb where Moses stood,
 And view the landscape o'er,
Not Jordan's stream, nor death's cold flood,
 Should fright us from the shore!

Isaac Watts (1674–1748)

255 LUTHER'S HYMN 87.87.887.

Present form of melody by MARTIN LUTHER
(1483–1546)

WE come unto our fathers' God;
  Their rock is our salvation;
The eternal arms, their dear abode,
  We make our habitation;
We bring thee, Lord, the praise they brought;
We seek thee as thy saints have sought
  In every generation.

2 Their joy unto their Lord we bring;
  Their song to us descendeth;
The Spirit who in them did sing
  To us his music lendeth;
His song in them, in us, is one;
We raise it high, we send it on,
  The song that never endeth.

3. Ye saints to come, take up the strain,
  Uplift the song for ever;
Unbroken be the golden chain,
  Unceasing the endeavour;
Safe in the same dear dwelling-place,
Rich with the same eternal grace,
  Bless the same boundless giver.

Thomas Hornblower Gill (1819–1906) and Compilers

See also

227	For all the saints		282	Sing Alleluia forth
228	For all thy saints		184	The Church's one foundation
229	Give me the wings		235	The Son of God goes forth
492	How bright these glorious spirits		449	Think, O Lord
231	Lord, who in thy perfect wisdom		539	Think, O Lord (CS)
523	Love, unto thine own (CS)		218	We hail thy presence glorious
181	Rejoice, O people		286	Ye holy angels bright

Many hymns under *Saints' Days* (Nos. 226–240) are also suitable.

256 ARTHOG 85.85.843.

GEORGE THALBEN-BALL

Unison

1. ANGEL-VOICES, ever singing,
    Round thy throne of light,
Angel-harps for ever ringing,
    Rest not day nor night;
Thousands only live to bless thee,
    And confess thee
        Lord of might.

2. Yea, we know that thou rejoicest
    O'er each work of thine;
Thou didst ears and hands and voices
    For thy praise design;
Craftsman's art and music's measure
    For thy pleasure
        All combine.

3. In thy house, great God, we offer
    Of thine own to thee,
And for thine acceptance proffer,
    All unworthily,
Hearts and minds and hands and
        voices,
    In our choicest
        Psalmody.

4. Honour, glory, might, and merit
    Thine shall ever be,
Father, Son, and Holy Spirit,
    Blessèd Trinity.
Of the best that thou hast given
    Earth and heaven
        Render thee.

Francis Pott (1832-1909)

257 LIEBSTER JESU 78.78.88.　　Melody by JOHANN RUDOLPH AHLE (1625–73)

Liebster Jesu, wir sind hier

BLESSED Jesus, at thy word
　We are gathered all to hear thee;
Let our minds and wills be stirred
　Now to seek and love and fear thee;
By thy teachings true and holy
Drawn from earth to love thee solely.

2 All our knowledge, sense, and sight
　Lie in deepest darkness shrouded,
Till thy Spirit breaks our night
　With the beams of truth unclouded;
Thou alone to God canst win us,
Thou must work all good within us.

3. Glorious Lord, thyself impart,
　Light of light, from God proceeding,
Open thou each mind and heart,
　Help us by thy Spirit's pleading,
Hear the cry thy Church now raises,
Lord, accept our prayers and praises.

Tobias Clausnitzer (1619–84)
Tr. Catherine Winkworth (1827–78) and Compilers

258 HAREWOOD 66.66.44.44. SAMUEL SEBASTIAN WESLEY (1810–76) (adapted)

Angularis fundamentum

CHRIST is our corner-stone,
　On him alone we build;
With his true saints alone
　The courts of heaven are filled;
　　On his great love
　　Our hopes we place
　　Of present grace
　And joys above.

2 O then with hymns of praise
　These hallowed courts shall ring;
Our voices we will raise
　The Three in One to sing;
　　And thus proclaim
　　In joyful song,
　　Both loud and long,
　That glorious name.

3 Here, gracious God, do thou
　For evermore draw nigh;
Accept each faithful vow,
　And mark each suppliant sigh;
　　In copious shower
　　On all who pray
　　Each holy day
　Thy blessings pour.

4. Here may we gain from heaven
　The grace which we implore;
And may that grace, once given,
　Be with us evermore;
　　Until that day
　　When all the blest
　　To endless rest
　Are called away.

7th or 8th cent. Tr. John Chandler (1806–76)
Based on Ephesians 2, 20–22

For another translation of these words see No. 445.

259 MANCHESTER C.M.   ROBERT WAINWRIGHT (1748–82)

DEAR Shepherd of thy people, hear;
    Thy presence now display;
As thou hast given a place for prayer,
    So give us hearts to pray.

2 Within these walls let holy peace,
    And love and concord dwell;
Here give the troubled conscience ease,
    The wounded spirit heal.

3. May we in faith receive thy word,
    In faith present our prayers,
And in the presence of our Lord
    Unburden all our cares.

John Newton (1725–1807) and Compilers

260 COELITES PLAUDANT 11.11.11.5.

Rouen Melody

FATHER, O hear us, seeking now to praise thee:
Thou art our hope, our confidence, our Saviour;
Thou art the refuge of the generations,
Lord God Almighty.

2 Maker of all things, loving all thy creatures,
God of all goodness, infinite in mercy,
Changeless, eternal, holiest and wisest,
Hear thou thy children.

3. Glory and honour, thanks and adoration
Still will we bring, O God of men and angels,
To thee, the holy, merciful, and mighty
Father, our Father. Amen.

Douglas Walmsley (1848–1940)

261 CRANSLEY 88.10.8.

GREVILLE COOKE (1894–   )

PREPARATION FOR WORSHIP

For a Country Church

HERE beauty dwells, and holiness,
Here reigns thy God to charm and bless.
Folded in loveliness of field and flower,
Take thou thy fill of peace and power.

2 Come in thy strength at morning prime,
Come thou to rest at eventime.
Here, in this quiet haven of happiness,
Ease thou thy soul of all distress.

3 Lift up thine eyes to heaven above,
Think on its wonder, grace, and love.
Doth not the beauty that around thee lies
Lend thee a glimpse of Paradise?

4. Calm be thy soul, and still thy heart.
Say thou a prayer ere thou depart.
Then from this earthly Eden of delight
Go forth in peace by day or night.

Greville Cooke (1894–   )

262 LINTON 65.65.

WALTER K. STANTON (1891–   )

JESUS, stand among us
In thy risen power;
Let this time of worship
Be a hallowed hour.

2. Bid the fears and sorrows
   From each soul depart;
   Breathe the Holy Spirit
   Into every heart.

William Pennefather (1816–73) and Compilers

263 SIMEON L.M.　　　　　　　　　SAMUEL STANLEY (1767–1822)

JESUS, where'er thy people meet,
　There they behold thy mercy-seat;
Where'er they seek thee thou art found,
And every place is hallowed ground.

2 For thou, within no walls confined,
　Inhabitest the humble mind;
　Such ever bring thee where they come,
　And going, take thee to their home.

3 Dear Shepherd of thy chosen few,
　Thy former mercies here renew;
　Here to our waiting hearts proclaim
　The beauty of thy saving name.

4 Here may we prove the power of prayer,
　To strengthen faith and sweeten care,
　To teach our faint desires to rise,
　And bring all heaven before our eyes.

5. Lord, we are few, but thou art near,
　Nor short thine arm, nor deaf thine ear;
　O rend the heavens, come quickly down,
　And make a thousand hearts thine own!

William Cowper (1731–1800)

264 MERTHYR TYDFIL 88.88.88.

JOSEPH PARRY (1841–1903)

VATER UNSER 88.88.88.

Later form of melody in
VALENTIN SCHUMANN's *Gesangbuch* (1539)
Harmony from JOHANN SEBASTIAN BACH (1685–1750)

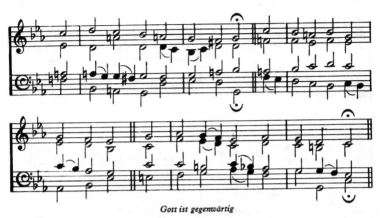

Gott ist gegenwärtig

LO, God is here! let us adore,
  And own how dreadful is this place:
Let all within us feel his power,
  And silent bow before his face:
Who know his power, his grace who prove,
Serve him with awe, with reverence love.

2 Lo, God is here! him, day and night,
    United choirs of angels sing;
  To him, enthroned above all height,
    Heaven's host their noblest praises bring:
  Disdain not, Lord, our meaner song,
  Who praise thee with a faltering tongue.

3. Being of beings, may our praise
    Thy courts with grateful fragrance fill;
  Still may we stand before thy face,
    Still hear and do thy sovereign will:
  To thee may all our thoughts arise,
  Ceaseless, accepted sacrifice.

Gerhard Tersteegen (1697–1769)
Tr. John Wesley (1703–91) and Compilers
Based on Genesis 28, 16–17

265 HENWOOD 87.3.4.8.   GEORGE THALBEN-BALL

MIGHT and glory, power and wisdom,
Make our Father wondrous great.
    We will now
    Before him bow,
And in his presence humbly wait.

2. Love and mercy, truth and patience,
    Make our Father wondrous kind.
        We will now
        Before him bow,
    And in the silence courage find.

Mildred Nevill (1889–   )

266 MIT FREUDEN ZART 87.87.887.

Later form of Hymn Melody of the
Bohemian Brethren

O DEAREST Lord, by all adored,
  Our trespasses confessing,
To thee this day thy children pray,
  The holy Faith professing.
Accept, O King, the gifts we bring,
Our songs of praise, the prayers we raise;
  And grant us, Lord, thy blessing.

Maurice Frederick Bell (1862–1947)

267 WAS LEBET, WAS
SCHWEBET 13.10.13.10.   *Rheinhardt MS.* (Üttingen, 1754)

O WORSHIP the Lord in the beauty of holiness,
  Bow down before him, his glory proclaim;
With gold of obedience, and incense of lowliness,
  Kneel and adore him, the Lord is his name.

2 Low at his feet lay thy burden of carefulness,
  High on his heart he will bear it for thee,
Comfort thy sorrows and answer thy prayerfulness,
  Guiding thy steps as may best for thee be.

3 Fear not to enter his courts in the slenderness
  Of the poor wealth thou would'st reckon as thine;
Truth in its beauty, and love in its tenderness,
  These are the offerings to lay on his shrine.

4 These, though we bring them in trembling and fearfulness,
  He will accept for the name that is dear;
Mornings of joy give for evenings of tearfulness,
  Trust for our trembling, and hope for our fear.

5. O worship the Lord in the beauty of holiness,
  Bow down before him, his glory proclaim;
With gold of obedience, and incense of lowliness,
  Kneel and adore him, the Lord is his name.

John Samuel Bewley Monsell (1811–75)

268 WATCHMAN S.M.   JAMES LEACH (1762–98)

STAND up, and bless the Lord,
    Ye people of his choice:
Stand up, and bless the Lord your God
    With heart and soul and voice.

2   Though high above all praise,
        Above all blessing high,
    Who would not fear his holy name,
        And praise and magnify?

3   O for the living flame
        From his own altar brought,
    To touch our lips, our minds inspire,
        And wing to heaven our thought!

4   God is our strength and song,
        And his salvation ours;
    Then be his love in Christ proclaimed
        With all our ransomed powers.

5.   Stand up, and bless the Lord,
        The Lord your God adore;
    Stand up, and bless his glorious name
        Henceforth for evermore.

James Montgomery (1771–1854)

See also

450	All people that on earth do dwell	458	How lovely are thy dwellings
188	Almighty God, thy word is cast	326	Lift up your hearts!
452	Before the almighty Father's throne	462	Lord of the worlds above
396	Behold, we come	331	My spirit longs for thee
122	Come, let us join our cheerful songs	465	O come, let us sing
487	Come, let us to the Lord	466	O God, give ear
5	From all that dwell	498	Where high the heavenly temple

O

269 LAUS DEO 87.87.
(REDHEAD 46)

RICHARD REDHEAD (1820–1901)

B RIGHT the vision that delighted
   Once the sight of Judah's seer;
Sweet the countless tongues united
   To entrance the prophet's ear.

2 Round the Lord in glory seated,
   Cherubim and Seraphim
Filled his temple, and repeated
   Each to each theˆalternate hymn:

Unison.

3 'Lord, thy glory fills the heaven;
　　Earth is with its fullness stored;
　Unto thee be glory given,
　　Holy, holy, holy, Lord.'

4 Heaven is still with glory ringing,
　　Earth takes up the angels' cry,
　'Holy, holy, holy,' singing,
　　'Lord of hosts, the Lord most high.'

5 With his seraph train before him,
　　With his holy Church below,
　Thus unite we to adore him,
　　Bid we thus our anthem flow:

Unison.

6. 'Lord, thy glory fills the heaven,
　　Earth is with its fullness stored;
　Unto thee be glory given,
　　Holy, holy, holy, Lord.'

Richard Mant (1776–1848)
Based on Isaiah 6, 1–3

270 HAMPTON LUCY 76.76. D. (Trochaic) WALTER K. STANTON (1891–)

COME, ye people, rise and sing
   Praise to God who made you,
And to heaven's eternal King
   Bring the prayers he bade you;
Bring your praise for mercies past,
   All his love confessing,
And on life, while life shall last,
   Ask your Father's blessing.

2 Praise we God the Father's name
   For our world's creation,
And his saving health proclaim
   Unto every nation;
Till, his name by all confessed,
   Every heart enthrone him,
And from furthest east and west
   All his children own him.

3 Praise we God the only Son,
   Who in mercy sought us;
Born to save a world undone,
   Out of death he brought us;
Here awhile he showed his love,
   Suffered uncomplaining,
Now he pleads for us above,
   Risen, ascended, reigning!

4 Grant us, Holy Ghost, we pray,
   More and more to know him,
More and more and every day
   In our lives to show him;
That with hearts by thee made brave,
   Strong and wise and tender,
We, with all the powers we have,
   Service meet may render.

5. Father, Son, and Holy Ghost,
   Help us to adore thee,
Till, with all the angel host,
   Low we fall before thee;
Till, throughout our earthly days
   Guided, loved, forgiven,
We can blend our songs of praise
   With the song of heaven!

Cyril Argentine Alington (1872–1955)

271 ARDEN C.M. GEORGE THALBEN-BALL

FILL thou my life, O Lord my God,
  In every part with praise,
That my whole being may proclaim
  Thy being and thy ways.

2 Not for the lip of praise alone,
    Nor ev'n the praising heart
  I ask, but for a life made up
    Of praise in every part.

3 Praise in the common things of life,
    Its goings out and in;
  Praise in each duty and each deed,
    However small and mean.

4 So shalt thou, gracious Lord, from me
    Receive the glory due;
  And so shall I begin on earth
    The song for ever new.

5. So shall no part of day or night
    From sacredness be free;
  But all my life, in every step,
    Be fellowship with thee.

Horatius Bonar (1808–89)

272 LUCERNA LAUDONIAE 77.77.77.   DAVID EVANS (1874-1948)

FOR the beauty of the earth,
  For the beauty of the skies,
For the love which from our birth
  Over and around us lies:
    Christ, our God, to thee we raise
    This our sacrifice of praise.

2 For the beauty of each hour
    Of the day and of the night,
  Hill and vale, and tree and flower,
    Sun and moon and stars of light:

3 For the joy of ear and eye,
    For the heart and mind's delight,
  For the mystic harmony
    Linking sense to sound and sight:

4 For the joy of human love,
    Brother, sister, parent, child,
  Friends on earth and friends above,
    For all gentle thoughts and mild:

5. For each perfect gift of thine
    To our race so freely given,
  Graces human and divine,
    Flowers of earth and buds of heaven:

Folliott Sandford Pierpoint (1835-1917)

273 CAROLYN 85.85.88.85.   HERBERT MURRILL (1909–52)

GOD OF LOVE 85.85.88.85.   HILARY PHILIP CHADWYCK-HEALEY (1888–   )

WORSHIP, THANKSGIVING, LOVE

GOD of love and truth and beauty,
　　Hallowed be thy name;
Fount of order, law, and duty,
　　Hallowed be thy name.
As in heaven thy hosts adore thee,
And their faces veil before thee,
So on earth, Lord, we implore thee,
　　Hallowed be thy name.

2 Lord, remove our guilty blindness,
　　Hallowed be thy name;
Show thy heart of lovingkindness,
　　Hallowed be thy name.
By our heart's deep-felt contrition,
By our mind's enlightened vision,
By our will's complete submission,
　　Hallowed be thy name.

3. In our worship, Lord most holy,
　　Hallowed be thy name;
In our work, however lowly,
　　Hallowed be thy name.
In each heart's imagination,
In the Church's adoration,
In the conscience of the nation,
　　Hallowed be thy name.

Timothy Rees, C.R. (1874–1939)

274 BINCHESTER C.M.   WILLIAM CROFT (1678–1727)

O quam juvat

HAPPY are they, they that love God,
  Whose hearts have Christ confessed,
Who by his Cross have found their life,
  And 'neath his yoke their rest.

2 Glad is the praise, sweet are the songs,
  When they together sing;
And strong the prayers that bow the ear
  Of heaven's eternal King.

3 Christ to their homes giveth his peace,
  And makes their loves his own:
But ah, what tares the evil one
  Hath in his garden sown.

4 Sad were our lot, evil this earth,
  Did not its sorrows prove
The path whereby the sheep may find
  The fold of Jesus' love.

5. Then shall they know, they that love him,
  How all their pain is good;
And death itself cannot unbind
  Their happy brotherhood.

Charles Coffin (1676–1749)
Par. Robert Bridges (1844–1930)

275 HERBERT 10.4.66.66.10.4.   HERBERT ARTHUR DYER (1878–1918)

LET all the world in every corner sing,
        My God and King!
The heavens are not too high,
His praise may thither fly;
The earth is not too low,
His praises there may grow.
Let all the world in every corner sing,
        My God and King!

2. Let all the world in every corner sing,
        My God and King!
The Church with psalms must shout,
No door can keep them out;
But, above all, the heart
Must bear the longest part.
Let all the world in every corner sing,
        My God and King!

George Herbert (1593–1632)

276 SONG 67 C.M.

Melody and Bass by ORLANDO GIBBONS (1583–1625)

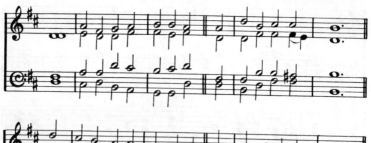

O Deus, ego amo te

MY God, I love thee; not because
   I hope for heaven thereby,
Nor yet because who love thee not
   Are lost eternally.

2 Thou, O my Jesus, thou didst me
   Upon the Cross embrace;
For me didst bear the nails and spear,
   And manifold disgrace,

3 And griefs and torments numberless,
   And sweat of agony;
Yea, death itself; and all for one
   Who was thine enemy.

4 Then why, O blessèd Jesus Christ,
   Should I not love thee well?
Not for the sake of winning heaven,
   Nor of escaping hell;

5 Not with the hope of gaining aught,
   Not seeking a reward;
But as thyself hast lovèd me,
   O ever-loving Lord?

6. So would I love thee, dearest Lord,
   And in thy praise will sing;
Solely because thou art my God,
   And my most loving King.

Coeleste Palmetum (1669) *from the Spanish*
Tr. Edward Caswall (1814–78)

277 NUN DANKET 67.67.66.66.

Present form of melody by
JOHANN CRÜGER (1598–1662)

Nun danket alle Gott

NOW thank we all our God,
  With heart and hands and
    voices,
Who wondrous things hath done,
In whom his world rejoices;
  Who from our mother's arms
    Hath blessed us on our way
With countless gifts of love,
  And still is ours to-day.

2 O may this bounteous God
  Through all our life be near us,
    With ever joyful hearts
And blessèd peace to cheer us;
  And keep us in his grace,
    And guide us when perplexed,
  And free us from all ills,
    In this world and the next.

3.   All praise and thanks to God
      The Father now be given,
        The Son, and him who reigns
      With them in highest heaven;
        The one eternal God,
          Whom earth and heaven adore;
        For thus it was, is now,
          And shall be evermore. Amen.

Martin Rinkart (1586–1649)
Tr. Catherine Winkworth (1827–78)
Based on Ecclesiasticus 50, 22–24

A - men.

278 ARDEN C.M.

GEORGE THALBEN-BALL

O FOR a thousand tongues to sing
    My dear Redeemer's praise,
The glories of my God and King,
    The triumphs of his grace!

2 Jesus, the name that charms our fears,
    That bids our sorrows cease;
'Tis music in the sinner's ears,
    'Tis life and health and peace.

3 He speaks: and, listening to his voice
    New life the dead receive,
The mournful broken hearts rejoice,
    The humble poor believe.

4 Hear him, ye deaf; his praise, ye dumb,
    Your loosened tongues employ;
Ye blind, behold your Saviour come;
    And leap, ye lame, for joy!

5. My gracious Master and my God,
    Assist me to proclaim
And spread through all the earth abroad
    The honours of thy name.

Charles Wesley (1707–88)

279 LAUDATE DOMINUM 10.10.11.11.

CHARLES HUBERT HASTINGS PARRY
(1848–1918)

O PRAISE ye the Lord! praise him in the height;
   Rejoice in his word, ye angels of light;
Ye heavens, adore him, by whom ye were made,
And worship before him, in brightness arrayed.

2 O praise ye the Lord! praise him upon earth,
   In tuneful accord, ye sons of new birth;
Praise him who hath brought you his grace from above,
Praise him who hath taught you to sing of his love.

3. O praise ye the Lord! thanksgiving and song
   To him be outpoured all ages along:
For love in creation, for heaven restored,
For grace of salvation, O praise ye the Lord!

Henry Williams Baker (1821–77)
Based on Psalms 148 & 150

280 OLD 124TH 10.10.10.10.10. Later form of melody from *Genevan Psalter* (1551)

Αἰνεῖτε, παῖδες, Κύριον

PRAISE ye the Lord, ye servants of the Lord:
   Praise ye his name; his lordly honour sing:
Thee we adore; to thee glad homage bring;
Thee we acknowledge; God to be adored
   For thy great glory, Sovereign, Lord, and King.

2. Father of Christ—of him whose work was done,
   When by his death he took our sins away—
To thee belongeth worship, day by day,
Yea, Holy Father, everlasting Son,
   And Holy Ghost, all praise be thine for aye!

Apostolic Constitutions (3rd cent.)
Tr. George Ratcliffe Woodward (1848–1934)
and Compilers

281 EIN' FESTE BURG 87.87.66.667.   Present form of melody by MARTIN LUTHER (1483–1546)

EIN' FESTE BURG

Present form of melody by MARTIN LUTHER (1483–1546)
Harmony chiefly from JOHANN SEBASTIAN BACH (1685–1750)

WORSHIP, THANKSGIVING, LOVE

R EJOICE to-day with one accord,
    Sing out with exultation:
Rejoice and praise our mighty Lord,
    Whose arm hath brought salvation;
       His works of love proclaim
       The greatness of his name;
       For he is God alone
       Who hath his mercy shown;
    Let all his saints adore him!

2. When in distress to him we cried,
    He heard our sad complaining;
O trust in him, whate'er betide,
    His love is all-sustaining;
       Triumphant songs of praise
       To him our hearts shall raise;
       Now every voice shall say,
       'O praise our God alway';
    Let all his saints adore him!

Henry Williams Baker (1821–77)

282 S. SEBASTIAN 10.10.7.

PERCY CARTER BUCK (1871–1947)

An end-less Al - le - lu - ia!

Alleluia piis edite laudibus

SING Alleluia forth in duteous praise,
Ye citizens of heaven; O sweetly raise
An endless Alleluia.

2 Ye powers, who stand before the eternal Light,
In hymning choirs re-echo to the height:

3 Ye who have gained at length your palms in bliss,
Victorious ones, your chant shall still be this:

4 There, in one grand acclaim, for ever ring
The strains which tell the honour of your King:

5 While thee, by whom were all things made, we praise
For ever, and tell out in sweetest lays:

6. Almighty Christ, to thee our voices sing
Glory for evermore; to thee we bring:

Mozarabic Breviary (5th–8th cent.)
Tr. John Ellerton (1826–93)

283 LEONI 66.84.D.

Adapted from a Hebrew melody

THE God of Abraham praise,
　Who reigns enthroned above,
Ancient of everlasting days,
　And God of love:
To him uplift your voice,
At whose supreme command
From earth we rise, and seek the joys
　At his right hand.

2* Though nature's strength decay,
　　And earth and hell withstand,
　To Canaan's bounds we urge our
　　　way
　　　At his command.
　　The watery deep we pass,
　　With Jesus in our view;
　And through the howling wilderness
　　　Our way pursue.

3 The goodly land we see,
　　With peace and plenty blest;
　A land of sacred liberty
　　　And endless rest;
　　There milk and honey flow,
　　And oil and wine abound,
　And trees of life for ever grow,
　　　With mercy crowned.

4 There dwells the Lord our King,
　The Lord our Righteousness,
Triumphant o'er the world and sin,
　The Prince of peace;
On Sion's sacred height
His kingdom he maintains,
And glorious with his saints in light
　For ever reigns.

5* Before the Three in One
　They all exulting stand,
And tell the wonders he hath done
　Through all their land:
The listening spheres attend,
And swell the growing fame,
And sing, in songs which never end,
　The wondrous name.

6* The God who reigns on high
　The great archangels sing,
And 'Holy, holy, holy,' cry,
　'Almighty King!
Who was, and is, the same,
And evermore shall be:
Eternal Father, great "I AM",
　We worship thee.'

7. The whole triumphant host
　　Give thanks to God on high;
　'Hail! Father, Son, and Holy Ghost,'
　　They ever cry:
　Hail! Abraham's God and mine!
　(I join the heavenly lays)
　All might and majesty are thine,
　　And endless praise.

Thomas Olivers (1725–99) and Compilers
Based on the Yigdal

284 ORIEL 87.87.87.

CASPAR ETT (1788–1847)

Gloriosi Salvatoris

To the name of our salvation
  Laud and honour let us pay,
Which for many a generation
  Hid in God's foreknowledge lay,
But with holy exultation
  We may sing aloud to-day.

2 Jesus is the name we treasure,
  Name beyond what words can tell;
Name of gladness, name of pleasure,
  Ear and heart delighting well;
Name of sweetness passing measure,
  Saving us from sin and hell.

3 'Tis the name that whoso preacheth
  Speaks like music to the ear;
Who in prayer this name beseecheth
  Sweetest comfort findeth near;
Who its perfect wisdom reacheth
  Heavenly joy possesseth here.

4 Jesus is the name exalted
  Over every other name;
In this name, whene'er assaulted,
  We can put our foes to shame;
Strength to them who else had halted,
  Eyes to blind, and feet to lame.

5. Therefore we, in love adoring,
  This most blessèd name revere,
Holy Jesus, thee imploring
  So to write it in us here,
That hereafter, heavenward soaring,
  We may sing with angels there.

c. 5th cent. Tr. John Mason Neale (1818–66)
and Compilers of Hymns A. & M.

285 PSALM 3. 667.667. D.
(O SEIGNEUR)

Composed or adapted by LOUIS BOURGEOIS
in *Genevan Psalter* (1551)

Beim frühen Morgenlicht

WHEN morning gilds the skies,
  My heart awaking cries,
    'May Jesus Christ be praised'.
When evening shadows fall,
This rings my curfew call,
    'May Jesus Christ be praised'.
When mirth for music longs,
This is my song of songs,
    'May Jesus Christ be praised'.
God's holy house of prayer
Hath none that can compare
    With 'Jesus Christ be praised'.

2 To him, my highest and best,
Sing I, when love-possest,
    'May Jesus Christ be praised'.
Whate'er my hands begin,
This blessing breaketh in,
    'May Jesus Christ be praised'.
No lovelier antiphon
In all high heaven is known
    Than 'Jesus Christ be praised'.
There to the͡eternal Word
The͡eternal psalm is heard,
    'O Jesus Christ be praised'.

3. Ye nations of mankind,
In this your concord find,
    'May Jesus Christ be praised'.
Let all the earth around
Ring joyous with the sound
    'May Jesus Christ be praised'
Sing, suns and stars of space,
Sing ye that see his face,
    Sing 'Jesus Christ be praised'.
God's whole creation o'er,
For aye and evermore,
    Shall Jesus Christ be praised.

19th cent. Tr. Edward Caswall (1814–78)
and Robert Bridges (1844–1930)

286 DARWALL'S 148TH 66.66.44.44.

JOHN DARWALL (1731–89)

YE holy angels bright,
    Who wait at God's right hand,
Or through the realms of light
    Fly at your Lord's command,
      Assist our song,
        Or else the theme
        Too high doth seem
      For mortal tongue.

2 Ye blessèd souls at rest,
    Who ran this earthly race,
And now, from sin released,
    Behold the Saviour's face,
      His praises sound,
        As in his light
        With sweet delight
      Ye do abound.

3 Ye saints, who toil below,
    Adore your heavenly King,
And onward as ye go
    Some joyful anthem sing:
      Take what he gives,
        And praise him still,
        Through good and ill,
      Who ever lives.

4. My soul, bear thou thy part,
    Triumph in God above,
And with a well-tuned heart
    Sing thou the songs of love.
      Let all thy days
        Till life shall end,
        Whate'er he send,
      Be filled with praise.

Richard Baxter (1615–91) *and others*

287 SHERSTON 10.10.11.11.　　　　WALTER K. STANTON (1891–)

Unison

LAUDATE DOMINUM 10.10.11.11.　　　　HENRY JOHN GAUNTLETT (1805–76)

YE servants of God, your Master proclaim,
And publish abroad his wonderful name:
The name all-victorious of Jesus extol;
His kingdom is glorious, and rules over all.

2 God ruleth on high, almighty to save;
And still he is nigh; his presence we have.
The great congregation his triumph shall sing,
Ascribing salvation to Jesus our King.

3 Salvation to God, who sits on the throne!
Let all cry aloud, and honour the Son:
The praises of Jesus the angels proclaim,
Fall down on their faces, and worship the Lamb.

4. Then let us adore, and give him his right:
All glory and power, all wisdom and might,
All honour and blessing, with angels above,
And thanks never-ceasing, and infinite love.

Charles Wesley (1707–88)

288 LASST UNS ERFREUEN 88.44.88. and Alleluias. Melody from *Geistliche Kirchengesang* (Cologne, 1623)

Al - le - lu - ia, Al - le - lu - ia, Al - le -

WORSHIP, THANKSGIVING, LOVE

-lu - ia, Al-le - lu - ia, Al-le - lu - ia!

Y E watchers and ye holy ones,
   Bright Seraphs, Cherubim, and Thrones,
   Raise the glad strain, Alleluia!
Cry out, Dominions, Princedoms, Powers,
Virtues, Archangels, Angels' choirs,
      Alleluia!

2 O higher than the Cherubim,
   More glorious than the Seraphim,
   Lead their praises, Alleluia!
   Thou Bearer of the eternal Word,
   Most gracious, magnify the Lord,
      Alleluia!

3 Respond, ye souls in endless rest,
   Ye Patriarchs and Prophets blest,
   Alleluia, Alleluia!
   Ye holy Twelve, ye Martyrs strong,
   All saints triumphant raise the song,
      Alleluia!

4. O friends, in gladness let us sing,
   Supernal anthems echoing,
   Alleluia, Alleluia!
   To God the Father, God the Son,
   And God the Spirit, Three in One,
      Alleluia!

John Athelstan Laurie Riley (1858–1945)

See also

2	All creatures of our God	169	Holy, holy, holy
117, 118	All hail the power	460	Jesus shall reign
119	All praise to thee, for thou	398	Most glorious Lord of life
120	At the name of Jesus	84	My song is love unknown
484	Behold the^amazing gift	469	O greatly blessed
123	Come ye faithful, raise the anthem	88	Praise to the Holiest
124	Crown him with many crowns	26	The Lord is King!
320	Enthrone thy God	314	Thee will I love
166	Father, in whom we live	94	To Christ, the Prince of peace
167	Father most holy	255	We come unto our fathers' God
455	God of mercy	95	We sing the praise
489	Hark how the^adoring hosts	541	What tongue can tell (CS)

Many hymns under *God: his Nature, Providence, and Works* (Nos. 1–22) are also suitable.

P

289 S. BERNARD C.M.　　Adapted from a melody in *Tochter Sion* (Cologne, 1741)

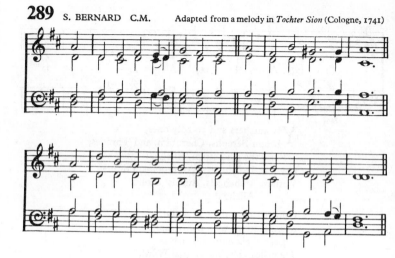

REPENTANCE AND FORGIVENESS

Quicunque certum quaeritis

ALL ye who seek for sure relief
　In trouble and distress,
Whatever sorrow vex the mind,
　Or guilt the soul oppress;

2 Jesus, who gave himself for you
　Upon the Cross to die,
Opens to you his sacred heart;
　O to that heart draw nigh.

3 Ye hear how kindly he invites;
　Ye hear his words so blest:
'All ye that labour come to me,
　And I will give you rest'.

4. O Jesus, joy of saints on high,
　Thou hope of sinners here,
Attracted by those loving words
　To thee we lift our prayer.

Aurelius Clemens Prudentius (348–c. 410)
Tr. Edward Caswall (1814–78)

290 DER TAG BRICHT AN L.M.

Melody probably by MELCHIOR VULPIUS
(c. 1560-1616)

FATHER of heaven, whose love profound
A ransom for our souls hath found,
Before thy throne we sinners bend:
To us thy pardoning love extend.

2 Almighty Son, incarnate Word,
Our Prophet, Priest, Redeemer, Lord,
Before thy throne we sinners bend:
To us thy saving grace extend.

3 Eternal Spirit, by whose breath
The soul is raised from sin and death,
Before thy throne we sinners bend:
To us thy quickening power extend.

4. Thrice Holy! Father, Spirit, Son,
Mysterious Godhead, Three in One,
Before thy throne we sinners bend:
Grace, pardon, life to us extend.

Edward Cooper (1770-1833)

291 LIBERA NOS 87.87.47.

CYRIL V. TAYLOR (1907–   )

JESUS, Lord of life and glory,
  Bend from heaven thy gracious ear;
While our waiting souls adore thee,
  Friend of helpless sinners, hear:
      By thy mercy,
      O deliver us, good Lord.

2 From the depth of nature's blindness,
    From the hardening power of sin,
  From all malice and unkindness,
    From the pride that lurks within,
        By thy mercy,
        O deliver us, good Lord.

3 When temptation sorely presses,
    In the day of Satan's power,
  In our times of deep distresses,
    In each dark and trying hour,
        By thy mercy,
        O deliver us, good Lord.

4 In the weary hours of sickness,
    In the times of grief and pain,
  When we feel our mortal weakness,
    When the creature's help is vain,
        By thy mercy,
        O deliver us, good Lord.

5. In the solemn hour of dying,
    In the awful judgment-day,
  May our souls, on thee relying,
    Find thee still our rock and stay:
        By thy mercy,
        O deliver us, good Lord.

John James Cummins (1795–1867)

292 SAFFRON WALDEN 888.6. ARTHUR HENRY BROWN (1830-1926)

WALFORD 888.6. GEORGE THALBEN-BALL

JUST as I am, without one plea
But that thy blood was shed for me,
And that thou bidd'st me come to thee,
    O Lamb of God, I come.

2 Just as I am, though tossed about,
With many a conflict, many a doubt,
Fightings and fears within, without,
    O Lamb of God, I come.

3 Just as I am, poor, wretched, blind;
Sight, riches, healing of the mind,
Yea, all I need, in thee to find,
    O Lamb of God, I come.

4 Just as I am, thou wilt receive,
Wilt welcome, pardon, cleanse, relieve;
Because thy promise I believe,
    O Lamb of God, I come.

5 Just as I am (thy love unknown
Has broken every barrier down),
Now to be thine, yea, thine alone,
    O Lamb of God, I come.

6. Just as I am, of that free love
The breadth, length, depth, and height to prove,
Here for a season, then above,
    O Lamb of God, I come.

Charlotte Elliott (1789–1871)

293 WINDSOR C.M.

DAMON's *Psalmes* (1591)

LORD, as to thy dear Cross we flee,
  And plead to be forgiven,
So let thy life our pattern be,
  And form our souls for heaven.

2 Help us, through good report and ill,
   Our daily cross to bear;
Like thee, to do our Father's will,
   Our brethren's griefs to share.

3 Let grace our selfishness expel,
   Our earthliness refine;
And in our hearts let kindness dwell,
   As free and true as thine.

4. Kept peaceful in the midst of strife,
   Forgiving and forgiven,
O may we lead the pilgrim's life,
   And follow thee to heaven.

John Hampden Gurney (1802–62) and Compilers

294 HUDDERSFIELD 77.75.

WALTER PARRATT (1841–1924)

L ORD of all, to whom alone
  All our hearts' desires are known,
When we stand before thy throne,
    Jesu, hear and save!

2 Son of Man, before whose eyes
  Every secret open lies,
  At thy great and last assize,
    Jesu, hear and save!

3 Saviour, who didst not condemn
  Those who touched thy garments' hem,
  Mercy show to us and them;
    Jesu, hear and save!

4. Lord, the way to sinners shown,
  Lord, the truth by sinners known,
  Love incarnate on the throne,
    Jesu, hear and save!

Cyril Argentine Alington (1872–1955)

295 ZENNOR 77.75.

GEORGE THALBEN-BALL

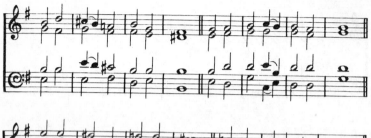

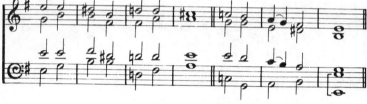

L ORD of mercy and of might,
Of mankind the life and light,
Maker, teacher infinite,
Jesu, hear and save!

2 Who, when sin's tremendous doom
Gave creation to the tomb,
Didst not scorn the Virgin's womb,
Jesu, hear and save!

3 Strong Creator, Saviour mild,
Humbled to a mortal child,
Captive, beaten, bound, reviled,
Jesu, hear and save!

4 Throned above celestial things,
Borne aloft on angels' wings,
Lord of lords, and King of kings,
Jesu, hear and save!

5. Who shalt yet come from on high,
Robed in might and majesty,
Hear us, help us when we cry:
Jesu, hear and save!

Reginald Heber (1783–1826)

296 REDHEAD 76 77.77.77.   RICHARD REDHEAD (1820–1901)

ROCK of ages, cleft for me,
Let me hide myself in thee;
Let the water and the blood,
From thy riven side which flowed,
Be of sin the double cure:
Cleanse me from its guilt and power.

2 Not the labours of my hands
Can fulfil thy law's demands;
Could my zeal no respite know,
Could my tears for ever flow,
All for sin could not atone:
Thou must save, and thou alone.

3 Nothing in my hand I bring;
Simply to thy Cross I cling;
Naked, come to thee for dress;
Helpless, look to thee for grace;
Foul, I to the fountain fly;
Wash me, Saviour, or I die.

4. While I draw this fleeting breath,
When mine eyes are closed in death,
When I soar through tracts unknown,
See thee on thy judgment-throne;
Rock of ages, cleft for me,
Let me hide myself in thee.

Augustus Montague Toplady (1740–78)

See also

79   Alone thou goest
502 Alone to sacrifice   (CS)
301 Beneath the cross of Jesus
487 Come, let us to the Lord
4   Come, O thou Traveller
7   God is love
106 Jesu, lover of my soul
520 Lighten the darkness   (CS)
342 Lo, now is our accepted day
12   My God, how wonderful thou art
331 My spirit longs for thee
345 Not for our sins alone

333 O for a closer walk
334 O for a heart
37   O heavenly Word
346 O kind Creator
530 O Lamb of God   (CS)
87   O Saviour, where shall guilty man
38   On Jordan's bank
15   Praise, my soul, the King of heaven
20   Souls of men
92   There is a green hill
97   When I survey

297 EIN' FESTE BURG 87.87.66.667.

Present form of melody by MARTIN LUTHER
(1483–1546)

EIN' FESTE BURG

Present form of melody by MARTIN LUTHER (1483–1546)
Harmony chiefly from JOHANN SEBASTIAN BACH (1685–1750)

FAITH AND TRUST

Ein' feste Burg ist unser Gott

A SAFE stronghold our God is
    still,
A trusty shield and weapon;
He'll help us clear from all the ill
    That hath us now o'ertaken.
        The ancient prince of hell
        Hath risen with purpose fell;
        Strong mail of craft and power
        He weareth in this hour;
        On earth is not his fellow.

2 With force of arms we nothing can,
    Full soon were we down-ridden;
But for us fights the proper Man,
    Whom God himself hath bidden.
        Ask ye, who is this same?
        Christ Jesus is his name,
        The Lord Sabaoth's Son;
        He, and no other one,
        Shall conquer in the battle.

3*And were this world all devils o'er,
    And watching to devour us,
We lay it not to heart so sore;
    Not they can overpower us.
        And let the prince of ill,
        Look grim as e'er he will,
        He harms us not a whit;
        For why his doom is writ;
        A word shall quickly slay him.

4.*God's word, for all their craft and
        force,
    One moment will not linger,
But, spite of hell, shall have its
        course;
    'Tis written by his finger.
        And though they take our life,
        Goods, honour, children, wife,
        Yet is their profit small;
        These things shall vanish all:
        The City of God remaineth!

Martin Luther (1483–1546)
Tr. Thomas Carlyle (1795–1881)
Based on Psalm 46

See also No. 454

298 EVENTIDE 10.10.10.10.

WILLIAM HENRY MONK (1823–89)

1. ABIDE with me; fast falls the eventide;
The darkness deepens; Lord, with me abide;
When other helpers fail, and comforts flee,
Help of the helpless, O abide with me.

2. Swift to its close ebbs out life's little day;
Earth's joys grow dim, its glories pass away;
Change and decay in all around I see;
O thou who changest not, abide with me.

3. I need thy presence every passing hour;
What but thy grace can foil the tempter's power?
Who like thyself my guide and stay can be?
Through cloud and sunshine, O abide with me.

4. I fear no foe, with thee at hand to bless;
Ills have no weight, and tears no bitterness;
Where is death's sting? where, grave, thy victory?
I triumph still, if thou abide with me.

5. Hold thou thy Cross before my closing eyes;
Shine through the gloom, and point me to the skies;
Heaven's morning breaks, and earth's vain shadows flee;
In life, in death, O Lord, abide with me.

Henry Francis Lyte (1793–1847)

See also No. 499 (CS)

FAITH AND TRUST

299 MEINE HOFFNUNG 87.87.337. Melody by JOACHIM NEANDER (1650–80)

Meine Hoffnung stehet feste

ALL my hope on God is founded;
  He doth still my trust renew,
Me through change and chance he
    guideth,
  Only good and only true.
    God unknown,
    He alone
  Calls my heart to be his own.

2 Pride of man and earthly glory,
    Sword and crown betray his trust;
  What with care and toil he buildeth,
    Tower and temple, fall to dust.
      But God's power,
      Hour by hour,
    Is my temple and my tower.

3 God's great goodness aye endureth,
    Deep his wisdom, passing thought:
  Splendour, light, and life attend
      him,
    Beauty springeth out of naught.
      Evermore
      From his store
    New-born worlds rise and adore.

4 Daily doth the almighty giver
    Bounteous gifts on us bestow;
  His desire our soul delighteth,
    Pleasure leads us where we go.
      Love doth stand
      At his hand;
    Joy doth wait on his command.

5. Still from man to God eternal
    Sacrifice of praise be done,
  High above all praises praising
    For the gift of Christ his Son.
      Christ doth call
      One and all:
    Ye who follow shall not fall.

Joachim Neander (1650–80)
Par. Robert Bridges (1844–1930)

300 S. PETERSBURG L.M.   Dmitri Stepanovitch Bortnianski (1751–1825)

AWAKE, our souls, away, our
  fears!
 Let every trembling thought be
  gone!
Awake, and run the heavenly race,
And put a cheerful courage on.

2 True, 'tis a strait and thorny road,
  And mortal spirits tire and faint;
But they forget the mighty God
  That feeds the strength of every
  saint.

3 O mighty God, thy matchless power
  Is ever new and ever young,
And firm endures, while endless
  years
 Their everlasting circles run.

4 From thee, the ever-flowing spring,
  Our souls shall drink a fresh
  supply;
While such as trust their native
  strength
 Shall melt away and droop and die.

5. Swift as the eagle cuts the air,
  We'll mount aloft to thine abode;
On wings of love our souls shall fly,
Nor tire along the heavenly road.

Isaac Watts (1674–1748)
Based on Isaiah 40, 28–31

301 HELDER 76.86.86.86.   Melody by BARTHOLOMAEUS HELDER (1585–1635)

BENEATH the cross of Jesus
  I fain would take my stand,
The shadow of a mighty rock
  Within a weary land;
A home within a wilderness,
  A rest upon the way,
From burning rays of noontide heat
  And burdens of the day.

2 Upon that cross of Jesus
  Mine eyes with awe can see
The very dying form of him
  Who suffered there for me.
And from a humbled heart, with shame,
  Two wonders I confess,
The depths of his redeeming love,
  And my own lovelessness.

3. Beneath thy cross, O Saviour,
  Redeemed by thee I stand,
The shadow of a mighty rock
  Within a weary land;
Content unto the world to die,
  To count all gain but loss,
My only shame a sinful heart,
  My glory all thy Cross.

Elizabeth Cecilia Clephane (1830–69) *and Compilers*

302 CANNOCK L.M.

WALTER K. STANTON (1891-   )

First Tune

FAITH AND TRUST

302 RUSHFORD L.M.

HENRY GEORGE LEY (1887–1962)

Second Tune

FIGHT the good fight with all thy might;
Christ is thy strength, and Christ thy right;
Lay hold on life, and it shall be
Thy joy and crown eternally.

2 Run the straight race through God's good grace,
Lift up thine eyes and seek his face;
Life with its way before thee lies,
Christ is the path, and Christ the prize.

3 Cast care aside, lean on thy Guide;
His boundless mercy will provide;
Trust, and thy trusting soul shall prove
Christ is its life and Christ its love.

4. Faint not nor fear, his arms are near;
He changeth not, and thou art dear;
Only believe, and thou shalt see
That Christ is all in all to thee.

John Samuel Bewley Monsell (1811–75)

303 ALL RED THE RIVER 77.77.77.   Chinese Verse Tune

GOD the Father's only Son,
And with him in glory one,
One in wisdom, one in might,
Absolute and infinite;
Jesu, I believe in thee,
Thou art Lord and God to me.

2 Preacher of eternal peace,
Christ, anointed to release,
Calling man from error's night
Into truth's eternal light;
Jesu, I believe in thee,
Christ the Prophet sent to me.

3 Low in deep Gethsemane,
High on dreadful Calvary,
In the garden, on the cross,
Making good our utter loss;
Jesu, I believe in thee,
Priest and Sacrifice for me.

4. Ruler of thy ransomed race,
And protector by thy grace,
Leader through our earthly strife,
And the goal of all our life;
Jesu, I believe in thee,
Christ, the King of kings to me.

Samuel John Stone (1839–1900)
and Compilers

304 WIGTOWN C.M.
Scottish Psalter (1635)

HE that is down needs fear no fall,
   He that is low, no pride;
He that is humble ever shall
   Have God to be his guide.

2 I am content with what I have,
   Little be it or much;
And, Lord, contentment still I crave,
   Because thou savest such.

3. Fullness to such a burden is
   That go on pilgrimage;
Here little, and hereafter bliss,
   Is best from age to age.

John Bunyan (1628–88)

305 KILMARNOCK C.M.

Melody by NEIL DOUGALL (1776–1862)

HOW are thy servants blest, O Lord!
　How sure is their defence!
Eternal wisdom is their guide,
　Their help omnipotence.

2 From all their griefs and dangers, Lord,
　Thy mercy sets them free,
While in the confidence of prayer
　Their souls take hold on thee.

3 In midst of dangers, fears, and death,
　Thy goodness we'll adore;
And praise thee for thy mercies past,
　And humbly hope for more.

4. Our life, while thou preserv'st that life,
　Thy sacrifice shall be;
And death, when death shall be our lot,
　Shall join our souls to thee.

Joseph Addison (1672–1719)

FAITH AND TRUST

306 ALBERTA 10.4.10.4.10.10.   WILLIAM HENRY HARRIS (1883–)

First Tune

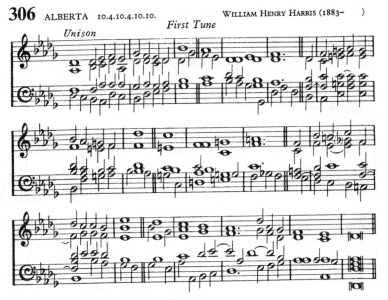

LEAD, kindly light, amid the encircling gloom,
    Lead thou me on;
The night is dark, and I am far from home,
    Lead thou me on.
Keep thou my feet; I do not ask to see
The distant scene; one step enough for me.

2 I was not ever thus, nor prayed that thou
    Should'st lead me on;
I loved to choose and see my path; but now
    Lead thou me on.
I loved the garish day, and, spite of fears,
Pride ruled my will: remember not past years.

3. So long thy power hath blessed me, sure it still
    Will lead me on,
O'er moor and fen, o'er crag and torrent, till
    The night is gone;
And with the morn those angel faces smile,
Which I have loved long since, and lost awhile.

John Henry Newman (1801–90)

Harmony version overleaf.

306 *(continued)* ALBERTA 10.4.10.4.10.10.   WILLIAM HENRY HARRIS (1883–)

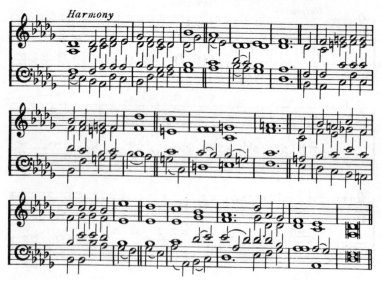

LEAD, kindly light, amid the encircling gloom,
    Lead thou me on;
The night is dark, and I am far from home,
    Lead thou me on.
Keep thou my feet; I do not ask to see
The distant scene; one step enough for me.

2 I was not ever thus, nor prayed that thou
    Should'st lead me on;
I loved to choose and see my path; but now
    Lead thou me on.
I loved the garish day, and, spite of fears,
Pride ruled my will: remember not past years.

3. So long thy power hath blessed me, sure it still
    Will lead me on,
O'er moor and fen, o'er crag and torrent, till
    The night is gone;
And with the morn those angel faces smile,
Which I have loved long since, and lost awhile.

John Henry Newman (1801–90)

FAITH AND TRUST

306 SANDON 10.4.10.4.10.10.
Second Tune

CHARLES HENRY PURDAY (1799–1885)

LEAD, kindly light, amid the encircling gloom,
　　　Lead thou me on;
The night is dark, and I am far from home,
　　　Lead thou me on.
Keep thou my feet; I do not ask to see
The distant scene; one step enough for me.

2　I was not ever thus, nor prayed that thou
　　　Should'st lead me on;
I loved to choose and see my path; but now
　　　Lead thou me on.
I loved the garish day, and, spite of fears,
Pride ruled my will: remember not past years.

3.　So long thy power hath blessed me, sure it still
　　　Will lead me on,
O'er moor and fen, o'er crag and torrent, till
　　　The night is gone;
And with the morn those angel faces smile,
Which I have loved long since, and lost awhile.

John Henry Newman (1801–90)

307 MANNHEIM 87.87.87.

Adapted from a Chorale by
FRIEDRICH FILITZ (1804–76)

LEAD us, heavenly Father, lead us
    O'er the world's tempestuous sea;
Guard us, guide us, keep us, feed us,
    For we have no help but thee;
Yet possessing every blessing
    If our God our Father be.

2 Saviour, breathe forgiveness o'er us;
    All our weakness thou dost know,
Thou didst tread this earth before us,
    Thou didst feel its keenest woe;
Lone and dreary, faint and weary,
    Through the desert thou didst go.

3. Spirit of our God, descending,
    Fill our hearts with heavenly joy,
Love with every passion blending,
    Pleasure that can never cloy:
Thus provided, pardoned, guided,
    Nothing can our peace destroy.

James Edmeston (1791–1867)

FAITH AND TRUST

308 SHELDONIAN 10.10.10.10.   CYRIL V. TAYLOR (1907–)

LEAD us, O Father, in the paths of peace:
　　Without thy guiding hand we go astray,
And doubts appal, and sorrows still increase;
　　Lead us through Christ, the true and living Way.

2 Lead us, O Father, in the paths of truth:
　　Unhelped by thee, in error's maze we grope,
While passion stains and folly dims our youth,
　　And age comes on uncheered by faith or hope.

3 Lead us, O Father, in the paths of right:
　　Blindly we stumble when we walk alone,
Involved in shadows of a darkening night;
　　With thee alone we journey safely on.

4. Lead us, O Father, to thy heavenly rest,
　　However rough and steep the pathway be,
Through joy or sorrow, as thou deemest best,
　　Until our lives are perfected in thee.

William Henry Burleigh (1812–71) and Compilers

309 MINIVER 10.11.11.12.   CYRIL V. TAYLOR (1907–   )

SNOWSHILL 10.11.11.12.   WALTER K. STANTON (1891–   )

FAITH AND TRUST

LORD of all hopefulness, Lord of all joy,
  Whose trust, ever childlike, no cares could destroy,
Be there at our waking, and give us, we pray,
Your bliss in our hearts, Lord, at the break of the day.

2 Lord of all eagerness, Lord of all faith,
  Whose strong hands were skilled at the plane and the lathe,
  Be there at our labours, and give us, we pray,
  Your strength in our hearts, Lord, at the noon of the day.

3 Lord of all kindliness, Lord of all grace,
  Your hands swift to welcome, your arms to embrace,
  Be there at our homing, and give us, we pray,
  Your love in our hearts, Lord, at the eve of the day.

4. Lord of all gentleness, Lord of all calm,
  Whose voice is contentment, whose presence is balm,
  Be there at our sleeping, and give us, we pray,
  Your peace in our hearts, Lord, at the end of the day.

Jan Struther (1901–53)

310 S. LEONARD   C.M.

HENRY SMART (1813–79)

O FOR a faith that will not shrink,
  Though pressed by many a foe;
That will not tremble on the brink
  Of poverty or woe;

2 That will not murmur or complain
  Beneath the chastening rod;
But in the hour of grief or pain
  Can lean upon its God;

3 A faith that shines more bright and clear
  When tempests rage without;
That when in danger knows no fear,
  In darkness feels no doubt;

4 A faith that keeps the narrow way
  Till life's last spark is fled,
And with a pure and heavenly ray
  Lights up the dying bed.

5. Lord, give me such a faith as this,
  And then, whate'er may come,
I taste e'en now the hallowed bliss
  Of an eternal home.

William Hiley Bathurst (1796–1877)

FAITH AND TRUST

311 ERFURT 886.D.   Melody by Georg Peter Weimar (1734–1800)

O LORD, how happy should we be
  If we could cast our care on thee,
    If we from self could rest,
And feel at heart that One above,
In perfect wisdom, perfect love,
    Is working for the best;

2 Could we but kneel, and cast our load,
  E'en while we pray, upon our God,
    Then rise with lightened cheer;
Sure that the Father, who is nigh,
To still the famished raven's cry,
    Will hear, and calm our fear.

3 We cannot trust him as we should;
  So chafes weak nature's restless mood
    To cast its peace away;
But birds and flowers around us preach,
And all the present evil teach
    Sufficient for the day.

4. Lord, make these faithless hearts of ours
  Such lessons learn from birds and flowers:
    Make them from self to cease,
Leave all things to a Father's will,
And taste, on him relying still,
    E'en in affliction, peace.

Joseph Anstice (1808–36) and Compilers
Based on S. Matthew 6, 25–32

312 CROWLE C.M.

Melody from *A Book of Psalmody* by JAMES GREEN
(c. 1690–1750)

O THOU in all thy might so far,
　In all thy love so near,
Beyond the range of sun and star,
　And yet beside us here:

2 What heart can comprehend thy name,
　　Or searching find thee out?
　Who art within, a quickening flame,
　　A presence round about.

3 More dear than all the things I know
　　Is childlike faith to me,
　That makes the darkest way I go
　　An open path to thee.

4. Yet though I know thee but in part,
　　I ask not, Lord, for more;
　Enough for me to know thou art,
　　To love thee, and adore.

Frederick Lucian Hosmer (1840–1929) *and Compilers*

313 S. MICHAEL   S.M.
(OLD 134TH)

Composed or adapted by
LOUIS BOURGEOIS in *Genevan Psalter* (1551)

Befiehl du deine Wege

PUT thou thy trust in God
  In duty's path go on;
Walk in his strength with faith and hope,
  So shall thy work be done.

2   Give to the winds thy fears;
      Hope, and be undismayed;
God hears thy sighs and counts thy tears,
      God shall lift up thy head.

3   Who points the clouds their course,
      Whom winds and seas obey,
He shall direct thy wandering feet,
      He shall prepare thy way.

4   Leave to his sovereign sway
      To choose and to command;
So shalt thou wondering own his way,
      How wise, how strong his hand.

5   Let us, in life and death,
      His steadfast truth declare,
And publish, with our latest breath,
      His love and guardian care.

Paulus Gerhardt (1607–76)
Tr. John Wesley (1703–91) *and others*

Q

314 HAMBLEDEN 89.89.D.   WALTER K. STANTON (1891–   )

PSALM 138

Melody from *Genevan Psalter* (? 1544). Harmony adapted from CLAUDE GOUDIMEL (d. 1572)

FAITH AND TRUST

THEE will I love, my God and King,
   Thee will I sing, my strength and tower:
For evermore thee will I trust,
   O God most just of truth and power;
Who all things hast in order placed,
   Yea, for thy pleasure hast created;
And on thy throne, unseen, unknown,
   Reignest alone in glory seated.

2 Set in my heart thy love I find;
   My wandering mind to thee thou leadest:
My trembling hope, my strong desire
   With heavenly fire thou kindly feedest.
Lo, all things fair thy path prepare,
   Thy beauty to my spirit calleth,
Thine to remain in joy or pain,
   And count it gain whate'er befalleth.

3. O more and more thy love extend,
   My life befriend with heavenly pleasure;
That I may win thy paradise,
   Thy pearl of price, thy countless treasure;
Since but in thee I can go free
   From earthly care and vain oppression,
This prayer I make for Jesus' sake,
   That thou me take in thy possession.

Robert Bridges (1844–1930)

315 EIA, EIA 76.76.46.
(ZU BETHLEHEM GEBOREN)

Melody from NORDSTERN's
Führer zur Seligkeit (1671)

Zu Bethlehem geboren

TO us in Bethlem city
　　Was born a little son;
In him all gentle graces
　　Were gathered into one,
　　　Eia, Eia,
　　Were gathered into one.

2 And all our love and fortune
　　Lie in his mighty hands;
Our sorrows, joys, and failures,
　　He sees and understands,
　　　Eia, Eia,
　　He sees and understands.

3 O Shepherd, ever near us,
　　We'll go where thou dost lead;
No matter where the pasture,
　　With thee at hand to feed,
　　　Eia, Eia,
　　With thee at hand to feed.

4. No grief shall part us from thee,
　　However sharp the edge:
We'll serve, and do thy bidding—
　　O take our hearts in pledge!
　　　Eia, Eia,
　　Take thou our hearts in pledge.

Cölner Psalter (1638)
Par. Percy Dearmer (1867–1936)

316 SLANE 10.11.11.11.

Irish Melody

Rob tu mo bhoile, a Comdi cride

BE thou my Vision, O Lord of my heart,
Be all else but naught to me, save that thou art;
Be thou my best thought in the day and the night,
Both waking and sleeping, thy presence my light.

2 Be thou my Wisdom, be thou my true Word;
Be thou ever with me, and I with thee, Lord;
Be thou my great Father, and I thy true son;
Be thou in me dwelling, and I with thee one.

3 Be thou my breastplate, my sword for the fight;
Be thou my whole armour, be thou my true might;
Be thou my soul's shelter, be thou my strong tower,
O raise thou me heavenward, great Power of my power.

4 Riches I heed not, nor man's empty praise,
Be thou mine inheritance now and always;
Be thou and thou only the first in my heart;
O Sovereign of heaven, my treasure thou art.

5. High King of heaven, thou heaven's bright Sun,
O grant me its joys, after victory is won;
Great Heart of my own heart, whatever befall,
Still be thou my Vision, O Ruler of all.

Ancient Irish. Tr. Mary Elizabeth Byrne (1881–1931)
Versified by Eleanor Henrietta Hull (1860–1935) and Compilers

317 S. THOMAS S.M. AARON WILLIAMS (1731-76)

BELIEVE not those who say
The upward path is smooth,
Lest thou shouldst stumble in the way
And faint before the truth.

2   It is the only road
Unto the realms of joy;
But he who seeks that blest abode
Must all his powers employ.

3   Arm, arm thee for the fight!
Cast useless loads away;
Watch through the darkest hours of night;
Toil through the hottest day.

4   To labour and to love,
To pardon and endure,
To lift thy heart to God above
And keep thy conscience pure;

5   Be this thy constant aim,
Thy hope, thy chief delight;
What matter who should whisper blame,
Or who should scorn or slight;

6.   If but thy God approve,
And if, within thy breast,
Thou feel the comfort of his love,
The earnest of his rest.

Anne Brontë (1820-49)

ASPIRATION

318 FRANCONIA S.M.

WILLIAM HENRY HAVERGAL (1793–1870). Founded
on a melody in KÖNIG's *Choralbuch* (1738)

Blest are the pure in heart,
For they shall see our God;
The secret of the Lord is theirs,
Their soul is Christ's abode.

2   The Lord, who left the heavens,
Our life and peace to bring,
To dwell in lowliness with men,
Their pattern and their King;

3   Still to the lowly soul
He doth himself impart,
And for his dwelling and his throne
Chooseth the pure in heart.

4.   Lord, we thy presence seek;
May ours this blessing be:
Give us a pure and lowly heart,
A temple meet for thee.

John Keble (1792–1866) and others

319 HERONGATE L.M.　　　　　　　　　　　English Traditional Melody

DEAR Master, in whose life I see
　　All that I long, but fail, to be,
Let thy clear light for ever shine,
To shame and guide this life of mine.

2. Though what I dream and what I do
　　In my poor days are always two,
　　Help me, oppressed by things undone,
　　O thou, whose deeds and dreams were one.

John Hunter (1848-1917)

320 S. BOTOLPH C.M.   Gordon Slater (1896–   )

ENTHRONE thy God within thy heart,
  Thy being's inmost shrine;
He doth to thee the power impart
  To live the life divine.

2 Seek truth in him with Christlike mind;
  With faith his will discern;
Walk on life's way with him, and find
  Thy heart within thee burn.

3 With love that overflows thy soul
  Love him who first loved thee;
Is not his love thy life, thy goal,
  Thy soul's eternity?

4. Serve him in his sufficing strength:
  Heart, mind, and soul employ;
And he shall crown thy days at length
  With everlasting joy.

William Joseph Penn (1875–1956)

321 SONG 1 10.10.10.10.10.10.

Melody and Bass by
ORLANDO GIBBONS (1583–1625)

ASPIRATION

ETERNAL Ruler of the ceaseless round
    Of circling planets singing on their way;
Guide of the nations from the night profound
    Into the glory of the perfect day;
Rule in our hearts, that we may ever be
Guided and strengthened and upheld by thee.

2 We are of thee, the children of thy love,
    The brothers of thy well-belovèd Son;
Descend, O Holy Spirit, like a dove
    Into our hearts, that we may be as one:
As one with thee, to whom we ever tend;
As one with him, our brother and our friend.

3 We would be one in hatred of all wrong,
    One in our love of all things sweet and fair,
One with the joy that breaketh into song,
    One with the grief that trembleth into prayer,
One in the power that makes the children free
To follow truth, and thus to follow thee.

4. O clothe us with thy heavenly armour, Lord,
    Thy trusty shield, thy sword of love divine;
Our inspiration be thy constant word;
    We ask no victories that are not thine:
Give or withhold, let pain or pleasure be;
Enough to know that we are serving thee.

John White Chadwick (1840–1904)

322 MENDIP C.M.

English Traditional Melody

Jesu, dulcis memoria

JESU, the very thought of thee
   With sweetness fills the breast;
But sweeter far thy face to see,
   And in thy presence rest.

2 No voice can sing, no heart can frame,
   Nor can the memory find
A sweeter sound than Jesus' name,
   The Saviour of mankind.

3 O hope of every contrite heart,
   O joy of all the meek;
To those who ask how kind thou art,
   How good to those who seek!

4 But what to those who find? Ah, this
   Nor tongue nor pen can show;
The love of Jesus, what it is
   None but his loved ones know.

5. Jesu, our only joy be thou,
   As thou our prize wilt be;
In thee be all our glory now,
   And through eternity.

11th cent. Tr. Edward Caswall (1814–78)

323

Mode i

HEREFORD L.M.

SAMUEL SEBASTIAN WESLEY (1810–76)

ASPIRATION

Jesu, dulcedo cordium

JESU, thou joy of loving hearts,
  Thou fount of life, thou light of men,
From the best bliss that earth imparts
  We turn unfilled to thee again.

2 Thy truth unchanged hath ever stood;
  Thou savest those that on thee call:
To them that seek thee, thou art good,
  To them that find thee, all in all.

3 We taste thee, O thou living bread,
  And long to feast upon thee still:
We drink of thee, the fountain-head,
  And thirst our souls from thee to fill.

4 Our restless spirits yearn for thee,
  Where'er our changeful lot is cast,
Glad when thy gracious smile we see,
  Blest when our faith can hold thee fast.

5. O Jesu, ever with us stay;
  Make all our moments calm and bright:
Chase the dark night of sin away;
  Shed o'er the world thy holy light.

11th cent. Tr. Ray Palmer (1808–87)

324 S. FULBERT C.M. HENRY JOHN GAUNTLETT (1805–76)

Amor Jesus dulcissimus

JESU, thy mercies are untold
  Through each returning day;
Thy love exceeds a thousandfold
  Whatever we can say;

2 That love which in thy Passion drained
    For us thy precious blood:
  That love whereby the saints have gained
    The vision of their God.

3 'Tis thou hast loved us from the womb,
    Pure source of all our bliss,
  Our only hope of life to come,
    Our happiness in this.

4. Lord, grant us, while on earth we stay,
    Thy love to feel and know;
  And, when from hence we pass away,
    To us thy glory show.

11th cent. Tr. Edward Caswall (1814–78)

325 GWALCHMAI 74.74.D. JOSEPH DAVID JONES (1827–70)

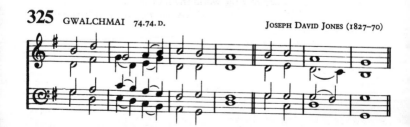

ASPIRATION

KING of glory, King of peace,
   I will love thee;
And, that love may never cease,
   I will move thee.
Thou hast granted my request,
   Thou hast heard me;
Thou didst note my working breast,
   Thou hast spared me.

2 Wherefore with my utmost art
   I will sing thee,
And the cream of all my heart
   I will bring thee.
Though my sins against me cried,
   Thou didst clear me,
And alone, when they replied,
   Thou didst hear me.

3. Seven whole days, not one in seven,
   I will praise thee;
In my heart, though not in heaven,
   I can raise thee.
Small it is, in this poor sort
   To enrol thee;
E'en eternity's too short
   To extol thee.

George Herbert (1593–1632)

326 WOODLANDS 10.10.10.10. WALTER GREATOREX (1877–1949)

ASPIRATION

'LIFT up your hearts!' We lift them, Lord, to thee;
  Here at thy feet none other may we see:
'Lift up your hearts!' E'en so, with one accord,
We lift them up, we lift them to the Lord.

2 Above the level of the former years,
  The mire of sin, the slough of guilty fears,
  The mist of doubt, the blight of love's decay,
  O Lord of light, lift all our hearts to-day!

3 Lift every gift that thou thyself hast given;
  Low lies the best till lifted up to heaven:
  Low lie the bounding heart, the teeming brain,
  Till, sent from God, they mount to God again.

4. Then, as the trumpet-call, in after years,
  'Lift up your hearts!' rings pealing in our ears,
  Still shall those hearts respond with full accord,
  'We lift them up, we lift them to the Lord!'

Henry Montagu Butler (1833–1918)

327 TANTUM ERGO 87.87.87. SAMUEL WEBBE the elder (1740–1816)

L ORD of beauty, thine the splen-
   dour
   Shown in earth and sky and sea,
Burning sun and moonlight tender,
   Hill and river, flower and tree;
Lest we fail our praise to render,
   Touch our eyes that we may see!

2 Lord of wisdom, whom obeying
   Mighty waters ebb and flow,
While unhasting, undelaying,
   Planets on their courses go;
In thy laws thyself displaying,
   Teach our minds thy truth to
   know!

3 Lord of life, alone sustaining
   All below and all above,
Lord of love, by whose ordaining
   Sun and stars sublimely move;
In our earthly spirits reigning,
   Lift our hearts, that we may
   love!

4. Lord of beauty, bid us own thee,
   Lord of truth, our footsteps guide,
Till as love our hearts enthrone thee,
   And, with vision purified,
Lord of all, when all have known
   thee,
   Thou in all art glorified!

Cyril Argentine Alington (1872–1955)

328 HYFRYDOL 87.87.D. Melody by ROWLAND HUGH PRICHARD (1811–87)

LOVE divine, all loves excelling,
  Joy of heaven, to earth come
    down,
Fix in us thy humble dwelling,
  All thy faithful mercies crown.
Jesu, thou art all compassion,
  Pure unbounded love thou art;
Visit us with thy salvation,
  Enter every trembling heart.

2 Come, almighty to deliver,
  Let us all thy life receive;
Suddenly return, and never,
  Never more thy temples leave.
Thee we would be always blessing,
  Serve thee as thy hosts above;
Pray, and praise thee without
    ceasing,
  Glory in thy perfect love.

3. Finish then thy new creation,
    Pure and sinless let us be;
  Let us see thy great salvation,
    Perfectly restored in thee,
  Changed from glory into glory,
    Till in heaven we take our place,
  Till we cast our crowns before thee,
    Lost in wonder, love, and praise.

Charles Wesley (1707–88)

See also No. 329

329 LOVE DIVINE 87.87. JOHN STAINER (1840-1901)

LOVE divine, all loves excelling,
 Joy of heaven, to earth come down,
Fix in us thy humble dwelling,
 All thy faithful mercies crown.

2 Jesu, thou art all compassion,
 Pure unbounded love thou art;
Visit us with thy salvation,
 Enter every trembling heart.

3 Come, almighty to deliver,
 Let us all thy life receive;
Suddenly return, and never,
 Never more thy temples leave.

4 Thee we would be always blessing,
 Serve thee as thy hosts above;
Pray, and praise thee without ceasing,
 Glory in thy perfect love.

5 Finish then thy new creation,
 Pure and sinless let us be;
Let us see thy great salvation,
 Perfectly restored in thee.

6. Changed from glory into glory,
 Till in heaven we take our place,
Till we cast our crowns before thee,
 Lost in wonder, love, and praise.

Charles Wesley (1707-88)

See also No. 328

ASPIRATION

330 SONG 20 S.M.   Melody and Bass by ORLANDO GIBBONS (1583–1625)

M Y Lord, my Life, my Love,
   To thee, to thee I call;
I cannot live if thou remove:
   Thou art my joy, my all.

2   My only sun to cheer
    The darkness where I dwell;
  The best and only true delight
    My song hath found to tell.

3   To thee in very heaven
    The angels owe their bliss;
  To thee the saints, whom thou hast called
    Where perfect pleasure is.

4   And how shall man, thy child,
    Without thee happy be?
  Who hath no comfort nor desire
    In all the world but thee.

5.   Return, my Love, my Life,
    Thy grace hath won my heart;
  If thou forgive, if thou return,
    I will no more depart.

Robert Bridges (1844–1930)
Based on Isaac Watts (1674–1748)

331 MARIA JUNG UND ZART 66.66. *Psalteriolum Harmonicum* (1642)

M Y spirit longs for thee
    Within my troubled breast,
Though I unworthy be
    Of so divine a guest:

2 Of so divine a guest
    Unworthy though I be,
Yet has my heart no rest
    Unless it come from thee:

3 Unless it come from thee,
    In vain I look around;
In all that I can see
    No rest is to be found:

4. No rest is to be found
    But in thy blessèd love:
O let my wish be crowned,
    And send it from above.

John Byrom (1692–1763)

ASPIRATION

*Last verse ♮

NEARER, my God, to thee,
   Nearer to thee!
E'en though it be a cross
   That raiseth me,
Still all my song would be,
'Nearer, my God, to thee,
   Nearer to thee!'

2 Though, like the wanderer,
   The sun gone down,
Darkness be over me,
   My rest a stone;
Yet in my dreams I'd be
Nearer, my God, to thee,
   Nearer to thee.

3 There let my way appear
   Steps unto heaven;
All that thou send'st to me
   In mercy given,
Angels to beckon me
Nearer, my God, to thee,
   Nearer to thee.

4. Then, with my waking thoughts
   Bright with thy praise,
Out of my stony griefs
   Bethel I'll raise;
So by my woes to be
Nearer, my God, to thee,
   Nearer to thee.

Sarah Flower Adams (1805-48)
Based on Genesis 28, 10-22

333 CAITHNESS C.M.   *Scottish Psalter* (1635)

O FOR a closer walk with God,
    A calm and heavenly frame;
A light to shine upon the road
    That leads me to the Lamb!

2 Return, O holy Dove, return,
    Dear messenger of rest;
I hate the sins that made thee mourn,
    And drove thee from my breast.

3 The dearest idol I have known,
    Whate'er that idol be,
Help me to tear it from thy throne
    And worship only thee.

4. So shall my walk be close with God,
    Calm and serene my frame;
So purer light shall mark the road
    That leads me to the Lamb.

William Cowper (1731–1800)

ASPIRATION

334 STOCKTON C.M.

Thomas Wright (1763–1829)

O FOR a heart to praise my God,
   A heart from sin set free;
A heart that always feels thy blood
   So freely shed for me;

2 A heart resigned, submissive, meek,
   My dear Redeemer's throne,
Where only Christ is heard to speak,
   Where Jesus reigns alone;

3 A humble, lowly, contrite heart,
   Believing, true, and clean,
Which neither life nor death can part
   From him that dwells within;

4 A heart in every thought renewed
   And full of love divine,
Perfect and right and pure and good:
   A copy, Lord, of thine.

5. Thy nature, gracious Lord, impart;
   Come quickly from above;
Write thy new name upon my heart,
   Thy new best name of love.

Charles Wesley (1707–88)

335 KOCHER 76.76.

JUSTIN HEINRICH KNECHT (1752–1817)

O HAPPY band of pilgrims,
  If onward ye will tread,
With Jesus as your fellow,
  To Jesus as your Head!

2 O happy if ye labour
  As Jesus did for men;
O happy if ye hunger
  As Jesus hungered then!

3 The cross that Jesus carried
  He carried as your due:
The crown that Jesus weareth,
  He weareth it for you.

4 The faith by which ye see him,
  The hope in which ye yearn,
The love that through all troubles
  To him alone will turn;

5 What are they but forerunners
  To lead you to his sight?
What are they but the foregleams
  Of uncreated light?

6 The trials that beset you,
  The sorrows ye endure,
The manifold temptations
  That death alone can cure;

7 What are they but his jewels
  Of right celestial worth?
What are they but the ladder
  Set up to heaven on earth?

8. O happy band of pilgrims,
  Look upward to the skies,
Where such a light affliction
  Shall win you such a prize!

John Mason Neale (1818–66)
and Compilers

ASPIRATION

Melody by WILLIAM WEALE (c. 1690–1727)

O HELP us, Lord; each hour of need
    Thy heavenly succour give;
Help us in thought and word and deed,
    Each hour on earth we live.

2 O help us, when our spirits bleed
    With contrite anguish sore;
And, when our hearts are cold and dead,
    O help us, Lord, the more.

3 O help us, through the prayer of faith,
    More firmly to believe;
For still the more the servant hath,
    The more shall he receive.

4. O help us, Jesus, from on high,
    We know no help but thee;
O help us so to live and die
    As thine in heaven to be.

Henry Hart Milman (1791–1868)

337 BONN 77.77.
(FESTUS)

Abridged from a melody in
FREYLINGHAUSEN's *Gesangbuch* (1704)

Pugnate, Christi milites

SOLDIERS, who are Christ's below,
Strong in faith resist the foe;
Boundless is the pledged reward
Unto them who serve the Lord.

2 'Tis no palm of fading leaves
That the conqueror's hand receives;
Joys are his, serene and pure,
Light that ever shall endure.

3 For the souls that overcome
Waits the beauteous heavenly home,
Where the blessèd evermore
Tread on high the starry floor.

4 Passing soon, and little worth,
Are the things that tempt on earth;
Heavenward lift thy soul's regard;
God himself is thy reward.

5. Father, who the crown dost give,
Saviour, by whose death we live,
Spirit, who our hearts dost raise,
Three in One, thy name we praise. Amen.

Bourges Breviary (1734)
Tr. John Haldenby Clark (1839–88)

A - men.

ASPIRATION

338 S. JAMES C.M.

RAPHAEL COURTEVILLE (? –1772)

THOU art the Way; by thee alone
From sin and death we flee:
And he who would the Father seek
Must seek him, Lord, by thee.

2 Thou art the Truth; thy word alone
True wisdom can impart;
Thou only canst inform the mind
And purify the heart.

3 Thou art the Life; the rending tomb
Proclaims thy conquering arm;
And those who put their trust in thee
Nor death nor hell shall harm.

4. Thou art the Way, the Truth, the Life,
Grant us that way to know,
That truth to keep, that life to win,
Whose joys eternal flow.

George Washington Doane (1799–1859)
Based on S. John 14, 6

See also

451	As pants the hart		525	My heart is filled	(CS)
484	Behold the amazing gift		526	My soul, there is a country	(CS)
488	Father of peace		468	O God, thou art my God	
512	God be in my head	(CS)	37	O heavenly Word	
458	How lovely are thy dwellings		130	Sing we triumphant hymns	
81	It is a thing most wonderful		537	Sunset and evening star	(CS)
518	Jesu, priceless treasure	(CS)	473	Teach me, O Lord, the perfect way	
519	Jesus is this dark world's light	(CS)	131	The eternal gates	
11	Lord of all being		186	Through the night of doubt	
462	Lord of the worlds above				

339 MIDIAN 11.11.11.11.

HUGH PERCY ALLEN (1869–1946)

Οὐ γὰρ βλέπεις τοὺς ταράττοντας

CHRISTIAN, dost thou see them on the holy ground,
How the hosts of evil prowl and prowl around?
Christian, up and smite them, counting gain but loss;
Smite them by the merit of the holy Cross.

2 Christian, dost thou feel them, how they work within,
Striving, tempting, luring, goading into sin?
*Christian, never tremble; cast away thy care;
Smite them by the virtue of unceasing prayer.

3 Christian, dost thou hear them, how they speak thee fair,
'Always fast and vigil, always watch and prayer'?
Christian, answer boldly, 'While I breathe, I pray':
Peace shall follow battle, night shall end in day.

4. 'Well I know thy trouble, O my servant true;
Thou art very weary; I was weary too;
But that toil shall make thee some day all mine own,
And the end of sorrow shall be near my throne.'

? *from the Greek of S. Andrew of Crete* (d. 761)
Tr. John Mason Neale (1818–66) *and Compilers*

* *During Lent these two lines may be sung as follows:*

Christian, never tremble; never be downcast;
Smite them by the virtue of the Lenten fast.

R

340 SAINTBURY 77.73.   WALTER K. STANTON (1891–   )

CHRISTIAN, seek not yet repose;
    Hear thy guardian angel say,
'Thou art in the midst of foes;
    Watch and pray.'

2 Principalities and powers,
    Mustering their unseen array,
Wait for thy unguarded hours:
    Watch and pray.

3 Gird thy heavenly armour on,
    Wear it ever night and day;
Ambushed lies the evil one:
    Watch and pray.

4. Watch, as if on that alone
    Hung the issue of the day;
Pray, that help may be sent down:
    Watch and pray.
                    Charlotte Elliott (1789–1871)

341 HEINLEIN 77.77.
       (AUS DER TIEFE)   MARTIN HERBST (1654–81)

Verses 1 to 4

BUCKLAND 77.77.   LEIGHTON GEORGE HAYNE (1836–83)

Verses 5 & 6

FORTY days and forty nights
    Thou wast fasting in the wild;
Forty days and forty nights
    Tempted, and yet undefiled:

2 Sunbeams scorching all the day;
    Chilly dewdrops nightly shed;
Prowling beasts about thy way;
    Stones thy pillow; earth thy bed.

3 Shall not we thy sorrow share,
    And from earthly joys abstain,
Fasting with unceasing prayer,
    Glad with thee to suffer pain?

4 And if Satan, vexing sore,
    Flesh or spirit should assail,
Thou, his vanquisher before,
    Grant we may not faint nor fail.

Change tune.

5 So shall we have peace divine;
    Holier gladness ours shall be;
Round us too shall angels shine,
    Such as ministered to thee.

6. Keep, O keep us, Saviour dear,
    Ever constant by thy side;
That with thee we may appear
    At the eternal Eastertide.

George Hunt Smyttan (1822–70)
Francis Pott (1832–1909)
Based on S. Mark 1, 12–13

342

Mode iii

PLAISTOW L.M.

Magdalen Hymns (c. 1760)

Ecce tempus idoneum

LO, now is our accepted day,
The time for purging sins away,
The sins of thought and deed and word,
That we have done against the Lord.

2 For he, the merciful and true,
Hath spared his people hitherto;
Not willing that the soul should die,
Though great its past iniquity.

3 Therefore, with fasting and with prayer,
Our sins and failures we declare;
With all good striving seek his face,
And lowly-hearted plead for grace.

4. Blest Three in One and One in Three,
Almighty God, we pray to thee,
That thou wouldst now vouchsafe to bless
Our fast with fruits of righteousness. Amen.

10th cent. Tr. John Mason Neale (1818–66)
Thomas Alexander Lacey (1853–1931) and others

343 ISTE CONFESSOR 11.11.11.5.
(ROUEN)

Rouen Melody

PRAYER AND SELF-DISCIPLINE

LONE in the desert, facing all temptation,
Jesus, our Saviour, grant to us salvation;
Hear now thy people making supplication:
Aid our endeavour.

2 Grant to us wisdom, Satan's wiles discerning,
From thy high triumphs at this season learning,
By prayer and fasting blessèd respite earning
From earthly passions.

3. Guard we our bodies, greed and sloth dispelling,
Guard we our minds, all pride and passion quelling,
Guard we our spirits by thine own indwelling,
So shall we serve thee.

Paul Gedge (1903–   )

344 S. HUGH C.M.   EDWARD JOHN HOPKINS (1818–1901)

LORD, teach us how to pray aright
　　With reverence and with fear;
Though dust and ashes in thy sight,
　　We may, we must draw near.

2 We perish if we cease from prayer;
　　O grant us power to pray;
And, when to meet thee we prepare,
　　Lord, meet us by the way.

3 God of all grace, we bring to thee
　　A broken contrite heart;
Give, what thine eye delights to see,
　　Truth in the inward part;

4 Faith in the only sacrifice
　　That can for sin atone;
To cast our hopes, to fix our eyes,
　　On Christ, on Christ alone;

5 Patience to watch and wait and weep,
　　Though mercy long delay;
Courage our fainting souls to keep,
　　And trust thee, though thou slay;

6. Give these, and then thy will be done;
　　Thus, strengthened with all might,
We, through thy Spirit and thy Son,
　　Shall pray, and pray aright.

James Montgomery (1771–1854)

PRAYER AND SELF-DISCIPLINE

345 FRILFORD 66.66.66.　　　　　　WILLIAM HAROLD FERGUSON (1874–1950)

NOT for our sins alone
　　Thy mercy, Lord, we sue;
Let fall thy pitying glance
　On our devotions too,
What we have done for thee,
And what we think to do.

2 The holiest hours we spend
　　In prayer upon our knees,
The times when most we deem
　Our songs of praise will please,
Thou searcher of all hearts,
Forgiveness pour on these.

3 And all the gifts we bring,
　　And all the vows we make,
And all the acts of love
　We plan for thy dear sake,
Into thy pardoning thought,
O God of mercy, take.

4 And most, when we, thy flock,
　　Before thine altar bend,
And strange, bewildering thoughts
　With those sweet moments blend,
By him whose death we plead,
Good Lord, thy help extend.

5. Bow down thine ear and hear!
　　Open thine eyes and see!
Our very love is shame,
　And we must come to thee
To make it, of thy grace,
　What thou would'st have it be.

Henry Twells (1823–1900)

346

Mode ii

BABYLON'S STREAMS L.M.

THOMAS CAMPION (1575–1619)

Audi, benigne Conditor

O KIND Creator, bow thine ear
　　To mark the cry, to know the tear
Before thy throne of mercy spent
In this thy holy fast of Lent.

2 Our hearts are open, Lord, to thee;
　Thou knowest our infirmity;
　Pour out on all who seek thy face
　Abundance of thy pardoning grace.

3 Our sins are many, this we know;
　Spare us, good Lord, thy mercy show;
　And, for the honour of thy name,
　Our fainting souls to life reclaim.

4 Give us the self-control that springs
　From discipline of outward things,
　That, fasting inward secretly,
　The soul may purely dwell with thee.

5. We pray thee, Holy Trinity,
　One God, unchanging Unity,
　That we from this our abstinence
　May reap the fruits of penitence. Amen.

Ascribed to S. Gregory the Great (540–604)
Tr. Thomas Alexander Lacey (1853–1931)

347 WIGTOWN C.M.

Scottish Psalter (1635)

PRAYER is the soul's sincere desire,
    Uttered or unexpressed;
The motion of a hidden fire
    That trembles in the breast.

2 Prayer is the simplest form of speech
    That infant lips can try;
Prayer the sublimest strains that reach
    The Majesty on high.

3 Prayer is the Christian's vital breath,
    The Christian's native air,
His watchword at the gates of death:
    He enters heaven with prayer.

4. O thou by whom we come to God,
    The Life, the Truth, the Way,
The path of prayer thyself hast trod:
    Lord, teach us how to pray.

James Montgomery (1771–1854)

348 S. ETHELDREDA C.M.   Thomas Turton (1780–1864)

SHEPHERD divine, our wants relieve
  In this our evil day;
To all thy tempted followers give
  The power to watch and pray.

2 Long as our fiery trials last,
  Long as the cross we bear,
O let our souls on thee be cast
  In never-ceasing prayer.

3 The spirit of interceding grace
  Give us in faith to claim;
To wrestle till we see thy face,
  And know thy hidden name.

4 Till thou thy perfect love impart,
  Till thou thyself bestow,
Be this the cry of every heart,
  'I will not let thee go'.

5 I will not let thee go, unless
  Thou tell thy name to me;
With all thy great salvation bless,
  And make me all like thee.

6. Then let me on the mountain-top
  Behold thine open face,
Where faith in sight is swallowed up,
  And prayer in endless praise.

Charles Wesley (1707–88)
Based on Genesis 32, 22–30

See also

135 Be thou my guardian
83 Lord, who throughout these forty days

466 O God, give ear
409 O splendour of God's glory

349 FERRY C.M.

GREEN's *Psalmody* (1731)

DEDICATION AND DISCIPLESHIP

BEHOLD us, Lord, a little space
From daily tasks set free,
And met within thy holy place
To rest awhile with thee.

2 Yet these are not the only walls
Wherein thou may'st be sought;
On homeliest work thy blessing falls,
In truth and patience wrought.

3 Thine is the loom, the forge, the mart,
The wealth of land and sea,
The worlds of science and of art,
Revealed and ruled by thee.

4. All work is prayer, if it be wrought
As thou wouldst have it done,
And prayer, by thee inspired and taught,
Itself with work is one.

John Ellerton (1826–93) and Compilers

350 EDOM 65.65.66.65.

Arranged by EDGAR PETTMAN (1865–1943)

CHRISTIAN, unflinching stand,
   Satan defying!
Outstretched is God's right hand,
   All power supplying;
Valiant as saints of old,
Proudly the Cross uphold,
Moved by his love untold
   To live for Jesus.

2 Stern is your fight with wrong;
   Christ stands beside you.
Hard grows the way and long;
   His hand will guide you.
Calmly each danger face,
Boldly his footsteps trace,
Seeking by God's good grace
   To live for Jesus.

3. Friends by your side may fall;
   Help and defend them.
Foes in distress may call;
   Comfort and tend them.
Give ear to them that plead;
Bind up the hearts that bleed;
Learn by each kindly deed
   To live for Jesus.

Edgecombe Walter Leachman (1870–1945)

CHRISTIAN LIFE AND DUTY: TOWARDS GOD

351 REPTON 86.886. CHARLES HUBERT HASTINGS PARRY (1848–1918)

ARNOLD 86.886. HERBERT MURRILL (1909–52)

DEAR Lord and Father of mankind,
 Forgive our foolish ways;
Re-clothe us in our rightful mind,
In purer lives thy service find,
 In deeper reverence praise.

2 In simple trust like theirs who heard,
 Beside the Syrian sea,
The gracious calling of the Lord,
Let us, like them, without a word
 Rise up and follow thee.

3 O Sabbath rest by Galilee,
 O calm of hills above,
Where Jesus knelt to share with thee
The silence of eternity,
 Interpreted by love!

4 Drop thy still dews of quietness,
 Till all our strivings cease;
Take from our souls the strain and stress,
And let our ordered lives confess
 The beauty of thy peace.

5. Breathe through the heats of our desire
 Thy coolness and thy balm;
Let sense be dumb, let flesh retire;
Speak through the earthquake, wind, and fire,
 O still small voice of calm!

John Greenleaf Whittier (1807–92)

352 SUSSEX 87.87.

Adapted from an English Traditional Melody

FATHER, hear the prayer we offer;
Not for ease that prayer shall be,
But for strength that we may ever
Live our lives courageously.

2 Not for ever in green pastures
Do we ask our way to be;
But the steep and rugged pathway
May we tread rejoicingly.

3 Not for ever by still waters
Would we idly rest and stay;
But would smite the living fountains
From the rocks along our way.

4. Be our strength in hours of weakness,
In our wanderings be our guide;
Through endeavour, failure, danger,
Father, be thou at our side.

Love Maria Willis (1824–1908) and others

353 GRAND ISLE Irregular.

JOHN HENRY HOPKINS (1861–1945)

DEDICATION AND DISCIPLESHIP

For Young Children

I SING a song of the saints of God,
    Patient and brave and true,
Who toiled and fought and lived and died
    For the Lord they loved and knew.
And one was a doctor, and one was a queen,
And one was a shepherdess on the green:
They were all of them saints of God; and I mean,
    God helping, to be one too.

2 They loved their Lord so good and dear,
    And his love made them strong;
And they followed the right, for Jesus' sake,
    The whole of their good lives long.
And one was a soldier, and one was a priest,
And one was slain by a fierce wild beast:
And there's not any reason, no, not the least,
    Why I shouldn't be one too.

3. They lived not only in ages past,
    There are hundreds of thousands still;
The world is bright with the joyous saints
    Who love to do Jesus' will.
You can meet them in school, or in lanes, or at sea,
In church, or in trains, or in shops, or at tea,
For the saints of God began just like me,
    And I mean to be one too.

Lesbia Scott (1898–   ) and others

354 WRAYSBURY 87.87.   EDWARD JOHN HOPKINS (1818–1901)

JESUS calls us! O'er the tumult
  Of our life's wild restless sea
Day by day his voice is sounding,
  Saying, 'Christian, follow me':

2 As of old Saint Andrew heard it
    By the Galilean lake,
  Turned from home and toil and kindred,
    Leaving all for his dear sake.

3 Jesus calls us from the worship
    Of the vain world's golden store,
  From each idol that would keep us,
    Saying, 'Christian, love me more'.

4 In our joys and in our sorrows,
    Days of toil and hours of ease,
  Still he calls, in cares and pleasures,
    'Christian, love me more than these'.

5. Jesus calls us! By thy mercies,
    Saviour, may we hear thy call,
  Give our hearts to thy obedience,
    Serve and love thee best of all.

Cecil Frances Alexander (1818–95) and Compilers
Based on S. Mark 1, 16–17

355 S. KILDA C.M.   WILLIAM ROBERT BROOMFIELD (1826–88)

LORD, it belongs not to my care
   Whether I die or live;
To love and serve thee is my share,
   And this thy grace must give.

2 If life be long, O make me glad
   The longer to obey:
If short, yet why should I be sad
   To welcome endless day?

3 Christ leads me through no darker rooms
   Than he went through before:
And he that to God's kingdom comes
   Must enter by this door.

4 Come, Lord, when grace hath made me meet
   Thy blessèd face to see;
For if thy work on earth be sweet,
   What will thy glory be?

5. My knowledge of that life is small,
   The eye of faith is dim;
But 'tis enough that Christ knows all,
   And I shall be with him.

                    Richard Baxter (1615–91) and Compilers

356 BELGRAVE C.M.

WILLIAM HORSLEY (1774–1858)

M Y God, accept my heart this day
  And make it always thine,
That I from thee no more may stray,
  No more from thee decline.

2 Before the Cross of him who died,
    Behold, I prostrate fall;
  Let every sin be crucified,
    And Christ be all in all.

3 Anoint me with thy heavenly grace,
    And seal me for thine own;
  That I may see thy glorious face,
    And worship near thy throne.

4 Let every thought and work and word
    To thee be ever given;
  Then life shall be thy service, Lord,
    And death the gate of heaven.

5. All glory to the Father be,
    All glory to the Son,
  All glory, Holy Ghost, to thee,
    While endless ages run. Amen.

Matthew Bridges (1800–94)

A - men.

357 MEYER 888.4.
(ES IST KEIN TAG)

Melody from
JOHANN MEYER'S *Seelenfreud* (1692)

M^Y God, my Father, make me strong,
When tasks of life seem hard and long,
To greet them with this triumph-song:
    Thy will be done.

2 Draw from my timid eyes the veil,
To show, where earthly forces fail,
Thy power and love must still prevail,
    Thy will be done.

3 With confident and humble mind,
Freedom in service I would find,
Praying through every toil assigned,
    Thy will be done.

4 Things deemed impossible I dare,
Thine is the call and thine the care;
Thy wisdom shall the way prepare,
    Thy will be done.

5 All power is here and round me now,
Faithful I stand in rule and vow,
While 'tis not I, but ever thou:
    Thy will be done.

6. Heaven's music chimes the glad days in,
Hope soars beyond death, pain, and sin,
Faith shouts in triumph, Love must win,
    Thy will be done.

Frederick Mann (1846–1928)

358 GRÄFENBERG 86.86. *Praxis Pietatis Melica* (1653)

O DEAREST Lord, thy sacred
head
  With thorns was pierced for me;
O pour thy blessing on my head,
  That I may think for thee.

2 O dearest Lord, thy sacred hands
  With nails were pierced for me;
O shed thy blessing on my hands,
  That they may work for thee.

3 O dearest Lord, thy sacred feet
  With nails were pierced for me;
O pour thy blessing on my feet,
  That they may follow thee.

4. O dearest Lord, thy sacred heart
  With spear was pierced for me;
O pour thy spirit in my heart,
  That I may live for thee.

Father Andrew, S.D.C. (1869–1946)

359 S. NICHOLAS C.M.   *First Tune*   Melody from HOLDROYD's *Spiritual Man's Companion* (1753)

359 MARTYRS C.M.   *Scottish Psalter (1615)*

Second Tune

O GOD of truth, whose living word
    Upholds whate'er hath breath,
Look down on thy creation, Lord,
    Enslaved by sin and death.

2 Set up thy standard, Lord, that we,
    Who claim a heavenly birth,
May march with thee to smite the lies
    That vex thy groaning earth.

3 But can we fight for truth and God,
    Poor slaves of lies and sin?
He who would wage that war on earth
    Must first be true within.

4 Then, God of truth, for whom we long,
    Thou who wilt hear our prayer,
Do thine own battle in our hearts,
    And slay the falsehood there.

5. So, tried in thy refining fire,
    From every lie set free,
In us thy perfect truth shall dwell,
    And we may fight for thee.

Thomas Hughes (1822–96) and others

360 WOLVERCOTE 76.76. D.   WILLIAM HAROLD FERGUSON (1874–1950)

Unison

O JESUS, I have promised
  To serve thee to the end;
Be thou for ever near me,
  My Master and my Friend;
I shall not fear the battle
  If thou art by my side,
Nor wander from the pathway
  If thou wilt be my guide.

2 O let me feel thee near me:
    The world is ever near;
  I see the sights that dazzle,
    The tempting sounds I hear;
  My foes are ever near me,
    Around me and within;
  But, Jesus, draw thou nearer,
    And shield my soul from sin.

3 O let me hear thee speaking
    In accents clear and still,
  Above the storms of passion,
    The murmurs of self-will;
  O speak to reassure me,
    To hasten or control;
  O speak, and make me listen,
    Thou guardian of my soul.

4 O Jesus, thou hast promised
    To all who follow thee,
  That where thou art in glory
    There shall thy servant be;
  And, Jesus, I have promised
    To serve thee to the end;
  O give me grace to follow,
    My Master and my Friend.

5. O let me see thy footmarks,
    And in them plant mine own;
  My hope to follow duly
    Is in thy strength alone;
  O guide me, call me, draw me,
    Uphold me to the end;
  And then in heaven receive me,
    My Saviour and my Friend.

John Ernest Bode (1816–74)

Harmony version overleaf.

360 WOLVERCOTE 76.76.D. WILLIAM HAROLD FERGUSON (1874–1950)

O JESUS, I have promised
    To serve thee to the end;
Be thou for ever near me,
    My Master and my Friend;
I shall not fear the battle
    If thou art by my side,
Nor wander from the pathway
    If thou wilt be my guide.

2 O let me feel thee near me:
    The world is ever near;
I see the sights that dazzle,
    The tempting sounds I hear;
My foes are ever near me,
    Around me and within;
But, Jesus, draw thou nearer,
    And shield my soul from sin.

3 O let me hear thee speaking
    In accents clear and still,
Above the storms of passion,
    The murmurs of self-will;
O speak to reassure me,
    To hasten or control;
O speak, and make me listen,
    Thou guardian of my soul.

4 O Jesus, thou hast promised
    To all who follow thee,
That where thou art in glory
    There shall thy servant be;
And, Jesus, I have promised
    To serve thee to the end;
O give me grace to follow,
    My Master and my Friend.

5. O let me see thy footmarks,
    And in them plant mine own;
My hope to follow duly
    Is in thy strength alone;
O guide me, call me, draw me,
    Uphold me to the end;
And then in heaven receive me,
    My Saviour and my Friend.

John Ernest Bode (1816–74)

361 WER NUR DEN LIEBEN GOTT 88.88.88.

Adapted from a melody by
GEORG NEUMARK (1621-81)

Liebe die du mich zum Bilde

O LOVE, who formedst me to wear
    The image of thy godhead here;
Who soughtest me with tender care
    Through all my wanderings wild and drear;
      O Love, I give myself to thee,
      Thine ever, only thine to be.

2 O Love, who ere life's earliest morn
    On me thy choice hast gently laid;
  O Love, who here as man wast born,
    And wholly like to us wast made:

3 O Love, who once in time wast slain,
    Pierced through and through with bitter woe;
  O Love, who wrestling thus didst gain
    That we eternal joy might know:

4. O Love, who once shalt bid me rise
    From out this dying life of ours;
  O Love, who once o'er yonder skies
    Shalt set me in the fadeless bowers:

Johann Scheffler (1624-77)
Tr. Catherine Winkworth (1827-78)

362 HEREFORD L.M.   SAMUEL SEBASTIAN WESLEY (1810–76)

O THOU who camest from above,
  The pure celestial fire to impart,
Kindle a flame of sacred love
  On the mean altar of my heart.

2 There let it for thy glory burn
    With ever-bright, undying blaze,
  And trembling to its source return
    In humble prayer and fervent praise.

3 Jesu, confirm my heart's desire
    To work and speak and think for thee;
  Still let me guard the holy fire,
    And still stir up thy gift in me.

4. Ready for all thy perfect will,
    My acts of faith and love repeat,
  Till death thy endless mercies seal,
    And make the sacrifice complete.

Charles Wesley (1707–88) *and others*
Based on Leviticus 6, 13

363 UNIVERSITY COLLEGE 77.77.   HENRY JOHN GAUNTLETT (1805–76)

O FT in danger, oft in woe,
 Onward, Christians, onward go;
Bear the toil, maintain the strife,
Strengthened with the Bread of life.

2 Let your drooping hearts be glad;
 March in heavenly armour clad;
 Fight, nor think the battle long:
 Victory soon shall tune your song.

3 Let not sorrow dim your eye,
 Soon shall every tear be dry;
 Let not fears your course impede, ,
 Great your strength, if great your need.

4. Onward then in battle move;
 More than conquerors ye shall prove;
 Though opposed by many a foe,
 Christian soldiers, onward go.

Henry Kirke White (1785–1806) *and others*

364 CARLISLE S.M.   CHARLES LOCKHART (1745-1815)

R ISE up, O men of God!
Have done with lesser things;
Give heart and soul and mind and strength
To serve the King of kings.

2   Rise up, O men of God!
His kingdom tarries long;
Bring in the day of brotherhood,
And end the night of wrong.

3   Rise up, O men of God!
The Church for you doth wait:
Her strength unequal to her task;
Rise up, and make her great!

4.   Lift high the Cross of Christ!
Tread where his feet have trod;
As brothers of the Son of Man
Rise up, O men of God!

William Pierson Merrill (1867-1954)

365 FROM STRENGTH
TO STRENGTH D.S.M.

EDWARD WOODALL NAYLOR (1867–1934)

SOLDIERS of Christ, arise,
  And put your armour on;
Strong in the strength which God supplies,
  Through his eternal Son;
  Strong in the Lord of hosts,
  And in his mighty power;
Who in the strength of Jesus trusts
  Is more than conqueror.

2 Stand, then, in his great might,
    With all his strength endued;
  And take, to arm you for the fight,
    The panoply of God.
    To keep your armour bright
    Attend with constant care,
  Still walking in your Captain's sight,
    And watching unto prayer.

3. From strength to strength go on;
    Wrestle and fight and pray;
  Tread all the powers of darkness down,
    And win the well-fought day;
    That, having all things done,
    And all your conflicts past,
  Ye may o'ercome, through Christ alone,
    And stand complete at last.

Charles Wesley (1707–88)
Based on Ephesians 6, 10-18

See also No. 366

366 S. ETHELWALD S.M.　　　　　　　　WILLIAM HENRY MONK (1823–89)

SOLDIERS of Christ, arise,
　And put your armour on;
Strong in the strength which God supplies,
　Through his eternal Son;

2　Strong in the Lord of hosts,
　　And in his mighty power;
Who in the strength of Jesus trusts
　Is more than conqueror.

3　Stand, then, in his great might,
　　With all his strength endued;
And take, to arm you for the fight,
　The panoply of God.

4　To keep your armour bright
　　Attend with constant care,
Still walking in your Captain's sight,
　And watching unto prayer.

5　From strength to strength go on;
　　Wrestle and fight and pray;
Tread all the powers of darkness down,
　And win the well-fought day.

6.　That, having all things done,
　　And all your conflicts past,
Ye may o'ercome, through Christ alone,
　And stand complete at last.

Charles Wesley (1707–88)
Based on Ephesians 6, 10–18

See also No. 365

367 HARTS 77.77.   BENJAMIN MILGROVE (1731–1810)

SOLDIERS of the Cross, arise!
　　Gird you with your armour bright;
Mighty are your enemies,
　　Hard the battle ye must fight.

2 O'er a faithless fallen world
　　Raise your banner in the sky;
Let it float there wide unfurled;
　　Bear it onward; lift it high.

3 'Mid the homes of want and woe,
　　Strangers to the living word,
Let the Saviour's herald go,
　　Let the voice of hope be heard.

4 Guard the helpless; seek the strayed;
　　Comfort troubles; banish grief;
In the might of God arrayed,
　　Scatter sin and unbelief.

5. Be the banner still unfurled,
　　Still unsheathed the Spirit's sword,
Till the kingdoms of the world
　　Are the Kingdom of the Lord.

William Walsham How (1823–97)

368 MORPETH 76.76.D.   Cyril V. Taylor (1907–)

MORNING LIGHT 76.76.D.   George James Webb (1803–87)

DEDICATION AND DISCIPLESHIP

STAND up, stand up for Jesus,
  Ye soldiers of the Cross!
Lift high his royal banner,
  It must not suffer loss.
From victory unto victory
  His army he shall lead,
Till every foe is vanquished,
  And Christ is Lord indeed.

2 Stand up, stand up for Jesus!
    The trumpet call obey;
  Forth to the mighty conflict
    In this his glorious day.
  Ye that are men, now serve him
    Against unnumbered foes;
  Let courage rise with danger,
    And strength to strength oppose.

3 Stand up, stand up for Jesus!
    Stand in his strength alone;
  The arm of flesh will fail you,
    Ye dare not trust your own.
  Put on the gospel armour,
    Each piece put on with prayer;
  When duty calls or danger,
    Be never wanting there!

4. Stand up, stand up for Jesus!
    The strife will not be long;
  This day the noise of battle,
    The next the victor's song.
  To him that overcometh,
    A crown of life shall be;
  He with the King of glory
    Shall reign eternally.

George Duffield (1818–88)
Based on Ephesians 6, 10–18

369 BRESLAU L.M.   Melody in *As hymnodus sacer* (Leipzig, 1625)

TAKE up thy cross, the Saviour said,
   If thou wouldst my disciple be;
Deny thyself, the world forsake,
   And humbly follow after me.

2 Take up thy cross; let not its weight
   Fill thy weak soul with vain alarm;
His strength shall bear thy spirit up,
   And brace thy heart, and nerve thine arm.

3 Take up thy cross, nor heed the shame,
   Nor let thy foolish pride rebel;
The Lord for thee the cross endured,
   To save thy soul from death and hell.

4 Take up thy cross then in his strength,
   And calmly every danger brave;
'Twill guide thee to a better home,
   And lead to victory o'er the grave.

5. Take up thy cross, and follow Christ,
   Nor think till death to lay it down;
For only he who bears the cross
   May hope to wear the glorious crown.

Charles William Everest (1814–77) and others
Based on S. Mark 8, 34

DEDICATION AND DISCIPLESHIP

For Young Children

THE wise may bring their learning,
  The rich may bring their wealth,
And some may bring their greatness,
  And some their strength and
    health:
We too would bring our treasures
  To offer to the King;
We have no wealth or learning,
  What gifts then shall we bring?

2 We'll bring the many duties
  We have to do each day;
We'll try our best to please him,
  At home, at school, at play:

And better are these treasures
  To offer to our King
Than richest gifts without them;
  Yet these we all may bring.

3. We'll bring him hearts that love him,
  We'll bring him thankful praise,
And souls for ever striving
  To follow in his ways:
And these shall be the treasures
  We offer to the King,
And these are gifts that ever
  Our grateful hearts may bring.

Book of Praise for Children (1881), *and Compilers*

371 MONKS GATE 65.65.66.65.   English Traditional Melody

WHO would true valour see,
    Let him come hither;
One here will constant be,
    Come wind, come weather;
There's no discouragement
Shall make him once relent
His first avowed intent
    To be a pilgrim.

2 Whoso beset him round
    With dismal stories,
Do but themselves confound;
    His strength the more is.
No lion can him fright,
He'll with a giant fight,
But he will have a right
    To be a pilgrim.

3. Hobgoblin nor foul fiend
    Can daunt his spirit;
He knows he at the end
    Shall life inherit.
Then fancies fly away;
He'll fear not what men say;
He'll labour night and day
    To be a pilgrim.

John Bunyan (1628–88)

372 NARENZA S.M.

Cöln Gesangbuch (1619). Adapted by
WILLIAM HENRY HAVERGAL (1793–1870)

YE servants of the Lord,
  Each in his office wait,
Observant of his heavenly word,
  And watchful at his gate.

2 Let all your lamps be bright,
    And trim the golden flame;
  Gird up your loins as in his sight,
    For aweful is his name.

3 Watch! 'tis your Lord's command,
    And while we speak, he's near;
  Mark the first signal of his hand,
    And ready all appear.

4 O happy servant he,
    In such a posture found!
  He shall his Lord with rapture see,
    And be with honour crowned.

5. Christ shall the banquet spread
    With his own royal hand,
  And raise that faithful servant's head
    Amidst the^angelic band.

Philip Doddridge (1702–51)
Based on S. Luke 12, 35–40

See also

120 At the name of Jesus	494 I'm not ashamed
316 Be thou my Vision	72 Jesus, good above all other
317 Believe not those	34 Lift up your heads, ye mighty gates
301 Beneath the cross of Jesus	266 O dearest Lord, by all adored
339 Christian, dost thou see them	215 Strengthen for service
23 Eternal God, whose power upholds	536 Strengthen for service
488 Father of peace	187 Thy hand, O God
406 Forth in thy name	

(CS)

373 SONG 46 10.10.   Melody and Bass by ORLANDO GIBBONS (1583–1625)

LOVE, UNITY, PEACE

BELOVÈD, let us love: for love is of God;
In God alone hath love its true abode.

2 Belovèd, let us love: for they who love,
They only are his sons, born from above.

3 Belovèd, let us love: for love is rest,
And he who loveth not abides unblest.

4 Belovèd, let us love: for love is light,
And he who loveth not dwelleth in night.

5. Belovèd, let us love: for only thus
Shall we behold that God who loveth us.

Horatius Bonar (1808–89)
Based on 1 John 4, 7

374 VIENNA 77.77.   Melody by JUSTIN HEINRICH KNECHT (1752–1817)

JESUS, Lord, we look to thee;
Let us in thy name agree;
Show thyself the Prince of peace;
Bid our strife for ever cease.

2 Make us of one heart and mind,
Courteous, pitiful, and kind,
Lowly, meek, in thought and word,
Altogether like our Lord.

3 Let us for each other care,
Each the other's burden bear;
To thy Church the pattern give,
Show how true believers live.

4. Free from anger and from pride,
Let us thus in God abide;
All the depths of love express,
All the height of holiness.

Charles Wesley (1707–88)

375 HALTON HOLGATE 87.87.

WILLIAM BOYCE (1710–79)

MAY the grace of Christ our Saviour,
And the Father's boundless love,
With the Holy Spirit's favour,
Rest upon us from above.

2. Thus may we abide in union
With each other and the Lord,
And possess, in sweet communion,
Joys which earth cannot afford.

John Newton (1725–1807)
Based on 2 Corinthians 13, 14

See also No. 524 (CS)

LOVE, UNITY, PEACE

376 INTERCESSOR 11.10.11.10.   CHARLES HUBERT HASTINGS PARRY (1848–1918)

O BROTHER man, fold to thy heart thy brother!
   Where pity dwells, the peace of God is there;
To worship rightly is to love each other,
   Each smile a hymn, each kindly deed a prayer.

2 For he whom Jesus loved hath truly spoken:
   The holier worship which he deigns to bless
Restores the lost, and binds the spirit broken,
   And feeds the widow and the fatherless.

3 Follow with reverent steps the great example
   Of him whose holy work was doing good;
So shall the wide earth seem our Father's temple,
   Each loving life a psalm of gratitude.

4. Then shall all shackles fall; the stormy clangour
   Of wild war-music o'er the earth shall cease;
Love shall tread out the baleful fire of anger,
   And in its ashes plant the tree of peace.

John Greenleaf Whittier (1807–92)
Based on S. James 1, 27

377 EVERTON 87.87. D.

HENRY SMART (1813–79)

SON of God, eternal Saviour,
    Source of life and truth and grace,
Son of Man, whose birth incarnate
    Hallows all our human race;
Thou, our Head, who, throned in glory,
    For thine own dost ever plead,
Fill us with thy love and pity;
    Heal our wrongs and help our need.

2 Bind us all as one together
    In thy Church's sacred fold,
Weak and healthy, poor and wealthy,
    Sad and joyful, young and old.
Is there want or pain or sorrow?
    Make us all the burden share.
Are there spirits crushed and broken?
    Teach us, Lord, to soothe their care.

3 As thou, Lord, hast lived for others,
　　So may we for others live;
Freely have thy gifts been granted,
　　Freely may thy servants give.
Thine the gold and thine the silver,
　　Thine the wealth of land and sea,
We but stewards of thy bounty,
　　Held in solemn trust for thee.

4. Come, O Christ, and reign among us,
　　King of love, and Prince of peace,
Hush the storm of strife and passion,
　　Bid its cruel discords cease;
Thou who prayedst, thou who willest
　　That thy people should be one,
Grant, O grant our hope's fruition:
　　Here on earth thy will be done.

Somerset Corry Lowry (1855–1932)

See also

29	All glory to God	398	Most glorious Lord of life
485	Behold, the mountain	526	My soul, there is a country (CS)
149	Come down, O Love divine	24	O day of God, draw nigh
23	Eternal God, whose power upholds	157	O Holy Spirit, Lord of grace
321	Eternal Ruler	158	O King enthroned on high
201	Father, we thank thee	25	O Lord our God, arise!
455	God of mercy	213	O thou, who at thy Eucharist
153	Gracious Spirit, Holy Ghost	472	Pray that Jerusalem
457	Hail to the Lord's Anointed	479	The Lord will come
52	It came upon the midnight clear	60	The maker of the sun
72	Jesus, good above all other	496	The race that long in darkness pined
460	Jesus shall reign	186	Through the night of doubt
308	Lead us, O Father	27	Thy kingdom come, O God
53	Love came down at Christmas	28	'Thy kingdom come!' On bended knee
524	May the grace of Christ (CS)	285	When morning gilds the skies

378 DUNFERMLINE C.M.

Scottish Psalter (1615)

THOSE IN NEED

HELP us to help each other, Lord,
  Each other's cross to bear;
Let each his friendly aid afford,
  And feel his brother's care.

2 Up into thee, our living Head,
  Let us in all things grow,
And by thy sacrifice be led
  The fruits of love to show.

3. Drawn by the loadstone of thy love,
  Let all our hearts agree;
And ever toward each other move,
  And ever move toward thee.

Charles Wesley (1707–88) *and Compilers*

THOSE IN NEED

379 S. ETHELDREDA C.M.

THOMAS TURTON (1780–1864)

JESUS, my Lord, how rich thy grace,
 How fair thy bounties shine!
What can my poverty bestow,
 When all the worlds are thine?

2 But thou hast needy brethren here,
 The partners of thy grace,
And wilt confess their humble names
 Before thy Father's face.

3 In them thou may'st be clothed and fed,
 And visited and cheered,
And in their accents of distress
 The Saviour's voice is heard.

4. Thy face with reverence and with love
 I in thy poor would see;
O let me rather beg my bread,
 Than hold it back from thee.

Philip Doddridge (1702–51)
Edward Osler (1798–1863) and others
Based on S. Matthew 25, 31–45

380 KENT L.M.

JOHANN FRIEDRICH LAMPE (1703-51)

LORD Christ, who on thy heart didst bear
     The burden of our shame and sin,
And now on high dost stoop to share
     The fight without, the fear within;

2 Thy patience cannot know defeat,
     Thy pity will not be denied,
Thy loving-kindness still is great,
     Thy tender mercies still abide.

3 O brother Man, for this we pray,
     Thou brother Man and sovereign Lord,
That we thy brethren, day by day,
     May follow thee and keep thy word;

4 That we may care, as thou hast cared,
     For sick and lame, for deaf and blind,
And freely share, as thou hast shared,
     In all the sorrows of mankind;

5. That ours may be the holy task
     To help and bless, to heal and save;
This is the happiness we ask,
     And this the service that we crave.

Henry Arnold Thomas (1848-1924) and Compilers

381 CRUCIS VICTORIA C.M.   MYLES BIRKET FOSTER (1851–1922)

O GOD, whose will is life and good
   For all of mortal breath,
Unite in bonds of brotherhood
   All those who fight with death.

2 Make strong their hands and hearts and wills
   To drive disease afar,
To battle with the body's ills,
   And wage thy holy war.

3 Where'er they heal the sick and blind,
   Christ's love may they proclaim:
Make known the good Physician's mind,
   And prove the Saviour's name.

4. Before them set thy holy will,
   That they, with heart and soul,
To thee may consecrate their skill,
   And make the sufferer whole.

       Hardwicke Drummond Rawnsley (1851–1920) and Compilers

382 S. MATTHEW D.C.M.

Modern form of melody by
WILLIAM CROFT (1678–1727)

THINE arm, O Lord, in days of old
    Was strong to heal and save;
It triumphed o'er disease and death,
    O'er darkness and the grave;
To thee they went, the blind, the dumb,
    The palsied and the lame,
The leper with his tainted life,
    The sick with fevered frame.

2 And lo, thy touch brought life and health,
    Gave speech and strength and sight;
And youth renewed and frenzy calmed
    Owned thee the Lord of light;
And now, O Lord, be near to bless,
    Almighty as of yore,
In crowded street, by restless couch,
    As by Gennesareth's shore.

3. Be thou our great deliverer still,
    Thou Lord of life and death;
Restore and quicken, soothe and bless
    With thine almighty breath;
To hands that work, and eyes that see,
    Give wisdom's heavenly lore,
That whole and sick, and weak and strong,
    May praise thee evermore.

Edward Hayes Plumptre (1821–91)

383 S. LEONARD 87.87.77. Melody by JOHANN CHRISTOPH BACH (1642–1703)

THOU to whom the sick and dying
 Ever came, nor came in vain,
Still with healing word replying
To the wearied cry of pain,
  Hear us, Jesu, as we meet,
  Suppliants at thy mercy-seat.

2 Still the weary, sick, and dying
   Need a brother's, sister's care;
 On thy higher help relying,
   May we now their burden share,
    Bringing all our offerings meet,
    Suppliants at thy mercy-seat.

3 May each child of thine be willing,
   Willing both in hand and heart,
 All the law of love fulfilling,
   Ever comfort to impart,
    Ever bringing offerings meet,
    Suppliant to thy mercy-seat.

4. So may sickness, sin, and sadness
   To thy healing virtue yield,
 Till the sick and sad, in gladness,
   Rescued, ransomed, cleansed, and healed,
    One in thee together meet,
    Pardoned at thy judgment-seat.

Godfrey Thring (1823–1903)

See also

70	A stranger once	306	Lead, kindly light
289	All ye who seek	332	Nearer, my God, to thee
412	At even, when the sun	310	O for a faith
300	Awake, our souls	466	O God, give ear
504	Cast thy burden (CS)	495	O God of Bethel
491	Hast thou not known	335	O happy band of pilgrims
142	How sweet the name	336	O help us, Lord
143	I heard the voice	311	O Lord, how happy
144	Jesu, guide our way	313	Put thou thy trust
145	Jesu, lover of my soul	377	Son of God, eternal Saviour
291	Jesus, Lord of life	498	Where high the heavenly temple stands

384 MELITA 88.88.88.　　　　　　　　　　　JOHN BACCHUS DYKES (1823–76)

ETERNAL Father, strong to save,
Whose arm hath bound the restless wave,
Who bidd'st the mighty ocean deep
Its own appointed limits keep;
　　O hear us when we cry to thee
　　For those in peril on the sea.

2 O Christ, whose voice the waters heard,
And hushed their raging at thy word,
Who walkedst on the foaming deep,
And calm amid the storm didst sleep;
　　O hear us when we cry to thee
　　For those in peril on the sea.

3 O Holy Spirit, who didst brood
Upon the waters dark and rude,
And bid their angry tumult cease,
And give, for wild confusion, peace;
　　O hear us when we cry to thee
　　For those in peril on the sea.

4. O Trinity of love and power,
Our brethren shield in danger's hour;
From rock and tempest, fire and foe,
Protect them wheresoe'er they go;
　　Thus evermore shall rise to thee
　　Glad hymns of praise from land and sea.

William Whiting (1825–78)

385 DIVA SERVATRIX 11.11.11.5.

Bayeux Melody

FATHER all-seeing, friend of all creation,
  Life of thy children, still thy love revealing,
For all our loved ones, now far absent from us,
    We are appealing.

2 Working or playing, Lord, be thou their leader;
    And, if alarm or sickness should oppress them,
  Teach them to trust thee, knowing that in all things
      Thy love will bless them.

3 In all temptation be their strength and comfort;
    Guide them in weakness, sanctifying, shielding;
  Through him who, tempted every day as we are,
      Lived without yielding.

4. When they are lonely, be thou their companion,
    Hold them in safety, strengthen their endeavour;
  Grant them to follow where thy voice shall call them,
      Now and for ever.

Maud Anna Bell (1868–1957)

386 BUSHMEAD 85.83.

CYRIL V. TAYLOR (1907–   )

H OLY Father, in thy mercy
    Hear thy children's prayer;
Keep our loved ones, now far distant,
    In thy care.

2 Jesus, Saviour, let thy presence
    Be their light and guide;
Keep, O keep them, in their weakness,
    At thy side.

3 When in sorrow, when in danger,
    When in loneliness,
In thy love look down and comfort
    Their distress.

4 May the joy of thy salvation
    Be their strength and stay;
May they love and may they praise thee
    Day by day.

5 Holy Spirit, let thy teaching
    Sanctify their life;
Send thy grace, that they may conquer
    In the strife.

6. Father, Son, and Holy Spirit,
    God the One in Three,
Bless them, guard them, save them, keep them
    Near to thee.

Isabella Stephana Stevenson (1843–90) *and Compilers*

See also

495 O God of Bethel
468 O God, thou art my God

Many hymns under *Faith and Trust* (Nos. 297–315) are also suitable.

387 JERUSALEM D.L.M.

CHARLES HUBERT HASTINGS PARRY (1848–1918)
(arranged by GEORGE THALBEN-BALL)

And did those feet in an-cient time Walk up-on England's moun-tains green? And was the ho — ly Lamb of

387 (*continued*)

dark sa-tan-ic mills?

(add to Sw. & Gt.)

f a tempo   *ff*

2. Bring me my bow of burn-ing gold! Bring me my

ar-rows of de - sire! Bring me my spear! O clouds, un-

-fold! Bring me my char-i-ot of fire! I will not cease from men-tal fight, Nor shall my sword sleep in my hand, Till we have built Je-ru-sa-lem In England's

387 (*continued*)

green and pleas-ant land.

AND did those feet in ancient time
  Walk upon England's mountains green?
And was the holy Lamb of God
  On England's pleasant pastures seen?
And did the countenance divine
  Shine forth upon our clouded hills?
And was Jerusalem builded here
  Among those dark satanic mills?

2. Bring me my bow of burning gold!
    Bring me my arrows of desire!
  Bring me my spear! O clouds, unfold!
    Bring me my chariot of fire!
  I will not cease from mental fight,
    Nor shall my sword sleep in my hand,
  Till we have built Jerusalem
    In England's green and pleasant land.

William Blake (1757–1827)

388 SALONICA 4.10.10.10.4.

JOHN SEBASTIAN SCOTT (1881–)

Unison

C OME, labour on!
Who dares stand idle on the harvest plain,
While all around him waves the golden grain,
And to each servant doth the master say,
    'Go, work to-day'?

2 Come, labour on!
Away with gloomy doubt and faithless fear!
No arm so weak but may do service here:
By hands the feeblest can our God fulfil
    His righteous will.

3 Come, labour on!
No time for rest, till glows the western sky
Till the long shadows o'er our pathway lie,
And a glad sound comes with the setting sun,
    'Servant, well done!'

4. Come, labour on!
The toil is pleasant and the harvest sure;
Blessèd are those who to the end endure:
How full their joy, how deep their rest shall be,
    O Lord, with thee!

                        Jane Borthwick (1813–97)

T

389 CHARING 88.87.   STUDLEY LESLIE RUSSELL (1901–   )

FATHER, who on man dost shower
  Gifts of plenty from thy dower,
To thy people give the power
  All thy gifts to use aright.

2 Lift from this and every nation
  All that brings us degradation;
  Quell the forces of temptation;
    Put thine enemies to flight.

3 Be with us, thy strength supplying,
  That with energy undying,
  Every foe of man defying,
    We may rally to the fight.

4 Thou who art our captain ever,
  Lead us on to great endeavour;
  May thy Church the world deliver:
    Give us wisdom, courage, might.

5. Father, who hast sought and found us,
  Son of God, whose love has bound us,
  Holy Spirit, in us, round us,
    Hear us, Godhead infinite!

Percy Dearmer (1867–1936)

390 CRUDWELL 11.10.11.10. (Dactylic).   WALTER K. STANTON (1891–)

GOD of eternity, Lord of the ages,
    Father, and Spirit, and Saviour of men,
Thine is the glory of time's numbered pages;
    Thine is the power to revive us again.

2 Thankful we come to thee, Lord of the nations,
    Praising thy faithfulness, mercy, and grace,
Shown to our fathers in past generations,
    Pledge of thy love to our people and race.

3 Head of the Church on earth, risen, ascended,
    Thine is the honour that dwells in this place:
As thou hast blessed us through years that have ended,
    Still lift upon us the light of thy face.

4. Pardon our sinfulness, God of all pity,
    Call to remembrance thy mercies of old;
Strengthen thy Church to abide as a city
    Set on a hill for a light to thy fold.

Ernest Northcroft Merrington (1876–1953)

391 GRAFTON 87.87.87.

French Melody

G OD of grace and God of glory,
   On thy people pour thy power;
Now fulfil thy Church's story;
   Bring her bud to glorious flower.
Grant us wisdom, grant us courage,
   For the facing of this hour.

2 Lo, the hosts of evil round us
   Scorn thy Christ, assail his ways;
From the fears that long have bound
   us
   Free our hearts to faith and praise.
Grant us wisdom, grant us courage,
   For the living of these days.

3 Cure thy children's warring madness,
   Bend our pride to thy control;
Shame our wanton selfish gladness,
   Rich in goods and poor in soul.
Grant us wisdom, grant us courage,
   Lest we miss thy kingdom's goal.

4. Set our feet on lofty places,
   Gird our lives that they may be
Armoured with all Christ-like graces
   In the fight to set men free.
Grant us wisdom, grant us courage,
   That we fail not man nor thee.

Harry Emerson Fosdick (1878–1969) *and Compilers*

392 NATIONAL ANTHEM 664.6664. *Thesaurus Musicus* (1745)

A Prayer for Queen and Empire

GOD save our gracious Queen,
Long live our noble Queen,
   God save the Queen!
Send her victorious,
Happy and glorious,
Long to reign over us;
   God save the Queen!

2 Thy choicest gifts in store
On her be pleased to pour,
   Long may she reign;
May she defend our laws,
And ever give us cause
To sing with heart and voice
   God save the Queen!

3. Of many a race and birth
From utmost ends of earth,
   God save us all!
Bid strife and hatred cease,
Bid hope and joy increase,
Spread universal peace,
   God save us all!
Anon.

393 RHUDDLAN 87.87.87.

Welsh Traditional Melody

JUDGE eternal, throned in splendour,
　Lord of lords and King of kings,
With thy living fire of judgment
　Purge this realm of bitter things:
Solace all its wide dominion
　With the healing of thy wings.

2 Still the weary folk are pining
　For the hour that brings release;
And the city's crowded clangour
　Cries aloud for sin to cease;
And the homesteads and the woodlands
　Plead in silence for their peace.

3. Crown, O God, thine own endeavour;
　Cleave our darkness with thy sword;
Feed the faint and hungry heathen
　With the richness of thy word;
Cleanse the body of this empire
　Through the glory of the Lord.

Henry Scott Holland (1847-1918)

394 KING'S LYNN 76.76.D. English Traditional Melody

Unison

O GOD of earth and altar,
  Bow down and hear our cry;
Our earthly rulers falter,
  Our people drift and die;
The walls of gold entomb us,
  The swords of scorn divide,
Take not thy thunder from us,
  But take away our pride.

2 From all that terror teaches,
    From lies of tongue and pen,
  From all the easy speeches
    That comfort cruel men,

From sale and profanation
  Of honour and the sword,
From sleep and from damnation,
  Deliver us, good Lord!

3. Tie in a living tether
    The prince and priest and thrall;
  Bind all our lives together,
    Smite us and save us all;
  In ire and exultation,
    Aflame with faith, and free,
  Lift up a living nation,
    A single sword to thee.

Gilbert Keith Chesterton (1874–1936)

395 DONNE SECOURS 11.10.11.10.
(PSALM 12)

Composed or adapted by Louis Bourgeois
in *Genevan Psalter* (1547)

SERVICE AND CITIZENSHIP

THE King, O God, his heart to thee upraiseth;
  With him the nation bows before thy face;
With high thanksgiving thee thy glad Church praiseth,
  Our strength thy spirit, our trust and hope thy grace.

2 Unto great honour, glory undeservèd,
    Hast thou exalted us, and drawn thee nigh;
  Nor, from thy judgments when our feet had swervèd,
    Didst thou forsake, nor leave us, Lord most high.

3 In thee our fathers trusted and were savèd;
    In thee destroyèd thrones of tyrants proud;
  From ancient bondage freed the poor enslavèd;
    To sow thy truth poured out their saintly blood.

4 Unto our minds give freedom and uprightness;
    Let strength and courage lead o'er land and wave;
  To our souls' armour grant celestial brightness,
    Joy to our hearts, and faith beyond the grave.

5. Our plenteous nation still in power extending,
    Increase our joy, uphold us by thy word;
  Beauty and wisdom all our ways attending,
    Good will to man and peace through Christ our Lord.

Robert Bridges (1844–1930)

See also

349	Behold us, Lord, a little space	380	Lord Christ, who on thy heart
23	Eternal God, whose power	376	O brother man
273	God of love and truth	85	O crucified Redeemer
379	Jesus, my Lord, how rich	359	O God of truth
34	Lift up your heads, ye mighty gates	377	Son of God

396 DUNFERMLINE C.M.

Scottish Psalter (1615)

SUNDAY

BEHOLD, we come, dear Lord, to thee,
    And bow before thy throne;
We come to offer on our knee
    Our vows to thee alone.

2 Whate'er we have, whate'er we are,
    Thy bounty freely gave;
Thou dost us here in mercy spare,
    And wilt hereafter save.

3 Come then, my soul, bring all thy powers,
    And grieve thou hast no more;
Bring every day thy choicest hours,
    And thy great God adore.

4. But, above all, prepare thine heart
    On this, his own blest day,
In its sweet task to bear thy part,
    And sing and love and pray.

John Austin (1613–69)

397 S. MAWES 88.88.88. WALTER K. STANTON (1891–   )

COME, let us with our Lord arise,
Our Lord, who made both earth and skies;
Who died to save the world he made,
And rose triumphant from the dead;
He rose, the Prince of life and peace,
And sealed the day for ever his.

2. This is the day the Lord hath made,
That all may see his love displayed,
May feel his Resurrection's power,
And rise again to fall no more,
In perfect righteousness renewed,
And filled with all the life of God.

Charles Wesley (1707–88) *and Compilers*

398 FARLEY CASTLE 10.10.10.10.   HENRY LAWES (1596–1662)

(v.4 starts here)

M OST glorious Lord of life, that on this day
Didst make thy triumph over death and sin,
And having harrowed hell, didst bring away
Captivity thence captive, us to win:

2 This joyous day, dear Lord, with joy begin,
And grant that we, for whom thou diddest die,
Being with thy dear blood clean washed from sin,
May live for ever in felicity:

3 And that thy love we, weighing worthily,
May likewise love thee for the same again;
And for thy sake, that all like dear didst buy,
With love may one another entertain.

4. So let us love, dear Love, like as we ought,
Love is the lesson which the Lord us taught.

Edmund Spenser (c. 1552–99)

399 FALCON STREET S.M.

Later form of melody by ISAAC SMITH
(c. 1725–c. 1800)

1. THIS is the day of light:
   Let there be light to-day;
   O Dayspring, rise upon our night,
   And chase its gloom away.

2. This is the day of rest:
   Our failing strength renew;
   On weary brain and troubled breast
   Shed thou thy freshening dew.

3. This is the day of peace:
   Thy peace our spirits fill;
   Bid thou the blasts of discord cease,
   The waves of strife be still.

4. This is the day of prayer:
   Let earth to heaven draw near;
   Lift up our hearts to seek thee there,
   Come down to meet us here.

5. This is the first of days:
   Send forth thy quickening breath,
   And wake dead souls to love and praise,
   Thou vanquisher of death.

John Ellerton (1826–93)

400 BROMSGROVE C.M.

Later form of melody from
Psalmodia Evangelica (1789)

THIS is the day the Lord hath made;
    He calls the hours his own;
Let heaven rejoice, let earth be glad,
    And praise surround the throne.

2 This day he rose and left the dead,
    And Satan's empire fell;
This day the saints his triumphs spread,
    And all his wonders tell.

3 Hosanna to the anointed King,
    To David's holy Son!
O help us, Lord; descend and bring
    Salvation from thy throne.

4. Hosanna in the highest strains
    The Church on earth can raise;
The highest heavens in which he reigns
    Shall give him nobler praise.

Isaac Watts (1674–1748) and Compilers
Based on Psalm 118

See also No. 325 King of glory

401 TRURO L.M.   *Psalmodia Evangelica* (1789)

A<small>LL</small> praise to thee, who safe hast kept
And hast refreshed me whilst I slept;
Grant, Lord, when I from death shall wake,
I may of endless light partake.

2 Lord, I my vows to thee renew,
Disperse my sins as morning dew;
Guard my first springs of thought and will,
And with thyself my spirit fill.

3 Direct, control, suggest, this day
All I design or do or say;
That all my powers, with all their might,
In thy sole glory may unite.

4. Praise God, from whom all blessings flow;
Praise him, all creatures here below;
Praise him above, ye heavenly host;
Praise Father, Son, and Holy Ghost. Amen.

Thomas Ken (1637–1711)

A - men.

402 HEATHLANDS 77.77.77.

HENRY SMART (1813–79)

A<small>T</small> thy feet, O Christ, we lay
Thine own gift of this new day;
Doubt of what it holds in store
Makes us crave thine aid the more;
Lest it prove a time of loss,
Mark it, Saviour, with thy Cross.

2 If it flow on calm and bright,
Be thyself our chief delight;
If it bring unknown distress,
Good is all that thou canst bless;
Only, while its hours begin,
Pray we, keep them clear of sin.

3 Fain would we thy word embrace,
Live each moment on thy grace,
All our selves to thee consign,
Fold up all our wills in thine,
Think and speak and do and be
Simply that which pleases thee.

4. Hear us, Lord, and that right soon;
Hear, and grant the choicest boon
That thy love can e'er impart,
Loyal singleness of heart;
So shall this and all our days,
Christ our God, show forth thy
praise.

William Bright (1824–1901)

403 MORNING HYMN L.M.   François Hippolyte Barthélémon (1741–1808)

AWAKE, my soul, and with the sun
Thy daily stage of duty run;
Shake off dull sloth, and joyful rise
To pay thy morning sacrifice.

2 Thy precious time mis-spent redeem,
Each present day thy last esteem;
Improve thy talent with due care,
For the great day thyself prepare.

3 In conversation be sincere,
Keep conscience as the noon-tide clear;
Think how all-seeing God thy ways
And all thy secret thoughts surveys.

4 By influence of the light divine
Let thy own light to others shine;
Reflect all heaven's propitious rays
In ardent love and cheerful praise.

5. Praise God, from whom all blessings flow;
Praise him, all creatures here below;
Praise him above, ye heavenly host;
Praise Father, Son, and Holy Ghost. Amen.

Thomas Ken (1637–1711)

A - men.

404 MEINE ARMUTH 847. D.

JOHANN ANASTASIUS FREYLINGHAUSEN
(1670–1739)

MORNING

Seele du musst munter werden

COME, my soul, thou must be waking;
　　　Now is breaking
　　O'er the earth another day:
　Come to him who made this splendour;
　　　See thou render
　　All thy feeble strength can pay.

2 Gladly hail the light returning;
　　　Ready burning
　　Be the incense of thy powers:
　For the night is safely ended;
　　　God hath tended
　　With his care thy helpless hours.

3 Pray that he may prosper ever
　　　Each endeavour
　　When thine aim is good and true;
　But that he may ever thwart thee,
　　　And convert thee,
　　From the ill thou wouldst pursue.

4. May'st thou then on life's last morrow,
　　　Free from sorrow,
　　Pass away in slumber sweet;
　And, released from death's dark sadness,
　　　Rise in gladness,
　　That far brighter sun to greet.

Friedrich Rudolf Ludwig von Canitz (1654–99)
Tr. Henry James Buckoll (1803–71) *and Compilers*

405 CHRISTE SANCTORUM 11.11.11.5.

Melody by
FRANÇOIS DE LA FEILLÉE (1808)

Nocte surgentes

FATHER, we praise thee, now the night is over;
  Active and watchful, stand we all before thee;
Singing, we offer prayer and meditation:
      Thus we adore thee.

2 Monarch of all things, fit us for thy mansions;
  Banish our weakness, health and wholeness sending;
Bring us to heaven, where thy saints united
      Joy without ending.

3. All-holy Father, Son, and equal Spirit,
  Trinity blessèd, send us thy salvation;
Thine is the glory, gleaming and resounding
      Through all creation. Amen.

Ascribed to S. Gregory the Great (540-604)
Tr. Percy Dearmer (1867-1936)

406 ANGELS' SONG   L.M.
(SONG 34)

Melody and Bass by
ORLANDO GIBBONS (1583–1625)

FORTH in thy name, O Lord, I go,
   My daily labour to pursue;
Thee, only thee, resolved to know,
   In all I think or speak or do.

2 The task thy wisdom hath assigned
   O let me cheerfully fulfil,
In all my works thy presence find,
   And prove thy good and perfect will.

3 Thee may I set at my right hand,
   Whose eyes my inmost substance see,
And labour on at thy command,
   And offer all my works to thee.

4 Give me to bear thy easy yoke,
   And every moment watch and pray,
And still to things eternal look,
   And hasten to thy glorious day;

5. For thee delightfully employ
   Whate'er thy bounteous grace hath given,
And run my course with even joy,
   And closely walk with thee to heaven.

Charles Wesley (1707–88) *and others*

407 S. TIMOTHY C.M.

HENRY WILLIAMS BAKER (1821–77)
arranged by WILLIAM HENRY MONK (1823–89)

MY Father, for another night
    Of quiet sleep and rest,
For all the joy of morning light,
    Thy holy name be blest.

2 Now with the new-born day I give
    Myself anew to thee,
That as thou willest I may live,
    And what thou willest be.

3 Whate'er I do, things great or small,
    Whate'er I speak or frame,
Thy glory may I seek in all,
    Do all in Jesus' name.

4. My Father, for his sake, I pray,
    Thy child accept and bless;
And lead me by thy grace to-day
    In paths of righteousness.

Henry Williams Baker (1821–77)

408 MELCOMBE L.M.   SAMUEL WEBBE the elder (1740–1816)

O timely happy, timely wise,
Hearts that with rising morn arise,
Eyes that the beam celestial view
Which evermore makes all things new.

[In *The Christian Year* the above lines (not to be sung) precede the hymn.]

MORNING

NEW every morning is the love
　Our wakening and uprising prove;
Through sleep and darkness safely brought,
Restored to life and power and thought.

2 New mercies, each returning day,
　Hover around us while we pray;
　New perils past, new sins forgiven,
　New thoughts of God, new hopes of heaven.

3 If on our daily course our mind
　Be set to hallow all we find,
　New treasures still, of countless price,
　God will provide for sacrifice.

4 Old friends, old scenes, will lovelier be,
　As more of heaven in each we see;
　Some softening gleam of love and prayer
　Shall dawn on every cross and care.

5 The trivial round, the common task,
　Would furnish all we ought to ask,
　Room to deny ourselves, a road
　To bring us daily nearer God.

6. Only, O Lord, in thy dear love
　Fit us for perfect rest above;
　And help us, this and every day,
　To live more nearly as we pray.

John Keble (1792–1866)

409

ORLANDO L.M.   GEORGE THALBEN-BALL

MORNING

Splendor paternae gloriae

O SPLENDOUR of God's glory bright,
Who bringest forth the light from light;
O Light of light, light's fountain spring;
O Day, our days enlightening;

2 Come, very Sun of truth and love,
Come in thy radiance from above,
And shed the Holy Spirit's ray
On all we think or do to-day.

3 Likewise to thee our prayers ascend,
Father of glory without end,
Father of sovereign grace, for power
To conquer in temptation's hour.

4 Teach us to work with all our might;
Beat back the devil's threatening spite;
Turn all to good that seems most ill;
Help us our calling to fulfil.

5. All praise to God the Father be,
All praise, eternal Son, to thee,
Whom with the Spirit we adore,
For ever and for evermore. Amen.

S. Ambrose (? 340–97)
Tr. Compilers of Hymns A. & M.

410 TEMPLE 66.84.   HENRY WALFORD DAVIES (1869–1941)

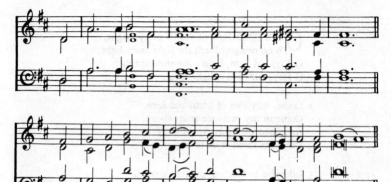

Jam lucis orto sidere

THE star of morn has risen:
  O Lord, to thee we pray;
O uncreated Light of light,
  Guide thou our way.

2 Sinless be tongue and hand,
    And innocent the mind;
  Let simple truth be on our lips,
    Our hearts be kind.

3 As day rolls swiftly on,
    Still, Lord, our guardian be;
  And keep the entry of our hearts
    From evil free.

4. Grant that our daily toil
    May to thy glory tend;
  And as our hours begin with thee,
    So may they end.

c. 8th cent.
Tr. Greville Phillimore (1821–84) and Compilers

See also
137 Christ, whose glory fills the skies
285 When morning gilds the skies

411 S. PETER C.M.   ALEXANDER ROBERT REINAGLE (1799–1877)

Labente jam solis rota

AS now the sun's declining rays
    At eventide descend,
So life's brief day is sinking down
    To its appointed end.

2. Lord, on the Cross thine arms were stretched
    To draw thy people nigh;
O grant us then that Cross to love,
    And in those arms to die.

Charles Coffin (1676–1749)
Tr. John Chandler (1806–76) *and others*

412 ANGELUS L.M.

Cantica Spiritualia (1847), founded on a melody by GEORG JOSEPH (*c.* 1657)

AT even, when the sun did set,
 The sick, O Lord, around thee lay;
O in what divers pains they met!
 O with what joy they went away!

2 Once more 'tis eventide, and we,
 Oppressed with various ills, draw near;
What if thy form we cannot see?
 We know and feel that thou art here.

3 O Saviour Christ, our woes dispel;
 For some are sick, and some are sad,
And some have never loved thee well,
 And some have lost the love they had.

4 And none, O Lord, have perfect rest,
 For none are wholly free from sin;
And they who fain would serve thee best
 Are conscious most of wrong within.

5 O Saviour Christ, thou too art man;
 Thou hast been troubled, tempted, tried;
Thy kind but searching glance can scan
 The very wounds that shame would hide.

6. Thy touch has still its ancient power,
 No word from thee can fruitless fall;
Hear in this solemn evening hour,
 And in thy mercy heal us all.

Henry Twells (1823–1900)
Based on S. Mark 1, 32

413 TE LUCIS

First Tune

Mode viii

Te lucis ante terminum

BEFORE the ending of the day,
Creator of the world, we pray
That with thy wonted favour thou
Wouldst be our guard and keeper now.

2 From all ill dreams defend our eyes,
From nightly fears and fantasies;
Tread under foot our ghostly foe,
That no pollution we may know.

3. O Father, that we ask be done,
Through Jesus Christ, thine only Son;
Who, with the Holy Ghost and thee,
Doth live and reign eternally. Amen.

Before 8th cent.
Tr. John Mason Neale (1818–66)

A - men.

413 TE LUCIS

ON FERIAS

Second Tune

Mode viii

Te lucis ante terminum

BEFORE the ending of the day,
Creator of the world, we pray
That with thy wonted favour thou
Wouldst be our guard and keeper now.

2 From all ill dreams defend our eyes,
From nightly fears and fantasies;
Tread under foot our ghostly foe,
That no pollution we may know.

3. O Father, that we ask be done,
Through Jesus Christ, thine only Son;
Who, with the Holy Ghost and thee,
Doth live and reign eternally. Amen.

Before 8th cent.
Tr. John Mason Neale (1818–66)

U

414 TALLIS' CANON L.M.

THOMAS TALLIS (*c.* 1510–*c.* 1585)

GLORY to thee, my God, this night
For all the blessings of the light;
Keep me, O keep me, King of kings,
Beneath thy own almighty wings.

2 Forgive me, Lord, for thy dear Son,
The ill that I this day have done,
That with the world, myself, and thee,
I, ere I sleep, at peace may be.

3 Teach me to live, that I may dread
The grave as little as my bed;
Teach me to die, that so I may
Rise glorious at the aweful day.

4 O may my soul on thee repose,
And with sweet sleep mine eyelids close,
Sleep that may me more vigorous make
To serve my God when I awake.

5 When in the night I sleepless lie,
My soul with heavenly thoughts supply;
Let no ill dreams disturb my rest,
No powers of darkness me molest.

6. Praise God, from whom all blessings flów,
Praise him, all creatures here below,
Praise him above, ye heavenly host,
Praise Father, Son, and Holy Ghost. Amen.

Thomas Ken (1637–1711)

415 AR HYD Y NOS 84.84.88.84.

Welsh Traditional Melody

GOD, that madest earth and heaven,
　　Darkness and light;
Who the day for toil hast given,
　　For rest the night;
May thine angel-guards defend us,
Slumber sweet thy mercy send us,
Holy dreams and hopes attend us,
　　This livelong night.

2. Guard us waking, guard us sleeping;
　　And, when we die,
May we in thy mighty keeping
　　All peaceful lie;
When the last dread call shall wake us,
Do not thou, our God, forsake us,
But to reign in glory take us
　　With thee on high.

Reginald Heber (1783–1826)
Richard Whately (1787–1863)

416 LESSINGTON Irregular.   REGINALD S. THATCHER (1888–1957)

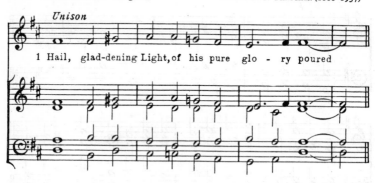

Unison

1 Hail, glad-dening Light, of his pure glo - ry poured

Who is th'im-mor-tal Fa-ther, heaven - ly, blest,

Ho - li-est of ho-lies, Je - sus Christ, our Lord.

EVENING

Unison

2 Now we are come to the sun's hour of rest,

Trebles sing Descant

The lights of eve - ning round us shine,

We hymn the Fa-ther, Son, and Ho-ly Spi-rit di - vine.

Harmony

3. Wor - thiest art thou at all times to be sung

416 (*continued*)

With un-de-fil-èd tongue, Son of our God, giv-er of life, a-lone;

Unison

There-fore in all the world thy glo-ries, Lord, they own.

Descant

Φῶς ἱλαρόν

HAIL, gladdening Light, of his pure glory poured
Who is the immortal Father, heavenly, blest,
Holiest of holies, Jesus Christ, our Lord.

2 Now we are come to the sun's hour of rest,
The lights of evening round us shine,
We hymn the Father, Son, and Holy Spirit divine.

3. Worthiest art thou at all times to be sung
With undefilèd tongue,
Son of our God, giver of life, alone;
Therefore in all the world thy glories, Lord, they own.

3rd cent. or earlier. Tr. John Keble (1792–1866)

See also No. 514 (CS)

417 CARSAIG 77.75.

GEORGE THALBEN-BALL

HOLY Father, cheer our way,
With thy love's perpetual ray:
Grant us every closing day
   Light at evening time.

2 Holy Saviour, calm our fears
When earth's brightness disappears;
Grant us in our later years
   Light at evening time.

3 Holy Spirit, be thou nigh
When in mortal pains we lie;
Grant us, as we come to die,
   Light at evening time.

4. Holy, blessèd Trinity,
Darkness is not dark with thee;
Those thou keepest always see
   Light at evening time.

Richard Hayes Robinson (1842–92)
Based on Zechariah 14, 7

418 CHRISTE SANCTORUM 11.11.11.5.

Melody by
FRANÇOIS DE LA FEILLÉE (1808)

Die Nacht ist kommen

NOW it is evening; time to cease from labour;
Father, according to thy will and pleasure,
Through the night-season, have thy faithful people
 Safe in thy keeping.

2 Far from our dwellings drive the evil spirits;
Under the shadow of thy wings protect us;
Be thou our guardian through the hours of darkness,
 Strong to defend us.

3 Call we, ere sleeping, on the name of Jesus;
Rise we at day-break, strong to serve thee better;
Order our goings, well begun and ended,
 All to thy glory.

4 Fountain of goodness, bless the sick and needy;
Visit the captive, solace the afflicted;
Shelter the stranger, lull the babe to slumber,
 Foster the orphan.

5. Father, who neither slumberest nor sleepest,
Thou, to whom darkness is as clear as noon-day,
Have us this night-time, for the sake of Jesus,
 Safe in thy keeping.

Petrus Herbert (died 1571)
Tr. George Ratcliffe Woodward (1848–1934) and Compilers

EVENING

419 EUDOXIA 65.65.   SABINE BARING-GOULD (1834-1924)

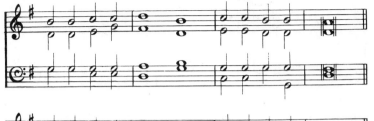

For Young Children

N<small>OW</small> the day is over,
  Night is drawing nigh,
Shadows of the evening
  Steal across the sky.

2 Now the darkness gathers,
    Stars begin to peep,
  Birds and beasts and flowers
    Soon will be asleep.

3 Jesus, give the weary
    Calm and sweet repose;
  With thy tenderest blessing
    May mine eyelids close.

4 Grant to little children
    Visions bright of thee;
  Guard the sailors tossing
    On the deep blue sea.

5 Comfort every sufferer
    Watching late in pain;
  Those who plan some evil
    From their sin restrain.

6 Through the long night-watches
    May thine angels spread
  Their white wings above me,
    Watching round my bed.

7 When the morning wakens,
    Then may I arise
  Pure and fresh and sinless
    In thy holy eyes.

8. Glory to the Father,
    Glory to the Son,
  And to thee, blest Spirit,
    Whilst all ages run. Amen.

Sabine Baring-Gould (1834-1924)

See also No. 420

A - men.

420 EUDOXIA 65.65.　　　　　　　　SABINE BARING-GOULD (1834–1924)

NOW the day is over,
　　Night is drawing nigh,
Shadows of the evening
　　Steal across the sky.

2 Jesus, give the weary
　　Calm and sweet repose;
With thy tenderest blessing
　　May mine eyelids close.

3 Comfort every sufferer
　　Watching late in pain;
Those who plan some evil
　　From their sin restrain.

4 When the morning wakens,
　　Then may I arise
Pure and fresh and sinless
　　In thy holy eyes.

5. Glory to the Father,
　　Glory to the Son,
And to thee, blest Spirit,
　　Whilst all ages run. Amen

Sabine Baring-Gould (1834–1924)

See also No. 419

A - men.

421

Christe, qui lux es et dies

O CHRIST, who art the light and day,
Thou drivest night and gloom away;
O Light of light, whose word doth show
The light of heaven to us below;

2 All-holy Lord, in humble prayer
We ask to-night thy watchful care:
O grant us calm repose in thee,
A quiet night from perils free.

3 Asleep though wearied eyes may be,
Still keep the heart awake to thee;
Let thy right hand outstretched above
Guard those who serve the Lord they love.

4. All praise to God the Father be,
All praise, eternal Son, to thee,
Whom with the Spirit we adore,
For ever and for evermore. Amen.

6th cent. Tr. William John Copeland (1804–85)
and Compilers of Hymns A. & M.

Metrical tune and words overleaf.

A - men.

421 REX GLORIOSE L.M.

Andernach Gesangbuch (1608)

Christe, qui lux es et dies

O CHRIST, who art the light and day,
Thou drivest night and gloom away;
O Light of light, whose word doth show
The light of heaven to us below;

2 All-holy Lord, in humble prayer
We ask to-night thy watchful care:
O grant us calm repose in thee,
A quiet night from perils free.

3 Asleep though wearied eyes may be,
Still keep the heart awake to thee;
Let thy right hand outstretched above
Guard those who serve the Lord they love.

4. All praise to God the Father be,
All praise, eternal Son, to thee,
Whom with the Spirit we adore,
For ever and for evermore. Amen.

6th cent. Tr. *William John Copeland* (1804-85)
and *Compilers of Hymns A. & M.*

A - men.

422 SEELENBRÄUTIGAM 55.88.55.   ADAM DRESE (1620–1701)

R OUND me falls the night;
    Saviour, be my light:
Through the hours in darkness shrouded
Let me see thy face unclouded;
    Let thy glory shine
    In this heart of mine.

2   Earthly work is done,
    Earthly sounds are none;
Rest in sleep and silence seeking,
Let me hear thee softly speaking;
    In my spirit's ear
    Whisper, 'I am near'.

3.   Blessèd, heavenly Light,
    Shining through earth's night;
Voice that oft of love hast told me;
Arms so strong to clasp and hold me;
    Thou thy watch wilt keep,
    Saviour, o'er my sleep.

                    William Romanis (1824–99)

423 COOLINGE 10.10.10.10.

Cyril V. Taylor (1907–)

SAVIOUR, again to thy dear name we raise
With one accord our parting hymn of praise.
Guard thou the lips from sin, the hearts from shame,
That in this house have called upon thy name.

2 Grant us thy peace, Lord, through the coming night;
Turn thou for us its darkness into light;
From harm and danger keep thy children free,
For dark and light are both alike to thee.

3 Grant us thy peace throughout our earthly life;
Peace to thy Church from error and from strife;
Peace to our land, the fruit of truth and love;
Peace in each heart, thy Spirit from above:

4. Thy peace in life, the balm of every pain;
Thy peace in death, the hope to rise again;
Then, when thy voice shall bid our conflict cease,
Call us, O Lord, to thine eternal peace.

John Ellerton (1826–93)

424 BIRLING L.M. From an early-19th-century MS.

'Tis gone, that bright and orbèd blaze,
Fast fading from our wistful gaze:
Yon mantling cloud has hid from sight
The last faint pulse of quivering light.

In darkness and in weariness
The traveller on his way must press;
No gleam to watch on tree or tower,
Whiling away the lonesome hour.

[In *The Christian Year* the above verses (not to be sung) begin the hymn.]

SUN of my soul, thou Saviour dear,
It is not night if thou be near:
O may no earth-born cloud arise
To hide thee from thy servant's eyes.

2 When the soft dews of kindly sleep
My wearied eyelids gently steep,
Be my last thought, how sweet to rest
For ever on my Saviour's breast.

3 Abide with me from morn till eve,
For without thee I cannot live;
Abide with me when night is nigh,
For without thee I dare not die.

4 If some poor wandering child of thine
Have spurned to-day the voice divine,
Now, Lord, the gracious work begin;
Let him no more lie down in sin.

5 Watch by the sick; enrich the poor
With blessings from thy boundless store;
Be every mourner's sleep to-night
Like infant's slumbers, pure and light.

6. Come near and bless us when we wake,
Ere through the world our way we take;
Till in the ocean of thy love
We lose ourselves in heaven above.

John Keble (1792–1866)

425 HOMINUM AMATOR 76.76.88. WILLIAM HAROLD FERGUSON (1874–1950)

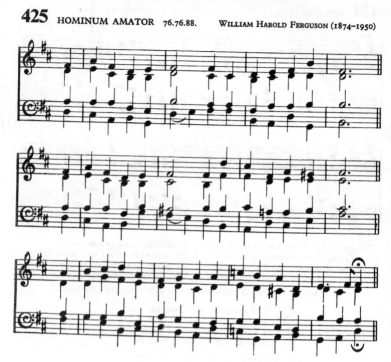

EVENING

Τὴν ἡμέραν διελθών

THE day is past and over;
  All thanks, O Lord, to thee;
I pray thee now that sinless
  The hours of dark may be.
O Jesus, keep me in thy sight,
And guard me through the coming night.

2   The joys of day are over;
  I lift my heart to thee,
And pray thee that offenceless
  The hours of dark may be.
O Jesus, make their darkness light,
And guard me through the coming night.

3   The toils of day are over;
  I raise the hymn to thee,
And pray that free from peril
  The hours of dark may be.
O Jesus, keep me in thy sight,
And guard me through the coming night.

4.   Be thou my soul's preserver,
  For thou alone dost know
How many are the perils
  Through which I have to go.
Lover of men, O hear my call,
And guard and save me from them all.

? 6th cent.
Tr. John Mason Neale (1818–66) *and others*

For another translation of these words see No. 509 (CS)

426 GOTT WILL'S MACHEN 98.98.

Adapted from JOHANN LUDWIG STEINER
(1688–1761)

S. CLEMENT 98.98.

CLEMENT COTTERILL SCHOLEFIELD (1839–1904)

EVENING

THE day thou gavest, Lord, is ended,
   The darkness falls at thy behest;
To thee our morning hymns ascended,
   Thy praise shall sanctify our rest.

2 We thank thee that thy Church unsleeping,
   While earth rolls onward into light,
Through all the world her watch is keeping,
   And rests not now by day or night.

3 As o'er each continent and island
   The dawn leads on another day,
The voice of prayer is never silent,
   Nor dies the strain of praise away.

4 The sun that bids us rest is waking
   Our brethren 'neath the western sky,
And hour by hour fresh lips are making
   Thy wondrous doings heard on high.

5. So be it, Lord! thy throne shall never,
   Like earth's proud empires, pass away;
Thy kingdom stands, and grows for ever,
   Till all thy creatures own thy sway.

John Ellerton (1826–93)

427 O WELT ICH MUSS DICH LASSEN
(INNSBRUCK) 776.778.

Traditional German Melody, possibly by
HEINRICH ISAAK (c. 1455–1520)

O WELT ICH MUSS DICH LASSEN
(INNSBRUCK) 776.778.

The same, adapted by JOHANN SEBASTIAN BACH
(1685–1750)

EVENING

Nun ruhen alle Wälder

THE duteous day now closeth,
  Each flower and tree reposeth,
    Shade creeps o'er wild and wood:
Let us, as night is falling,
On God our Maker calling,
  Give thanks to him, the Giver good.

2 Now all the heavenly splendour
  Breaks forth in starlight tender
    From myriad worlds unknown;
And man, the marvel seeing,
Forgets his selfish being,
  For joy of beauty not his own.

3. Awhile his mortal blindness
  May miss God's loving-kindness,
    And grope in faithless strife:
But when life's day is over
Shall death's fair night discover
  The fields of everlasting life.

Paulus Gerhardt (1607–76)
Par. Robert Bridges (1844–1930)

428 S. COLUMBA 64.66.   HERBERT STEPHEN IRONS (1834-1905)

Sol praeceps rapitur

THE sun is sinking fast,
  The daylight dies;
Let love awake, and pay
  Her evening sacrifice.

2 As Christ upon the Cross
  His head inclined,
And to his Father's hands
  His parting soul resigned;

3 So now herself my soul
  Would wholly give
Into his sacred charge
  In whom all spirits live;

4 So now beneath his eye
  Would calmly rest,
Without a wish or thought
  Abiding in the breast;

5 Save that his will be done,
  Whate'er betide,
Dead to herself, and dead
  In him to all beside.

6 Thus would I live; yet now
  Not I, but he
In all his power and love
  Henceforth alive in me:

7. One sacred Trinity,
  One Lord divine;
Myself for ever his,
  And he for ever mine.

? 19*th cent. Tr. Edward Caswall* (1814-78)

See also

509 Darkening night (CS)
514 Hail! gladdening Light (CS)
527 Now cheer our hearts (CS)

NEW YEAR

429 INNOCENTS 77.77. *From The Parish Choir (1850)*

FOR thy mercy and thy grace,
  Faithful through another year,
Hear our song of thankfulness,
  Father and Redeemer, hear.

2 In our weakness and distress,
  Rock of strength, be thou our stay;
In the pathless wilderness
  Be our true and living way.

3. Keep us faithful, keep us pure,
  Keep us evermore thine own;
Help, O help us to endure;
  Fit us for the promised crown.

Henry Downton (1818–85)

430 ABBEY C.M.   *Scottish Psalter (1615)*

NEW YEAR

O THOU, whom neither time nor space
      Can limit, hold, or bind,
Look down from heaven, thy dwelling-place,
      With mercy on mankind.

2 Another year has now begun:
      Thy loving care renew;
Forgive the ill that we have done,
      The good we failed to do.

3 In doubt or danger all our days
      Be near to guard us still;
Let all our thoughts and all our ways
      Be governed by thy will.

4. O help us on this earth to live
      From selfish passions free;
And at the last in mercy give
      Immortal life with thee.

Horace Smith (1836–1922) and Compilers

See also

487 Come, let us to the Lord
352 Father, hear the prayer
244 From glory to glory
390 God of eternity
140 Guide me
459 I to the hills
144 Jesu, guide our way
277 Now thank we all our God

181 Rejoice, O people
364 Rise up, O men of God!
 26 The Lord is King!
481 Through all the changing scenes
186 Through the night of doubt
255 We come unto our fathers' God
371 Who would true valour see

Many hymns under *God: his Nature, Providence, and Works* (Nos. 1–22) and *Faith and Trust* (Nos. 297–315) are also suitable.

PLOUGH SUNDAY

431 SUSSEX 87.87. Adapted from an English Traditional Melody

B^Y the rutted roads we follow,
    Fallow fields are rested now;
All along the waking country
    Soil is waiting for the plough.

2 In the yard the plough is ready,
    Ready to the ploughman's hand,
Ready for the crow-straight furrow,
    Farmer's sign across God's land.

3 God, in this good land you lend us,
    Bless the service of the share;
Light our thinking with your wisdom,
    Plant your patience in our care.

4. This is first of all man's labours,
    Man must always plough the earth;
God, be with us at the ploughing,
    Touch our harvest at its birth.

John Arlott (1914–   )

See also

2	All creatures of our God	495	O God of Bethel
455	God of mercy	471	O worship the King
463	My soul, praise the Lord!	444	We plough the fields

432 MANCHESTER C.M.   ROBERT WAINWRIGHT (1748–82)

ROGATIONTIDE

LORD, while for all mankind we pray
   Of every clime and coast,
O hear us for our native land,
   The land we love the most.

2 O guard our shores from every foe;
   With peace our borders bless;
With prosperous times our cities crown,
   Our fields with plenteousness.

3 Unite us in the sacred love
   Of knowledge, truth, and thee;
And let our hills and valleys shout
   The songs of liberty.

4. Lord of the nations, thus to thee
   Our country we commend;
Be thou her refuge and her trust,
   Her everlasting friend.

John Reynell Wreford (1800–81)

433 WAREHAM L.M.

Later version of melody by
WILLIAM KNAPP (1698–1768)

REJOICE, O land, in God thy might;
His will obey, him serve aright;
For thee the saints uplift their voice:
Fear not, O land, in God rejoice.

2 Glad shalt thou be, with blessing crowned,
With joy and peace thou shalt abound;
Yea, love with thee shall make his home
Until thou see God's kingdom come.

3. He shall forgive thy sins untold:
Remember thou his love of old;
Walk in his way, his word adore,
And keep his truth for evermore.

Robert Bridges (1844–1930)
Based on Joel 2, 21

434 CHRISTCHURCH 66.66.88.   CHARLES STEGGALL (1826–1905)

To thee our God we fly
For mercy and for grace;
O hear our lowly cry,
And hide not thou thy face.
O Lord, stretch forth thy mighty hand,
And guard and bless our fatherland.

2 Arise, O Lord of hosts!
   Be jealous for thy name,
And drive from out our coasts
   The sins that put to shame:

3 Thy best gifts from on high
   In rich abundance pour,
That we may magnify
   And praise thee more and more:

4*The powers ordained by thee
   With heavenly wisdom bless;
May they thy servants be,
   And rule in righteousness:

5*The Church of thy dear Son
   Inflame with love's pure fire;
Bind her once more in one,
   And life and truth inspire:

6*The pastors of thy fold
   With grace and power endue,
That faithful, pure, and bold,
   They may be pastors true:

7*O let us love thy house,
   And sanctify thy day,
Bring unto thee our vows,
   And loyal homage pay:

8*Give peace, Lord, in our time;
    O let no foe draw nigh,
Nor lawless deed of crime
    Insult thy majesty:

9. Though all unworthy, still
    Thy people, Lord, are we;
And for our God we will
    None other have but thee:

William Walsham How (1823–97) and Compilers

435 RODMELL C.M.   English Traditional Melody

WE watched the winter turn its back,
    Its grip is loosened now,
And shoot and leaf have signed their green
    On brown of field and bough.

2 From ambushed frost that kills by night,
    And storm with bludgeoned hand,
From soft and secret-moving blight,
    Dear God, protect our land.

3. And send soft rain to feed the crops,
    Sun-warm them gold and red;
So grant the prayer we learned from Christ,
    Give us our daily bread.

John Arlott (1914–   )

See also

2   All creatures of our God
455   God of mercy
495   O God of Bethel

436 HOLYROOD S.M.

JAMES WATSON (1816–80)

LAMMAS

FAIR waved the golden corn
In Canaan's pleasant land,
When full of joy, some shining morn,
Went forth the reaper-band.

2 To God so good and great
Their cheerful thanks they pour;
Then carry to his temple-gate
The choicest of their store.

3 For thus the holy word
Spoken by Moses ran:
'The first-ripe ears are for the Lord,
The rest he gives to man.'

4. Like Israel, Lord, we give
Our earliest fruits to thee,
And pray that, long as we shall live,
We may thy servants be.

John Hampden Gurney (1802–62) and Compilers
Based on Exodus 22, 29

437 STONEGATE 11.10.11.10.   CYRIL V. TAYLOR (1907–)

LORD, by whose breath all souls and seeds are living
   With life that is and life that is to be,
First-fruits of earth we offer with thanksgiving
   For fields in flood with summer's golden sea.

2 Lord of the earth, accept these gifts in token
   Thou in thy works art to be all-adored,
From whom the light as daily bread is broken,
   Sunset and dawn as wine and milk are poured.

3. Poor is our praise, but these shall be our psalter;
   Lo, like thyself they rose up from the dead;
Lord, give them back when at thy holy altar
   We feed on thee, who art our living bread.

Andrew Young (1885–)

438 WINDERMERE S.M.

ARTHUR SOMERVELL (1863–1937)

WE give thee but thine own,
Whate'er the gift may be;
All that we have is thine alone,
A trust, O Lord, from thee.

2. May we thy bounties thus
As stewards true receive,
And gladly, as thou blessest us,
To thee our first-fruits give.

William Walsham How (1823–97)

See also

2 All creatures of our God	14 O Lord of heaven
3 All things bright	471 O worship the King
272 For the beauty of the earth	442 Sing to the Lord of harvest
461 Let us, with a gladsome mind	443 To thee, O Lord
463 My soul, praise the Lord!	444 We plough the fields
266 O dearest Lord, by all adored	

439 S. GEORGE 77.77.D.
(WINDSOR)

GEORGE JOB ELVEY (1816–93)

COME, ye thankful people, come,
Raise the song of harvest-home:
All is safely gathered in,
Ere the winter storms begin;
God, our Maker, doth provide
For our wants to be supplied:
Come to God's own temple, come,
Raise the song of harvest-home.

2 All this world is God's own field,
Fruit unto his praise to yield;
Wheat and tares together sown,
Unto joy or sorrow grown;
First the blade, and then the ear,
Then the full corn shall appear:
Lord of harvest, grant that we
Wholesome grain and pure may be.

3 For the Lord our God shall come,
And shall take his harvest home;
From his field shall in that day
All offences purge away;
Give his angels charge at last
In the fire the tares to cast;
But the fruitful ears to store
In his garner evermore.

4. Even so, Lord, quickly come
To thy final harvest-home:
Gather thou thy people in,
Free from sorrow, free from sin;
There, for ever purified,
In thy presence to abide:
Come, with all thine angels, come,
Raise the glorious harvest-home.

Henry Alford (1810–71)
Based on S. Matthew 13, 37–43

X

440 SHIPSTON 87.87.   English Traditional Melody

GOD, whose farm is all creation,
    Take the gratitude we give;
Take the finest of our harvest,
    Crops we grow that men may live.

2 Take our ploughing, seeding, reaping,
    Hopes and fears of sun and rain,
All our thinking, planning, waiting,
    Ripened in this fruit and grain.

3. All our labour, all our watching,
    All our calendar of care,
In these crops of your creation,
    Take, O God: they are our prayer.

John Arlott (1914–   )

HARVEST

Melody from *Hymn Tunes of the United Brethren* (1824)
Arranged by JOHN WILKES (1785–1869)

PRAISE, O praise our God and King;
Hymns of adoration sing:
For his mercies still endure
Ever faithful, ever sure.

2 Praise him that he made the sun
Day by day his course to run:

3 And the silver moon by night,
Shining with her gentle light:

4 Praise him that he gave the rain
To mature the swelling grain:

5 And hath bid the fruitful field
Crops of precious increase yield:

6 Praise him for our harvest-store,
He hath filled the garner-floor:

7 And for richer food than this,
Pledge of everlasting bliss:

8. Glory to our bounteous King;
Glory let creation sing;
Glory to the Father, Son,
And blest Spirit, Three in One.
Amen.

Henry Williams Baker (1821–77)

A - men.

442 ELLACOMBE 76.76.D.   *Mainz Gesangbuch* (1833)

HARVEST

SING to the Lord of harvest,
   Sing songs of love and praise;
With joyful hearts and voices
   Your alleluias raise.
By him the rolling seasons
   In fruitful order move;
Sing to the Lord of harvest
   A song of happy love.

2 By him the clouds drop fatness,
   The desert's bloom and spring,
The hills leap up in gladness,
   The valleys laugh and sing.
He filleth with his fullness
   All things with large increase,
He crowns the year with goodness,
   With plenty and with peace.

3. Bring to his sacred altar
   The gifts his goodness gave,
The golden sheaves of harvest,
   The souls he died to save.
Your hearts lay down before him
   When at his feet ye fall,
And with your lives adore him,
   Who gave his life for all.

John Samuel Bewley Monsell (1811–75)
Based on Psalm 65

443 MEGERRAN 87.87.D.

WALTER K. STANTON (1891–   )

HARVEST

To thee, O Lord, our hearts we raise
   In hymns of adoration,
To thee bring sacrifice of praise
   With shouts of exultation.
Bright robes of gold the fields adorn,
   The hills with joy are ringing,
The valleys stand so thick with corn
   That even they are singing.

2 And now, on this our festal day,
   Thy bounteous hand confessing,
Upon thine altar, Lord, we lay
   The first-fruits of thy blessing.
By thee the souls of men are fed
   With gifts of grace supernal,
Thou, who dost give us earthly bread,
   Give us the bread eternal.

3 We bear the burden of the day,
   And often toil seems dreary;
But labour ends with sunset ray,
   And rest comes for the weary.
May we, the angel-reaping o'er,
   Stand at the last accepted,
Christ's golden sheaves, for evermore
   To garners bright elected.

4. O blessèd is that land of God,
   Where saints abide for ever;
Where golden fields spread far and broad,
   Where flows the crystal river.
The strains of all its holy throng
   With ours to-day are blending;
Thrice blessèd is that harvest-song
   Which never hath an ending.

William Chatterton Dix (1837–98)

444 WIR PFLÜGEN 76.76.D.66.84.

Melody by JOHANN ABRAHAM PETER SCHULZ
(1747–1800)

HARVEST

Wir pflügen und wir streuen

WE plough the fields, and scatter
   The good seed on the land,
But it is fed and watered
   By God's almighty hand;
He sends the snow in winter,
   The warmth to swell the grain,
The breezes and the sunshine,
   And soft refreshing rain.
      All good gifts around us
         Are sent from heaven above;
      Then thank the Lord, O thank the Lord,
         For all his love.

2 He only is the maker
   Of all things near and far;
He paints the wayside flower,
   He lights the evening star;
The winds and waves obey him,
   By him the birds are fed;
Much more to us, his children,
   He gives our daily bread:

3. We thank thee then, O Father,
   For all things bright and good,
The seed-time and the harvest,
   Our life, our health, our food;
Accept the gifts we offer
   For all thy love imparts,
And, what thou most desirest,
   Our humble, thankful hearts:

Matthias Claudius (1740–1815)
Tr. Jane Montgomery Campbell (1817–78) and others

See also

2 All creatures of our God
3 All things bright
272 For the beauty of the earth
461 Let us, with a gladsome mind
327 Lord of beauty
463 My soul, praise the Lord!
277 Now thank we all our God
266 O dearest Lord, by all adored
14 O Lord of heaven
471 O worship the King
19 Sing to the Lord a joyful song

445

Mode ii

ORIEL 87.87.87.

CASPAR ETT (1788–1847)

Angularis fundamentum

CHRIST is made the sure foundation,
　Christ the head and corner-stone,
Chosen of the Lord, and precious,
　Binding all the Church in one,
Holy Sion's help for ever,
　And her confidence alone.

2 All that dedicated city
　Dearly loved of God on high,
In exultant jubilation
　Pours perpetual melody,
God the One in Three adoring
　In glad hymns eternally.

3 To this temple, where we call thee,
　Come, O Lord of hosts, to-day;
With thy wonted loving-kindness
　Hear thy servants as they pray;
And thy fullest benediction
　Shed within its walls alway.

4 Here vouchsafe to all thy servants
　What they ask of thee to gain,
What they gain from thee for ever
　With the blessèd to retain,
And hereafter in thy glory
　Evermore with thee to reign.

5. Laud and honour to the Father,
　Laud and honour to the Son,
Laud and honour to the Spirit,
　Ever Three and ever One;
One in might, and One in glory,
　While unending ages run. Amen.

7th or 8th cent.
Tr. John Mason Neale (1818–66)
Based on Ephesians 2, 20–22

For another translation of these words see No. 258.

446 COELITES PLAUDANT 11.11.11.5.

Rouen Melody

DEDICATION FESTIVAL

Christe cunctorum Dominator alme

ONLY-BEGOTTEN, Word of God eternal,
Lord of creation, merciful and mighty,
Hear now thy servants, when their joyful voices
  Rise to thy presence.

2 This is thy temple; here thy presence-chamber;
Here may thy servants, at the mystic banquet,
Humbly adoring, take thy body broken,
  Drink of thy chalice.

3 Here in our sickness healing grace aboundeth,
Light in our blindness, in our toil refreshment:
Sin is forgiven, hope o'er fear prevaileth,
  Joy over sorrow.

4 Hallowed this dwelling where the Lord abideth,
This is none other than the gate of heaven;
Strangers and pilgrims, seeking homes eternal,
  Pass through its portals.

5 Lord, we beseech thee, as we throng thy temple,
By thy past blessings, by thy present bounty,
Favour thy children, and with tender mercy
  Hear our petitions.

6. God in Three Persons, Father everlasting,
Son co-eternal, ever-blessèd Spirit,
Thine be the glory, praise, and adoration,
  Now and for ever. Amen.

Mozarabic Breviary. Tr. Maxwell Julius Blacker (1822–88)
and Compilers of The Hymnal (U.S.A. 1940)

See also

171	Behold the temple	180	O thou not made with hands
258	Christ is our corner-stone	472	Pray that Jerusalem
173	City of God	181	Rejoice, O people
174	Faith of our fathers	281	Rejoice to-day
176	Glorious things	183	The Church of God
458	How lovely are thy dwellings	184	The Church's one foundation
264	Lo, God is here!	187	Thy hand, O God
462	Lord of the worlds above	541	What tongue can tell (CS)
277	Now thank we all our God		

447 LES COMMANDEMENS DE DIEU 98.98.

Composed or adapted by LOUIS BOURGEOIS
in *Genevan Psalter* (1547)

BURIAL

GO, happy soul, thy days are ended,
   Thy pilgrimage on earth below:
Go, by angelic guard attended,
   To God's own Paradise now go.

2 Go; Christ, the Shepherd good, befriend thee,
   Who gave his life thy soul to win;
'Tis even he that shall defend thee,
   Thy going out and coming in.

3. Go forth in peace: farewell to sadness:
   May rest in Paradise be thine;
In Jesus' presence there is gladness:
   Light everlasting on thee shine.

George Ratcliffe Woodward (1848–1934) and Compilers

448 S. VALENTINE 77.77.88. WILLIAM HAROLD FERGUSON (1874–1950)

NOW the labourer's task is o'er;
Now the battle-day is past;
Now upon the farther shore
Lands the voyager at last.
Father, in thy gracious keeping
Leave we now thy servant sleeping.

2 There the tears of earth are dried;
There its hidden things are clear;
There the work of life is tried
By a juster judge than here:

3 There the sinful souls, that turn
To the Cross their dying eyes,
All the love of Christ shall learn
At his feet in Paradise:

4. There no more the powers of hell
Can prevail to mar their peace;
Christ the Lord shall guard them well,
He who died for their release:

John Ellerton (1826–93)

449 CASWALL 65.65.

FRIEDRICH FILITZ (1804–76)

Yesu Bin Mariamu

THINK, O Lord, in mercy
On the souls of those
Who, in faith gone from us,
Now in death repose.

2 Here, 'mid stress and conflict,
Toils can never cease;
There, the warfare ended,
Bid them rest in peace.

3 Often were they wounded
In the deadly strife;
Heal them, good Physician,
With the balm of life.

4 Every taint of evil,
Frailty, and decay,
Good and gracious Saviour,
Cleanse and purge away.

5 Rest eternal grant them,
  After weary fight;
Shed on them the radiance
  Of thy heavenly light.

6. Lead them onward, upward,
  To the holy place,
Where thy saints, made perfect,
  Gaze upon thy face.

Written in Swahili
Tr. Edmund Stuart Palmer (1856–1931)

See also

486	Blest be the everlasting God		248	Jerusalem the golden
241	Brief life		106	Jesus lives!
507	Christ who knows all his sheep	(CS)	249	Let saints on earth
243	For those we love		250	Light's abode
244	From glory to glory		526	My soul, there is a country	(CS)
511	Give rest, O Christ	(CS)	251	O dear and heavenly city
245	He wants not friends		252	O what their joy
246	How mighty are the Sabbaths		537	Sunset and evening star	(CS)
82	It is finished		254	There is a land
247	Jerusalem, my happy home		539	Think, O Lord, in mercy	(CS)

450 OLD HUNDREDTH L.M.

Composed or adapted by LOUIS BOURGEOIS
in *Genevan Psalter* (1551)

PSALM 100

A<small>LL</small> people that on earth do dwell,
  Sing to the Lord with cheerful voice;
Him serve with mirth, his praise forth tell,
Come ye before him and rejoice.

2 *See next page.*

3 O enter then his gates with praise,
  Approach with joy his courts unto;
Praise, laud, and bless his name always,
  For it is seemly so to do.

4. *See next page.*

METRICAL PSALMS

OLD HUNDREDTH L.M.   Harmony by JOHN DOWLAND (1563-1626)

1 *See previous page.*

2 Know that the Lord is God indeed;
   Without our aid he did us make;
   We are his folk, he doth us feed;
   And for his sheep he doth us take.

3 *See previous page.*

4. For why the Lord our God is good:
   His mercy is for ever sure;
   His truth at all times firmly stood,
   And shall from age to age endure.

William Kethe (died 1594)
as in Day's Psalter, and Scottish Psalter (1564)

See also No. 452

451 MARTYRDOM C.M.

HUGH WILSON (1766-1824)

PSALM 42

AS pants the hart for cooling streams,
When heated in the chase,
So longs my soul, O God, for thee,
And thy refreshing grace.

2 For thee, my God, the living God,
My thirsty soul doth pine:
O when shall I behold thy face,
Thou Majesty divine?

3 Why restless, why cast down, my soul?
Hope still, and thou shalt sing
The praise of him who is thy God,
Thy health's eternal spring.

4. To Father, Son, and Holy Ghost,
The God whom we adore,
Be glory, as it was, is now,
And shall be evermore. Amen.

Nahum Tate (1652-1715) and Nicholas Brady (1659-1726)
in New Version (1696)

A - men.

452 OLD HUNDREDTH L.M.

Composed or adapted by LOUIS BOURGEOIS
in *Genevan Psalter* (1551)

PSALM 100

BEFORE the almighty Father's throne,
  Ye nations, bow with sacred joy;
Know that the Lord is God alone,
  He can create, and he destroy.

2 *See next page.*

3 We'll crowd thy gates with thankful songs,
    High as the heavens our voices raise;
  And earth, with her ten thousand tongues,
    Shall fill thy courts with sounding praise.

4. *See next page.*

452 *(continued)*

OLD HUNDREDTH L.M. Harmony by John Dowland (1563–1626)

1 *See previous page.*

2 His sovereign power, without our aid,
　Made us of clay and formed us men:
　And when like wandering sheep we strayed,
　He brought us to his fold again.

3 *See previous page.*

4. Wide as the world is thy command,
　Vast as eternity thy love,
　Firm as a rock thy truth shall stand,
　When rolling years shall cease to move.

Isaac Watts (1674–1748)
John Wesley (1703–91) and Compilers

See also No. 450

453 HIC BREVE VIVITUR 76.76.   Melody by ALFRED PETTET (1790–1837)

PSALM 27

G OD is my strong salvation;
   What foe have I to fear?
In darkness and temptation
   My light, my help, is near.

2 Though hosts encamp around me,
   Firm to the fight I stand;
What terror can confound me,
   With God at my right hand?

3 Place on the Lord reliance;
   My soul, with courage wait;
His truth be thine affiance,
   When faint and desolate.

4. His might thine heart shall strengthen,
   His love thy joy increase;
Mercy thy days shall lengthen;
   The Lord will give thee peace.

James Montgomery (1771–1854)

454 STROUDWATER C.M.

WILLIAM ANCHORS
A Choice Collection (c. 1721)

PSALM 46

G OD is our refuge and our strength,
    In straits a present aid;
Therefore, although the earth remove,
    We will not be afraid:

2 Though hills amidst the seas be cast;
    Though waters roaring make,
And troubled be; yea, though the hills
    By swelling seas do shake.

3 A river is, whose streams do glad
    The city of our God;
The holy place, wherein the Lord
    Most High hath his abode.

4. God in the midst of her doth dwell;
    Nothing shall her remove:
The Lord to her an helper will,
    And that right early, prove.

Scottish Psalter (1650)

See also No. 297

455 HEATHLANDS 77.77.77.   HENRY SMART (1813-79)

PSALM 67

GOD of mercy, God of grace,
Show the brightness of thy face;
Shine upon us, Saviour, shine,
Fill thy Church with light divine;
And thy saving health extend
Unto earth's remotest end.

2 Let the people praise thee, Lord;
Be by all that live adored;
Let the nations shout and sing
Glory to their Saviour King;
At thy feet their tribute pay,
And thy holy will obey.

3. Let the people praise thee, Lord;
Earth shall then her fruits afford;
God to man his blessing give,
Man to God devoted live;
All below, and all above,
One in joy and light and love.

Henry Francis Lyte (1793-1847)

456 S. ANDREW C.M.

Tanzer's *New Harmony of Sion* (1764)

PSALM 19

GOD'S law is perfect, and converts
    The soul in sin that lies:
God's testimony is most sure,
    And makes the simple wise.

2 The statutes of the Lord are right,
    And do rejoice the heart:
The Lord's command is pure, and doth
    Light to the eyes impart.

3 Unspotted is the fear of God,
    And doth endure for ever:
The judgments of the Lord are true
    And righteous altogether.

4 Moreover, they thy servant warn
    How he his life should frame:
A great reward provided is
    For them that keep the same.

5. The words which from my mouth proceed,
    The thoughts sent from my heart,
Accept, O Lord, for thou my Strength
    And my Redeemer art.

Scottish Psalter (1615)

457 CRÜGER 76.76. D.

JOHANN CRÜGER (1598–1662)

PSALM 72

HAIL to the Lord's Anointed,
　　Great David's greater Son!
Hail, in the time appointed,
　　His reign on earth begun!
He comes to break oppression,
　　To set the captive free;
To take away transgression,
　　And rule in equity.

2 He comes with succour speedy
　　To those who suffer wrong;
To help the poor and needy,
　　And bid the weak be strong;
To give them songs for sighing,
　　Their darkness turn to light,
Whose souls, condemned and dying,
　　Were precious in his sight.

3 He shall come down like showers
　　Upon the fruitful earth,
And love, joy, hope, like flowers,
　　Spring in his path to birth:
Before him on the mountains
　　Shall peace the herald go;
And righteousness in fountains
　　From hill to valley flow.

4 Kings shall fall down before him,
　　And gold and incense bring;
All nations shall adore him,
　　His praise all people sing;
To him shall prayer unceasing
　　And daily vows ascend;
His kingdom still increasing,
　　A kingdom without end.

5. O'er every foe victorious,
　　He on his throne shall rest,
From age to age more glorious,
　　All-blessing and all-blest:
The tide of time shall never
　　His covenant remove;
His name shall stand for ever;
　　That name to us is Love.

James Montgomery (1771–1854)

See also No. 460

458 HARINGTON C.M.
(RETIREMENT)

HENRY HARINGTON (1727-1816)

PSALM 84

H OW lovely are thy dwellings fair!
O Lord of hosts, how dear
The pleasant tabernacles are,
Where thou dost dwell so near.

2 My soul doth long and almost die
Thy courts, O Lord, to see;
My heart and flesh aloud do cry,
O living God, for thee.

3 Happy who in thy house reside,
Where thee they ever praise;
Happy whose strength in thee doth bide,
And in their hearts thy ways.

4 They journey on from strength to strength
With joy and gladsome cheer,
Till all before our God at length
In Sion do appear.

5. For God, the Lord, both sun and shield,
Gives grace and glory bright;
No good from them shall be withheld
Whose ways are just and right.

See also No. 462

John Milton (1608–74)

459 FRENCH C.M.
(DUNDEE)

Scottish Psalter (1615)
as given in RAVENSCROFT's *Psalter* (1621)

PSALM 121

I TO the hills will lift mine eyes,
From whence doth come mine aid.
My safety cometh from the Lord,
Who heaven and earth hath made.

2 Thy foot he'll not let slide, nor will
He slumber that thee keeps;
Behold, he that keeps Israel,
He slumbers not, nor sleeps.

3 The Lord thee keeps, the Lord thy shade
On thy right hand doth stay:
The moon by night thee shall not smite,
Nor yet the sun by day.

4. The Lord shall keep thy soul; he shall
Preserve thee from all ill:
Henceforth thy going out and in
God keep for ever will.

Scottish Psalter (1650)

460 GALILEE L.M.　　　　　　　　　PHILIP ARMES (1836–1908)

PSALM 72

JESUS shall reign where'er the sun
Doth his successive journeys run;
His kingdom stretch from shore to shore,
Till moons shall wax and wane no more.

2 People and realms of every tongue
Dwell on his love with sweetest song,
And infant voices shall proclaim
Their early blessings on his name.

3 Blessings abound where'er he reigns;
The prisoner leaps to lose his chains;
The weary find eternal rest,
And all the sons of want are blest.

4. Let every creature rise and bring
Peculiar honours to our King;
Angels descend with songs again,
And earth repeat the long amen.

Isaac Watts (1674–1748)

See also No. 457

461 MONKLAND 77.77.

Melody from *Hymn Tunes of the United Brethren* (1824)
Arranged by JOHN WILKES (1785–1869)

PSALM 136

LET us, with a gladsome mind,
Praise the Lord, for he is kind:
For his mercies aye endure,
Ever faithful, ever sure.

2 Let us blaze his name abroad,
For of gods he is the God:

3 He, with all-commanding might,
Filled the new-made world with light:

4 He the golden-tressèd sun
Caused all day his course to run:

5 And the hornèd moon by night,
'Mid her spangled sisters bright:

6 All things living he doth feed;
His full hand supplies their need:

7. Let us then with gladsome mind
Praise the Lord, for he is kind:

John Milton (1608–74) and others

See also No. 6

Y

462 MORETON 66.66.44.44.

J. HODGSON CREED (1904–   )

PSALM 84

LORD of the worlds above,
   How pleasant and how fair
The dwellings of thy love,
   Thy earthly temples, are!
     To thine abode
      My heart aspires
     With warm desires
    To see my God.

2 O happy souls that pray
   Where God appoints to hear!
O happy men that pay
   Their constant service there!
     They praise thee still;
      And happy they
     That love the way
    To Sion's hill.

3 They go from strength to strength,
   Through this dark vale of tears,
Till each arrives at length,
   Till each in heaven appears:
     O glorious seat,
      When God our King
     Shall thither bring
    Our willing feet!

4. God is our sun and shield,
   Our light and our defence;
With gifts his hands are filled,
   We draw our blessings thence.
     Thrice happy he,
      O God of hosts,
     Whose spirit trusts
    Alone in thee.

Isaac Watts (1674–1748) and Compilers

See also No. 458

463 OLD 104TH 55.55.65.65.

RAVENSCROFT'S *Psalter* (1621)

PSALM 104

M Y soul, praise the Lord!
  O God, thou art great:
In fathomless works
Thyself thou dost hide.
Before thy dark wisdom
  And power uncreate,
Man's mind, that dare praise thee,
  In fear must abide.

2 This earth where we dwell,
   That journeys in space,
   With air as a robe
   Thou wrappest around:
Her countries she turneth
   To greet the sun's face,
Then plungeth to slumber
   In darkness profound.

3 All seemeth so sure,
   Yet nought doth remain:
   Unending their change
   Obeys thy decree.
The valleys of ocean
   Stand up a dry plain,
Thou whelmest the mountains
   Beneath the deep sea.

4 The clouds gather rain
   And melt o'er the land,
   Then back to the sun
   Are drawn by his shine:
Whereby the corn springeth
   Through toil of man's hand,
And vineyards that gladden
   His heart with good wine.

5 All beasts of the field
   Rejoice in their life;
   Among the tall trees
   Are light birds on wing;
With strains of their music
   The woodlands are rife;
They nest in thick branches
   And welcome sweet spring.

6 Lo, there is thy sea,
   Whose bosom below
   With creatures doth teem,
   Scaled fishes and finned.
Above, the ships laden
   With merchandise go,
Nor fear the wild waters,
   Nor rage of rude wind.

7. O God, thou art great!
   No greatness I see,
   Except thee alone,
   Thy praise to record.
On all thy works musing
   My pleasure shall be:
My joy shall be singing
   'My soul, praise the Lord!'

Robert Bridges (1844–1930)

See also No. **471**

464 OLD 124TH 10.10.10.10.10.

Later form of melody from
Genevan Psalter (1551)

PSALM 124

Or peut bien dire Israel maintenant

NOW Israel may say, and that truly,
    If that the Lord had not our cause maintained;
    If that the Lord had not our right sustained,
When cruel men against us furiously
Rose up in wrath, to make of us their prey;

2 Then certainly they had devoured us all,
    And swallowed quick, for ought that we could deem;
    Such was their rage, as we might well esteem.
And as fierce floods before them all things drown,
So had they brought our soul to death quite down.

3 The raging streams, with their proud swelling waves,
    Had then our soul o'erwhelmèd in the deep;
    But blest be God, who doth us safely keep,
And hath not given us for a living prey
Unto their teeth, and bloody cruelty.

4. Even as a bird out of the fowler's snare
    Escapes away, so is our soul set free:
    Broke are their nets, and thus escapèd we,
Therefore our help is in the Lord's great name,
Who heaven and earth by his great power did frame.

Theodore of Beza (1519–1605)
Tr. William Whittingham (?–1579) *as in Anglo-Genevan Psalter* (1564)
and revised in Scottish Psalter (1650)

465 BON ACCORD C.M.　　　　　　　　*Scottish Psalter (Aberdeen, 1625)*

1. O come, let us sing to the Lord: come, let us ev'ry one A joy-ful noise make to the Rock of our sal-va-tion, of our sal-va-tion.

PSALM 95

O COME, let us sing to the Lord:
　　Come, let us every one
A joyful noise make to the Rock
　　Of our salvation.

2 Let us before his presence come
　　With praise and thankful voice;
　Let us sing psalms to him with grace,
　　And make a joyful noise.

3 For God, a great God and great King
　　Above all gods he is.
　Depths of the earth are in his hand,
　　The strength of hills is his.

4 To him the spacious sea belongs,
　For he the same did make;
The dry land also from his hands
　Its form at first did take.

5. O come, and let us worship him,
　Let us bow down withal,
And on our knees before the Lord
　Our Maker let us fall.

Scottish Psalter (1615)

466 S. DAVID C.M.   RAVENSCROFT'S *Psalter (1621)*

PSALM 61

O GOD, give ear unto my cry;
　Unto my prayer attend.
From the utmost corner of the land
　My cry to thee I'll send.

2 What time my heart is overwhelmed
　And in perplexity,
Do thou me lead unto the rock
　That higher is than I.

3 For thou hast for my refuge been
　A shelter by thy power;
And for defence against my foes
　Thou hast been a strong tower.

4. And so will I perpetually
　Sing praise unto thy name;
That having made my vows, I may
　Each day perform the same.

Scottish Psalter (1650)

467 S. ANNE C.M.   WILLIAM CROFT (1678–1727)

PSALM 90

O GOD, our help in ages past,
    Our hope for years to come,
Our shelter from the stormy blast,
    And our eternal home;

2 Under the shadow of thy throne
    Thy saints have dwelt secure;
Sufficient is thine arm alone,
    And our defence is sure.

3 Before the hills in order stood,
    Or earth received her frame,
From everlasting thou art God,
    To endless years the same.

4 A thousand ages in thy sight
    Are like an evening gone,
Short as the watch that ends the night
    Before the rising sun.

5 Time, like an ever-rolling stream,
    Bears all its sons away;
They fly forgotten, as a dream
    Dies at the opening day.

6. O God, our help in ages past,
    Our hope for years to come,
Be thou our guard while troubles last,
    And our eternal home.

Isaac Watts (1674–1748)

468 CANNONS L.M.　　　　　　　GEORGE FREDERICK HANDEL (1685-1759)

PSALM 63

O GOD, thou art my God alone,
　Early to thee my soul shall cry,
A pilgrim in a land unknown,
　A thirsty land whose springs are dry.

2 Yet through this rough and thorny maze
　I follow hard on thee, my God;
Thine hand unseen upholds my ways;
　I safely tread where thou hast trod.

3 Thee, in the watches of the night,
　When I remember on my bed,
Thy presence makes the darkness light;
　Thy guardian wings are round my head.

4 Better than life itself thy love,
　Dearer than all beside to me;
For whom have I in heaven above,
　Or what on earth, compared with thee?

5. Praise, with my heart, my mind, my voice,
　For all thy mercy I will give;
My soul shall still in God rejoice;
　My tongue shall bless thee while I live.

James Montgomery (1771-1854)

469 WARWICK C.M.

SAMUEL STANLEY (1767–1822)

PSALM 89

O GREATLY blessed the people are
    The joyful sound that know;
In brightness of thy face, O Lord,
    They ever on shall go.

2 They in thy name shall all the day
    Rejoice exceedingly;
And in thy righteousness shall they
    Exalted be on high.

3 Because the glory of their strength
    Doth only stand in thee;
And in thy favour shall our horn
    And power exalted be.

4. For God is our defence, and he
    To us doth safety bring:
The Holy One of Israel
    Is our almighty King.

Scottish Psalter (1650)

470 DUKE STREET L.M.　　　　　　　　　　　　JOHN HATTON (?–1793)

PSALM 145

O LORD, thou art my God and King;
　　Thee will I magnify and praise:
I will thee bless, and gladly sing
　　Unto thy holy name always.

2 Each day I rise I will thee bless,
　　And praise thy name time without end:
Much to be praised, and great God is;
　　His greatness none can comprehend.

3 Race shall thy works praise unto race,
　　The mighty acts show done by thee;
I will speak of the glorious grace
　　And honour of thy majesty.

4 Thy wondrous works I will record:
　　By men the might shall be extolled
Of all thy dreadful acts, O Lord:
　　And I thy greatness will unfold.

5. They utter shall abundantly
　　The memory of thy goodness great;
And shall sing praises cheerfully,
　　Whilst they thy righteousness relate.

John Craig (1512–1600) in Scottish Psalter (1564)
revised in Scottish Psalter (1650)

See also Nos. 13, 19

471 HANOVER 10.10.11.11.   Probably by WILLIAM CROFT (1678–1727)

PSALM 104

O WORSHIP the King, all glorious above;
O gratefully sing his power and his love:
Our shield and defender, the ancient of days,
Pavilioned in splendour, and girded with praise.

2 O tell of his might, O sing of his grace;
Whose robe is the light, whose canopy space;
His chariots of wrath the deep thunder-clouds form,
And dark is his path on the wings of the storm.

3 This earth, with its store of wonders untold,
Almighty, thy power hath founded of old;
Hath stablished it fast by a changeless decree,
And round it hath cast, like a mantle, the sea.

4 Thy bountiful care what tongue can recite?
It breathes in the air, it shines in the light;
It streams from the hills, it descends to the plain,
And sweetly distils in the dew and the rain.

5 Frail children of dust, and feeble as frail,
   In thee do we trust, nor find thee to fail;
   Thy mercies how tender, how firm to the end,
   Our maker, defender, redeemer, and friend.

6. O measureless might, ineffable love,
   While angels delight to hymn thee above,
   Thy humbler creation, though feeble their lays,
   With true adoration shall sing to thy praise.

Robert Grant (1779-1838)

See also No. 463

472 ABERDEEN C.M.
(S. PAUL)

CHALMERS' *Collection* (Aberdeen, 1749)

PSALM 122

PRAY that Jerusalem may have
   Peace and felicity:
Let them that love thee and thy peace
   Have still prosperity.

2 Therefore I wish that peace may still
     Within thy walls remain,
   And ever may thy palaces
     Prosperity retain.

3. Now, for my friends' and brethren's sakes,
     'Peace be in thee', I'll say;
   And for the house of God our Lord,
     I'll seek thy good alway.

Scottish Psalter (1650)

473 YORK C.M.

Scottish Psalter (1615)
Arranged by JOHN MILTON (*c.* 1563–1647)

PSALM 119, 33–37

TEACH me, O Lord, the perfect way
  Of thy precepts divine,
And to observe it to the end
  I shall my heart incline.

2 Give understanding unto me,
    So keep thy law shall I;
  Yea, ev'n with my whole heart I shall
    Observe it carefully.

3 In thy law's path make me to go,
    For I delight therein.
  My heart unto thy testimonies,
    And not to greed, incline.

4. Turn thou away my sight and eyes
    From viewing vanity;
  And in thy good and holy way
    Be pleased to quicken me.

Scottish Psalter (1615)

474 UNIVERSITY C.M.　　　　　　　　　　? JOHN RANDALL (1715–99)

PSALM 23

THE God of love my Shepherd is,
　And he that doth me feed;
While he is mine and I am his,
　What can I want or need?

2 He leads me to the tender grass,
　Where I both feed and rest;
Then to the streams that gently pass:
　In both I have the best.

3 Or if I stray, he doth convert,
　And bring my mind in frame;
And all this not for my desert,
　But for his holy name.

4 Yea, in death's shady black abode
　Well may I walk, not fear;
For thou art with me, and thy rod
　To guide, thy staff to bear.

5. Surely thy sweet and wondrous love
　Shall measure all my days;
And, as it never shall remove,
　So neither shall my praise.

George Herbert (1593–1632)

See also Nos. 475, 477, 480

METRICAL PSALMS

475 DOMINUS REGIT ME 87.87.

JOHN BACCHUS DYKES (1823–76)

S. COLUMBA 87.87.

Irish Melody

PSALM 23

THE King of love my Shepherd is,
   Whose goodness faileth never:
I nothing lack if I am his,
   And he is mine for ever.

2 Where streams of living waters flow
   My ransomed soul he leadeth;
And where the verdant pastures grow
   With food celestial feedeth.

3 Perverse and foolish oft I strayed;
   But yet in love he sought me,
And on his shoulder gently laid,
   And home, rejoicing, brought me.

4 In death's dark vale I fear no ill,
   With thee, dear Lord, beside me;
Thy rod and staff my comfort still,
   Thy Cross before to guide me.

5 Thou spread'st a table in my sight;
   Thy unction grace bestoweth;
And O, what transport of delight
   From thy pure chalice floweth!

6. And so through all the length of days
   Thy goodness faileth never:
Good Shepherd, may I sing thy praise
   Within thy house for ever.

Henry Williams Baker (1821–77)

See also Nos. 474, 477, 48

476 STROUDWATER C.M.

WILLIAM ANCHORS
A Choice Collection (c. 1721)

PSALM 93

THE Lord doth reign, and clothed is he
  With majesty most bright;
His works do show him clothed to be,
  And girt about with might.

2 The world is also stablishèd,
    That it cannot depart.
  Thy throne is fixed of old, and thou
    From everlasting art.

3 The floods, O Lord, have lifted up,
    They lifted up their voice;
  The floods have lifted up their waves,
    And made a mighty noise.

4 But yet the Lord, that is on high,
    Is more of might by far
  Than noise of many waters is,
    Or great sea-billows are.

5. Thy testimonies every one
    In faithfulness excel;
  And holiness for ever, Lord,
    Thine house becometh well.

Scottish Psalter (1650)

477 SURREY 88.88.88.

HENRY CAREY (1690–1743)

PSALM 23

THE Lord my pasture shall prepare,
    And feed me with a shepherd's care;
His presence shall my wants supply,
And guard me with a watchful eye;
My noonday walks he shall attend,
And all my midnight hours defend.

2 When in the sultry glebe I faint,
    Or on the thirsty mountain pant,
To fertile vales and dewy meads
My weary wandering steps he leads,
Where peaceful rivers, soft and slow,
Amid the verdant landscape flow.

3 Though in a bare and rugged way
    Through devious lonely wilds I stray,
Thy bounty shall my pains beguile;
The barren wilderness shall smile,
With sudden greens and herbage crowned,
And streams shall murmur all around.

4. Though in the paths of death I tread,
    With gloomy horrors overspread,
My steadfast heart shall fear no ill,
For thou, O Lord, art with me still;
Thy friendly crook shall give me aid,
And guide me through the dreadful shade.

Joseph Addison (1672–1719)

See also Nos. 474, 475, 480

478 CROFT'S 136TH 66.66.44.44.   WILLIAM CROFT (1678–1727)

PSALM 148

THE Lord of heaven confess;
　On high his glory raise:
Him let all angels bless,
　Him all his armies praise.
　　Him glorify
　　　Sun, moon, and stars;
　　Ye higher spheres,
And cloudy sky.

2 Praise God from earth below,
　Ye dragons, and ye deeps:
Fire, hail, clouds, wind, and snow,
　Whom in command he keeps.
　　Praise ye his name,
　　　Hills great and small,
　　Trees low and tall,
Beasts wild and tame.

3. O let God's name be praised
　Above both earth and sky;
For he his saints hath raised,
　And set their horn on high;
　　Yea, they that are
　　Of Israel's race,
　　Are in his grace,
And ever dear.

George Wither (1588–1667)

See also Nos. 16, 483

479 S. STEPHEN C.M.
(NEWINGTON)

WILLIAM JONES (1726–1800)

PSALMS 82, 85, 86

THE Lord will come, and not be slow,
　His footsteps cannot err;
Before him righteousness shall go,
　His royal harbinger.

2 Truth from the earth, like to a flower,
　Shall bud and blossom then;
And justice, from her heavenly bower,
　Look down on mortal men.

3 Rise, God, judge thou the earth in might,
　This wicked earth redress;
For thou art he who shalt by right
　The nations all possess.

4 The nations all whom thou hast made
　Shall come, and all shall frame
To bow them low before thee, Lord,
　And glorify thy name.

5. For great thou art, and wonders great
　By thy strong hand are done:
Thou in thy everlasting seat
　Remainest God alone.

John Milton (1608–74)

480 CRIMOND C.M.

Melody by JESSIE SEYMOUR IRVINE (1836–87)

PSALM 23

THE Lord's my Shepherd, I'll not want.
  He makes me down to lie
In pastures green: he leadeth me
  The quiet waters by.

2 My soul he doth restore again,
  And me to walk doth make
Within the paths of righteousness,
  E'en for his own name's sake.

3 Yea, though I walk in death's dark vale,
  Yet will I fear none ill:
For thou art with me, and thy rod
  And staff me comfort still.

4 My table thou hast furnishèd
  In presence of my foes;
My head thou dost with oil anoint,
  And my cup overflows.

5. Goodness and mercy all my life
  Shall surely follow me:
And in God's house for evermore
  My dwelling-place shall be.

Scottish Psalter (1650)

See also Nos. 474, 475, 477

481 WILTSHIRE C.M.

GEORGE SMART (1776–1867)

PSALM 34

THROUGH all the changing
  scenes of life,
In trouble and in joy,
The praises of my God shall still
  My heart and tongue employ.

2 O magnify the Lord with me,
  With me exalt his name;
When in distress to him I called,
  He to my rescue came.

3 The hosts of God encamp around
  The dwellings of the just;
Deliverance he affords to all
  Who on his succour trust.

4 O make but trial of his love;
  Experience will decide
How blest they are, and only they,
  Who in his truth confide.

5 Fear him, ye saints, and you will then
  Have nothing else to fear;
Make you his service your delight
  Your wants shall be his care.

6. To Father, Son, and Holy Ghost,
  The God whom we adore,
Be glory, as it was, is now,
  And shall be evermore. Amen.

Nahum Tate (1652–1715) and Nicholas Brady (1659–1726)
in New Version (1696)

A - men.

482 LONDON NEW C.M.

Scottish Psalter (1635)
as given in PLAYFORD's *Psalms* (1671)

PSALM 36

THY mercy, Lord, is in the heavens,
　Thy truth doth reach the clouds:
Thy justice is like mountains great,
　Thy judgments deep as floods.

2 Lord, thou preservest man and beast,
　How precious is thy grace!
Therefore in shadow of thy wings
　Men's sons their trust shall place.

3 They with the fatness of thy house
　Shall be well satisfied;
From rivers of thy pleasures thou
　Wilt drink to them provide.

4 Because of life the fountain pure
　Remains alone with thee;
And in that purest light of thine
　We clearly light shall see.

5. Thy loving-kindness unto them
　Continue that thee know;
And still on men upright in heart
　Thy righteousness bestow.

Scottish Psalter (1650)

See also No. 9

483 DARWALL'S 148TH 66.66.44.44.   JOHN DARWALL (1731–89)

PSALM 148

YE boundless realms of joy,
  Exalt your Maker's fame,
His praise your song employ
  Above the starry frame;
    Your voices raise,
    Ye Cherubim,
    And Seraphim,
    To sing his praise.

2 Thou moon that rul'st the night,
    And sun that guid'st the day,
  Ye glittering stars of light,
    To him your homage pay;
      His praise declare,
      Ye heavens above,
      And clouds that move
      In liquid air.

3 Let them adore the Lord,
    And praise his holy name,
  By whose almighty word
    They all from nothing came;

And all shall last,
  From changes free;
  His firm decree
  Stands ever fast.

4 United zeal be shown
    His wondrous fame to raise,
  Whose glorious name alone
    Deserves our endless praise;
      Earth's utmost ends
      His power obey;
      His glorious sway
      The sky transcends.

5. His chosen saints to grace,
    He sets them up on high,
  And favours Israel's race,
    Who still to him are nigh;
      O therefore raise
      Your grateful voice,
      And still rejoice
      The Lord to praise.

Nahum Tate (1652–1715) and Nicholas Brady (1659–1726)
in New Version (1696)

See also Nos. 16, 478

484 S. STEPHEN C.M.
(NEWINGTON)

WILLIAM JONES (1726–1800)

I JOHN 3 1–4

BEHOLD the amazing gift of love
  The Father hath bestowed
On us, the sinful sons of men,
  To call us sons of God.

2 Concealed as yet this honour lies,
  By this dark world unknown,
A world that knew not when he came,
  Even God's eternal Son.

3 High is the rank we now possess;
  But higher we shall rise;
Though what we shall hereafter be
  Is hid from mortal eyes.

4 Our souls, we know, when he appears,
  Shall bear his image bright;
For all his glory, full disclosed,
  Shall open to our sight.

5. A hope so great and so divine
  May trials well endure;
And purge the soul from sense and sin,
  As Christ himself is pure.

Scottish Paraphrases (1781)

485 GLASGOW C.M.   MOORE's *Psalm-Singer's Pocket Companion* (1756)

ISAIAH 2, 2–6

BEHOLD, the mountain of the Lord
  In latter days shall rise
On mountain tops above the hills,
  And draw the wondering eyes.

2 To this the joyful nations round,
  All tribes and tongues shall flow;
Up to the hill of God, they'll say,
  And to his house we'll go.

3 The beam that shines from Sion hill
  Shall lighten every land;
The King who reigns in Salem's towers
  Shall all the world command.

4 Among the nations he shall judge;
  His judgments truth shall guide;
His sceptre shall protect the just,
  And quell the sinner's pride.

5 No strife shall rage, nor hostile feuds
  Disturb those peaceful years;
To ploughshares men shall beat their swords,
  To pruning-hooks their spears.

6. Come then, O God's own people, come
  To worship at his shrine;
And, walking in the light of God,
  With holy beauties shine.

Scottish Paraphrases (1781) *and Compilers*

486 BISHOPTHORPE C.M.   JEREMIAH CLARKE (1670–1707)

I PETER I, 3–5

Blest be the everlasting God,
    The Father of our Lord;
Be his abounding mercy praised,
    His majesty adored.

2 When from the dead he raised his Son,
    And called him to the sky,
He gave our souls a lively hope
    That they should never die.

3 To an inheritance divine
    He taught our hearts to rise;
'Tis uncorrupted, undefiled,
    Unfading in the skies.

4. Saints by the power of God are kept,
    Till the salvation come:
We walk by faith as strangers here,
    But Christ shall call us home.

*Isaac Watts (1674–1748) and William Cameron (1751–1811)
    as in Scottish Paraphrases (1781)*

487 KILMARNOCK C.M.   Melody by NEIL DOUGALL (1776–1862)

HOSEA 6, 1–4

COME, let us to the Lord our God
    With contrite hearts return;
Our God is gracious, nor will leave
    The desolate to mourn.

2 His voice commands the tempest forth,
    And stills the stormy wave;
And, though his arm be strong to smite,
    'Tis also strong to save.

3 Long hath the night of sorrow reigned;
    The dawn shall bring us light;
God shall appear, and we shall rise
    With gladness in his sight.

4 Our hearts, if God we seek to know,
    Shall know him, and rejoice;
His coming like the morn shall be,
    Like morning songs his voice.

5 As dew upon the tender herb,
    Diffusing fragrance round;
As showers that usher in the spring,
    And cheer the thirsty ground;

6. So shall his presence bless our souls,
    And shed a joyful light;
That hallowed morn shall chase away
    The sorrows of the night.

John Morison (1749–98)
as in Scottish Paraphrases (1781)

488 CAITHNESS C.M.

Scottish Psalter (1635)

HEBREWS 13, 20-21

FATHER of peace, and God of love,
  We own thy power to save,
That power by which our Shepherd rose
  Victorious o'er the grave.

2 Him from the dead thou brought'st again,
    When, by his sacred blood,
  Confirmed and sealed for evermore
    The eternal covenant stood.

3 O may thy Spirit seal our souls,
    And mould them to thy will,
  That our weak hearts no more may stray,
    But keep thy precepts still.

4. That to perfection's sacred height
    We nearer still may rise,
  And all we think, and all we do,
    Be pleasing in thine eyes.

Philip Doddridge (1702-51)
as in Scottish Paraphrases (1781)

489 S. MAGNUS C.M.
(NOTTINGHAM)

Probably by JEREMIAH CLARKE (1670–1707)

REVELATION 5, 9–13

HARK how the adoring hosts above,
  With songs surround the throne!
Ten thousand thousand are their tongues,
  But all their hearts are one.

2 Worthy the Lamb that died, they cry,
  To be exalted thus;
Worthy the Lamb, let us reply;
  For he was slain for us.

3 To him be power divine ascribed,
  And endless blessings paid;
Salvation, glory, joy, remain
  For ever on his head!

4 Thou hast redeemed us with thy blood
  And set the prisoners free;
Thou mad'st us kings and priests to God,
  And we shall reign with thee.

5 From every kindred, every tongue,
  Thou brought'st thy chosen race;
And distant lands and isles have shared
  The riches of thy grace.

6 Let all that dwell above the sky,
  Or on the earth below,
With fields and floods and ocean's shores,
  To thee their homage show.

7. To him who sits upon the throne,
  The God whom we adore,
And to the Lamb that once was slain,
  Be glory evermore. Amen.

Isaac Watts (1674–1748)
as in Scottish Paraphrases (1781)

490 BRISTOL C.M.

RAVENSCROFT's *Psalter* (1621)

S. LUKE 4, 18–19

HARK, the glad sound, the Saviour comes,
　The Saviour promised long!
Let every heart prepare a throne,
　And every voice a song.

2 He comes the prisoners to release
　In Satan's bondage held;
The gates of brass before him burst,
　The iron fetters yield.

3 He comes the broken heart to bind,
　The bleeding soul to cure,
And with the treasures of his grace
　To enrich the humble poor.

4. Our glad hosannas, Prince of peace,
　Thy welcome shall proclaim,
And heaven's eternal arches ring
　With thy belovèd name.

Philip Doddridge (1702–51)

491 BEDFORD PARK C.M.   CYRIL V. TAYLOR (1907–   )

Why pourest thou forth thine anxious plaint,
  Despairing of relief,
As if the Lord o'erlooked thy cause,
  And did not heed thy grief?

[The above verse (not to be sung) begins this Paraphrase.]

ISAIAH 40, 27–31

Hast thou not known, hast thou not heard,
  That firm remains on high
The everlasting throne of him
  Who formed the earth and sky?

2 Art thou afraid his power shall fail
    When comes thy evil day?
  And can an all-creating arm
    Grow weary or decay?

3 Supreme in wisdom as in power
    The Rock of Ages stands;
  Though him thou canst not see, nor trace
    The working of his hands.

4 He gives the conquest to the weak,
    Supports the fainting heart;
  And courage in the evil hour
    His heavenly aids impart.

5. Mere human power shall fast decay,
    And youthful vigour cease;
  But they who wait upon the Lord
    In strength shall still increase.

                    Isaac Watts (1674–1748)
                    as in Scottish Paraphrases (1781)

492 ROCHESTER C.M.　　　CHARLES HYLTON STEWART (1884–1932)

REVELATION 7, 13–17

H OW bright these glorious spirits
　　　shine!
　Whence all their white array?
How came they to the blissful seats
　Of everlasting day?

2 Lo, these are they from sufferings
　　great
　Who came to realms of light,
And in the blood of Christ have
　　washed
　Those robes that shine so bright.

3 Now with triumphal palms they
　　stand
　Before the throne on high,
And serve the God they love, amidst
　The glories of the sky.

4 Hunger and thirst are felt no more,
　Nor suns with scorching ray;
God is their sun, whose cheering
　　beams
　Diffuse eternal day.

5 The Lamb which dwells amidst the
　　throne
　Shall o'er them still preside,
Feed them with nourishment divine,
　And all their footsteps guide.

6. In pastures green he'll lead his flock
　Where living streams appear;
And God the Lord from every eye
　Shall wipe off every tear.

? William Cameron (1751–1811) and Isaac Watts (1674–1748)
as in Scottish Paraphrases (1781)

493 IRISH C.M.

Melody from *A Collection*
of Hymns and Sacred Poems (Dublin, 1749)

ISAIAH 26, 1-4

H OW glorious Sion's courts appear,
    The city of our God!
His throne he hath established here,
    Here fixed his loved abode.

2 Its walls, defended by his grace,
    No power shall e'er o'erthrow,
Salvation is its bulwark sure
    Against the⌢assaulting foe.

3 Lift up the everlasting gates,
    The doors wide open fling;
Enter, ye nations, who obey
    The statutes of our King.

4 Here shall ye taste unmingled joys,
    And dwell in perfect peace,
Ye, who have known Jehovah's name,
    And trusted in his grace.

5. Trust in the Lord, for ever trust,
    And banish all your fears;
Strength in the Lord Jehovah dwells,
    Eternal as his years.

Scottish Paraphrases (1781)

494 JACKSON C.M.

THOMAS JACKSON (1715–81)

2 TIMOTHY I, 12

I'M not ashamed to own my Lord,
 Or to defend his cause,
Maintain the glory of his Cross,
 And honour all his laws.

2 Jesus, my Lord, I know his name,
 His name is all my boast;
Nor will he put my soul to shame,
 Nor let my hope be lost.

3 I know that safe with him remains.
 Protected by his power,
What I've committed to his trust,
 Till the decisive hour.

4. Then will he own his servant's name
 Before his Father's face,
And in the new Jerusalem
 Appoint my soul a place.

Isaac Watts (1674–1748)
as in Scottish Paraphrases (1781)

495 SALZBURG C.M.   JOHANN MICHAEL HAYDN (1737–1806)

GENESIS 28, 20–22

O GOD of Bethel, by whose hand
  Thy people still are fed;
Who through this weary pilgrimage
  Hast all our fathers led:

2 Our vows, our prayers, we now present
  Before thy throne of grace:
God of our fathers, be the God
  Of their succeeding race.

3 Through each perplexing path of life
  Our wandering footsteps guide;
Give us each day our daily bread,
  And raiment fit provide.

4. O spread thy covering wings around,
  Till all our wanderings cease,
And at our Father's loved abode
  Our souls arrive in peace.

Philip Doddridge (1702–51) and John Logan (1748–88)
as in Scottish Paraphrases (1781)

496 FRENCH C.M.
(DUNDEE)

Scottish Psalter (1615)
as given in RAVENSCROFT's *Psalter* (1621)

ISAIAH 9, 2–8

THE race that long in darkness pined
   Have seen a glorious light;
The people dwell in day, who dwelt
   In death's surrounding night.

2 To hail thy rise, thou better Sun,
   The gathering nations come,
Joyous, as when the reapers bear
   The harvest-treasures home.

3 To us a Child of hope is born,
   To us a Son is given;
Him shall the tribes of earth obey,
   Him all the hosts of heaven.

4 His name shall be the Prince of peace,
   For evermore adored;
The Wonderful, the Counsellor,
   The great and mighty Lord.

5. His power increasing still shall spread;
   His reign no end shall know:
Justice shall guard his throne above,
   And peace abound below.

John Morison (1749–98)
as in Scottish Paraphrases (1781)

497 S. ANDREW C.M.   TANZER's *New Harmony of Sion* (1764)

ROMANS 8, 34-39

THE Saviour died, but rose again
   Triumphant from the grave;
And pleads our cause at God's right hand,
   Omnipotent to save.

2 Who then can e'er divide us more
   From Jesus and his love,
Or break the sacred chain that binds
   The earth to heaven above?

3 Let troubles rise and terrors frown,
   And days of darkness fall;
Through him all dangers we'll defy,
   And more than conquer all.

4. Nor death nor life, nor earth nor hell,
   Nor time's destroying sway,
Can e'er efface us from his heart,
   Or make his love decay.

Scottish Paraphrases (1781)

498 KENT L.M.

JOHANN FRIEDRICH LAMPE (1703–51)

HEBREWS 4, 14–16

WHERE high the heavenly temple stands,
The house of God not made with hands,
A great High Priest our nature wears,
The guardian of mankind appears.

2 He who for men their surety stood,
And poured on earth his precious blood,
Pursues in heaven his mighty plan,
The Saviour and the Friend of man.

3 Though now ascended up on high,
He bends on earth a brother's eye;
Partaker of the human name,
He knows the frailty of our frame.

4 In every pang that rends the heart,
The Man of Sorrows had a part;
He sympathizes with our grief,
And to the sufferer sends relief.

5. With boldness, therefore, at the throne,
Let us make all our sorrows known;
And ask the aids of heavenly power
To help us in the evil hour.

Scottish Paraphrases (1781)

CHOIR SETTINGS

499 CONGLETON 10.10.10.10.   *The Standard Psalm Tune-book* (1852)

ABIDE with me; fast falls the eventide:
The darkness deepens; Lord, with me abide;
When other helpers fail, and comforts flee,
Help of the helpless, O abide with me.

2 Swift to its close ebbs out life's little day;
Earth's joys grow dim, its glories pass away;
Change and decay in all around I see;
O thou who changest not, abide with me.

3 I need thy presence every passing hour;
What but thy grace can foil the tempter's power?
Who like thyself my guide and stay can be?
Through cloud and sunshine, O abide with me.

4 I fear no foe, with thee at hand to bless;
Ills have no weight, and tears no bitterness;
Where is death's sting? Where, grave, thy victory?
I triumph still, if thou abide with me.

5. Hold thou thy Cross before my closing eyes;
Shine through the gloom, and point me to the skies:
Heaven's morning breaks, and earth's vain shadows flee;
In life, in death, O Lord, abide with me.

Henry Francis Lyte (1793–1847)

500 HERZLIEBSTER JESU 11.11.11.5.

Later form of melody by
JOHANN CRÜGER (1598–1662)

Herzliebster Jesu

AH, holy Jesus, how hast thou offended,
   That man to judge thee hath in hate pretended?
By foes derided, by thine own rejected,
   O most afflicted.

2 Who was the guilty? Who brought this upon thee?
   Alas, my treason, Jesus, hath undone thee.
   'Twas I, Lord Jesus, I it was denied thee:
      I crucified thee.

3. Lo, the good Shepherd for the sheep is offered;
   The slave hath sinnèd, and the Son hath suffered;
   For man's atonement, while he nothing heedeth,
      God intercedeth.

Johann Heermann (1505–1647)
Par. Robert Bridges (1844–1930)

501 WARUM SOLLT' ICH MICH
DENN GRÄMEN 83.36. D.

Melody by JOHANN GEORG EBELING (1637–76)
Adapted and harmonized by JOHANN SEBASTIAN
BACH (1685–1750)

WARUM SOLLT' ICH MICH
DENN GRÄMEN 83.36. D.

The same, harmonized by the Compilers

CHOIR SETTINGS.

Fröhlich soll mein Herze springen

ALL my heart this night rejoices,
   As I hear,
   Far and near,
Sweetest angel voices;
'Christ is born', their choirs are singing,
   Till the air,
   Everywhere,
Now with joy is ringing.

2 Hark, a voice from yonder manger,
   Soft and sweet,
   Doth entreat,
'Flee from woe and danger;
Brethren, come; from all doth grieve you
   You are freed;
   All you need
I will surely give you.'

3. Come then, let us hasten yonder;
   Here let all,
   Great and small,
Kneel in awe and wonder;
Love him who with love is yearning;
   Hail the star
   That from far
Bright with hope is burning.

Paulus Gerhardt (1607–76)
Tr. Catherine Winkworth (1827–78)

502 REMENHAM 10.10.10.10.

WALTER K. STANTON (1891–)

Solus ad victimam procedis, Domine

ALONE to sacrifice thou goest, Lord,
  Giving thyself to Death whom thou hast slain.
For us thy wretched folk is any word,
  Who know that for our sins this is thy pain?

2 For they are ours, O Lord, our deeds, our deeds,
  Why must thou suffer torture for our sin?
Let our hearts suffer in thy Passion, Lord,
  That very suffering may thy mercy win.

3 This is the night of tears, the three days' space,
  Sorrow abiding of the eventide,
Until the day break with the risen Christ,
  And hearts that sorrowed shall be satisfied.

4. So may our hearts share in thine anguish, Lord,
  That they may sharers of thy glory be;
Heavy with weeping may the three days pass,
  To win the laughter of thine Easter Day.

Peter Abelard (1079–1142)
Tr. Helen Waddell (1889–1965)

Another translation of these words will be found at No. 79

503 RENDEZ À DIEU 98.98.D.
(PSALM 118)

Melody composed or adapted by
LOUIS BOURGEOIS in *Genevan Psalter* (1543)

Bread of the world, in mer-cy bro-ken, Wine of the soul, in mer-cy shed, By whom the words of life were spo-ken, And in whose death our sins are dead: Look on the heart by sor-row bro-ken, Look on the tears by sin-ners shed; And be thy feast to us the to-ken That by thy grace our souls are fed.

Reginald Heber (1783–1826)

504 CAST THY BURDEN Irregular.

Melody from *Meiningen*
Gesangbuch (1693), adapted and harmonized by
FELIX MENDELSSOHN-BARTHOLDY (1809–47)

C̲AST thy burden upon the Lord,
  And he shall sustain thee.
He never will suffer the righteous to fall:
  He is at thy right hand.
Thy mercy, Lord, is great;
  And far above the heavens.
Let none be made ashamèd,
  That wait upon thee.

? *William Bartholomew* (1793–1867)

505 JESUS, UNSER TROST
UND LEBEN Irregular.

Melody Anon. (1714)
Bass by Johann Sebastian Bach (1685–1750)

Al - le - lu - ia, Al-le-lu - ia.

Jesus, unser Trost und Leben

CHRIST, our helper and life-giver,
Did himself to death deliver;
    Now, all glorious from the strife,
    Brings us victory, brings us life,
Death's cruel bands asunder rending,
Crowned with glory never ending,
    Alleluia, Alleluia.

2 Nobly through the fight he bore him,
Satan's armies fled before him;
    Not a fiend can shame us more,
    Rage his anger ne'er so sore.
Wherefore Sion now rejoices,
Pealing out with myriad voices,
    Alleluia, Alleluia.

3. New again in youth and beauty
Earth takes up her tuneful duty;
    All things living far and wide
    Don the dress of Eastertide.
E'en the seas for joy are singing,
Clear o'er vale and mount is ringing
    Alleluia, Alleluia.

Ernst Christoph Homburg (1605–81)
Tr. Geoffrey William Daisley (1877–1939)

506 NUN LASST UNS
GOTT 77.77.

Melody by NICOLAUS SELNECKER (1528–92)
Harmonized by JOHANN SEBASTIAN BACH (1685–1750)

CHRIST was the Word who spake it:
He took the bread and brake it:
And what his word doth make it,
That I believe and take it.

16th cent.

CHOIR SETTINGS

507 CAMBRIDGE 66.65.65.

CHARLES WOOD (1866–1926)

Rather slowly

ORGAN

Ped.

Voices

1 Christ who knows all his sheep Will all in safe-ty
take this spi-rit:We trust thy love and

keep, He will not lose one soul, Nor ev-er
me-rit. Take home the wand-'ring sheep, For thou hast

fail us; Nor we the prom-ised goal, Though hell as-
sought it; This soul in safe-ty keep, For thou hast

small notes Org.

Unison

-sail us. 2 I know my God is
bought it.

ORGAN

FINE (small notes)

507 (*continued*)

just; To him I whol - ly trust All that I have and am, All that I hope for: All's sure and seen to him, Which here I grope for.

3. Lord Je - sus

CHRIST who knows all his sheep
　Will all in safety keep,
　He will not lose one soul,
　　Nor ever fail us;
　Nor we the promised goal,
　　　Though hell assail us.

2 I know my God is just;
　To him I wholly trust
　　All that I have and am,
　　　All that I hope for:
　All's sure and seen to him,
　　　Which here I grope for.

3. Lord Jesus, take this spirit:
　We trust thy love and merit.
　　Take home the wandering sheep,
　　　For thou hast sought it;
　This soul in safety keep,
　　　For thou hast bought it.

Richard Baxter (1615–91)

CHOIR SETTINGS

508 VENI CREATOR 88.88.88.
(ATTWOOD)

THOMAS ATTWOOD (1765–1838)

Verses 1, 2, (see opposite page for Verse 3)

CHOIR SETTINGS

Veni, Creator Spiritus

COME, Holy Ghost, our souls inspire,
And lighten with celestial fire;
Thou the anointing Spirit art,
Who dost thy sevenfold gifts impart.
Thy blessèd unction from above
Is comfort, life, and fire of love.

2 Enable with perpetual light
The dullness of our blinded sight:
Anoint and cheer our soilèd face
With the abundance of thy grace:
Keep far our foes, give peace at home;
Where thou art guide no ill can come.

3. Teach us to know the Father, Son,
And thee, of both, to be but one;
That through the ages all along
This may be our endless song:
Praise to thy eternal merit,
Father, Son, and Holy Spirit.

? 9th cent. Par. John Cosin (1594–1672)

509 PSALM 38 847. D.

Melody composed or adapted by
LOUIS BOURGEOIS in *Genevan Psalter* (1542)
Set by HARRY ELLIS WOOLDRIDGE (1845–1917)

CHOIR SETTINGS

Τὴν ἡμέραν διελθών

DARKENING night the land doth cover;
    Day is over:
We give thanks, O thou Most High;
While with wonted hymn we adore thee,
    And implore thee
For the light that doth not die.

2* Like a day our short life hasteth,
    Soon it wasteth;
Cometh surely its sad eve.
O do thou that eve enlighten,
    Save and brighten;
Nor old age of joy bereave.

3* Come no pain nor pity near it,
    Bless and cheer it,
That in peace we our peace win;
As thou wilt do thou us gather,
    Gracious Father,
Only without shame and sin.

4. Now we pray for rest, that sleeping
    In thy keeping,
We may joy in the sun's ray;
So through death's last darkness take us,
    So awake us
To heaven's everlasting day.

? 6th cent. Tr. Robert Bridges (1844–1930)

For another translation of these words see No. 425

510 SCHMÜCKE DICH 88.88.D. Melody by JOHANN CRÜGER (1598–1662)

CHOIR SETTINGS

PART I

DECK thyself, my soul, with gladness,
Leave the gloomy haunts of sadness,
Come into the daylight's splendour,
There with joy thy praises render
Unto him whose grace unbounded
Hath this wondrous banquet founded:
High o'er all the heavens he reigneth,
Yet to dwell with thee he deigneth.

2. Now I sink before thee lowly,
Filled with joy most deep and holy,
As with trembling awe and wonder
On thy mighty works I ponder;
How, by mystery surrounded,
Depths no man hath ever sounded,
None may dare to pierce unbidden
Secrets that with thee are hidden.

PART 2

1 Sun, who all my life dost brighten;
Light, who dost my soul enlighten;
Joy, the sweetest man e'er knoweth;
Fount, whence all my being floweth:
At thy feet I cry, my Maker,
Let me be a fit partaker
Of this blessèd food from heaven,
For our good, thy glory, given.

2. Jesus, bread of life, I pray thee,
Let me gladly here obey thee;
Never to my hurt invited,
Be thy love with love requited:
From this banquet let me measure,
Lord, how vast and deep its treasure;
Through the gifts thou here dost give me,
As thy guest in heaven receive me.

Johann Franck (1618–77)
Tr. Catherine Winkworth (1827–78)

CHOIR SETTINGS

511 KIEFF MELODY Irregular.   *Edited by* WALTER PARRATT (1841–1924)

Со святыми упокой, Христе

Μετὰ τῶν ἁγίων ἀνάπαυσον, Χριστέ

Give rest, O Christ, to thy ser-vant with thy saints:

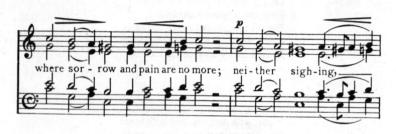

where sor – row and pain are no more; nei-ther sigh-ing,

but life ev-er-last – ing. Thou on-ly art im-mor-tal,

the Cre-a-tor and Ma-ker of man: and we are mor-tal,

form-ed of the earth, and un-to earth shall we re-turn:

for so thou didst or-dain, when thou cre-a-tedst me,

511 (*continued*)

say - ing, Dust thou art, and un-to dust shalt thou re-turn.

All we go down to the dust; and, weeping o'er the grave,

we make our song: Al-le-lu-ia, Al-le-lu-ia, Al-le-lu - ia.

Tr. William John Birkbeck (1859–1916)

512 ACINOM Irregular.

WALTER K. STANTON (1891–   )

God be in my head, and in my un-der-stand-ing;

God be in mine eyes, and in my look-ing;

God be in my mouth, and in my speak-ing;

God be in my heart, and in my think-ing;

God be at mine end, and my de-part-ing.

Horae B.V.M. (London, 1514)

513 GOTT LEBET
NOCH Irregular.

Melody by
JOHANN ANASTASIUS FREYLINGHAUSEN (1670–1739)
Bass by JOHANN SEBASTIAN BACH (1685–1750)

Gott lebet noch

GOD liveth still:
    Soul, why takest thought of ill?
God is good, and God's compassion
    Never turns from earth away;
His protecting hand will fashion
    Right from wrong, health from decay.
Though we see not how, from sorrow
Blessing shapes he for the morrow.
    So, my soul, reck naught of ill:
    God is living, living still.

2.   God liveth still:
    Soul, why fearest aught of ill?
Though thy cross be sore oppressing,
    To thy God direct thy way.
He will pour on thee his blessing,
    To thy feet be staff and stay.
For his truth endureth ever,
His compassion faileth never.
    So, my soul, reck naught of ill:
    God is living, living still.

Johann Friedrich Zihn (1650–1719)
Tr. Geoffrey William Daisley (1877–1939)

CHOIR SETTINGS

514 SEBASTE Irregular.   JOHN STAINER (1840–1901)

φῶς ἱλαρόν

1 Hail, gladdening Light, of his pure glo-ry poured

Who is the immortal Fa - ther, heav'n-ly, blest,

Ho - li-est of ho-lies, Je-sus Christ, our Lord.

2 Now we are come to the sun's hour of rest,

The lights of ev'-ning round us shine, We hymn the Fa-ther,

CHOIR SETTINGS

Son, and Ho-ly Spi-rit di-vine. 3. Worthiest art thou at all times to be sung With un-de-fil-èd tongue, Son of our God, giv-er of life, a-lone;— There-fore in all the world thy glor-ies Lord, they own.

3rd cent. (or earlier)
Tr. John Keble (1792–1866)

515 DELGANEY Irregular.

PERCY CARTER BUCK (1871-1947)

1 In to this world of sor - row, In - to this
val - ley of rue and sad-ness, Came Christ, our dear Con -
so - ler, And brought men glad - - - ness.
And brought men glad - ness.

2 Now is the time of his com - ing, Now are our
hearts with joy re - plete; But to lead men to
hea - ven, He bread of tears did eat.
He bread of tears did eat.

Anon.

516 ES IST VOLLBRACHT Irregular.

Melody ANON. (1714). Bass by
JOHANN SEBASTIAN BACH (1685–1750)

Es ist vollbracht

IT is finishèd! ah, grant, O Lord,
My heart may ne'er forget this
word,
That Jesus at the consummation
Of his great work for our salvation
Spake, as he saw that work accom-
plishèd,
This last great word—It is finishèd.

2. It is finishèd! ah, Jesu, Lord,
Grant I may ne'er forget that
word;
But make it my ensample ever,
To put good end to each endeavour;
Remembering all my life how Jesus
said
With his last breath—It is finishèd.

*Johann Eusebius Schmidt (1669–1745)
Tr. Geoffrey William Daisley (1877–1939)
Based on S. John 19, 30*

517 SONG 13 77.77.

Melody and Bass by
ORLANDO GIBBONS (1583–1625)

Dignare me, O Jesu, rogo te

JESU, grant me this, I pray,
Ever in thy heart to stay;
Let me evermore abide
Hidden in thy wounded side.

2 If the evil one prepare,
Or the world, a tempting snare,
I am safe when I abide
In thy heart and wounded side.

3 If the flesh, more dangerous still,
Tempt my soul to deeds of ill,
Naught I fear when I abide
In thy heart and wounded side.

4. Death will come one day to me;
Jesu, cast me not from thee:
Dying, let me still abide
In thy heart and wounded side.

17th cent. Tr. Henry Williams Baker (1821–77)

518 JESU, MEINE
FREUDE 665.D.786.

German Traditional Melody, adapted by JOHANN CRÜGER
(1598–1662). Further adapted and harmonized by
JOHANN SEBASTIAN BACH (1685–1750)

Jesu, meine Freude

JESU, priceless treasure,
Source of purest pleasure,
   Truest friend to me;
Ah, how long I've panted,
And my heart hath fainted,
   Thirsting, Lord, for thee!
Thine I am, O spotless Lamb,
I will suffer naught to hide thee,
   Naught I ask beside thee.

2. Hence, all fears and sadness,
For the Lord of gladness,
   Jesus, enters in;
Those who love the Father,
Though the storms may gather,
   Still have peace within;
Yea, whate'er I here must bear,
Still in thee lies purest pleasure,
   Jesu, priceless treasure!

*Johann Franck (1618–77)
Tr. Catherine Winkworth (1827–78)*

519 JESUS IST DAS
SCHÖNSTE LICHT Irregular.

Melody ANON. (1704). Bass by
JOHANN SEBASTIAN BACH (1685–1750)

Jesus ist das schönste Licht

JESUS is this dark world's light,
  Jesus is his Father's pleasure,
If his words do tell aright;
  So let him be all my treasure.
Sweet is Jesus' touch and sure,
  Setting all my love a-burning,
Satisfying all my yearning
  For a peace that shall endure.

2. Jesu, rest and peace of mine,
  Jesu, Jesu, seek and find me.
With the cords of love divine
  To thyself, sweet Jesu, bind me.
Ever will I turn to thee,
  For thou only shalt possess me.
Though all hell's fierce powers
    oppress me,
  Thine for ever will I be.

Christian Friedrich Richter (1676–1711)
Tr. Geoffrey William Daisley (1877–1939)

520 SONG 24 10.10.10.10.

Melody and Bass by
ORLANDO GIBBONS (1583–1625)

LIGHTEN the darkness of our life's long night,
    Through which we blindly stumble to the day.
Shadows mislead us: Father, send thy light
    To set our footsteps in the homeward way.

2 Lighten the darkness of our self-conceit,
    The subtle darkness that we love so well,
Which shrouds the path of wisdom from our feet,
    And lulls our spirits with its baneful spell.

3 Lighten our darkness when we bow the knee
    To all the gods we ignorantly make
And worship, dreaming that we worship thee,
    Till clearer light our slumbering souls awake.

4. Lighten our darkness when we fail at last,
    And in the midnight lay us down to die;
We trust to find thee when the night is past,
    And daylight breaks across the morning sky.

Frances Owen (1842–83)

521 JESUS IST MEIN
AUFENTHALT 78.78.77.

Melody ANON. Harmonized by
JOHANN SEBASTIAN BACH (1685–1750)

LOVE of love, and Light of light,
    Heavenly Father, all maintaining;
Wisdom hid in highest height,
    To thy creature fondly deigning;
Maker wonderful and just,
Thou hast called my heart to trust.

2 What are life's unnumbered cares,
    Sorrow, torment, passing measure?
O'er my short-lived pains and fears
    Surely ruleth thy good pleasure.
Boundless is thy love for me,
Boundless then my trust shall be.

3. Every burden weigheth light,
    Since in thee my hope abideth;
Sweetly bright my darkest night,
    While on thee my mind confideth.
Give thy gift, I thee implore,
Thee to trust for evermore.

Robert Bridges (1844–1930)

522 SONG 22 10.10.10.10.

Melody and Bass by
ORLANDO GIBBONS (1583–1625)

Amor Patris et Filii

LOVE of the Father, Love of God the Son,
From whom all came, in whom was all begun;
Who formest heavenly beauty out of strife,
Creation's whole desire and breath of life:

2 Thou the all-holy, thou supreme in might,
Thou dost give peace, thy presence maketh right;
Thou with thy favour all things dost enfold,
With thine all-kindness free from harm wilt hold.

3 Hope of all comfort, splendour of all aid,
That dost not fail nor leave the heart afraid:
To all that cry thou dost all help accord,
The angels' armour, and the saints' reward.

4 Purest and highest, wisest and most just,
There is no truth save only in thy trust;
Thou dost the mind from earthly dreams recall,
And bring, through Christ, to him for whom are all.

5. Eternal glory, all men thee adore,
Who art and shalt be worshipped evermore:
Us whom thou madest, comfort with thy might,
And lead us to enjoy thy heavenly light.

12th cent. Par. Robert Bridges (1844–1930)

523 CHASTLETON 847.D.

WALTER K. STANTON (1891–)

CHOIR SETTINGS

LOVE, unto thine own who camest
  Condescending,
 Whom thine own receivèd not:
Light, that shinedst in the darkness,
  But the darkness
 Thy splendour perceivèd not:

2 O blessèd were they who saw thee,
  Who were chosen
 First saints of thy saving word:
Blessèd they who have not seen thee,
  Yet believing
 Are callèd by thee, O Lord.

3 Like stars in the night appearing,
  Some are shining,
 Leaders high of man's desire:
Saints are some, in silent temples
  Ever burning,
 Bright lamps of love's living fire.

4 Thou hidest them, Love almighty,
  In thy presence,
 From this world's provoking wrongs:
Sheltered in thy quiet haven
  Thou dost keep them
 From strife of ungodly tongues.

5. Love, unto thine own who camest,
  May thy servants
 Thy great love receive aright:
Grant, O grant that out of darkness
  All creation
 May come to thy marvellous light.

Robert Bridges (1844–1930)

524 GOTT DES
HIMMELS 87.87.

Melody by HEINRICH ALBERT (1604–51)
Harmonized by JOHANN SEBASTIAN BACH (1685–1750)

MAY the grace of Christ our
Saviour,
And the Father's boundless love,
With the Holy Spirit's favour,
Rest upon us from above.

2. Thus may we abide in union
With each other and the Lord,
And possess in sweet communion
Joys which earth cannot afford.

John Newton (1725–1807)
Based on 2 Corinthians 13, 14

525 INNSBRUCK 776.77.10.

HEINRICH ISAAK (c. 1455–1520)

O Welt, ich muss dich lassen

MY heart is filled with longing,
And thick the thoughts come thronging,
Of my eternal home:
That all desire fulfilleth,
And woe and terror stilleth:
Ah, thither fain, thither fain would I come.

2   Creation knows no staying,
And, with the world decaying,
Love may itself decay:
Yea, as the earth grows older,
Her grace and beauty moulder,
Her joy of life passeth, passeth away.

3. But thou, O Love supremest,
Who man from woe redeemest,
My Maker, thee I pray,
My soul, with night surrounded,
Above the abyss unsounded
Lead forth to light, lead to thy heavenly day.

Par. Robert Bridges (1844–1930)

526 CHRISTUS DER IST
MEIN LEBEN 76.76.

Melody by MELCHIOR VULPIUS (c. 1560–1616)
Harmonized by JOHANN SEBASTIAN BACH (1685–1750)

MY soul, there is a country
Far beyond the stars,
Where stands a wingèd sentry
All skilful in the wars.

2 There, above noise and danger,
Sweet peace sits, crowned with smiles,
And one born in a manger
Commands the beauteous files.

3 He is thy gracious friend,
And—O my soul, awake!—
Did in pure love descend,
To die here for thy sake.

4 If thou canst get but thither,
There grows the flower of peace,
The rose that cannot wither,
Thy fortress and thy ease.

5. Leave then thy foolish ranges,
For none can thee secure
But one, who never changes,
Thy God, thy life, thy cure.

Henry Vaughan the Silurist (1622–95)

CHOIR SETTINGS

527 ACH BLEIB BEI UNS L.M.
(CALVISIUS)

Founded on a melody by SETH CALVISIUS
(1556–1615)
Harmonized by JOHANN SEBASTIAN BACH
(1685–1750)

Ach bleib bei uns, Herr Jesu Christ

NOW cheer our hearts this eventide,
Lord Jesus Christ, and with us bide;
Thou that canst never set in night,
Our heavenly sun, our glorious light.

2. May we and all who bear thy name
By gentle love thy Cross proclaim:
Thy gift of peace on earth secure,
And for thy truth the world endure.

Robert Bridges (1844–1930)
Based on Nicolaus Selnecker (1532–92)

528 OXFORD C.M.

Melody by JAMES MORRIS COOMBS (1769–1820)

O GOD unseen, yet ever near,
Thy presence may we feel;
And thus inspired with holy fear,
Before thine altar kneel.

2 Here may thy faithful people know
The blessings of thy love,
The streams that through the desert flow,
The manna from above.

3 We come, obedient to thy word,
To feast on heavenly food;
Our meat the body of the Lord,
Our drink his precious blood.

4. Thus may we all thy word obey,
For we, O God, are thine;
And go rejoicing on our way,
Renewed with strength divine.

Edward Osler (1798–1863)

529 O JESULEIN SÜSS Irregular.

Melody ANON. (1650). Bass by JOHANN
SEBASTIAN BACH (1685–1750)

O Jesulein süss

O JESU so meek, O Jesu so kind,
  Thou hast fulfilled thy Father's mind;
Hast come from heaven down to earth
  In human flesh through human birth.
O Jesu so meek, O Jesu so kind.

2. O Jesu so good, O Jesu so meek,
  To do thy will is all we seek:
For all we are or have is thine:
  Do thou our hearts to thee incline.
O Jesu so good, O Jesu so meek.

Valentin Thilo (1607–62)
Tr. Geoffrey William Daisley (1877–1939)

530 O LAMM GOTTES 77.77.77.9.

Rheinfels Gesangbuch (1666). Set by
GEORGE RATCLIFFE WOODWARD (1849–1934)

O Lamm Gottes unschuldig

O LAMB of God all-holy,
  Who on the Cross didst suffer,
And, patient still and lowly,
  Thyself to scorn didst offer:
Our sins by thee were taken,
Or hope had us forsaken:
  Have mercy upon us, O Jesu.

Nicolas Decius (1519–41)
Tr. Arthur Tozer Russell (1806–74)

CHOIR SETTINGS

531 DESMOND 88.88.88.   GEORGE HEATH-GRACIE (1896–   )

O LEAD my blindness by the hand,
　　Lead me to thy familiar feast,
Not here or now to understand,
　　Yet even here and now to taste,
How the eternal Word of heaven
On earth in broken bread is given.

2 We, who this holy precinct round
　　In one adoring circle kneel,
May we in one intent be bound,
　　And one serene devotion feel;
And grow around thy sacred shrine
Like tendrils of the deathless vine.

3. We, who with one blest food are fed,
　　Into one body may we grow,
And one pure life from thee, the Head,
　　Informing all the members, flow;
One pulse be felt in every vein,
One law of pleasure and of pain.

William Ewart Gladstone (1809–98)

CHOIR SETTINGS

532 CHRISTMAS CAROL D.C.M. Irregular.

HENRY WALFORD DAVIES
(1869–1941)

CHOIR SETTINGS

O LITTLE town of Bethlehem,
   How still we see thee lie!
Above thy deep and dreamless sleep
   The silent stars go by:
Yet in thy dark streets shineth
   The everlasting Light;
The hopes and fears of all the years
   Are met in thee to-night.

2 O morning stars, together
   Proclaim the holy birth,
And praises sing to God the King,
   And peace to men on earth.
For Christ is born of Mary;
   And, gathered all above,
While mortals sleep, the angels keep
   Their watch of wondering love.

3 How silently, how silently,
   The wondrous gift is given!
So God imparts to human hearts
   The blessings of his heaven.
No ear may hear his coming;
   But in this world of sin,
Where meek souls will receive him, still
   The dear Christ enters in.

4. O holy Child of Bethlehem,
   Descend to us, we pray;
Cast out our sin, and enter in,
   Be born in us to-day.
We hear the Christmas angels
   The great glad tidings tell:
O come to us, abide with us,
   Our Lord Immanuel.

Phillips Brooks (1835–93)

533 PASSION CHORALE 76.76.D.

Melody by HANS LEO HASSLER (1564–1612)
Adapted and harmonized by JOHANN
SEBASTIAN BACH (1685–1750)

O Haupt voll Blut und Wunden

O SACRED head, sore wounded,
  Defiled and put to scorn;
O kingly head, surrounded
  With mocking crown of thorn:
What sorrow mars thy grandeur?
  Can death thy bloom deflower?
O countenance whose splendour
  The hosts of heaven adore!

2. In thy most bitter Passion
  My heart to share doth cry,
With thee for my salvation
  Upon the Cross to die.
Ah, keep my heart thus movèd
  To stand thy Cross beneath,
To mourn thee, well-belovèd,
  Yet thank thee for thy death.

From Salve caput cruentatum (? Arnulf von Loewen, 1200–50)
Tr. Paulus Gerhardt (1607–76). Par. Robert Bridges (1844–1930)

534 LOBE DEN HERREN 14.14.4.7.8.

Melody from *Stralsund Gesangbuch* (1665)
Harmonized by JOHANN SEBASTIAN BACH
(1685–1750)

CHOIR SETTINGS

Lobe den Herren

PRAISE to the Lord, the Almighty, the King of creation;
O my soul, praise him, for he is thy health and salvation:
> All ye who hear,
> Brothers and sisters, draw near,
Praise him in glad adoration.

2 Praise to the Lord, who o'er all things so wondrously reigneth,
Shelters thee under his wings, yea, so gently sustaineth:
> Hast thou not seen?
> All that is needful hath been
Granted in what he ordaineth.

3 Praise to the Lord, who doth prosper thy work and defend thee;
Surely his goodness and mercy here daily attend thee:
> Ponder anew
> What the Almighty can do
Whc with his love doth befriend thee.

4. Praise to the Lord, O let all that is in me adore him!
All that hath life and breath come now with praises before him!
> Let the amen
> Sound from his people again:
Gladly for aye we adore him!

Joachim Neander (1650–80)
Tr. Catherine Winkworth (1827–78) *and Compilers*
Based on Psalms 103 & 150

535 HYMNUS EUCHARISTICUS L.M. BENJAMIN ROGERS (1614–98)

S EE, Father, thy belovèd Son
  Whom here we now present to thee;
The all-sufficient sacrifice,
  The sinner's one and only plea.

2. Through him we pray for all we love,
    For all by pain or sin oppressed;
For souls departed in thy fear:
    O grant them thine eternal rest.

William Henry Hammond Jervois (1852–1905)

CHOIR SETTINGS

Melody Anon. (1625)
Harmonized by Johann Sebastian Bach
(1685–1750)

536 ACH GOTT UND HERR 87.87.

STRENGTHEN for service, Lord, the hands
    That holy things have taken;
Let ears that now have heard thy songs
    To clamour never waken.

2 Lord, may the tongues which 'Holy' sang
    Keep free from all deceiving;
The eyes which saw thy love be bright,
    Thy blessèd hope perceiving.

3. The feet that tread thy holy courts
    From light do thou not banish;
The bodies by thy body fed
    With thy new life replenish.

Liturgy of Malabar
Tr. C. W. Humphreys, Percy Dearmer (1867–1936), and others

B b

CHOIR SETTINGS

537 FRESHWATER Irregular.

CHARLES HUBERT HASTINGS PARRY
(1848–1918)

1. Sun-set and eve-ning star, And one clear call for me!
2. Twi-light and eve-ning bell, And af-ter that the dark!

And may there be no moan-ing of the bar, When
And may there be no sad-ness of fare-well, When

I put out to sea, But such a tide as mov-ing seems a-
I ____ em-bark; For, though from out our bourne of time and

-sleep, Too full for sound and foam, When that which drew from
place, The flood may bear me far, I hope to see my

out the bound-less deep Turns a-gain home.
Pi-lot face to face When I have crossed the bar.

Alfred, Lord Tennyson (1809–92)

538 SHENG EN 98.98.
(GOD'S GRACE)

Melody by Su Yin-Lan (1934)

救世之身爲衆生擘

THE bread of life, for all men broken!
   He drank the cup on Golgotha.
His grace we trust, and spread with reverence
   This holy feast, and thus remember.

2 With godly fear we seek thy presence;
   Our hearts are sad, people distressed.
Thy holy face is stained with bitter tears,
   Our human pain still bearest thou with us.

3. O Lord, we pray, come thou among us,
   Lighten our eyes, brightly appear!
Immanuel, heaven's joy unending,
   Our life with thine for ever blending.

Timothy Tingfang Lew (1891–1947)
Tr. Walter Reginald Oxenham Taylor (1890–   )

First tune

539 SPARSHOLT 65.65.D.　　　　　　　　　WALTER K. STANTON (1891–　　)

Yesu Bin Mariamu

THINK, O Lord, in mercy,
　On the souls of those
Who, in faith gone from us,
　Now in death repose.
Here, 'mid stress and conflict,
　Toils can never cease;
There, the warfare ended,
　Bid them rest in peace.

2 Often were they wounded
　In the deadly strife;
Heal them, good Physician,
　With the balm of life.

Every taint of evil,
　Frailty and decay,
Good and gracious Saviour,
　Cleanse and purge away.

3. Rest eternal grant them,
　After weary fight;
Shed on them the radiance
　Of thy heavenly light.
Lead them onward, upward,
　To the holy place,
Where thy saints, made perfect,
　Gaze upon thy face.

Written in Swahili. Tr. Edmund Stuart Palmer (1856–1931)

Second tune

539 REQUIEM 65.65.D.   J. ERIC HUNT (1903–   )

Yesu Bin Mariamu

THINK, O Lord, in mercy,
  On the souls of those
Who, in faith gone from us,
  Now in death repose.
Here, 'mid stress and conflict,
  Toils can never cease;
There, the warfare ended,
  Bid them rest in peace.

2 Often were they wounded
  In the deadly strife;
Heal them, good Physician,
  With the balm of life.

Every taint of evil,
  Frailty and decay,
Good and gracious Saviour,
  Cleanse and purge away.

3. Rest eternal grant them,
  After weary fight;
Shed on them the radiance
  Of thy heavenly light.
Lead them onward, upward,
  To the holy place,
Where thy saints, made perfect,
  Gaze upon thy face.

Written in Swahili. Tr. Edmund Stuart Palmer (1856–1931)

540 RHYDDID 76.76.D.

Welsh Melody

WE hail thy presence glorious
　O Christ, our great High Priest,
O'er sin and death victorious,
　At thy thanksgiving feast;
As thou art interceding
　For us in heaven above,
Thy Church on earth is pleading
　Thy perfect work of love.

2 Through thee in every nation
　Thine own their hearts upraise,
Offering one pure oblation,
　One sacrifice of praise:
With thee, in blest communion,
　The living and the dead,
Are joined in closest union,
　One body with one Head.

3 O living bread from heaven,
　Jesu, our Saviour good,
Who thine own self hast given
　To be our souls' true food;

For us thy body broken
　Hung on the cross of shame;
This bread its hallowed token
　We break in thy dear name.

4 O stream of love unending,
　Poured from the one true vine,
With our weak nature blending
　The strength of life divine;
Our thankful faith confessing
　In thy life-blood outpoured,
We drink this cup of blessing,
　And praise thy name, O Lord.

5. May we, thy word believing,
　Thee through thy gifts receive,
That, thou within us living,
　We all to God may live;
Draw us from earth to heaven,
　Till sin and sorrow cease,
Forgiving and forgiven,
　In love and joy and peace.

Richard Godfrey Parsons (1882–1948)

541 WIE SCHÖN
LEUCHTET 887.D.48.48.

Melody by PHILIPP NICOLAI (1556–1608)
Harmonized by GEORG GOTTFRIED WAGNER
(1698–1756)

WHAT tongue can tell thy greatness, Lord,
    That art in all the world adored,
  The world by thee created?
Through all this temple praise abounds;
Unceasing praise to thee resounds,
    By every voice repeated.
        Amen, Amen,
        So is 'Holy, holy, holy'
        Ever ringing,
Where the angel choirs are singing.

? *Alfred Angel*

542 LEGEND Irregular.

PETER ILITCH TSCHAIKOWSKY (1840–93)

1 When Je-sus Christ was yet a child He had a gar - den small and wild, Where-in he cher-ished ro-ses fair, And wove them in - to gar-lands there. 2 Now once, as sum - mer-time drew nigh, There came a

troop of chil-dren by, And see-ing ro-ses on the tree, With shouts they plucked them mer - ri - ly.

3 'Do you bind ro-ses in your hair?' They cried, in
'Do you bind ro-ses in your hair?' They cried, in
3 'Do you bind ro-ses in your hair?' They cried in

scorn, to Je-sus there. The boy said hum-bly: 'Take, I

542 (continued)

pray, All but the nak-ed thorns a-way.' Then of the

thorns they made a crown, And with rough fin-gers pressed it

down, Till on his fore-head fair and young Red drops of

blood ____ like ro-ses sprung.

like ro-ses sprung, like ro-ses sprung.

Alexei Nikolaievich Plechtchéev (1825–93)
Tr. Geoffrey Dearmer (1893–)

HYMNS FOR USE IN PROCESSION

ADVENT

All glory to God in the sky, 29.
Hills of the north, rejoice, 33.
Lift up your heads, ye mighty gates, 34.
Lo! he comes with clouds descending, 35.
O come, O come, Immanuel, 36.

CHRISTMAS

Christians, awake, salute the happy morn, 46.
From east to west, from shore to shore, 47.
Hark, the herald-angels sing, 50.
It came upon the midnight clear, 52.
O Christ, Redeemer of our race, 54.
O come, all ye faithful, 55.
O little town of Bethlehem, 56.
Of the Father's love begotten, 57.
Once in royal David's city, 58.
Sing, O sing, this blessèd morn!, 59.

EPIPHANY

As with gladness men of old, 62.
From the eastern mountains, 65.
Hail to the Lord's Anointed, 457.
O worship the Lord in the beauty of holiness, 267.
What star is this with beams so bright, 69.

PASSION SUNDAY

The royal banners forward go, 91.

PALM SUNDAY

All glory, laud, and honour, 77, 78.
Praise to the Holiest in the height, 88.
Ride on! ride on in majesty!, 89.
Sing, my tongue, the glorious battle, 90.

EASTER

Alleluia! Hearts to heaven, 98.
His cheering message from the grave, 104.
Light's glittering morn bedecks the sky, 108.
O sons and daughters, let us sing, 110.
The Lamb's high banquet doth invite, 113.

ROGATIONTIDE

To thee our God we fly, 434.

ASCENSIONTIDE

All hail the power of Jesus' name, 117.
All praise to thee, for thou, O King divine, 119.
Alleluia! sing to Jesus, 197.
At the name of Jesus, 120.
Crown him with many crowns, 124.
Hail the day that sees him rise, 125.
Lord, enthroned in heavenly splendour, 206.
See the Conqueror mounts in triumph, 129.

WHIT SUNDAY

Come, thou Holy Spirit, come, 152.
Hail, blest Spirit, Lord eternal, 154.
Thy hand, O God, has guided, 187.
To thee, O Comforter divine, 164.
(See also under *Dedication Festival* and *The Church, its Commission and Work.*)

TRINITY SUNDAY

Come, ye people, rise and sing, 270.
Holy, holy, holy, Lord God Almighty!, 169.
I bind unto myself to-day, 170.
Immortal, invisible, God only wise, 10.

FESTIVALS OF THE BLESSED VIRGIN MARY

The God whom earth and sea and sky, 239.

SAINTS' DAYS

Disposer supreme, and Judge of the earth, 226.
For all the saints who from their labours rest, 227.
How mighty are the Sabbaths, 246.
Light's abode, celestial Salem, 250.
Lo, round the throne, a glorious band, 230.
Lord, who in thy perfect wisdom, 231.
O what their joy and their glory must be, 252.
The Son of God goes forth to war, 235.
Who are these, like stars appearing, 236.

MICHAELMAS

Stars of the morning, so gloriously bright, 238.

Ye watchers and ye holy ones, 288.

DEDICATION FESTIVAL

Behold the temple of the Lord!, 171.

Christ is made the sure foundation, 445.

Faith of our fathers, taught of old, 174.

Glorious things of thee are spoken, 176.

Only-begotten, Word of God eternal, 446.

Rejoice, O people, in the mounting years, 181.

The Church's one foundation, 184.

Thy hand, O God, has guided, 187.

HARVEST THANKSGIVING

Come, ye thankful people, come, 439.

Let us, with a gladsome mind, 461.

My soul, praise the Lord!, 463.

O Lord of heaven and earth and sea, 14.

O worship the King, all glorious above, 471.

Praise, O praise our God and King, 441.

To thee, O Lord, our hearts we raise, 443.

We plough the fields, and scatter, 444.

THE CHURCH, ITS COMMISSION AND WORK

Behold the temple of the Lord!, 171.

Eternal God, whose power upholds, 23.

God is working his purpose out, 177.

Hills of the north, rejoice, 33.

Lift up your heads, ye gates of brass, 178.

Rejoice, O people, in the mounting years, 181.

Thy hand, O God, has guided, 187.

GENERAL

A safe stronghold our God is still, 297.

All creatures of our God and King, 2.

All hail the power of Jesus' name, 117.

All praise to thee, for thou, O King divine, 119.

Alleluia! sing to Jesus, 197.

At the name of Jesus, 120.

Come, ye people, rise and sing, 270.

Faith of our fathers, taught of old, 174.

For the might of thine arm, 242.

Holy, holy, holy, Lord God Almighty!, 169.

How mighty are the Sabbaths, 246.

I bind unto myself to-day, 170.

Let us, with a gladsome mind, 461.

Lord, enthroned in heavenly splendour, 206.

My soul, praise the Lord!, 463.

Now thank we all our God, 277.

O Jesus, I have promised, 360.

O Lord of heaven and earth and sea, 14.

O what their joy and their glory must be, 252.

O worship the King, all glorious above, 471.

Praise, my soul, the King of heaven, 15.

Praise to the Holiest in the height, 88.

Praise to the Lord, the Almighty, the King of creation, 17.

Rejoice, O people, in the mounting years, 181.

Sing praise to God who reigns above, 18.

Stand up, stand up for Jesus, 368.

The God of Abraham praise, 283.

Through the night of doubt and sorrow, 186.

Thy hand, O God, has guided, 187.

We hail thy presence glorious, 218.

Who is he in yonder stall, 75.

Ye boundless realms of joy, 483.

Ye watchers and ye holy ones, 288.

INDEX OF SCRIPTURE PASSAGES

OLD TESTAMENT

Genesis 1, 3 185
    28, 10–22 . . . 332
    28, 16–17 . . . 264
    28, 20–22 . . . 495
    32, 22–30 . . 4, 348
Exodus 22, 29 . . . 436
Leviticus 6, 13 . . . 362
Numbers 24, 17 . . . 69
Psalms 19, 1–6 . . . 21
    19, 7–14 . . . 456
    22, 1 . . . 93
    23 . 474, 475, 477, 480
    27 . . . 453
    34 . . . 481
    36, 5–9 . . 9, 482
    42 . . . 451
    46 . . 297, 454
    61 . . . 466
    63 . . . 468
    65 . . . 442
    67 . . . 455
    72 . . 457, 460
    82 . . . 479
    84 . . 458, 462
    85 . . . 479
    86 . . . 479
    87 . . . 176
    89 . . . 469
    90 . . . 467
    93 . . . 476
    95 . . . 465
    100 . . 450, 452
    103 . . 15, 17, 534
    104 . . 463, 471
    117 . . . 5
    118 . . . 400
    119, 33–37 . . 473
    121 . . . 459
    122 . . . 472
    124 . . . 464
    136 . . 6, 461
    145 . . 13, 19, 470
    148 . 16, 279, 478, 483
    150 . 17, 279, 534
Isaiah 2, 2–6 . . . 485
    6, 1–3 . . . 269
    9, 2–8 . . . 496
    26, 1–4 . . . 493
    33, 20–21 . . . 176
    40, 27–31 . . 300, 491

Hosea 6, 1–4 487
Joel 2, 21 433
Habakkuk 2, 14 . . . 177
Zechariah 14, 7 . . . 417

APOCRYPHA

Ecclesiasticus 50, 22–24 . . 277

NEW TESTAMENT

S. Matthew 2, 1–10 . . 65, 69
    2, 1–11 . . 62, 64
    6, 25–32 . . . 311
    13, 37–43 . . . 439
    25, 1–13 . . . 40
    25, 31–45 . . . 379
    27, 45–46 . . . 93
S. Mark 1, 12–13 . . . 341
    1, 16–17 . . . 354
    1, 32 . . . 412
    4, 3–9 . . . 188
    8, 34 . . . 369
    10, 13–16 . . . 71
S. Luke 2, 8–14 . . . 61
    2, 8–11 . . . 46
    2, 13–14 . . . 52
    2, 51 . . . 68
    4, 18–19 . . . 490
    12, 35–40 . . . 372
S. John 14, 6 . . . 338
    14, 16 . . . 160
    17, 11 . . . 213
    19, 30 . . . 516
Acts 2, 1–4 . . . 162
Romans 8, 11 . . . 106
    8, 34–39 . . . 497
1 Corinthians 13 . . . 153
2 Corinthians 13, 14 . 375, 524
Galatians 6, 14 . . . 97
Ephesians 2, 20–22 . 258, 445
    6, 10–18 . 365, 366, 368
Philippians 2, 5–11 . . 119
    2, 9–11 . . . 120
1 Timothy 1, 17 . . . 10
2 Timothy 1, 12 . . . 494
Hebrews 4, 14–16 . . 498
    4, 15–16 . . . 134
    10, 1–14 . . . 214
    13, 20–21 . . . 488
S. James 1, 27 . . . 376
1 Peter 1, 3–5 . . . 486
    3, 18–19 . . . 82

NEW TESTAMENT (contd.)

1 John 3, 1–4 .	.	.	.	484
4, 7 .	.	.	.	373
Revelation 4, 8–11 .	.	.	.	169
5, 9–10 .	.	.	.	230

Revelation 5, 9–13 .	.	.	489
5, 11–13 .	.	.	122
7, 13–17 .	230,	236,	492

INDEX OF ORIGINAL FIRST LINES OF TRANSLATED HYMNS

CHINESE

See No. 538.

DANISH

Igjennem Nat og Trængsel, 186.

FRENCH

Or peut bien dire Israel maintenant, 464.

GAELIC

Atomriug indiu niurt tren, 170.
Crist lim, Crist reum, Crist im degaid, 136.
Leanabh an aigh, 45.
Rob tu mo bhoile, a Comdi cride, 316.

GERMAN

Ach bleib bei uns, Herr Jesu Christ, 527.
Befiehl du deine Wege, 313.
Beim frühen Morgenlicht, 285.
Christe du Beistand, 179.
Christus ist erstanden, 101.
Die Nacht ist kommen, 418.
Ein' feste Burg ist unser Gott, 297.
Es ist vollbracht, 516.
Fröhlich soll mein Herze springen, 501.
Gott ist gegenwärtig, 264.
Gott lebet noch, 513.
Herzliebster Jesu, 500.
Jesu, geh' voran, 144.
Jesu, meine Freude, 518.
Jesu, unser Trost und Leben, 505.
Jesus ist das schönste Licht, 519.
Jesus lebt, 106.
Liebe die du mich zum Bilde, 361.
Liebster Jesu, wir sind hier, 257.
Lobe den Herren, 17, 534.
Macht hoch die Thür, das Thor macht weit, 34.
Meine Hoffnung stehet feste, 299.
Nun danket alle Gott, 277.
Nun ruhen alle Wälder, 427.
O Haupt voll Blut und Wunden, 86, 533.
O Jesulein süss, 529.
O Lamm Gottes unschuldig, 530.
O Traurigkeit, O Herzeleid, 96.
O Welt, ich muss dich lassen, 525.

Schmücke dich, 510.
Schönster Herr Jesu, 138, 139.
Seele du musst munter werden, 404.
Sei Lob und Ehr' dem höchsten Gut, 18.
Vom Himmel hoch da komm ich her, 48.
Wachet auf! ruft uns die Stimme, 40.
Walte fürder, nah und fern, 182.
Wer sind die vor Gottes Throne, 236.
Wie schön leuchtet der Morgenstern, 141.
Wir pflügen und wir streuen, 444.
Zu Bethlehem geboren, 315.

GREEK

Αἰνεῖτε, παῖδες, Κύριον, 280.
Ἄισωμεν πάντες λαοί, 102.
Ἀναστάσεως ἡμέρα, 112.
Ἀπὸ δόξης εἰς δόξαν πορευόμενοι, 244.
Βασιλεῦ οὐράνιε, Παράκλητε, 158.
Μέγα καὶ παράδοξον θαῦμα, 41.
Μετὰ τῶν ἁγίων ἀνάπαυσον, Χριστέ, 511.
Οὐ γὰρ βλέπεις τοὺς ταράττοντας, 339.
Σιγησάτω πᾶσα σὰρξ βροτεία, 204.
Τὴν ἡμέραν διελθών, 425, 509.
Φῶς ἱλαρόν, 416, 514.
Φωστῆρες τῆς ἀΰλου, 238.

ITALIAN

Discendi, Amor santo, 149.
Laudato sia Dio mio Signore, 2.

LATIN

A Patre unigenitus, 67.
A solis ortus cardine, 47.
Ad cenam Agni providi, 113.
Adeste, fideles, 55.
Adesto, sancta Trinitas, 165.
Adoro te devote, 217.
Aeterna Christi munera, 234.
Aeterne Rex altissime, 121.
Alleluia piis edite laudibus, 282.
Amor Jesus dulcissimus, 324.
Amor Patris et Filii, 522.
Angularis fundamentum, 258, 445.
Audi, benigne Conditor, 346.
Aurora lucis rutilat, 107, 108.
Beata nobis gaudia, 162.
Caelestis O Jerusalem, 251.
Chorus novae Jerusalem, 116.

LATIN (contd.)

Christe cunctorum Dominator alme, 446.
Christe, qui lux es et dies, 421.
Christe, Redemptor omnium, 54.
Claro paschali gaudio, 111.
Conditor alme siderum, 31.
Corde natus ex Parentis, 57.
Deus tuorum militum, 232.
Dignare me, O Jesu, rogo te, 517.
Ecce tempus idoneum, 342.
Finita jam sunt proelia, 114.
Gloria, laus, et honor, 77, 78.
Gloriosi Salvatoris, 284.
Hic breve vivitur, 241.
Hymnum canamus gloriae, 130.
In domo Patris, 233.
Instantis adventum Dei, 39.
Jam desinant suspiria, 49.
Jam lucis orto sidere, 410.
Jerusalem luminosa, 250.
Jesu, dulcedo cordium, 323.
Jesu, dulcis memoria, 322.
Jesu, nostra redemptio, 126.
Jordanis oras praevia, 38.
Labente jam solis rota, 411.
Nocte surgentes, 405.
O amor quam ecstaticus, 73.
O Deus, ego amo te, 276.
O esca viatorum, 209.
O filii et filiae, 110.
O fons amoris, Spiritus, 157.
O Pater sancte, 167.
O quam juvat, 274.
O quanta qualia sunt illa Sabbata, 246, 252.
O salutaris hostia, 212.
O sola magnarum urbium, 64.
Pange, lingua, gloriosi Corporis mysterium, 208.
Pange, lingua, gloriosi proelium certaminis, 90.

Pugnate, Christi milites, 337.
Quae stella sole pulchrior, 69.
Quem terra, pontus, aethera, 239.
Quicunque certum quaeritis, 289.
Satus Dei, volens tegi, 68.
Sermone blando Angelus, 104.
Solus ad victimam procedis, Domine, 79, 502.
Sol praeceps rapitur, 428.
Splendor paternae gloriae, 409.
Stabat Mater dolorosa, 80.
Summi Parentis Filio, 94.
Supreme quales arbiter, 226.
Tantum ergo sacramentum, 208.
Te lucis ante terminum, 413.
Urbs Sion aurea, 248.
Veni, Creator Spiritus, 151, 508.
Veni, sancte Spiritus, 152.
Veni, veni, Immanuel, 36.
Verbum supernum prodiens, a Patre, 37.
Verbum supernum prodiens, nec Patris, 216.
Vexilla Regis prodeunt, 91.

RUSSIAN

See Nos. 511, 542.

SWAHILI

Yesu Bin Mariamu, 449, 539.

SYRIAC

See Nos. 215, 536.

WELSH

Arglwydd arwain trwy'r anialwch, 140.

ALPHABETICAL INDEX OF TUNES

Abbey, 430.
Abbot's Leigh, 7, 176.
Aberdeen (S. Paul), 472.
Aberystwyth, 145[1].
Abridge, 135.
Ach bleib bei uns, 527.
Ach Gott und Herr, 215, 536.
Acinom, 512.
Ad inferos, 82.
Adeste fideles, 55.
Adoro te, 217.
Aeterna Christi munera, 234.
Affection, 69[2].
Albano, 214.
Alberta, 306[1].
All red the river, 303.
All Saints, 236.
All things bright, 3.
Angels' Song (Song 34), 224, 245, 406.
Angelus, 412.
Animae hominum, 20.
Arden, 271, 278.
Arfon, 93[1].
Ar hyd y nos, 415.
Arnold, 351[2].
Arthog, 256.
Ascendit Deus, 133.
Aurelia, 184.
Austrian Hymn, 16.
Ave virgo virginum, 102.

Babylon's Streams, 346[2].
Bangor, 79, 196.
Bedford, 336.
Bedford Park, 491.
Belgrave, 22, 356.
Bellwoods, 24.
Beweley, 192.
Binchester, 274.
Birling, 424.
Bishopthorpe, 486.
Bon accord, 465.
Bonn (Festus), 337.
Breslau, 369.
Bristol, 490.
Bromsgrove (Dyer), 235.
Bromsgrove (Psalmodia), 400.
Bryn Calfaria, 140[2].
Buckland, 146, 194, 341[2].

Bunessan, 45.
Bushmead, 386.

Caithness, 333, 488.
Cambridge, 507.
Cannock, 302[1].
Cannons, 468.
Capel, 183.
Capetown, 153.
Carlisle, 364.
Carolyn, 273[1].
Carsaig, 417.
Cast thy burden, 504.
Caswall, 203[2], 449.
Charing, 389.
Charterhouse, 200.
Chastleton, 523.
Christchurch, 434.
Christe fons jugis, 220.
Christe sanctorum, 405, 418.
Christi Mutter, 80[1].
Christmas Carol, 532.
Christus der ist mein Leben, 251, 526.
Christus ist erstanden, 100.
Church Triumphant, 26.
Clifton, 134, 188.
Coelites plaudant, 260, 446.
Congleton, 499.
Coolinge, 423.
Corona, 124.
Cradle Song, 43[2].
Cranham, 51.
Cransley, 261.
Crimond, 480.
Croft's 136th, 478.
Cromer, 225.
Crowle, 312.
Crucis victoria, 178, 381.
Crudwell, 390.
Crüger, 457.
Cuddesdon, 65, 120.

Dank sei Gott, 221.
Darwall's 148th, 286, 483.
Das neugeborne Kindelein, 74.

Deirdre, 136.
Delganey, 515.
Der Tag bricht an, 290.
Desmond, 531.
Deus tuorum militum, 111[2], 232[2].
Diva Servatrix, 385.
Divinum mysterium, 57.
Dix, 62.
Dominus regit me, 475[1].
Donne secours, 395.
Down Ampney, 149.
Du fond de ma pensée, 233.
Duke Street, 470.
Dunfermline, 378, 396.

Easter Hymn, 105.
Eastleach, 253.
Ebenezer, 197.
Edom, 350.
Eia, eia, 315.
Ein' feste Burg, 281, 297.
Eirene, 179.
Eisenach, 73.
Ellacombe, 112, 442.
Engedi, 87.
Engelberg, 119.
Erfurt, 311.
Es ist ein' Ros' entsprungen, 41.
Es ist vollbracht, 516.
Eudoxia, 203[1], 419, 420.
Eventide, 298.
Everton, 377.
Ewing, 248.
Exultate Deo, 99.

Falcon Street, 399.
Farley Castle, 398.
Ferry, 349.
Fitzwilliam, 71.
Forest Green, 56.
Franconia, 318.
French (Dundee), 249, 459, 496.
Freshwater, 537.
Frilford, 345.
From strength to strength, 365.
Fulda, 95.

Galilee, 460.
Glasgow, 485.
Gloucester, 205.
God of love, 273².
Golden Treasury, 180.
Gonfalon Royal, 91².
Gopsal, 128.
Gott des Himmels, 524.
Gott lebet, 513.
Gott sei dank, 155.
Gott will's machen, 426¹.
Gräfenberg, 358.
Grafton, 391.
Grand Isle, 353.
Gwalchmai, 325.
Gweedore, 199.

Halton Holgate, 375.
Hambleden, 314¹.
Hampton, 148.
Hampton Lucy, 270.
Hanover, 226, 471.
Harewood, 258.
Harington (Retirement), 458.
Harts, 367.
Hawkhurst, 150.
Heathlands, 402, 455.
Heinlein, 341¹.
Helder, 301.
Helmsley, 35.
Henwood, 265.
Herbert, 275.
Hereford, 323², 362.
Herongate, 81, 319.
Herr Jesu Christ, 47².
Herzliebster Jesu, 500.
Hic breve vivitur, 453.
Highwood, 32.
Hollingside, 145².
Holyrood, 436.
Hominum Amator, 425.
Horsley, 92.
Huddersfield, 294.
Hyfrydol, 328.
Hymnus Eucharisticus, 535.

Illsley, 165², 222.
In allen meinen Thaten, 209.
In Babilone, 231.
Innocents, 429.
Innsbruck, 525.
Intercessor, 376.
Irby, 58.
Iris, 42.

Irish, 28, 493.
Iste Confessor (Angers), 167².
Iste Confessor (Rouen), 343.

Jabbok, 4.
Jackson, 494.
Jerusalem, 387.
Jesmian, 63¹.
Jesu, meine Freude, 518.
Jesus ist das schönste Licht, 519.
Jesus ist mein Aufenthalt, 521.
Jesus, unser Trost, 505.
Jubilate Deo, 59¹.

Kent, 380, 498.
Kieff Melody, 511.
Kilmarnock, 305, 487.
Kingley Vale, 206.
Kingsfold, 143.
King's Lynn, 394.
Kocher, 335.

Ladywell, 117.
Lancing, 230.
Lasst uns erfreuen, 2, 108, 288.
Laudate Dominum (Gauntlett), 287².
Laudate Dominum (Parry), 279.
Laus Deo, 269.
Legend, 542.
Leoni, 283.
Les commandemens de Dieu, 201, 447.
Lessington, 416.
Libera nos, 291.
Lichfield, 29.
Liebster Jesu, 257.
Linton, 262.
Little Cornard, 33.
Liverpool, 332.
Livingstone, 177.
Llanfair, 125.
Llangloffan, 85.
Llangollen, 5¹.
Lobe den Herren, 17, 534.
London New, 8, 482.
Love divine, 329.
Love incarnate, 53.
Lower Marlwood, 34.
Loxton, 59².
Lucerna Laudoniae, 272.

Lucerne, 171.
Luther's Hymn, 255.

Manchester, 259, 432.
Mannheim, 307.
Marching, 186.
Maria jung und zart, 331.
Marston Street, 154.
Martyrdom, 451.
Martyrs, 359².
Mead House, 98.
Megerran, 443.
Meine Armuth, 404.
Meine Hoffnung, 299.
Meirionydd, 219.
Melcombe, 163, 408.
Melita, 384.
Melling, 182.
Mendelssohn, 50.
Mendip, 254, 322.
Merthyr Tydfil, 264¹.
Merton, 66.
Metzler's Redhead, 126.
Meyer (Es ist kein Tag), 357.
Midian, 339.
Miles Lane, 118.
Milton Abbas, 172.
Miniver, 309¹.
Mit Freuden zart, 266.
Monkland, 441, 461.
Monks Gate, 371.
Montesano, 107².
Moreton, 462.
Morning Hymn, 403.
Morning Light, 368².
Morpeth, 368¹.
Moscow, 185.
Mowsley, 106².
Mylor, 76.

Narenza, 372.
National Anthem, 392.
Nativity, 122.
Neander, 123.
New Year's Day, 147.
Nicaea, 169.
Noel, 52.
Norman, 121.
Normandy, 43¹.
Northumbria, 181.
Nun danket, 277.
Nun freut euch, 18.
Nun lasst uns Gott, 506.
Nyland, 191.

O filii et filiae, 110.
O Jesu Christ, 212².
O Jesulein süss, 529.
O Lamm Gottes, 530.
O Traurigkeit, 96.
O Welt, ich muss dich lassen (Innsbruck), 427.
Old 100th, 450, 452.
Old 104th, 463.
Old 124th, 280, 464.
Oriel, 284, 445².
Orlando, 9, 409².
Oxford, 528.

Pange, lingua (Plainsong) 90¹, 90², 208¹, 208².
Passion Chorale, 86, 533.
Pearsall, 246.
Picardy, 204.
Pilgrimage, 140¹.
Plainsong (see Metrical Index).
Plaistow, 342².
Portland, 14.
Praise my soul, 15.
Psalm 3, 285.
Psalm 36 (68), 174.
Psalm 38, 509.
Psalm 47, 84.
Psalm 125, 31².
Psalm 138, 314².

Quem pastores, 72, 240.

Ratisbon, 137.
Ravenshaw, 190.
Ready Token, 63².
Redhead 76, 296.
Regent Square, 127, 250².
Regnator orbis, 252.
Remenham, 502.
Rendez à Dieu, 503.
Repton, 351¹.
Requiem, 539².
Resonet in laudibus, 75.
Rex gloriae, 129.
Rex gloriose, 421².
Rhuddlan, 393.
Rhyddid, 540.
Richmond, 88, 173.
Ripponden, 243.
Rochester, 492.
Rockingham, 97, 207.
Rodmell, 60, 435.
Rushford, 302².
Ryburn, 211.

S. Albinus, 106¹.
S. Alphege, 223, 241.
S. Andrew, 456, 497.
S. Anne, 467.
S. Austin, 247.
S. Bartholomew, 13, 54², 239².
S. Bernard, 289.
S. Botolph, 320.
S. Cecilia, 27.
S. Clement, 426².
S. Columba (Irish), 475².
S. Columba (Irons), 428.
S. Cuthbert, 160.
S. David, 466.
S. Denio, 10.
S. Etheldreda, 348, 379.
S. Ethelwald, 366.
S. Flavian, 210.
S. Fulbert, 116, 324.
S. George (Gauntlett), 49, 94.
S. George (Windsor), 439.
S. Helena, 228.
S. Hugh, 344.
S. James, 338.
S. Kilda, 355.
S. Leonard (Bach), 383.
S. Leonard (Smart), 131, 310.
S. Magnus (Nottingham), 132, 489.
S. Mary, 83.
S. Matthew, 382.
S. Mawes, 397.
S. Michael, 313.
S. Nicholas, 359¹.
S. Patrick, 170.
S. Peter, 142, 411.
S. Petersburg, 300.
S. Sebastian, 282.
S. Stephen, 193, 479, 484.
S. Theodulph, 77, 78.
S. Thomas (trad.), 90³, 208³.
S. Thomas (Williams), 317.
S. Timothy, 156, 407.
S. Valentine, 448.
S. Venantius, 159.
Saffron Walden, 292¹.
Saintbury, 340.
Salonica, 388.
Salzburg, 495.
Samson, 162².
Sandon, 306².

Sandys, 166.
Schmücke dich, 510.
Schönster Herr Jesu, 138.
Sebaste, 514.
Seelenbräutigam, 144, 422.
Sheen, 244.
Sheldonian, 308.
Sheng En, 538.
Shere, 25.
Sherston, 287¹.
Shipston, 168, 440.
Silchester, 139.
Simeon, 263.
Sine Nomine, 227.
Sirius, 21.
Slane, 316.
Snowshill, 309².
Solemnis haec festivitas, 19, 104².
Solothurn, 237.
Song 1, 213, 321.
Song 13, 517.
Song 20, 330.
Song 22, 522.
Song 24, 520.
Song 46, 373.
Song 67, 229, 276.
Southwell, 189.
Sparsholt, 539¹.
Stabat Mater, 80¹.
Stockton, 334.
Stonegate, 437.
Stracathro, 1.
Stroudwater, 454, 476.
Stuttgart, 30, 64.
Surrey, 70, 477.
Sursum corda, 202.
Sussex, 352, 431.

Tallis' Canon, 414.
Tallis' Ordinal, 68, 157.
Tambaram, 175.
Tantum ergo, 327.
Tanworth, 242.
Te lucis, 413¹, 413².
Temple, 158, 410.
The King's Majesty, 89¹.
This endris nyght, 44.
Thornbury, 187.
Trisagion, 238.
Truro, 401.
Tugwood, 5², 113², 130.
Tyrolese, 370.

Uffingham, 11, 37².
Unde et memores, 198.

University, 474.
University College, 363.

Vater unser, 264².
Veni Creator (Attwood), 508.
Veni Creator (Plainsong), 151¹, 151².
Veni, Immanuel, 36.
Veni, sancte Spiritus, 152.
Verbum supernum (Plainsong), 37¹, 212¹, 216.
Vernus, 109.
Vexilla Regis, 91¹.
Victory, 114.
Vienna, 374.
Vigil, 195.
Vom Himmel hoch, 48.
Vruechten, 115.
Vulpius, 103.

Wachet auf, 40.
Walford, 292².

Wareham, 67², 433.
Warrington, 6.
Warum sollt' ich, 501.
Warwick, 469.
Was lebet, 267.
Watchman, 268.
Wellington Square, 23.
Wer nur den lieben Gott, 361.
Westminster, 12.
Whitsun, 164.
Wie schön leuchtet (Mendelssohn), 141.
Wie schön leuchtet (Wagner), 541.
Wigtown, 304, 347.
Wiltshire, 481.
Winchester New, 38, 89².
Winchester Old, 61.
Windermere, 39, 438.
Windsor, 293.
Winscombe, 93².
Wir pflügen, 444.
Wolvercote, 360.

Wood End, 161.
Woodlands, 326.
Wordsworth, 218.
Wraysbury, 354.
Würtemburg, 101.

York, 473.
Yorkshire, 46.

Zennor, 295.

The following are used twice, but the settings are different

Ach Gott und Herr, 215, 536.
Christus der ist mein Leben, 251, 526.
Lobe den Herren, 17, 534.
Passion Chorale, 86, 533.
Wie schön leuchtet, 141, 541.

METRICAL INDEX OF TUNES

S.M.
Bellwoods, 24.
Carlisle, 364.
Falcon Street, 399.
Franconia, 318.
Hampton, 148.
Holyrood, 436.
Narenza, 372.
S. Ethelwald, 366.
S. George (Gauntlett), 49, 94.
S. Helena, 228.
S. Michael, 313.
S. Thomas (Williams), 317.
Sandys, 166.
Shere, 25.
Song 20, 330.
Watchman, 268.
Windermere, 39, 438.

D.S.M.
Corona, 124.
From strength to strength, 365.

C.M.
Abbey, 430.
Aberdeen (S. Paul), 472.
Abridge, 135.
Albano, 214.
Arden, 271, 278.
Bangor, 79, 196.
Bedford, 336.
Bedford Park, 491.
Belgrave, 22, 356.
Binchester, 274.
Bishopthorpe, 486.
Bon accord, 465.
Bristol, 490.
Bromsgrove (Dyer), 235.
Bromsgrove (Psalmodia), 400.
Caithness, 333, 488.
Capel, 183.
Clifton, 134, 188.
Crimond, 480.
Crowle, 312.
Crucis victoria, 178, 381.
Dunfermline, 378, 396.
Ferry, 349.
French (Dundee), 249, 459, 496.

Glasgow, 485.
Harington (Retirement), 458.
Horsley, 92.
Irish, 28, 493.
Jackson, 494.
Kilmarnock, 305, 487.
London New, 8, 482.
Manchester, 259, 432.
Martyrdom, 451.
Martyrs, 359[2].
Mendip, 254, 322.
Metzler's Redhead, 126.
Miles Lane, 118.
Nativity, 122.
Oxford, 528.
Richmond, 88, 173.
Rochester, 492.
Rodmell, 60, 435.
S. Andrew, 456, 497.
S. Anne, 467.
S. Austin, 247.
S. Bernard, 289.
S. Botolph, 320.
S. David, 466.
S. Etheldreda, 348, 379.
S. Flavian, 210.
S. Fulbert, 116, 324.
S. Hugh, 344.
S. James, 338.
S. Kilda, 355.
S. Leonard (Smart), 131, 310.
S. Magnus (Nottingham), 132, 489.
S. Mary, 83.
S. Nicholas, 359[1].
S. Peter, 142, 411.
S. Stephen (Newington), 193, 479, 484.
S. Timothy, 156, 407.
Salzburg, 495.
Song 67, 229, 276.
Southwell, 189.
Stockton, 334.
Stracathro, 1.
Stroudwater, 454, 476.
Tallis' Ordinal, 68, 157.
This endris nyght, 44.
University, 474.
Warwick, 469.
Westminster, 12.
Wigtown, 304, 347.

Wiltshire, 481.
Winchester Old, 61.
Windsor, 293.
York, 473.

D.C.M.
Christmas Carol, 532.
Forest Green, 56.
Kingsfold, 143.
Ladywell, 117.
Noel, 52.
S. Matthew, 382.
Wellington Square, 23.

L.M.
Ach bleib bei uns (Calvisius), 527.
Aeterna Christi munera, 234.
Affection, 69[2].
Angels' Song (Song 34), 224, 245, 406.
Angelus, 412.
Babylon's Streams, 346[2].
Birling, 424.
Breslau, 369.
Cannock, 302[1].
Cannons, 468.
Church Triumphant, 26.
Cromer, 225.
Der Tag bricht an, 290.
Deus tuorum militum, 111[2], 232[2].
Duke Street, 470.
Eisenach, 73.
Fulda, 95.
Galilee, 460.
Gloucester, 205.
Gonfalon Royal, 91[2].
Hawkhurst, 150.
Hereford, 323[2], 362.
Herongate, 81, 319.
Herr Jesu Christ, 47[2].
Hymnus Eucharisticus, 535.
Illsley, 165[2], 222.
Kent, 380, 498.
Lancing, 230.
Llangollen, 5[1].
Melcombe, 163, 408.
Montesano, 107[2].

L.M. (contd.)
Morning Hymn, 403.
Mylor, 76.
O Jesu Christ, 212².
Old 100th, 450, 452.
Orlando, 9, 409².
Plaistow, 342².
Psalm 125, 31².
Rex gloriose, 421².
Rockingham, 97, 207.
Rushford, 302².
S. Bartholomew, 13, 54², 239².
S. Petersburg, 300.
S. Venantius, 159.
Samson, 162².
Simeon, 263.
Solemnis haec festivitas, 19, 104².
Solothurn, 237.
Tallis' Canon, 414.
The King's Majesty, 89¹.
Truro, 401.
Tugwood, 5², 113², 130.
Uffingham, 11, 37².
Veni Creator (Plainsong), 151.
Verbum supernum (Plainsong), 37¹, 212¹, 216.
Vexilla Regis, 91¹.
Vom Himmel hoch, 48.
Wareham, 67², 433.
Warrington, 6.
Winchester New, 38, 89².

D.L.M.
Jerusalem, 387.
S. Patrick, 170.
Sirius, 21.

447.76.
O Traurigkeit, 96.

4.10.10.10.4.
Salonica, 388.

55.53.D.
Bunessan, 45.

55.55.65.65.
Old 104th, 463.

555.11.
New Year's Day, 147.

55.88.55.
Seelenbräutigam, 144, 422.

569.558.
Schönster Herr Jesu, 138.
Silchester, 139.

64.64.664.
Liverpool, 332.

64.66.
S. Columba (Irons), 428.

65.65.
Caswall, 203, 449.
Eudoxia, 203, 419, 420.
Linton, 262.

65.65.D.
Cuddesdon, 65, 120.
Requiem, 539².
Sparsholt, 539¹.

65.65.66.65.
Edom, 350.
Monks Gate, 371.

664.6664.
Milton Abbas, 172.
Moscow, 185.
National Anthem, 392.

665.D.786.
Jesu, meine Freude, 518.

66.65.65.
Cambridge, 507.

66.66.
Beweley, 192.
Maria jung und zart, 331.
Ravenshaw, 190.
S. Cecilia, 27.

66.66.44.44.
Croft's 136th, 478.
Darwall's 148th, 286, 483.
Harewood, 258.
Moreton, 462.
Psalm 47, 84.

66.66.66.
Frilford, 345.
Golden Treasury, 180.

66.66.88.
Christchurch, 434.
Gopsal, 128.
Gweedore, 199.
Little Cornard, 33.

667.667.D.
Psalm 3 (O Seigneur), 285.

66.84.
Temple, 158, 410.

66.84.D.
Leoni, 283.

66.11.D.
Down Ampney, 149.

67.67.
Love incarnate, 53.

67.67.66.66.
Nun danket, 277.

67.67.D.
Vruechten, 115.

68.88.88.
Christus ist erstanden, 100.

74.74.D.
Easter Hymn, 105.
Gwalchmai, 325.
Llanfair, 125.

76.76.
Christus der ist mein Leben, 251, 256.
Hic breve vivitur, 453.
Kocher, 335.
S. Alphege, 223, 241.
S. Theodulph, 78.

76.76.46.
Eia, eia, 315.

76.76.676.
Es ist ein' Ros' entsprungen, 41.

76.76.D.
All things bright, 3.
Aurelia, 184.
Ave, virgo virginum, 102.

METRICAL INDEX OF TUNES

76.76.D. (contd.)

Crüger, 457.
Dank sei Gott, 221.
Du fond de ma pensée, 233.
Ellacombe, 112, 442.
Ewing, 248.
Hampton Lucy, 270.
King's Lynn, 394.
Meirionydd, 219.
Morning Light, 368[2].
Morpeth, 368[1].
Nyland, 191.
Passion Chorale, 86, 533.
Pearsall, 246.
Rhyddid, 540.
S. Theodulph, 77.
Thornbury, 187.
Tyrolese, 370.
Wolvercote, 360.
Wordsworth, 218.

76.76.D.66.84.

Wir pflügen, 444.

76.76.88.

Hominum Amator, 425.

76.86.86.86.

Helder, 301.

76.86.D.

Eastleach, 253.
Llangloffan, 85.

776.D.

In allen meinen Thaten, 209.

776.778.

O Welt, ich muss dich lassen (Innsbruck), 427.

776.77.10.

Innsbruck, 525.

77.73.

Saintbury, 340.

77.75.

Capetown, 153.
Carsaig, 417.
Huddersfield, 294.
Zennor, 295.

77.77.

Bonn (Festus), 337.

Buckland, 146, 194, 341.
Gott sei Dank, 155.
Harts, 367.
Heinlein, 341.
Innocents, 429.
Melling, 182.
Monkland, 441, 461.
Nun lasst uns Gott, 506.
Song 13, 517.
University College, 363.
Vienna, 374.

77.77.4.

Würtemburg, 101.

77.77.77.

All red the river, 303.
Arfon, 93[1].
Charterhouse, 200.
Dix, 62.
Heathlands, 402, 455.
Jubilate Deo, 59[1].
Loxton, 59[2].
Lucerna Laudoniae, 272.
Ratisbon, 137.
Redhead 76, 296.
Winscombe, 93[2].

777.D.

Veni, sancte Spiritus, 152.

77.77.77.9.

O Lamm Gottes, 530.

77.77.D.

Aberystwyth, 145[1].
Hollingside, 145[2].
S. George (Windsor), 439.
Wood End, 161.

7777.7777.77.

Mendelssohn, 50.

77.77.88.

S. Valentine, 448.

77.88. and Refrain.

Resonet in laudibus, 75.

78.78.4.

Mowsley, 106[2].
S. Albinus, 106[1].

78.78.77.

Jesus ist mein Aufenthalt, 521.

78.78.88.

Liebster Jesu, 257.

83.36.D.

Warum sollt' ich, 501.

847.D.

Chastleton, 523.
Meine Armuth, 404.
Psalm 38, 509.

84.84.884.

Lower Marlwood, 34.

84.84.88.84.

Ar hyd y nos, 415.

85.83.

Bushmead, 386.

85.85.843.

Arthog, 256.

85.85.88.85.

Carolyn, 273[1].
God of love, 273[2].

86.84.

S. Cuthbert, 160.

86.86.

Gräfenberg, 358.

86.886.

Arnold, 351[2].
Engedi, 87.
Repton, 351[1].

87.3.4.8.

Henwood, 265.

87.83.

Vigil, 195.

87.87.

Ach Gott und Herr, 215, 536.
Ad inferos, 82.
Animae hominum, 20.
Dominus regit me, 475[1].
Gott des Himmels, 524.
Halton Holgate, 375.

87.87. (contd.)

Laus Deo, 269.
Love divine, 329.
Marching, 186.
Merton, 66.
Norman, 121.
S. Columba (Irish), 475[2].
Shipston, 168, 440.
Stuttgart, 30, 64.
Sussex, 352, 431.
Wraysbury, 354.

87.87.337.

Meine Hoffnung, 299.

87.87.47.

Bryn Calfaria, 140[2].
Helmsley, 35.
Iris, 42.
Kingley Vale, 206.
Libera nos, 291.
Pilgrimage, 140[1].

87.87.66.667.

Ein' feste Burg, 281, 297.

87.87.77.

All Saints, 236.
Irby, 58.
S. Leonard (Bach), 383.

87.87.87.

Grafton, 391.
Mannheim, 307.
Neander, 123.
Oriel, 284, 445[2].
Pange, lingua (Plainsong), 90[1], 208[1].
Picardy, 204.
Praise my soul, 15.
Regent Square, 127, 250[2].
Rhuddlan, 393.
S. Thomas (trad.), 90[3], 208[3].
Tantum ergo, 327.

87.87.877.

Divinum mysterium, 57.

87.87.D.

Abbot's Leigh, 7, 176.
Austrian Hymn, 16.
Ebenezer, 197.
Everton, 377.

Hyfrydol, 328.
In Babilone, 231.
Mead House, 98.
Megerran, 443.
Rex gloriae, 129.

87.87.887.

Luther's Hymn, 255.
Mit Freuden zart, 266.
Nun freut euch, 18.

88.44.88. and Alleluias

Lasst uns erfreuen, 2, 108, 288.

886.

Whitsun, 164.

886.D.

Erfurt, 311.

88.77.

Quem pastores, 240.

887.D.

Ascendit Deus, 133.
Christi Mutter, 80.
Lucerne, 171.
Stabat Mater, 80.

887.D.48.48.

Wie schön leuchtet, 541.

887.D.84.48.

Wie schön leuchtet, 141.

887.887.D.

Psalm 36 (68), 174.

888. and Alleluias

O filii et filiae, 110.

888.4.

Meyer (Es ist kein Tag), 357.
Portland, 14.
Ripponden, 243.
Victory, 114.
Vulpius, 103.

88.86.46.

Exultate Deo, 99.

888.6.

Fitzwilliam, 71.
Saffron Walden, 292[1].
Walford, 292[2].

88.87.

Charing, 389.

888.7.

Quem pastores, 72.

88.88.

Deirdre, 136.

88.88.7.

Marston Street, 154.

88.88.88.

Das neugeborne Kindelein, 74.
Desmond, 531.
Jabbok, 4.
Melita, 384.
Merthyr Tydfil, 264[1].
Ryburn, 211.
S. Mawes, 397.
Surrey, 70, 477.
Vater unser, 264[2].
Veni Creator (Attwood), 508.
Veni, Immanuel, 36.
Wer nur den lieben Gott, 361.

88.88.D.

Lichfield, 29.
Schmücke dich, 510.

88.10.8.

Cransley, 261.

89.89.D.

Hambleden, 314[1].
Psalm 138, 314[2].

98.98.

Gott will's machen, 426[1].
Les commandemens de Dieu, 201, 447.
S. Clement, 426[2].
Sheng En, 538.

98.98.D.

Rendez à Dieu, 503.

10.4.66.66.10.4.

Herbert, 275.

10.4.10.4.10.10.

Alberta, 306[1].
Sandon, 306[2].

10.10.
Song 46, 373.

10.10.7.
S. Sebastian, 282.

10.10.10. with Alleluias.
Engelberg, 119.

10.10.10.4.
Sine nomine, 227.

10.10.10.10.
Adoro te, 217.
Congleton, 499.
Coolinge, 423.
Eventide, 298.
Farley Castle, 398.
Regnator orbis, 252.
Remenham, 502.
Sheldonian, 308.
Song 22, 522.
Song 24, 520.
Sursum corda, 202.
Trisagion, 238.
Woodlands, 326.

10.10.10.10.4.
Tambaram, 175.

10.10.10.10.10.
Old 124th, 280, 464.

10.10.10.10.10.10.
Northumbria, 181.
Song 1, 213, 321.
Unde et memores, 198.
Yorkshire, 46.

10.10.11.11.
Hanover, 226, 471.
Laudate Dominum
(Gauntlett), 287[2].

Laudate Dominum
(Parry), 279.
Sherston, 287[1].

10.11.11.11.
Slane, 316.

10.11.11.12.
Miniver, 309[1].
Snowshill, 309[2].

11.10.10.5.6.
Vernus, 109.

11.10.11.10.
Crudwell, 390.
Donne secours, 395.
Highwood, 32.
Intercessor, 376.
Jesmian, 63[1].
Ready Token, 63[2].
Stonegate, 437.

11.11.11.5.
Christe Fons jugis, 220.
Christe sanctorum, 405,
    418.
Coelites plaudant, 260,
    446.
Diva Servatrix, 385.
Eirene, 179.
Herzliebster Jesu, 500.
Iste Confessor (Angers),
    167[2].
Iste Confessor (Rouen),
    343.

11.11.11.11.
Cradle Song, 43[2].
Midian, 339.
Normandy, 43[1].
S. Denio, 10.

11.12.12.10.
Nicaea, 169.

13.10.13.10.
Was lebet, 267.

14.14.4.78.
Lobe den Herren, 17,
    534.

14.14.14.15.
Sheen, 244.

Irregular
Acinom, 512.
Adeste fideles, 55.
Cast thy burden, 504.
Cranham, 51.
Delganey, 515.
Es ist vollbracht, 516.
Freshwater, 537.
Gott lebet noch, 513.
Grand Isle, 353.
Jesus ist das schönste
    Licht, 519.
Jesus, unser Trost, 505.
Kieff Melody, 511.
Legend, 542.
Lessington, 416.
Livingstone, 177.
O Jesulein süss, 529.
Sebaste, 514.
Tanworth, 242.
Wachet auf, 40.

Plainsong
Mode i, 54[1], 91[1], 162[1],
    323[1], 409[1].
Mode ii, 69[1], 239[1], 250[1],
    346[1], 421[1], 445[1].
Mode iii, 47[1], 90[1], 90[2],
    165[1], 208[1], 208[2], 342[1].
Mode iv, 31[1], 167[1].
Mode viii, 37[1], 67[1], 104[1],
    107[1], 111[1], 113[1], 151[1],
    151[2], 212[1], 216, 232[1],
    413[1], 413[2].

INDEX OF COMPOSERS, ARRANGERS, AND SOURCES OF TUNES

Ahle, J. H., 257.
Albert, H., 524.
Allen, H. P., 206, 339.
Allison's *Psalter*, 31².
Anchors *Collection*, 454, 476.
Andernach Gesangbuch, 421².
Angers Melody, 19, 104², 167².
Anon., 55, 215, 424, 505, 516, 518, 519, 521, 529, 536.
Armes, P., 460.
As hymnodus sacer, 369.
Attwood, T., 508.
Ave Hierarchia, 190.

Bach, J. C., 383.
Bach, J. S., 40, 74, 86, 221, 264², 281, 297, 427, 501, 505, 506, 513, 516, 518, 519, 521, 524, 526, 527, 529, 533, 534, 536.
Baker, H. W., 156, 407.
Baring-Gould, S., 203¹, 419, 420.
Barthélémon, F. H., 403.
Bayeux Melody, 385.
Bishop, J., 165², 222.
Blanchet, A., 20.
Bohemian Brethren, 266.
Bortnianski, D. S., 300.
Bourgeois, L., 201, 285, 313, 395, 447, 450, 452, 503, 509.
Boyce, W., 375.
Broadwood, L., 143.
Broomfield, W. R., 355.
Brown, A. H., 292¹.
Buck, P. C., 91², 282, 515.
Butts, T., 147.

Calvisius, S., 527.
Campion, T., 346².
Cantica Spiritualia, 412.
Carey, H., 70, 477.
Chadwyck-Healey, H. P., 273².
Chalmers' *Collection*, 472.
Chinese Verse Tune, 303.
Christliche Lieder, 18.
Clarke, J., 11, 37², 132, 486, 489.
Clifton, J. C., 134, 188.
Cocker, N., 211, 243.
Collection of Hymns, Dublin, 28, 493.
Cöln Gesangbuch, 372.
Cooke, G., 261.
Coombs, J. M., 528.

Cooper, A. S., 200.
Corner's *Gesangbuch*, 80².
Courteville, R., 338.
Creed, J. H., 462.
Croft, W., (?) 226, 274, 382, 467, (?) 471, 478.
Crüger, J., 277, 457, 500, 510, 518.
Cummings, W. H., 50.

Damon's *Psalmes*, 293.
Darmstadt Gesangbuch, 236.
Darwall, J., 286, 483.
Davies, H. Walford, 158, 410, 532.
Day's *Psalter*, 210.
Doles' *Choralbuch*, 121.
Dougall, N., 305, 487.
Dowland, J., 450, 452.
Drese, A., 144, 422.
Duncalf, H., 13, 54², 239².
Dutch Melody, 115, 231.
Dyer, H. A., 235, 275.
Dykes, J. B., 145², 160, 169, 384, 475¹.

Ebeling, J. G., 501.
Elliott, J. W., 26.
Elvey, G. J., 140¹, 439.
English Carol, 44.
English Melody, 35, 55.
English Traditional Melody, 52, 56, 60, 71, 81, 143, 168, 183, 247, 254, 319, 322, 352, 371, 394, 431, 435, 440.
Este's *Psalter*, 61.
Ett, C., 284, 445².
Evans, D., 272.
Ewing, A., 248.

Fawcett, J., 182.
Ferguson, W. H., 65, 117, 120, 230, 345, 360, 425, 448.
Filitz, F., 153, 203², 307, 449.
Finnish Melody, 191.
Foster, M. B., 178, 381.
French Melody, 80¹, 391.
French Missal, 36.
French or Flemish Melody, 42.
French Traditional Carol, 204.
Freylinghausen, J. A., 404, 513.
Freylinghausen's *Gesangbuch*, 155, 337.

Gaelic Melody, 45.
Gardiner's *Sacred Melodies*, 95.

COMPOSERS, ARRANGERS, AND SOURCES OF TUNES

Gatty, N., 5[2], 113[2], 130.
Gauntlett, H. J., 49, 58, 94, 106[1], 116, 150, 223, 241, 287[2], 324, 363.
Geistliche Kirchengesang, 2, 108, 288.
Genevan Psalter, 201, 280, 285, 313, 314[2], 395, 447, 450, 452, 464, 503, 509.
George, G., 89[1].
German Carol Melody, 75.
German Melody, 41, 72, 240, 427.
German Traditional Melody, 518.
Giardini, F. de, 185.
Gibbons, O., 213, 224, 229, 245, 276, 321, 330, 373, 406, 517, 520, 522.
Goss, J., 15.
Goudimel, C., 314[2].
Greatorex, W., 326.
Green, J., 312.
Green's *Psalmody*, 349.
Greenwood's *Psalmody*, 69[2].
Grenoble Melody, 111[2], 232[2].
Guidetti, 234.
Gwyllt, I., 332.

Handel, G. F., 128, 162[2], 468.
Harington, H., 458.
Harmonia Sacra, 147.
Harris, W. H., 306[1].
Harrison, R., 6.
Harwood, B., 34, 187.
Hassler, H. L., 86, 533.
Hatton, J., 470.
Haus Kirchen Cantorei, 212[2].
Havergal, W. H., 318, 372.
Haweis, T., 88, 173.
Haydn, F. J., 16.
Haydn, J. M., 495.
Hayne, L. G., 27, 146, 194, 341[2].
Heath-Gracie, G. H., 531.
Hebrew Melody, 283.
Helder, B., 301.
Helmore, T., 36.
Herbst, M., 341[1].
Hodges, E., 205.
Holdroyd's *Companion*, 359[1].
Holst, G., 51, 244.
Hopkins, E. J., 344, 354.
Hopkins, J. H., 353.
Hopkirk, J., 24.
Horsley, W., 22, 92, 356.
Hunt, J. E., 539[2].
Hutcheson, C., 1.
Hymn Melody of Bohemian Brethren, 266.

Irish Melody, 136, 170, 316, 475[2].
Irons, H. S., 189, 428.

Irvine, J. S., 480.
Isaak, H., 427, 525.

Jackson, T., 494.
Jones, J. D., 325.
Jones, W., 193, 479, 484.
Joseph, G., 412.

Kieff Melody, 511.
Kirkpatrick, W., 43[2].
Knapp, W., 67[2], 433.
Knecht, J. H., 335, 374.
Kocher, C., 62.
König, J. B., 318.

La Feillée, F. de, 252, 405, 418.
Lahee, H., 122.
Lampe, J. F., 380, 498.
Law, J., 107[2].
Lawes, H., 84, 398.
Leach, J., 268.
Leisentritt's *Gesangbuch*, 102.
Ley, H. G., 302[2].
Lloyd, J. A., 225.
Lloyd, W., 219.
Lockhart, C., 364.
Luther, M., 48, 255, 281, 297.
Lyra Davidica, 105.

Magdalen Hymns, 342[2].
Mainz Gesangbuch, 112, 442.
Meiningen Gesangbuch, 504.
Mendelssohn-Bartholdy, F., 50, 141, 504.
Meyer, J., 357.
Milgrove, B., 228, 367.
Miller, E., 97, 207.
Milton, J., 473.
Monk, W. H., 3, 66, 114, 156, 190, 198, 218, 298, 366, 407.
Moore's *Companion*, 485.
Murrill, H., 273[1], 351[2].
Musikalisches Handbuch, 38, 89[2].

Naylor, E. W., 365.
Neander, J., 123, 299.
Neumark, G., 361.
Nicolai, P., 40, 141, 541.
Nordstern's *Führer zur Seligkeit*, 315.
Normandy Carol, 43[1].
Novello, V., 214.
Nürnberg Gesangbuch, 47[2].

Owen, W., 140[2].

Palestrina, G., 114.
Parish Choir, The, 429.

Parratt, W., 294, 511.
Parry, C. H. H., 279, 351[1], 376, 387, 537.
Parry, J., 145[1], 264[1].
Pearsall, R. L., 246.
Pettet, A., 453.
Pettman, E., 53, 350.
Piae Cantiones, 57.
Plainsong (*see* Metrical Index).
Playford's *Psalms*, 8, 482.
Praetorius, M., 41.
Praxis Pietatis Melica, 358.
Prichard, R. H., 328.
Prys' *Psalter*, 83.
Psalmodia Evangelica, 400, 401.
Psalmodia Sacra, 30, 64.
Psalteriolum Harmonicum, 331.
Purday, C. H., 306[2].

Randall, J., (?) 474.
Ravenscroft's *Psalter*, 249, 459, 463, 466, 490, 496.
Redhead, R., 126, 269, 296.
Reinagle, A. R., 142, 411.
Rheinfels Gesangbuch, 530.
Rheinhardt MS., 267.
Rogers, B., 535.
Rosenmüller, J., 101.
Rouen Melody, 159, 220, 260, 343, 446.
Russell, S. L., 389.

Sandys' *Collection*, 166.
Sangster, W. H., 82.
Schein, J. H., 73.
Schicht, J. G., 133.
Scholefield, C. C., 426[2].
Schop, J., 96.
Schultz, J. A. P., 444.
Schumann's *Gesangbuch*, 264[2].
Scott, J. S., 388.
Scottish Psalter, 8, 249, 304, 333, 347, 359[2], 378, 396, 430, 459, 465, 473, 482, 488, 496.
Selby, B. Luard, 164.
Selnecker, N., 506.
Shaw, M., 33, 186.
Shrubsole, W., 118.
Silesian Folk Song, 138.
Sion's Harp, 209.
Slater, G., 320.
Smart, G., 481.
Smart, H., 127, 129, 131, 238, 250[2], 310, 377, 402, 455.
Smith, A. M., 202.
Smith, I., 135, 399.

Solesmes Melody, 217.
Somervell, A., 39, 438.
Stainer, J., 329, 514.
Standard Psalm Tune-book, 499.
Stanford, C. V., 119.
Stanley, S., 263, 469.
Stanton, W. K., 29, 59[2], 63[2], 76, 93[2], 99, 109, 139, 161, 177, 181, 253, 262, 270, 287[1], 302[1], 309[2], 314[1], 340, 390, 397, 443, 502, 512, 523, 539[1].
Steggall, C., 434.
Steiner, J. L., 426[1].
Stewart, C. Hylton, 124, 492.
Stralsund Gesangbuch, 17, 534.
Strasburg Psalter, 174, 233.
Sullivan, A. S., 52.
Swiss Melody, 237.

Tallis, T., 68, 157, 414.
Tanzer, W., 79, 196.
Tanzer's *New Harmony*, 456, 497.
Taylor, C. V., 4, 7, 14, 98, 106[2], 154, 175, 176, 179, 180, 192, 242, 291, 308, 309[1], 368[1], 386, 423, 437, 491.
Terry, R. R., 32.
Teschner, M., 77, 78.
Thalben-Ball, G., 9, 21, 59[1], 63[1], 195, 256, 265, 271, 278, 292[2], 295, 409[2], 417.
Thatcher, R. S., 416.
Thesaurus Musicus, 392.
Thiman, E. H., 25, 172.
Tochter Sion, 289.
Trier Gesangbuch, 100.
Tschaikowsky, P. I., 542.
Turle, J., 12.
Turton, T., 348, 379.
Tyrolese Carol, 370.

United Brethren Hymns, 441, 461.

Vaughan Williams, R., 149, 227.
Vesperale Romanum, 151[2].
Vulpius, M., 74, 103, 251, 290, 526.

Wagner, G. G., 541.
Wainwright, J., 46.
Wainwright, R., 259, 432.
Warrack, G., 23.
Watson, J., 436.
Weale, W., 336.
Webb, G. J., 368[2].
Webbe, S. (the elder), 152, 163, 327, 408.
Webbe, S. (the younger), 88, 173.

Webbe's *Motetts*, 90[3], 110, 208[3].
Weimar, G. P., 311.
Weisse, M., 190.
Welsh Hymn Melody, 5[1], 93[1].
Welsh Melody, 10, 85, 540.
Welsh Traditional Melody, 393, 415.
Werner, *Choralbuch*, 137.
Wesley, S. S., 87, 184, 199, 258, 323[2], 362.
Wilkes, J., 441, 461.
Williams, A., 317.

Williams' *Psalmody*, 148.
Williams, R., 125.
Williams, T. J., 197.
Wilson, H., 451.
Wood, C., 507.
Woodward, G. R., 530.
Wooldridge, H. E., 509.
Wright, T., 334.
Würtemberg Gesangbuch, 171.

Yin-Lan, S., 538.

INDEX OF AUTHORS, TRANSLATORS,
AND SOURCES OF WORDS

(Translators in brackets)

Abelard, P., 79, 246, 252, 502.
Adams, S. F., 332.
Addison, J., 21, 22, 305, 477.
Ainger, A. C., 177.
Alexander, C. F., 3, 58, 92, 131, 354.
[Alexander, C. F.], 136, 170.
Alford, H., 193, 253, 439.   [327.
Alington, C. A., 103, 222, 270, 294,
[Alston, A. E.], 167.
Andrew, Father, 358.
Angel, A. (?), 541.
Anglo-Genevan Psalter, 464.
Anon., 43, 138, 139, 392, 506, 515
Anstice, J., 311.
Apostolic Constitutions, 280.
Arlott, J., 431, 435, 440.
Armstrong, J., 225.
Auber, H., 160.
Austin, J., 396.

Bahnmaier, J. F., 182.
Baker, H. W., 156, 190, 279, 281, 407,
    441, 475.
[Baker, H. W.], 54, 57, 517.
Baring-Gould, S., 419, 420.
[Baring-Gould, S.], 186.
Bartholomew, W. (?), 504.
Bathurst, W. H., 310.
Baxter, R., 245, 286, 355, 507.
Bayly, A. F., 181.
Bede, The Venerable, 130.
Bell, M. A., 385.
Bell, M. F., 266.
Beza, Theodore of, 464.
[Birkbeck, W. J.], 511
[Blacker, M. J.], 446.
Blake, W., 387.
Bode, J. E., 360.
Bonar, H., 143, 202, 271, 373.
Book of Praise for Children, 370.
Borthwick, J., 388.
Bourges Breviary, 337.
Bourne, G. H., 206.
Brady, N., 451, 481, 483.
Bridges, M., 124, 356.
Bridges, R., 314, 330, 395, 433, 463,
    521, 523, 527.
[Bridges, R.], 113, 285, 509; (Par.) 86,
    274, 299, 427, 500, 522, 525, 533
Bright, W., 198, 214, 402.
Brontë, A., 317.

Brooke, S. A., 71.
[Brooke, W. T.], 55.
Brooks, P., 56, 532.
Browne, S., 150.
[Brownlie, J.], 158.
[Buckoll, H. J.], 404.
Bunyan, J., 304, 371.
Burkitt, F. C., 161.
Burleigh, W. H., 308.
Butler, H. M., 326.
[Byrne, M. E.], 316.
Byrom, J., 46, 331.

Cameron, W., 486, (?) 492.
[Campbell, J. M.], 444.
[Campbell, R.], 116.
Canitz, F. R. L. von, 404.
[Carlyle, T.], 297.
[Caswall, E.], 64, 80, 94, 152, 208, 212,
    276, 285, 289, 322, 324, 428.
Cawood, J., 188.
Cennick, J., 35.
Chadwick, J. W., 321.
[Chandler, J.], 38, 39, 68, 69, 126, 157,
    258, 411.
Chesterton, G. K., 394.
Clare, J., 70.
[Clark, J. H.], 337.
Claudius, M., 444.
Clausnitzer, T., 257.
Clephane, E. C., 301.
Cluny, Bernard of, 241, 248.
Coeleste Palmetum, 276.   [411.
Coffin, C., 38, 39, 49, 69, 157, 274,
Coles, V. S. S., 219.
Cölner Psalter, 315.
Conder, J., 26, 200.
Contakion, Russian, 511.
Cooke, G., 261.
Cooper, E., 290.
[Copeland, W. J.], 421.
[Cosin, J.], 151, 508.
Cotterill, T., 125.
Cowper, W., 8, 263, 333.
[Cox, F. E.], 18, 106, 236.
Craig, J., 470.
Crossman, S., 84.
Crum, J. M. C., 109.
Cummins, J. J., 291.
                                    [529.
[Daisley, G. W.], 505, 513, 516, 519,

Day's *Psalter*, 450.
[Dearmer, G.], 542.
Dearmer, P., 72, 389.
[Dearmer, P.], 215, 315, 405, 536.
Decius, N., 530.
Didache, The, 201.
Dix, W. C., 62, 197, 443.
Doane, G. W., 338.
Doddridge, P., 207, 372, 379, 488, 490, 495.
Downton, H., 429.
[Draper, W. H.], 2.
Duffield, G., 368.

Edmeston, J., 307.
Ellerton, J., 93, 221, 349, 399, 423, 426, 448.
[Ellerton, J.], 47, 282.
Elliott, C., 292, 340.
Everest, C. W., 369.

Faber, F. W., 12, 20, 203.
F. B. P., 247.
Fortunatus, V., 90, 91, (?) 239.
Fosdick, H. E., 391.
Foundling Hospital Collection, 16, 163.
Franck, J., 510, 518.

Gedge, P., 343.
Gellert, C. F., 106.
Gerhardt, P., 313, 427, 501.
[Gerhardt, P.], 86, 533.
Gill, T. H., 255.
Gladstone, W. E., 211, 531.
Grant, R., 471.
Gurney, J. H., 74, 293, 436.

Hanby, B. R., 75.
Hatch, E., 148.
Havergal, F. R., 164.
Heber, R., 63, 169, 235, 240, 295, 415, 503.
Heerman, J., 500.
Hensley, L., 27.
Herbert, G., 275, 325, 474.
Herbert, P., 418.
Hernaman, C. F., 83.
Hill, R., 230.
Holland, H. S., 393.
Holmes, O. W., 11.
Homburg, E. C., 505.
Horne, C. S., 242.
Hosmer, F. L., 28, 312.
Housman, L., 60.
How, W. W., 81, 191, 227, 367, 434, 438.

Hughes, T., 359.
[Hull, E. H.], 316.
[Humphreys, C. W.], 215, 244, 536.
Hunter, J., 319.
Hupton, J., 123.
[*Hymnal, The* (U.S.A. 1940), Compilers of], 446.
[*Hymns A. & M.*, Compilers of], 37, 38, 47, 54, 67, 91, 107, 108, 111, 126, 152, 157, 165, 208, 212, 216, 232, 284, 322, 409, 421.

Ingemann, B. S., 186.
Irish, 316.

Jervois, W. H. H., 220, 535.
Johnson, S., 173.

Keble, J., 318, 408, 424.
[Keble J.], 416, 514.
Kelly, T., 95, 127, 132, 171.
Kempis, T. à, (?) 73, (?) 233, 250.
Ken, T., 401, 403, 414.
Kethe, W., 450.

Lacey, T. A., 174.
[Lacey, T. A.], 104, 342, 346.
Latin Acrostic Poem, 67.
Leachman, E. W., 350.
Leeson, J. E., 146, 194.
Lew, T. T., 538.
[Littledale, R. F.], 149.
Liturgy of Malabar, 215, 536.
Liturgy of S. James, 204, 244.
Loewen, A. von, (?) 86, (?) 533.
Logan, J., 495.
Longfellow, S., 155.
Löwenstern, M. A. von, 179.
Lowry, S. C., 377.
Luther, M., 48, 297.
Lyra Davidica, 105.
Lyte, H. F., 15, 298, 455, 499.

[Macbean, L.], 45.
Macdonald, M., 45.
Maclagan, W. D., 82.
Madan, M., 35, 50.
Mann, F., 357.
Mant, R., 228, 269.
Marriott, J., 185.
Mason, A. J., 205.
Matheson, G., 175.
May, C. E., 87.
Merrill, W. P., 364.
Merrington, E. N., 390.
Milman, H. H., 89, 336.

Milton, J., 458, 461, 479.
Monsell, J. S. B., 19, 267, 302, 442.
Montgomery, J., 42, 159, 178, 196, 224, 268, 344, 347, 453, 457, 468.
Morison, J., 487, 496.
[Moultrie, G.], 204.
Mozarabic Breviary, 282, 446.
Muirhead, L., 183.
Myers, F. W. H., 32.

Neale, J. M., 76, 123, 237, 335.
[Neale, J. M.], 31, 36, 41, 57, 77, 78, 90, 91, 102, 107, 108, 110, 111, 112, 152, 212, 216, 232, 233, 234, 238, 239, 241, 248, 250, 252, 284, 339, 342, 413, 425, 445.
Neander, J., 17, 299, 534.
Nevill, M., 265.
Newman, J. H., 88, 168, 306.
Newton, J., 142, 176, 259, 375, 524.
Nicolai, P., 40, 141.
Noel, C., 120.

[Oakeley, F.], 55.
Oakley, C. E., 33.
Olivers, T., 283.
Osler, E., 210, 379, 528.
Owen, F., 520.

Page, T. E., 195.
Palgrave, F. T., 180.
[Palmer, E. S.], 449, 539.
[Palmer, R.], 323.
Paris Breviary, 251.
Parsons, R. G., 218, 540.
Penn, W. J., 320.
Pennefather, W., 262.
Pentecostarion, 158.
Perronet, E., 117, 118.
Pestel, T., 44.
[Phillimore, G.], 410.
Pierpoint, F. S., 272.
Piggott, W. C., 243.
Plechtchéev, A. N., 542.
Plumptre, E. H., 187, 382.
[Pollock, T. B.], 67.
Pott, F., 256, 341.
[Pott, F.], 114.
Prudentius, A. C., 57, 64, 289.
[Pusey, P.], 179.

Rawnsley, H. D., 381.
Rees, T., 7, 85, 231, 273.
Richter, C. F., 519.
Riley, A., 288.
[Riley, A.], 209.

Rinkart, M., 277.
Rippon, J., 117, 118.
Rist, J., 96.
[Roberts, R. E.], 162.
Robinson, R. H., 417.
Romanis, W., 422.
Rossetti, C., 51, 53.
Russell, A. T., 133.
[Russell, A. T.], 144, 530.

S. Ambrose, (?) 232, 234, 409.
S. Andrew of Crete (?), 339.
S. Francis of Assisi, 2.
S. Fulbert of Chartres, 116.
S. Germanus, 41.
S. Gregory, 346, 405.
S. John of Damascus, 102, 112.
S. Joseph the Hymnographer, 238.
S. Theodulph, 77, 78.
S. Thomas Aquinas, 208, 212, 216, 217.
Santeuil, J.-B. de, 68, 226.
Sarum Use (Horae B.V.M.), 512.
Scheffler, J., 361.
Schenk, H. T., 236.
Schlegel, J. A., 141.
Schmidt, J. E., 516.
Schutz, J. J., 18.
Scott, L., 353.
Scott, R. B. Y., 24.
Scottish Paraphrases, 484, 485, 486, 487, 488, 489, 491, 492, 493, 494, 495, 496, 497, 498.
Scottish Psalter, 450, 454, 456, 459, 464, 465, 466, 469, 470, 472, 473, 476, 480, 482.
Sears, E. H., 52.
Sedulius, C., 47.
Shillito, C., 99.
Siena, B. de, 149.
Smith, H., 430.
Smith, W. C., 10.
Smyttan, G. H., 341.
Spenser, E., 398.
Steele, A., 189.
Stevenson, I. S., 386.
[Stevenson, L.], 138, 139.
Stone, S. J., 184, 303.
Struther, Jan, 309.
Swahili, 449, 539.
Symphonia Sirenum, 114.

Tate, N., 61, 451, 481, 483.
[Taylor, W. R. O.], 538.
[Tearle, M.], 192.
Tennyson, A., Lord, 537.

Tersteegen, G., 264.
Thilo, V., 529.
Thomas, H. A., 380.
Thring, G., 65, 124, 383
Tisserand, J., 110.
Toplady, A. M., 296.
Tucker, F. B., 119.
[Tucker, F. B.], 79, 201
Turton, W. H., 213.
Tweedy, H. H., 23.
Twells, H., 345, 412.

Vaughan, H., 526.

[Waddell, H.], 246, 502.
Wallis, S. J., 154.
Walmsley, D., 260.
Wardlaw, R., 25.
Watts, I., 5, 6, 9, 13, 97, 100, 122, 134,
    229, 254, 300, 400, 452, 460, 462,
    467, 486, 489, 491, 492, 494.
[Webb, B.], 73, 130.
Weisse, M., 101.
Weissel, G., 34.
Welch, E. A., 223.
Wesley, C., 4, 29, 30, 35, 50, 125, 128,
    137, 145, 147, 166, 199, 249, 278,
    287, 328, 329, 334, 348, 362, 365,
    366, 374, 378, 397, 406.
Wesley, J., 452.

[Wesley, J.], 264, 313.
Whately, R., 415.
White, H. K., 363.
Whitefield, G., 50.
Whiting, W., 384.
Whittier, J. G., 1, 351, 376.
[Whittingham, W.], 464.
Williams, I., 135.
[Williams, I.], 226, 251.
[Williams, P.], 140.
Williams, W., 140.
Willis, L. M., 352.
[Winkworth, C.], 17, 34, 40, 48, 96,
    101, 141, 182, 257, 277, 361, 501,
    510, 518, 534.
Wither, G., 478.
Wolcott, S., 172.
Woodd, B., 66.
[Woodford, J. R.], 49, 121, 217.
Woodward, G. R., 115, 447.
[Woodward, G. R.], 280, 418.
Wordsworth, C., 14, 59, 98, 129,
    153.
Wreford, J. R., 432.

Yigdal, The, 283.
Young, A., 437.

Zihn, J. F., 513.
Zinzendorf, N. L. von, 144.

INDEX OF FIRST LINES

(Choir Settings in italics)

First Line	Number	Name of Tune
A great and mighty wonder	41	Es ist ein' Ros' entsprungen
A safe stronghold our God is still	297	Ein' feste Burg
A stranger once did bless the earth	70	Surrey
A time to watch, a time to pray	76	Mylor
Abide with me; fast falls the eventide	298	Eventide
Abide with me; fast falls the eventide	499	Congleton
According to thy gracious word	196	Bangor
Ah, holy Jesus, how hast thou offended	500	Herzliebster Jesu
All as God wills, who wisely heeds	1	Stracathro
All creatures of our God and King	2	Lasst uns erfreuen
All glory, laud, and honour (8-line)	77	S. Theodulph
All glory, laud, and honour (4-line)	78	S. Theodulph
All glory to God in the sky	29	Lichfield
All hail the power of Jesus' name (8-line)	117	Ladywell
All hail the power of Jesus' name (4-line)	118	Miles Lane
All my heart this night rejoices	501	Warum sollt' ich
All my hope on God is founded	299	Meine Hoffnung
All people that on earth do dwell	450	Old 100th
All praise to thee, for thou, O King divine	119	Engelberg
All praise to thee, who safe hast kept	401	Truro
All things bright and beautiful	3	All things bright
All ye who seek for sure relief	289	S. Bernard
Alleluia, Alleluia! Hearts to heaven	98	Mead House
Alleluia! sing to Jesus	197	Ebenezer
Almighty God, thy word is cast	188	Clifton
Alone thou goest forth, O Lord	79	Bangor
Alone to sacrifice thou goest, Lord	502	Remenham
And did those feet in ancient time	387	Jerusalem
And now, O Father, mindful of the love	198	Unde et memores
Angel voices, ever singing	256	Arthog
Angels, from the realms of glory	42	Iris
Around the throne of God a band	237	Solothurn
As now the sun's declining rays	411	S. Peter
As pants the hart for cooling streams	451	Martyrdom
As with gladness men of old	62	Dix
At even, when the sun did set	412	Angelus
At the Cross, her station keeping	80	1. Stabat Mater
		2. Christi Mutter
At the name of Jesus	120	Cuddesdon
At thy feet, O Christ, we lay	402	Heathlands
Author of life divine	199	Gweedore
Awake, my soul, and with the sun	403	Morning Hymn
Awake, our souls, away, our fears!	300	S. Petersburg
Away in a manger, no crib for a bed	43	1. Normandy
		2. Cradle Song
Away with gloom, away with doubt!	99	Exultate Deo
Away with our fears	147	New Year's Day

INDEX OF FIRST LINES

First Line	Number	Name of Tune
Be near us, Holy Trinity	165	1. Mode iii
		2. Illsley
Be thou my guardian and my guide	135	Abridge
Be thou my Vision, O Lord of my heart	316	Slane
Before the^almighty Father's throne	452	Old 100th
Before the ending of the day	413	Te lucis (Mode viii)
Behold the^amazing gift of love	484	S. Stephen (Newington)
Behold, the great Creator makes	44	This endris nyght
Behold, the mountain of the Lord	485	Glasgow
Behold the temple of the Lord!	171	Lucerne
Behold us, Lord, a little space	349	Ferry
Behold, we come, dear Lord, to thee	396	Dunfermline
Believe not those who say	317	S. Thomas (Williams)
Belovèd, let us love: for love is of God	373	Song 46
Beneath the cross of Jesus	301	Helder
Blessèd Jesus, at thy word	257	Liebster Jesu
Blest are the pure in heart	318	Franconia
Blest be the everlasting God	486	Bishopthorpe
Bread of heaven, on thee we feed	200	Charterhouse
Bread of the world, in mercy broken	503	Rendez à Dieu
Breathe on me, Breath of God	148	Hampton
Brief life is here our portion	241	S. Alphege
Bright the vision that delighted	269	Laus Deo
Brightest and best of the sons of the morning	63	1. Jesmian
		2. Ready Token
By the rutted roads we follow	431	Sussex
Cast thy burden upon the Lord	504	Cast thy burden
Child in the manger	45	Bunessan
Christ, above all glory seated	121	Norman
Christ be with me, Christ within me	136	Deirdre
Christ for the world we sing!	172	Milton Abbas
Christ is made the sure foundation	445	1. Mode ii
		2. Oriel
Christ is our corner-stone	258	Harewood
Christ, our helper and life-giver	505	Jesus, unser Trost
Christ the Lord is risen!	100	Christus ist erstanden
Christ the Lord is risen again	101	Würtemburg
Christ was the Word who spake it	506	Nun lasst uns Gott
Christ who knows all his sheep	507	Cambridge
Christ, whose glory fills the skies	137	Ratisbon
Christian, dost thou see them	339	Midian
Christian, seek not yet repose	340	Saintbury
Christian, unflinching stand	350	Edom
Christians, awake, salute the happy morn	46	Yorkshire
City of God, how broad and far	173	Richmond
Come down, O Love divine	149	Down Ampney
Come, gracious Spirit, heavenly Dove	150	Hawkhurst
Come, Holy Ghost, our souls inspire	151	1. Veni Creator (Mode viii)
		2. ditto (Mechlin)
Come, Holy Ghost, our souls inspire	508	Veni Creator (Attwood)
Come, labour on!	388	Salonica
Come, let us join our cheerful songs	122	Nativity
Come, let us to the Lord our God	487	Kilmarnock
Come, let us with our Lord arise	397	S. Mawes

INDEX OF FIRST LINES

First Line	Number	Name of Tune
Come, my soul, thou must be waking	404	Meine Armuth
Come, O thou Traveller unknown	4	Jabbok
Come, thou Holy Spirit, come	152	Veni, sancte Spiritus
Come, thou long-expected Jesus	30	Stuttgart
Come, ye faithful, raise the anthem	123	Neander
Come, ye faithful, raise the strain	102	Ave virgo virginum
Come, ye people, rise and sing	270	Hampton Lucy
Come, ye thankful people, come	439	S. George (Windsor)
Creator of the starry height	31	1. Mode iv
		2. Psalm 125
Crown him with many crowns	124	Corona
Darkening night the land doth cover	509	Psalm 38
Dear Lord and Father of mankind	351	1. Repton
		2. Arnold
Dear Master, in whose life I see	319	Herongate
Dear Shepherd of thy people, hear	259	Manchester
Deck thyself, my soul, with gladness	510	Schmücke dich
Defend, O Lord, and keep	192	Beweley
Disposer supreme, and Judge of the earth	226	Hanover
Earth has many a noble city	64	Stuttgart
Enthrone thy God within thy heart	320	S. Botolph
Eternal Father, strong to save	384	Melita
Eternal God, whose power upholds	23	Wellington Square
Eternal Ruler of the ceaseless round	321	Song 1
Fair waved the golden corn	436	Holyrood
Fairest Lord Jesus	138	Schönster Herr Jesu
Fairest Lord Jesus	139	Silchester
Faith of our fathers, taught of old	174	Psalm 36 (68)
Father all-seeing, friend of all creation	385	Diva Servatrix
Father, hear the prayer we offer	352	Sussex
Father, in whom we live	166	Sandys
Father most holy, merciful and loving	167	1. Mode iv
		2. Iste Confessor (Angers)
Father, O hear us, seeking now to praise thee	260	Coelites plaudant
Father of heaven, whose love profound	290	Der Tag bricht an
Father of mercies, in thy word	189	Southwell
Father of peace, and God of love	488	Caithness
Father, we praise thee, now the night is over	405	Christe sanctorum
Father, we thank thee who hast planted	201	Les commandemens de Dieu
Father, who on man dost shower	389	Charing
Fight the good fight with all thy might	302	1. Cannock
		2. Rushford
Fill thou my life, O Lord my God	271	Arden
Firmly I believe and truly	168	Shipston
For all the saints who from their labours rest	227	Sine nomine
For all thy saints, O Lord	228	S. Helena
For the beauty of the earth	272	Lucerna Laudoniae
For the might of thine arm we bless thee	242	Tanworth
For those we love within the veil	243	Ripponden
For thy mercy and thy grace	429	Innocents
Forth in thy name, O Lord, I go	406	Angels' Song (Song 34)
Forty days and forty nights	341	Heinlein & Buckland

INDEX OF FIRST LINES

First Line	Number	Name of Tune
From all that dwell below the skies	5	1. Llangollen
		2. Tugwood
From east to west, from shore to shore	47	1. Mode iii
		2. Herr Jesu Christ
From glory to glory advancing	244	Sheen
From the eastern mountains.	65	Cuddesdon
Gather us in, thou love that fillest all	175	Tambaram
Give heed, my heart, lift up thine eyes	48	Vom Himmel hoch
Give me the wings of faith to rise	229	Song 67
Give rest, O Christ	511	Kieff Melody
Give to our God immortal praise	6	Warrington
Glorious things of thee are spoken	176	Abbot's Leigh
Glory to thee, my God, this night	414	Tallis' Canon
Go, happy soul, thy days are ended	447	Les commandemens de Dieu
God be in my head	512	Acinom
God from on high hath heard	49	S. George (Gauntlett)
God is love: let heaven adore him	7	Abbot's Leigh
God is my strong salvation	453	Hic breve vivitur
God is our refuge and our strength	454	Stroudwater
God is working his purpose out	177	Livingstone
God liveth still	513	Gott lebet
God moves in a mysterious way	8	London New
God of eternity, Lord of the ages	390	Crudwell
God of grace and God of glory	391	Grafton
God of love and truth and beauty	273	1. Carolyn
		2. God of love
God of mercy, God of grace	455	Heathlands
God save our gracious Queen	392	National Anthem
God that madest earth and heaven	415	Ar hyd y nos
God the Father's only Son	303	All red the river
God, whose farm is all creation	440	Shipston
God's law is perfect, and converts	456	S. Andrew
Good Christian men, rejoice and sing!	103	Vulpius
Gracious Spirit, Holy Ghost	153	Capetown
Guide me, O thou great Redeemer	140	1. Pilgrimage
		2. Bryn Calfaria
Hail, blest Spirit, Lord eternal	154	Marston Street
Hail, gladdening Light	416	Lessington
Hail, gladdening Light	514	Sebaste
Hail the day that sees him rise	125	Llanfair
Hail, thou source of every blessing	66	Merton
Hail to the Lord's Anointed	457	Crüger
Happy are they, they that love God	274	Binchester
Hark how the adoring hosts above	489	S. Magnus (Nottingham)
Hark, the glad sound, the Saviour comes	490	Bristol
Hark, the herald-angels sing	50	Mendelssohn
Hark what a sound, and too divine for hearing	32	Highwood
Hast thou not known, hast thou not heard	491	Bedford Park
He that is down needs fear no fall	304	Wigtown
He wants not friends that hath thy love	245	Angels' Song (Song 34)
Help us to help each other, Lord	378	Dunfermline
Here beauty dwells, and holiness	261	Cransley
Here, O my Lord, I see thee face to face	202	Sursum Corda

First Line	Number	Name of Tune
High in the heavens, eternal God	9	Orlando
Hills of the north, rejoice	33	Little Cornard
His cheering message from the grave	104	1. Mode viii
		2. Solemnis haec festivitas
Holy Father, cheer our way	417	Carsaig
Holy Father, in thy mercy	386	Bushmead
Holy, holy, holy, Lord God Almighty!	169	Nicaea
Holy Spirit, truth divine	155	Gott sei dank
How are thy servants blest, O Lord!	305	Kilmarnock
How bright these glorious spirits shine!	492	Rochester
How brightly beams the morning star!	141	Wie schön leuchtet
How glorious Sion's courts appear	493	Irish
How lovely are thy dwellings fair!	458	Harington (Retirement)
How mighty are the Sabbaths	246	Pearsall
How sweet the name of Jesus sounds	142	S. Peter
I bind unto myself to-day	170	S. Patrick
I heard the voice of Jesus say	143	Kingsfold
I sing a song of the saints of God	353	Grand Isle
I to the hills will lift mine eyes	459	French (Dundee)
I'm not ashamed to own my Lord	494	Jackson
Immortal, invisible, God only wise	10	S. Denio
In the bleak mid-winter	51	Cranham
In token that thou shalt not fear	193	S. Stephen (Newington)
Into this world of sorrow	515	Delganey
It came upon the midnight clear	52	Noel
It fell upon a summer day	71	Fitzwilliam
It is a thing most wonderful	81	Herongate
It is finishèd! ah, grant, O Lord	516	Es ist vollbracht
It is finished! blessèd Jesus	82	Ad inferos
Jerusalem (*see* 'And did those feet')		
Jerusalem, my happy home	247	S. Austin
Jerusalem the golden	248	Ewing
Jesu, grant me this, I pray	517	Song 13
Jesu, guide our way	144	Seelenbräutigam
Jesu, lover of my soul	145	1. Aberystwyth
		2. Hollingside
Jesu, our hope, our heart's desire	126	Metzler's Redhead
Jesu, priceless treasure	518	Jesu, meine Freude
Jesu, the very thought of thee	322	Mendip
Jesu, thou joy of loving hearts	323	1. Mode i
		2. Hereford
Jesu, thy mercies are untold	324	S. Fulbert
Jesus, blessèd Saviour	203	Eudoxia & Caswall
Jesus calls us! O'er the tumult	354	Wraysbury
Jesus Christ is risen to-day	105	Easter Hymn
Jesus, good above all other	72	Quem pastores laudavere
Jesus is this dark world's light	519	Jesus ist das schönste Licht
Jesus lives! thy terrors now	106	1. S. Albinus
		2. Mowsley
Jesus, Lord of life and glory	291	Libera nos
Jesus, Lord, we look to thee	374	Vienna
Jesus, my Lord, how rich thy grace	379	S. Etheldreda
Jesus shall reign where'er the sun	460	Galilee
Jesus, stand among us	262	Linton

INDEX OF FIRST LINES

First Line	Number	Name of Tune
Jesus, where'er thy people meet	263	Simeon
Judge eternal, throned in splendour	393	Rhuddlan
Just as I am, without one plea	292	1. Saffron Walden
		2. Walford
King of glory, King of peace	325	Gwalchmai
Lead, kindly light, amid the encircling gloom	306	1. Alberta
		2. Sandon
Lead us, heavenly Father, lead us	307	Mannheim
Lead us, O Father, in the paths of peace	308	Sheldonian
Let all mortal flesh keep silence	204	Picardy
Let all the world in every corner sing	275	Herbert
Let saints on earth in concert sing	249	French (Dundee)
Let us, with a gladsome mind	461	Monkland
Lift up your heads, ye gates of brass	178	Crucis victoria
Lift up your heads, ye mighty gates	34	Lower Marlwood
Lift up your hearts! We lift them, Lord, to thee	326	Woodlands
Lighten the darkness of our life's long night	520	Song 24
Light's abode, celestial Salem	250	1. Mode ii
		2. Regent Square
Light's glittering morn bedecks the sky	107	1. Mode viii
		2. Montesano
Light's glittering morn bedecks the sky	108	Lasst uns erfreuen
Lo, God is here! let us adore	264	1. Merthyr Tydfil
		2. Vater unser
Lo! he comes with clouds descending	35	Helmsley
Lo, now is our accepted day	342	1. Mode iii
		2. Plaistow
Lo, round the throne, a glorious band	230	Lancing
Lone in the desert, facing all temptation	343	Iste Confessor (Rouen)
Look down upon us, God of grace	205	Gloucester
Look, ye saints, and see how glorious	127	Regent Square
Lord, as to thy dear Cross we flee	293	Windsor
Lord, by whose breath all souls and seeds are living	437	Stonegate
Lord Christ, who on thy heart didst bear	380	Kent
Lord, enthroned in heavenly splendour	206	Kingley Vale
Lord, it belongs not to my care	355	S. Kilda
Lord of all being, throned afar	11	Uffingham
Lord of all hopefulness, Lord of all joy	309	1. Miniver
		2. Snowshill
Lord of all, to whom alone	294	Huddersfield
Lord of beauty, thine the splendour	327	Tantum ergo
Lord of mercy and of might	295	Zennor
Lord of our life, and God of our salvation	179	Eirene
Lord of the worlds above	462	Moreton
Lord, pour thy Spirit from on high	224	Angels' Song (Song 34)
Lord, teach us how to pray aright	344	S. Hugh
Lord, thy word abideth	190	Ravenshaw
Lord, while for all mankind we pray	432	Manchester
Lord, who in thy perfect wisdom	231	In Babilone
Lord, who throughout these forty days	83	S. Mary
Love came down at Christmas	53	Love incarnate
Love divine, all loves excelling (8-line)	328	Hyfrydol
Love divine, all loves excelling (4-line)	329	Love divine

INDEX OF FIRST LINES

First Line	Number	Name of Tune
Love of love, and Light of light	521	Jesus ist mein Aufenthalt
Love of the Father, Love of God the Son	522	Song 22
Love, unto thine own who camest	523	Chastleton
Loving Shepherd of thy sheep	146	Buckland
Loving Shepherd of thy sheep (Baptism)	194	Buckland
May the grace of Christ our Saviour	375	Halton Holgate
May the grace of Christ our Saviour	524	Gott des Himmels
Might and glory, power and wisdom	265	Henwood
Most glorious Lord of life, that on this day	398	Farley Castle
My Father, for another night	407	S. Timothy
My God, accept my heart this day	356	Belgrave
My God, and is thy table spread	207	Rockingham
My God, how wonderful thou art	12	Westminster
My God, I love thee; not because	276	Song 67
My God, my Father, make me strong	357	Meyer (Es ist kein Tag)
My God, my King, thy various praise	13	S. Bartholomew
My heart is filled with longing	525	Innsbruck
My Lord, my life, my love	330	Song 20
My song is love unknown	84	Psalm 47
My soul, praise the Lord!	463	Old 104th
My soul, there is a country	526	Christus der ist mein Leben
My spirit longs for thee	331	Maria jung und zart
Nearer, my God, to thee	332	Liverpool
New every morning is the love	408	Melcombe
Not for our sins alone	345	Frilford
Now cheer our hearts this eventide	527	Ach bleib bei uns (Calvisius)
Now Israel may say, and that truly	464	Old 124th
Now it is evening; time to cease from labour	418	Christe sanctorum
Now my tongue, the mystery telling	208	1. Pange, lingua (Mode iii)
		2. Ibid. (Mechlin)
		3. S. Thomas (trad.)
Now thank we all our God	277	Nun danket
Now the day is over (For young children)	419	Eudoxia
Now the day is over	420	Eudoxia
Now the green blade riseth from the buried grain	109	Vernus
Now the labourer's task is o'er	448	S. Valentine
O brother man, fold to thy heart thy brother!	376	Intercessor
O Christ, Redeemer of our race	54	1. Mode i
		2. S. Bartholomew
O Christ, who art the light and day	421	1. Mode ii
		2. Rex gloriose
O come, all ye faithful	55	Adeste fideles
O come, let us sing to the Lord	465	Bon accord
O come, O come, Immanuel	36	Veni, Immanuel
O crucified Redeemer	85	Llangloffan
O day of God, draw nigh	24	Bellwoods
O dear and heavenly city	251	Christus der ist mein Leben
O dearest Lord, by all adored	266	Mit Freuden zart
O dearest Lord, thy sacred head	358	Gräfenberg
O Father, all creating	221	Dank sei Gott
O Father, by whose sovereign sway	222	Illsley
O food of men wayfaring	209	In allen meinen Thaten

INDEX OF FIRST LINES

First Line	*Number*	*Name of Tune*
O for a closer walk with God	333	Caithness
O for a faith that will not shrink	310	S. Leonard (Smart)
O for a heart to praise my God	334	Stockton
O for a thousand tongues to sing	278	Arden
O God, give ear unto my cry	466	S. David
O God of Bethel, by whose hand	495	Salzburg
O God of earth and altar	394	King's Lynn
O God of truth, whose living word	359	1. S. Nicholas
		2. Martyrs
O God, our help in ages past	467	S. Anne
O God, thou art my God alone	468	Cannons
O God, thy soldiers' faithful Lord	232	1. Mode viii
		2. Deus tuorum militum
O God unseen, yet ever near	210	S. Flavian
O God unseen, yet ever near	528	Oxford
O God, whose will is life and good	381	Crucis victoria
O greatly blessed the people are	469	Warwick
O happy band of pilgrims	335	Kocher
O heavenly Word, eternal Light	37	1. Verbum supernum (Mode viii)
		2. Uffingham
O help us, Lord; each hour of need	336	Bedford
O Holy Ghost, thy people bless	156	S. Timothy
O Holy Spirit, Lord of grace	157	Tallis' Ordinal
O Jesu so meek, O Jesu so kind	529	O Jesulein süss
O Jesus, I have promised	360	Wolvercote
O kind Creator, bow thine ear	346	1. Mode ii
		2. Babylon's Streams
O King enthroned on high	158	Temple
O Lamb of God all-holy	530	O Lamm Gottes
O lead my blindness by the hand	211	Ryburn
O lead my blindness by the hand	531	Desmond
O little town of Bethlehem	56	Forest Green
O little town of Bethlehem	532	Christmas Carol
O Lord, how happy should we be	311	Erfurt
O Lord of heaven and earth and sea	14	Portland
O Lord our God, arise!	25	Shere
O Lord, thou art my God and King	470	Duke Street
O love, how deep, how broad, how high!	73	Eisenach
O love, who formedst me to wear	361	Wer nur den lieben Gott
O praise ye the Lord!	279	Laudate Dominum (Parry)
O sacred head, sore wounded	86	Passion Chorale
O sacred head, sore wounded	533	Passion Chorale
O saving victim, opening wide	212	1. Verbum supernum (Mode viii)
		2. O Jesu Christ
O Saviour, where shall guilty man	87	Engedi
O sons and daughters, let us sing	110	O filii et filiae
O spirit of the living God	159	S. Venantius
O splendour of God's glory bright	409	1. Mode i
		2. Orlando
O thou in all thy might so far	312	Crowle
O thou not made with hands	180	Golden Treasury
O thou, who at thy Eucharist didst pray	213	Song 1
O thou who camest from above	362	Hereford
O thou who makest souls to shine	225	Cromer

INDEX OF FIRST LINES

First Line	Number	Name of Tune
O thou, whom neither time nor space	430	Abbey
O what their joy and their glory must be	252	Regnator orbis
O Word of God incarnate	191	Nyland
O worship the King, all glorious above	471	Hanover
O worship the Lord in the beauty of holiness	267	Was lebet
Of the Father's love begotten	57	Divinum mysterium
Oft in danger, oft in woe	363	University College
On Jordan's bank the Baptist's cry	38	Winchester New
Once in royal David's city	58	Irby
Once, only once, and once for all	214	Albano
Only-begotten, Word of God eternal	446	Coelites plaudant
Our blest Redeemer, ere he breathed	160	S. Cuthbert
Our Father's home eternal	233	Du fond de ma pensée
Our Lord, his Passion ended	161	Wood End
Praise, my soul, the King of heaven	15	Praise my soul
Praise, O praise our God and King	441	Monkland
Praise the Lord! ye heavens, adore him	16	Austrian Hymn
Praise to the Holiest in the height	88	Richmond
Praise to the Lord, the Almighty	17	Lobe den Herren
Praise to the Lord, the Almighty	534	Lobe den Herren (Bach)
Praise ye the Lord, ye servants of the Lord	280	Old 124th
Pray that Jerusalem may have	472	Aberdeen (S. Paul)
Prayer is the soul's sincere desire	347	Wigtown
Put thou thy trust in God	313	S. Michael
Rejoice, O land, in God thy might	433	Wareham
Rejoice, O people, in the mounting years	181	Northumbria
Rejoice! the Lord is King	128	Gopsal
Rejoice! the year upon its way	162	1. Mode i
		2. Samson
Rejoice to-day with one accord	281	Ein' feste Burg
Ride on! ride on in majesty!	89	1. The King's Majesty
		2. Winchester New
Rise up, O men of God!	364	Carlisle
Rock of ages, cleft for me	296	Redhead 76
Round me falls the night	422	Seelenbräutigam
Saviour, again to thy dear name we raise	423	Coolinge
See, Father, thy belovèd Son	535	Hymnus Eucharisticus
See the Conqueror mounts in triumph	129	Rex gloriae
Shepherd divine, our wants relieve	348	S. Etheldreda
Sing Alleluia forth in duteous praise	282	S. Sebastian
Sing, my tongue, the glorious battle	90	1. Pange, lingua (Mode iii)
		2. Ibid. (Mechlin)
		3. S. Thomas (trad.)
Sing, O sing, this blessèd morn!	59	1. Jubilate Deo
		2. Loxton
Sing praise to God who reigns above	18	Nun freut euch
Sing to the Lord a joyful song	19	Solemnis haec festivitas
Sing to the Lord of harvest	442	Ellacombe
Sing we triumphant hymns of praise	130	Tugwood
Soldier, go! thy vow is spoken	195	Vigil
Soldiers of Christ, arise (8-line)	365	From strength to strength
Soldiers of Christ, arise (4-line)	366	S. Ethelwald
Soldiers of the Cross, arise!	367	Harts
Soldiers, who are Christ's below	337	Bonn (Festus)

INDEX OF FIRST LINES

First Line	Number	Name of Tune
Son of God, eternal Saviour	377	Everton
Souls of men, why will ye scatter	20	Animae hominum
Spirit of mercy, truth, and love	163	Melcombe
Spread, O spread, thou mighty word	182	Melling
Stand up, and bless the Lord	268	Watchman
Stand up, stand up for Jesus	368	1. Morpeth
		2. Morning Light
Stars of the morning, so gloriously bright	238	Trisagion
Strengthen for service, Lord, the hands	215	Ach Gott und Herr
Strengthen for service, Lord, the hands	536	Ach Gott und Herr (Bach)
Sun of my soul, thou Saviour dear	424	Birling
Sunset and evening star	537	Freshwater
Take up thy cross, the Saviour said	369	Breslau
Teach me, O Lord, the perfect way	473	York
Ten thousand times ten thousand	253	Eastleach
That Easter-tide with joy was bright	111	1. Mode viii
		2. Deus tuorum militum
The advent of our King	39	Windermere
The bread of life, for all men broken!	538	Sheng En
The Church of God a kingdom is	183	Capel
The Church's one foundation	184	Aurelia
The day is past and over	425	Hominum Amator
The day of Resurrection	112	Ellacombe
The day thou gavest, Lord, is ended	426	1. Gott will's machen
		2. S. Clement
The duteous day now closeth	427	O Welt, ich muss dich lassen (Innsbruck)
The eternal gates lift up their heads	131	S. Leonard (Smart)
The eternal gifts of Christ the King	234	Aeterna Christi munera
The Father's sole-begotten Son	67	1. Mode viii
		2. Wareham
The God of Abraham praise	283	Leoni
The God of love my Shepherd is	474	University
The God whom earth and sea and sky	239	1. Mode ii
		2. S. Bartholomew
The head that once was crowned with thorns	132	S. Magnus (Nottingham)
The heavenly Word, proceeding forth	216	Verbum supernum (Mode viii)
The King, O God, his heart to thee upraiseth	395	Donne secours
The King of love my Shepherd is	475	1. Dominus regit me
		2. S. Columba (Irish)
The Lamb's high banquet doth invite	113	1. Mode viii
		2. Tugwood
The Lord ascendeth up on high	133	Ascendit Deus
The Lord doth reign, and clothed is he	476	Stroudwater
The Lord is King! lift up thy voice	26	Church Triumphant
The Lord my pasture shall prepare	477	Surrey
The Lord of heaven confess	478	Croft's 136th
The Lord will come, and not be slow	479	S. Stephen (Newington)
The Lord's my Shepherd, I'll not want	480	Crimond
The maker of the sun and moon	60	Rodmell
The race that long in darkness pined	496	French (Dundee)
The royal banners forward go	91	1. Vexilla Regis (Mode i)
		2. Gonfalon Royal

INDEX OF FIRST LINES

First Line	Number	Name of Tune
The Saviour died, but rose again	497	S. Andrew
The Son of God goes forth to war	235	Bromsgrove (Dyer)
The Son of God his glory hides	68	Tallis' Ordinal
The spacious firmament on high	21	Sirius
The star of morn has risen	410	Temple
The strife is o'er, the battle done	114	Victory
The sun is sinking fast	428	S. Columba (Irons)
The wise may bring their learning	370	Tyrolese
Thee we adore, O hidden Saviour, thee	217	Adoro te
Thee will I love, my God and King	314	1. Hambleden
		2. Psalm 138
There is a green hill far away	92	Horsley
There is a land of pure delight	254	Mendip
Thine arm, O Lord, in days of old	382	S. Matthew
Think, O Lord, in mercy	449	Caswall
Think, O Lord, in mercy	539	1. Sparsholt
		2. Requiem
This is the day of light	399	Falcon Street
This is the day the Lord hath made	400	Bromsgrove (Psalmodia)
This joyful Eastertide	115	Vruechten
Thou art the Way; by thee alone	338	S. James
Thou to whom the sick and dying	383	S. Leonard (Bach)
Thou, whose almighty word	185	Moscow
Throned upon the aweful tree	93	1. Arfon
		2. Winscombe
Through all the changing scenes of life	481	Wiltshire
Through the night of doubt and sorrow	186	Marching
Thy hand, O God, has guided	187	Thornbury
Thy kingdom come, O God	27	S. Cecilia
'Thy kingdom come!' On bended knee	28	Irish
Thy mercy, Lord, is in the heavens	482	London New
To Christ, the Prince of peace	94	S. George (Gauntlett)
To the name of our salvation	284	Oriel
To thee, O Comforter divine	164	Whitsun
To thee, O Lord, our hearts we raise	443	Megerran
To thee our God we fly	434	Christchurch
To us in Bethlem city	315	Eia, eia
Virgin-born, we bow before thee	240	Quem pastores laudavere
Wake, O wake! for night is flying	40	Wachet auf
We come unto our fathers' God	255	Luther's Hymn
We give thee but thine own	438	Windermere
We hail thy presence glorious	218	Wordsworth
We hail thy presence glorious	540	Rhyddid
We lift our hearts, O Father	223	S. Alphege
We plough the fields, and scatter	444	Wir pflügen
We pray thee, heavenly Father	219	Meirionydd
We saw thee not when thou didst come	74	Das neugeborne Kindelein
We sing the praise of him who died	95	Fulda
We watched the winter turn its back	435	Rodmell
What sorrow sore	96	O Traurigkeit

INDEX OF FIRST LINES

First Line	Number	Name of Tune
What star is this with beams so bright	69	1. Mode i
		2. Affection
What tongue can tell thy greatness, Lord	541	Wie schön leuchtet
When all thy mercies, O my God	22	Belgrave
When I survey the wondrous Cross	97	Rockingham
When Jesus Christ was yet a child	542	Legend
When morning gilds the skies	285	Psalm 3 (O Seigneur)
Where high the heavenly temple stands	498	Kent
Wherefore, O Father, we thy humble servants	220	Christe Fons jugis
While shepherds watched their flocks by night	61	Winchester Old
Who are these, like stars appearing	236	All Saints
Who is he in yonder stall	75	Resonet in laudibus
Who would true valour see	371	Monks Gate
With joy we meditate the grace	134	Clifton
Ye boundless realms of joy	483	Darwall's 148th
Ye choirs of new Jerusalem	116	S. Fulbert
Ye holy angels bright	286	Darwall's 148th
Ye servants of God, your Master proclaim	287	1. Sherston
		2. Laudate Dominum (Gauntlett)
Ye servants of the Lord	372	Narenza
Ye watchers and ye holy ones	288	Lasst uns erfreuen

SILVER LAKE COLLEGE LIBRARY
2406 SOUTH ALVERNO ROAD
MANITOWOC, WI 54220